A Submarine Story

The Memoirs of a Submarine Engineer

In Peace and in War

Periscope Publishing

Penzance

A Submariner's Story

The Memoirs of a Submarine Engineer

In Peace and in War

By

Lieutenant Joel C. E. Blamey DSC. DSM.

Foreword By

Vice Admiral Sir Ian McIntosh KBE. DSO. MBE. DSC.

First published in 2002 by
Periscope Publishing Ltd.
33 Barwis Terrace
Penzance
Cornwall TR18 2AW

A CIP record for this book is available from the British Library

ISBN No 1-904381-02-2

Printed in England by Antony Rowe Ltd
Eastbourne

Table of Contents

This book is dedicated to the memory of those many shipmates and good friends who, less fortunate than I, lost their lives in HM Submarines in the service of their country.

Foreword

The submarine branch of the Royal Navy has always been small in numbers in relation to the rest of the service, yet it has held within its ranks as plenteous a collection of markedly individual people at all levels, as could be imagined. For 'paradoxically' the unforgiving nature of the environment in which submariners live and work, the necessity of each man to rely implicitly upon others, and to subordinate his own desires or fears to the good of the whole submarine, seems to encourage rather than inhibit the development of strong individual characters. Some few, indeed border on the eccentric, yet never with that tinge of contrivance which one may detect sometimes in men forged in a less vigorous smithy. For in addition to the restraints imposed by the sea and by the submarine, they share a common life at such close quarters over prolonged periods that each man, from the commanding officer to the most junior rating, becomes so well known to the rest of the crew, that any pose must wither.

Like most submariners, I was privileged to serve under, or with some of these characters, and was enriched by the experience. In particular it was my good fortune to serve, in my first submarine appointment, with Joe Blamey, and I not only learned from him, but also gained a lifelong and valued friend. His length of service in submarines and the breadth of his experience put him in a special and rare category, and the account that he has written is a unique record, in peace and war, of submarine life viewed as an engineer. Not that there is so sharp a distinction between engineers and seamen as there is in surface ships, for in a submarine we all to a large extent, live both in the engine room and very close to the sea.

In *Porpoise* one of my responsibilities was for gunnery. Our 4″ gun mounting was cursed with an air-loaded run-out system by which, after the gun had recoiled when a round had been fired, an air-loaded piston and cylinder arrangement was supposed to restore the gun to its firing position ready for the next round to be loaded and fired. To function correctly, this required an air pressure of 350 pounds per square inch, but try as we would we could never get the cylinder to hold this modest pressure for any length of time. In consequence, when a round was fired, the gun regularly sat back on its haunches and by refusing to run out, prevented the next round from being fired. Joe became a key member of the gun crew, and armed with a heavy lead 'flogging hammer' would beat the gun back to its proper position muttering ' Get back you b.... r', as only a West-Countryman can say it.

Those who are fortunate enough to read Joe Blamey's fascinating narrative will realize very soon that versatility came naturally to him. They will meet many interesting and memorable characters delineated as in many cases I can attest but, though his own modesty would make him deny it, he himself is one of the greatest of all these characters, and rightly has both the respect and affection of all the many submariners who have known him amongst whom, happily, is me.

Ian McIntosh

Introduction

These days I often find myself looking back to my boyhood. (A sure sign of fast approaching maturity, they tell me). I look back to those long balmy days spent in the classroom, with my often exasperated physics master drumming amongst other things, the principles of Archimedes into my oft-times unreceptive skull. Little did I realize at that time, how these ancient principles were to have such a marked effect on my future life.

Archimedes told us that when a body is immersed, or partially immersed in a fluid, it loses weight equal to the weight it displaces. This principle is of course perfectly true, and on the face of it, quite straightforward. But when we come to apply the principles of our dear old philosopher to a working submarine, we soon find that there are a myriad of snags and complexities that have to be overcome before that submarine can operate properly.

Firstly, the weight of the fluid (in our case seawater), is controlled by its density, and density in turn is governed to a large degree by temperature. Both of these properties can vary considerably within a few miles of travel or a few feet of depth change. Apart from this, there are many other reasons or causes which would effectively change the weight of a body (in this case a submarine), in the seawater, and subsequently cause problems with its control. For instance, the changing weights as food, water, fuel etc is consumed, the change in weight as torpedoes are expended, the speed and angle at which the submarine is travelling through the water. All of these facets and many more, have been and will almost certainly continue to be, a matter of prime concern for submarine First Lieutenants and submarine Engineer Officers. But these problems are of course, just another part of the submariners everyday life, in much the same way as wind speeds, and air pressures etc, become part of a pilot's everyday life. On joining submarines I very soon discovered how to master the eccentricities of submarine control and learned that the constant need to apply appropriate corrections in order to maintain the principles of Archimedes becomes second nature to the submariner.

Joining the Royal Navy in 1920 as an Engine Room Artificer Apprentice, I personally, had no real previous knowledge of submarines or submariners, or the conditions under which they lived; indeed I had no special yen to gain any. Then in 1926 I was conscripted into the submarine branch, and into a whole new world. It was a world to which I soon became very attached, and one that I consequently went on to spend the next twenty- eight years in before finally returning to general service when approaching the ripe old age of fifty.

So why twenty- eight years? What was the attraction? Looking back now, I'm sure that it wasn't the general conditions under which we lived, and it certainly wasn't the very meagre extra pay that we received. No, it certainly was none of that! Perhaps I didn't even realize this at the time, but I believe now that the main attraction for me was the esprit de corps, that special brand of camaraderie that one finds in a submarine crew. Nowhere else in the world (with the possible exception of a space capsule patrolling the outer limits) would one find that particular mixture of natural inter- reliance and unspoken discipline found aboard a submarine at sea. Of course, I'm not saying that our submarine crews did not carry a fair allocation of rogues and dissidents, far from it, but these people, together with other particularly eccentric characters that seemed to abound in the submarine service, all help to weave that special net of camaraderie, and they never failed to rise to the occasion when the need arose. So I would say that above all else, this was the overriding reason for my comparatively long association with the submarine world. My unbroken service of twenty-eight years in submarines was I understand, something of a record at that time.

My book is a record of my full naval career, albeit mostly spent in the submarine service. I have had many good times, and, as you will see, many not so good times. Events gone by can of course never be changed although looking back now, even if it were possible, I do not believe I would change any part of my service life. But then of course, I was one of the lucky ones! Even so, I have lost many brave friends and colleagues over the years, both through enemy action and peacetime accidents, and if I had the power to change that, then of course I would.

It was my intention when I decided to commit my rather extraordinary experiences in the service of HM submarines to paper, that my story should be kept as non-technical as possible, although this in itself is difficult, since a submarine is an extremely sophisticated and technical piece of machinery. Indeed I dare say that the few words that I have written up to now may seem technical to the uninitiated. However, a certain amount of 'tech talk' is I'm afraid, unavoidable.

As the urge to write did not descend upon me until I had almost reached the age of sixty-five, I deeply regret that my memory does not allow me to name all those magnificent submariners with whom it was my privilege to serve, or to know the ultimate rank or title of some of those mentioned. Mostly my words have been of praise or admiration, but in the very rare cases where there has been a lack of esteem, or fault to be found in a person, I have been careful to omit names. But of course, whatever I have written in this vein has been purely my own opinion.

I should perhaps say at this stage, that this book was originally intended only for the benefit of my family, a story that could be passed down the family tree. It was many years after completing it that I loaned it to certain of my friends to read, and subsequently these people have talked me into offering it for publication. I have made a conscious effort not to over glamorise my tale, in fact, being so well acquainted with the discomforts of submarine life and the rigours of war, there is probably a tendency to under-emphasise certain incidents.

I greatly appreciate, and sincerely thank Vice Admiral Sir Ian McIntosh KBE. CB. DSO. DSC. for his kindness in writing a foreword. I would also like to thank those very kind people who took it upon themselves to type the very lengthy original manuscript, my daughter Joan Lockley, my niece Margaret May, and my friend Iris Armstrong, whose husband 'Bob,' with much skill and patience, prepared the illustrations from some very indifferent photographs and prints. Finally I would like to thank my good friend and fellow ex-submariner John Kiff, who has spent many hours editing, re- typing and preparing this lengthy epistle, and making its publication a reality.

Joel. C. E. Blamey.

Part One - The Pre-War Years

At this time I felt like a poor swimmer who had been thrown in at the deep end. It was hard to imagine ever caring for this life, and to say that I had qualms about diving in one of these small and uncomfortable machines would be a major understatement.

Chapter One

I have no diary to help me in documenting my story. During the war years we were forbidden to keep diaries, and in any case I very much doubt that I would have ever found sufficient time to record the day-to-day happenings in my life during the period I write about now. Access to war patrol reports is still at this time restricted, and so I must rely very much on my memory and the memories of surviving friends and relatives in order to produce this account of my personal association with submarines and the submarine service.

My first encounter with submarines was in March 1925 when, having completed my four and a half years apprenticeship as a naval artificer, I was drafted to *HMS Valiant*, a battleship of the Queen Elizabeth class serving in the Mediterranean Fleet. To get there, I was given a 'working passage', which in the event turned out to be not an altogether pleasant experience.

My story starts when, together with several of my fellow fifth class Engine Room Artificers (E.R.A.'s), I humped my personal belongings aboard *HMS Princess Margaret*, berthed in Portsmouth harbour. The *'Princess Maggie'* as she was known, was an old passenger ship that had been converted to a minelayer, but she was well able to accommodate and employ us 'young rookies'. The next two weeks should have been an interesting and pleasant introduction to our sea-going lives, however this was not to be. In reality we largely were ignored, we felt that nobody really cared for us or even wanted us aboard. Altogether a most inauspicious start!

A fortnight, and several sea exercises later we found ourselves in Portland Harbour where eight of us, including myself were transferred to the battleship *HMS Royal Oak* of the Atlantic Fleet. *Royal Oak* was due to take part in spring manoeuvres before meeting up with the Mediterranean Fleet at Gibraltar early in March. We were aboard her for seven weeks in all before arriving at Gibraltar, having taken part in many exercises in the English Channel and the Bay of Biscay, culminating with combined fleet manoeuvres in the Atlantic.

We had been given a particularly miserable time in *Royal Oak*, mainly due to the senior C.E.R.A. (Chief Engine Room Artificer) who was notorious for the treatment of his juniors. This of course did nothing to improve our situation, and I began to wonder whether this was the lifestyle that I should expect for the future. But now of course, I look back on those days aboard *Royal Oak* as part of my learning curve, all good and very necessary experience

On arrival at Gibraltar, the four of us due to join *HMS Valiant* were bitterly disappointed to learn that she was still at Malta, not yet having completed a short refitting period. Our colleagues had been dispersed to their various ships, but we four could not remain in *Royal Oak*, as she was returning to the U.K. So we were ordered to hump our belongings across to the other side of the tidal basin, to a distinctly unsightly vessel named *HMS Lucia*. *Lucia* was an old cargo ship that had been captured from the Germans in the First World War and converted to a submarine parent ship. She, together with a flotilla of six submarines and a small tender, *Adamant,* were in the process of wending their way eastward to form the First Submarine Flotilla at Malta. Although clean and freshly painted, *Lucia* looked a 'real old tub' when compared to the spick and span *Royal Oak*. She was a coal burner, and just recently converted for her current role. The submarine service appeared to be 'the poor relations' of the navy at that time, and there were certainly no specially designed parent ships.

Having lugged our cases, hammocks and very heavy sea chests up the long and steep gangway to *Lucia's* quarterdeck, we awaited further instructions from the Officer of the Day as to our temporary accommodation. We were pleased for the opportunity to gather our breath, as lifting those sea chests was no mean feat. The chests were issued to artificer apprentices in lieu of kitbags in those days, and they were very well made of thick durable wood, reinforced with steel corners. A board was screwed over the front of the chest to prevent damage to the drawers in transit, and the complete chest weighed almost two hundredweight. Having only the rank of Leading Hand, 5th class E.R.A.s were not entitled to any help until they became acting 4th class, then assuming the rank of Chief Petty Officer. Apparently it was necessary to draft the four of us together because it required at least four lusty lads to haul one of these chests from the deck of a pitching motorboat, up the narrow ships gangway to the upper deck, a distance of at least twenty-five feet.

We were tired, hungry and thoroughly despondent when the messenger finally returned from the Officer of the Day to inform us that we would not after all be accommodated in *Lucia,* instead we would have to go through the whole transit routine again as we were now to be billeted in *Adamant,* the small tender lying just astern.

This was a cruel blow, we had had a pretty demanding and exhausting time since we left our training ship, and now it really did seem to us that we weren't wanted; certainly very few people appeared willing to help us in any way. We of course, were under the grand misapprehension that having endured and completed four and a half years of intensive training and further education, we were now important members of His Majesty's Royal Navy – it had taken us less than two weeks to discover that we were not! Another very important part of my learning curve!

On our arrival in *Adamant,* we were treated to a warmer reception by this tiny vessel. We were, and must have looked, completely worn out. Seeing our plight they quickly rustled up some supper for us in the E.R.A.s mess. Our sleeping accommodation was to be our hammocks slung above the machinery in the small engineers workshop under the quarterdeck, and our meals would be taken in the mess after the Chief and his three E.R.A.s had eaten theirs.

Adamant had at one time been a private yacht, and she still appeared a most unlikely naval vessel. Her main purpose was to assist in the submarine exercises, either by acting as target or by recovering the dummy torpedoes, which even in those days cost almost £3000 each. These torpedoes were fitted with 'blowing heads' instead of 'high explosive war heads', so that at the end of it's run of approximately five miles, water would be blown from the head of the torpedo using high pressure air, this would then enable the torpedo to float nose up on the surface while awaiting recovery.

Adamant had no accommodation for submarine crews; in fact she had little enough for her own crew's requirements. We four were very much supernumerary, and kept out of the way as much as we were able, although the engine room staff seemed a pleasant and a happy band. We were not required to keep watches during the voyage to Malta, but we were certainly not mollycoddled! The E.O. (engineer officer) found work for us aplenty, not only to keep us busily employed throughout the day but also into the first dogwatch and often into the last dog as well. We could not have our supper until the ships company E.R.A.'s had had theirs at 18:30, so we had to work until that time before cleaning ourselves and making ready to have our repast at 19:00. This did seem to us to be a little unnecessary, since most of the work we did was created for our benefit, nevertheless our life was heavenly when compared to being under the critical eye of the *Royal Oak* senior C.E.R.A. We saw very little of the engineer officer, who had himself been a submarine officer, and this was our first association with submarines and submariners. Many of *Adamant's* crew were either ex-submariners or spare crew.

Every day during the weeklong trip we were 'attacked' by the submarines in company with us. The sea was glassy calm and we could not resist popping our heads up through the workshop hatch to view these strange looking vessels breaking surface after having carried out an attack on either ourselves or *Lucia*. Early each day the submarines would receive orders to proceed ahead, in order to carry out these dummy attacks as we passed through the areas allocated to each one of them. It must have been very difficult to carry out an unseen attack, since throughout the whole of our passage to Malta there was barely a ripple on the surface of the sea, which made it very easy to detect the tell tale wake of a periscope. Dummy torpedoes were rarely fired during this passage, but the accuracy of each attack could still be assessed on board the parent ship.

On arrival at Malta, *Adamant* moored astern of *Lucia* in M'sida Creek (Marsamxett Harbour), and one by one we watched the submarines secure up alongside the parent ship, the senior C.O. taking the inside berth. The whole atmosphere seemed quite bewildering to us youngsters. To start with we were moored only a few yards from the shore with the many gondola like dghaises milling around like bees, either trying to sell their wares, or offering to take us ashore. The main thoroughfare around the narrow creek was thronged with Maltese sightseers dodging the hooting buses and the native horse drawn karrozzins.

But we youngsters hadn't long to enjoy this spectacle; later in the day the four of us were instructed to again hump all our belongings into a motorboat that had arrived alongside from *HMS Valiant*. Four others who had taken passage in *Lucia* then joined us on the long trip from M'sida Creek (the farthermost creek in Marsamxett harbour) out into the sea before entering the Grand Harbour through the breakwater to French Creek where *Valiant* was secured alongside Corradina Wharf. So yet again, we found ourselves humping our hammocks, toolboxes and chests aboard one of H.M.ships, but this time we hoped that our tenure would be a little more permanent.

Aboard *Valiant* the quarterdeck messenger was dispatched to inform the senior C.E.R.A. of the arrival of eight 5th class E.R.A.s. What would our new inquisitor be like? We certainly hadn't had much luck up to now - and it seemed that the senior chief, or indeed any C.E.R.A. could either make or mar our existence. Well we didn't have long to wait, - and thankfully, he was a toff! C.E.R.A. Nicholls, (Nick, to all except us 5th class) was a west countryman, tough but sympathetic, almost fatherly toward us young rookies. There were more than thirty in the mess, all C.P.O.s except us, and this included six C.E.R.A.s. They were a happy crowd; in fact it was a happy ships company from the captain to the most junior stoker. *Valiant* was in many ways much the same as *Royal Oak*, but there was a marked difference in the general atmosphere. We worked hard and played hard. I was very keen on sport of all types, and *Valiant*, for the next fifteen months won almost all of the fleet competitions and trophies, whether it was firing the 15" or 6" guns, regattas or marathons. Life was indeed very pleasant.

On this ship, with a crew of almost eighteen hundred men, I was to meet several officers and ratings with who I would have much association when I later joined the submarine service. One messmate, Phil King, was to join submarines on the same day as myself, and to be a shipmate of mine several times in the future. Also two stalwart members of a most extraordinary gunroom, Midshipmen 'Jacky' Slaughter and Hugh Bone were to join submarines at about the same time, the former was to be my captain on more than one occasion.

Submarines were forgotten during this period, and we concentrated on qualifying for the various certificates that would allow us to be advanced to 4th class artificers, and to carry the rank of C.P.O. I was also bent on getting into most of the ships sports teams - pretty keen competition in *Valiant*.

Valiant had been on station for over a year when we joined her, and was due to return to the U.K. in June 1926 for a long refit. In the meantime, the *Queen Elizabeth* had joined our squadron (which also included *Barham, Malaya* and *Warspite*), but owing to a serious electrical defect *Queen Elizabeth* was then ordered to take *Valliant's* place for refit in Portsmouth. As the *Queen Elizabeth's* crew had been on station for less than eighteen months they were to remain behind with *Valiant*, and

Valiant's crew were to steam *Queen Elizabeth* home. The two huge battleships came alongside each other and practically the whole of the two crews changed over – an extraordinary evolution. Not having been on station for eighteen months, we youngsters counted ourselves very lucky to stay with our shipmates and return to the U.K.

Almost as soon as we arrived at Portsmouth most of the crew including myself were drafted to Devonport Barracks (then *HMS Vivid*, later renamed *HMS Drake*), where we were given the Foreign Service leave to which we were entitled, in my case nearly three weeks, a fortnight for the first year, and one day for each subsequent month.

On return from leave I was summoned to the drafting office to be informed that subject to passing a rigorous medical examination, I was conscripted into the submarine service. There were six of us detailed for submarines, including Phil King and two others who had been in my artificers apprentice entry.

This draft didn't mean very much to me one way or the other, I vaguely understood that it was a voluntary service, but if they required conscripts, then it was all right with me. I was not in the least concerned about my physical fitness, although I was aware that the sight in my right eye was inferior to that of the left, and it was with a great sense of relief that I passed this examination as A1.

My mother was rather concerned about my draft to the submarine service, and it was most unfortunate that the day before we entrained for Portsmouth, the submarine *H29* sank alongside the wall in Devonport Dockyard, almost within sight of my home. Someone had been making adjustments to the trim while the hatches were still open, a very dangerous practice, but one that had happened before, and has happened since. Water had poured down the for'd hatch, and the C.E.R.A. who was the extremely capable and popular 'Sandy' Goodlet, with total disregard for his own safety, plunged down the hatch in an effort to shut it from the inside, a brave but abortive endeavour which cost him his life. Sadly several lives were lost in this accident, one in particular being George Elliot, a young engine fitter who lived near us and was a contemporary of mine at school. This disaster upset my mother a great deal, and made my parting the next day even more difficult.

So off we set to Portsmouth on the 13th of August 1926, again complete with our hammocks, sea chests and suitcases. On arrival at the Harbour Station we then crossed the harbour in a motor launch to join *HMS Dolphin* (Fort Blockhouse), a shore establishment lying on the seaward side of Haslar Creek. *Dolphin* was the depot for the submarine service, and the training school for submariners. We were shown into our mess, which was the whole of the ground floor of Bonadventure Block (Chiefs and Petty Officers had the first floor). We were told which watch we would be in, and then given a slinging billet for our hammocks, and finally some supper.

The Admiralty had only recently commenced conscription for service in submarines. Hitherto there had been sufficient volunteers, but now, with a rapidly expanding service, the volunteer quotas were becoming inadequate. The conscript period was for three years only, on completion of which conscripts would be returned to general service, thus forming a useful reserve. The volunteer period was for five years, but in most cases this was extended if the man concerned so desired. There were many with at least three times this period of service.

Fort Blockhouse, with the old parent ship *HMS Dolphin* tied up alongside, was a very unusual looking shore establishment comprising a number of odd buildings which had sprouted up around the original small fortress overlooking the western side of the entrance to Portsmouth harbour. New accommodation blocks and workshops having been added as and when required within the area bounded by the jetties on the one side, and the sea wall forming a rampart on the other, inside of which the main gate was situated, just beyond Bonadventure Block. The living accommodation, even for officers, was most inadequate for the numbers undergoing training, plus the spare submarine crew, and the crews of the eight or ten submarines that formed the 5th Submarine Flotilla. Captain S/M 5 was accommodated within the precincts, while the FLAG OFFICER SUBMARINES (F.O.S.M.) flew his flag from the old outdated parent ship *Dolphin*. Each building in Fort Blockhouse was named after an old parent ship or tender, and the submarines carried only pennant numbers.

The senior C.E.R.A. of the E.R.A.s mess was a huge tough character, very suitably named 'Bill' Sykes. Bill was a well-known figure throughout the submarine service, and he ruled the mess with a rod of iron, but more of the 'legendry' 'Bill' Sykes later.

Together with another six E.R.A.'s who had been conscripted from the Portsmouth and Chatham divisions, we commenced our submarine training almost immediately. The course lasted only three weeks in those days, during which time we attended a constant round of lectures on submarine construction and submarine machinery. For practical experience we went to sea in one of the little 'H' class submarines two or three times a week. These boats had a surface tonnage of only 440 tons, a length of 170 feet and a crew of twenty-two men. H29, which had recently sunk in Devonport, was a boat of this class. There were about ten of them still in commission at that time.

To say that I had qualms about diving in one of these small uncomfortable little submarines would be a major understatement. I can't say that I suffered from claustrophobia any more than the average person when shut up in a small space, but these were single hulled boats that rolled and pitched like the very devil in any sort of sea. Then there was the ever-present smell of diesel fuel permeating throughout the boat, mingling with the acrid stench of battery gas. We trainees, being additional to the crew, made space even more restricted, and when on the surface the noise of the main engines in this steel shell was deafening.

Leaving harbour at 08:00, we normally reached our exercise area about two hours later. There was a brief break for lunch either on the surface, or preferably dived, where at least we could retain the food in our bellies a little longer, and we returned to harbour at 18:00 – just in time to get cleaned up for supper in the mess.

It was late summer but the weather was generally poor, and if not actually sick, I felt anything but well on these sea trips, not yet being accustomed to the smell and the noise, the biggest causes of my distress. At that time it was hard to imagine ever caring for this life, but working hard between bouts of nausea I learned as much as possible about the main and auxiliary machinery, and the method of diving and carrying out the many evolutions that might be needed in emergency, such as the hand operation of normally power operated equipment.

There were two big advantages when a boat was dived, firstly the infernal din of the diesel engines would cease, and secondly there was little or no rolling. But since part of our training was the process of diving and surfacing we didn't remain dived for very long periods, and whereas the boat's crew broke into two watches soon after leaving harbour, we trainees were kept on duty the whole time.

At this time I felt very much like a poor swimmer thrown in at the deep end. There seemed so much to learn in such a short time and under such poor conditions. At the end of our short training period we were given a written examination, which we all succeeded in passing, after which we became eligible for draft to any type of submarine.

The submarine service was still quite small at that time, there was the one and only X1 of over 3600 tons dived, which beside her conventional torpedo armament, carried two twin 6" gun turrets. There were the few old 'H' class boats, less than thirty 'L' class (six of which carried a 4" gun platform at either end of their bridge structure). Two or three 'K' class, of about 1900 tons, which were propelled by steam turbine, two 'R' Class and three 'M' class, the forerunners of the mine laying submarines. Of this 'M' class, only M3 was completed as a minelayer. M1 was adapted to carry a 12" gun, and M2 was fitted out as a seaplane carrier.

The 'K' class, of which several were lost during the First World War, were designed as fast (23 knots) fleet submarines with two boilers, the funnel making this class very vulnerable when diving in haste. They carried two 4" guns.

Reference is made to the gun armament because it was an easy method of visual recognition, but the main armament of all submarines of that time was torpedo tubes – mostly six bow tubes. Guns were secondary armament, used in surprise attacks on vessels not worth a torpedo, not only because of the cost of a torpedo, but to conserve the torpedo for more worthwhile targets. In difficult attacks on important targets, a spread of sometimes six torpedoes would be fired in order to achieve a hit. Most submarines carried only twelve torpedoes.

I remained in Fort Blockhouse as spare crew for several moths before being drafted to a submarine. This gave me the chance to catch my breath and learn a little more about the job that I was about to embark upon, and the type of chaps that I was going to be shipmates with. I was employed mostly in the workshops and the floating dock repair party. There was a small floating dock attached to the establishment where submarines of the 5th flotilla could undergo their half yearly docking in order to carry out inspections and minor repairs. This included refitting all hull valves, renewing the anti-corrosion zinc plates, of which there were hundreds, changing propellers and removing hydroplanes, as well as scraping and painting the hull and external main ballast tanks. We also had to carry out checks and adjustments to torpedo bow cap and bow shutter clearances in order to ensure that the torpedoes did not foul when they were fired. Each torpedo tube had a bow cap, a bow shutter (a fairing plate to streamline the bow of the submarine when the torpedo tube was not in use), and a rear door. When a torpedo was fired the rear door was of course shut, and the bow cap and shutter were opened by telemotor (hydraulic) pressure.

There was invariably very much to be done in a very short time, and the boats crew were given the assistance of those submariners forming the spare crews. This was valuable experience for us, although we were seldom given work within the hull. As the winter of 1926 drew on, this external work on the floating dock became more and more arduous, when it wasn't raining it was bitterly cold – an east wind would blow straight up through the dock. This really was a perishing cold winter, and it seemed that the prevailing wind was from the northeast. Frequently dogged by ice and snow, working on the high and narrow staging around a boat could be extremely dangerous. It was not practical to wear gloves for most of the work and consequently the fingers quickly became numbed. On one occasion while working about fifteen feet up on some staging with E.R.A. Bill Kemp, I heard a yell and turned to see Bill falling headfirst to the bottom of the dock. He hit the steel bottom with a sickening thud and I thought that he surely must be killed. Sliding down the ladder that rested against the staging, I arrived at the dock bottom almost as soon as Bill had (or so it seemed). He was unconscious, blood pouring from a wound in the back of his head and from his nose. Refraining from moving him, I shouted loudly for help, which came immediately from all around. In a trice a stretcher had appeared and Bill was carted off to the sick bay. I thought that this must be the end of Bill, but like most submariners he was pretty tough. A few weeks in RN Hospital Haslar and he was back in harness once more. But after this accident Bill was inclined to get giddy spells and was subsequently drafted back to general service. I did bump into him many years later, and he assured me that he had completely recovered.

This accident brought forth a flood of orders intended for our safety. To start with, each one of us working on high staging was required to wear a stout lifeline around his waist, but we soon found that this wasn't practical as, in order to be properly mobile, we had to have at least six to eight feet of slack on the line, which meant that if we did fall, then we would get half way down before being bisected. Submariners in the main spurned this type of precaution, probably because they lived dangerously anyway!

I had been in the outfit long enough by this time to appreciate these established submariners. They were mostly a hard working, hard swearing and hard drinking lot, but I soon discovered what grand people they were. They were not only tough – toughness was an essential quality in the 'Trade' (as the submarine service was referred to) – but they were mostly men of great principal, staunch and very loyal. This became more manifest to me as the years rolled by. There were of course the exceptions, but these were few and far between.

So what prompted these men to volunteer? It certainly wasn't for comfort, or for an easy time. Extra pay was hardly an incentive, since this was barely sufficient to cover the extra expenses incurred, and if glamour or glory was expected, they were soon to be disappointed. I think that it could only be their spirit of adventure.

At that time, and certainly for many years to come, the extra pay was poor. We. C.P.O.s received an extra 2/6d per day, (12p), as 'danger money' In addition to this we received 1/3d (6p), when actually part of a submarine crew, and 1/3d for every twenty four hours spent at sea, or if we were forced to live aboard the submarine in the absence of a parent ship (termed as 'hard laying' money). So collectively this made a grand total of 5/- per day, or 25p in new money. Officers received a little more and junior ratings a little less, but as our clothing lasted a fraction of the time it would have done had we been in general service, we considered that by and large we were still out of pocket.

Stoppage of submarine pay was a frequent form of punishment for minor offences, but if this was a justifiable form of punishment for wrong doers, it was debatable whether or not it was strictly legal. Nobody seemed to mind very much, it was a small sum anyway and the offenders probably regarded themselves as fortunate. Actually we thought very little about pay, even though sometimes our general service colleagues chafed us about our 'huge bank balances' when we went ashore.

The Royal Navy had never lacked volunteers for arduous and hazardous tasks, and the shortage of volunteers for the submarine service was entirely due to lack of propaganda. Most navy men, like myself, knew little or nothing about submarines. Submariners were in a small closed service that, by the very nature of their work and environment, mixed little with others.

Anything more uncomfortable than a submarine on the surface in a rough sea is hard to imagine, and of course in those days before the advent of the snorkel, and indeed nuclear power, much of our time was spent on the surface. We wouldn't dive merely to dodge bad weather, as we would have to surface to recharge our batteries after fourteen hours anyway. Diving in a very rough sea was considered dangerous in any case, as whilst in the process of diving, a submarine is in a very unstable condition.

It was possible to remain dived for about twenty-four hours provided we proceeded at slow speed on one shaft with the two main motors on that shaft 'grouped down'. This meant that the motors were connected in series as opposed to being in parallel ('grouped up'), and gave a speed of one to one and a half knots, just sufficient to provide steerage way and to maintain the boats trim. Not having any form of air conditioning or being able to replace the oxygen in the boat, twenty four hours was just about the limit, by that time the oxygen content would be extremely low, and the CO_2 content very high.

I have laid stress on the discomfort and the squalid conditions under which we lived because this above all else was the thing that I noticed. This does not reflect discredit on the captains or the crews, or for that matter on the hierarchy of the service. Everything possible was done to keep these boats clean and habitable, but this was very much like trying to make a silk purse out of a sow's ear. Little could be done until living conditions came a little higher on the list of priorities. The submarine hull was constructed and then filled with masses of machinery, miles of pipe work and electric cable, then the batteries were installed, and finally the weapon systems. The accommodation was then squeezed into whatever space was left over, which was very little. It was apparent that crew comfort could only come with a larger submarine, and there were very good reasons at that time why submarines could not be larger.

As submarines were fighting units, fighting efficiency must be a paramount consideration. Nevertheless living conditions must have improved during the twenty-five years since their inception and my joining them. Much has been written about submarine 'heads' (toilets), always a bit of a joke - that is until you have to use one. Weird and frightening contraptions, fitted with a mass of valves, levers, non-return flaps and pressure gauges, all contained in a tiny space where there was hardly room to move. One almost needed a degree in engineering to operate these heads, and I always had the greatest admiration for newcomers to submarines who emerged from the 'heads' clean and in one piece. The system was designed to allow the user to blow his waste to sea using air pressure, but one had to very careful to follow instructions to the letter in order to prevent 'getting your own back' and this sometimes happened even to the most seasoned of submariners, especially if ones predecessor had not released the air pressure correctly. In the 'H' class, there was one 'head' allocated for the whole of the crew. This was situated at the after end of the engine room between the two engine clutches, and the officers had one forward. If one didn't feel seasick on arrival, the smell of oil fuel and bilge water sloshing around one's feet was often enough to ensure a good vomit in rough weather. There was much to be said for constipation.

Needless to say, being a junior E.R.A. it often fell to my lot to refit these 'heads' when they went wrong, which was quite frequently. Of course they really came under the care of the 'outside E.R.A.' (more affectionately known as the 'outside wrecker'), who was responsible for all the machinery outside of the engine room, but being usually a fairly senior E.R.A., whenever there was a problem with the 'heads', the 'wrecker' would invariably discover a more important defect requiring his attention.

I hadn't been in Fort Blockhouse very long when an E.R.A. Les (Jan) Honeywell, who organized the ratings rugby teams, enquired whether or not I was a rugby player. On learning that I was he quickly included me in the team, and I was later chosen to play for the *Dolphin* 1st team. This was quite an honour as *Dolphin* had a reputation of fielding two strong teams. Several internationals and many full navy caps have come from the submarine service.

But there was one drawback as far as I was concerned. Most of these weekly matches were played in the evenings, and I was obliged to stop work a little earlier than normal on match days in order to dash out to the Haslar playing field in time for the kick-off. My immediate boss was the notorious Bill Sykes, and Bill didn't approve of junior E.R.A.'s asking for time off to play games, but he had very little option. He would glower and mutter every time my request was submitted, even though I had volunteered to make up the time. He was a huge fellow, and very proud of the magnificent eagle that was tattooed across his broad back, he could also be a very frightening man, and his language had to be heard to be believed. He had a tough job in that he had a tough crowd to deal with, and was more than a little feared by his E.R.A.s, and most of the junior officers as well. Bill had been in the submarine service for fifteen years, and carried much weight, both literally and metaphorically. Because of his bulk he could easily have been used to adjust the trim on a smaller submarine. As time went by Bill seemed to mellow toward my rugby, and toward me. I had after all, volunteered to make up the time.

Bill had many admirable traits, and certainly did not lack courage. He eventually completed his twenty-two years for pension, and soon afterwards volunteered to be the engineer aboard one of the two submarines built by Vickers for delivery to the Chilean navy. He continued to serve the Chilean navy in this capacity for several years, a job that he would be capable of doing very efficiently, but I often wonder if they have ever recovered from Bill. He was an awkward cuss, and certainly not one to be dictated to, moreover the language barrier would not have helped. Bill Sykes was just one of the extraordinary characters one meets in submarines, and there were plenty of those about, not just in my branch, but in all branches, including the officers.

There was much work to be done at that time, the duty watch (we were duty every fourth night) always had to continue work until 18.30 and then, together with the duty watch of stokers, keep a four-hour watch on the diesel generators sometime during the night. Fort Blockhouse had to produce its own electricity in those days; it was many years before we had our power from the national grid.

Les Honeywell, who introduced me to rugby in *Dolphin*, hailed from the little market town of Newton Abbot in South Devon, and we later became great friends, having subsequently served in the same flotilla and played in the same rugger team several times. Les had volunteered for 'the trade' four years previously and was at that time, serving in *L25*, a single gun 'L' class submarine. When eventually I retired from the navy, and came to live in Newton Abbot we renewed our acquaintance and used to meet each week in the Market House Inn to settle world affairs. If only the heads of state did but heed our counsel!

Les's interest and hobby was collecting and collating writings, books and papers pertaining to the history of submarines, parent ships, and their crews. He had a library of almost four hundred books (excluding fiction). He is regarded as an authority on this subject nationally, and even internationally – having translated many books and documents into English. He has also been of great help to the curators of the R.N. library and the museum and library at HMS *Dolphin*, as well as the BBC.

Early in 1927 I was drafted to the submarine *L52*, which was nearing the end of an extensive refit at Portsmouth Dockyard, and I spent the next few weeks commuting between the Dockyard (to work) and Fort Blockhouse (to eat and sleep). Bernard Gavin, a contemporary of mine who joined submarines with me, and Ted Burgess, who was a little older, but fairly new to 'the Trade', were drafted at the same time, and this is where we met another extraordinary character, 'Chinky' Rice. 'Chinky' was *L52s* C.E.R.A. and had been standing by her throughout the refit. She was still in a bit of a mess when we joined her, but this gave us a good opportunity to see all the various pieces of her machinery that were being replaced, to trace through her numerous systems, and to witness the many tests and trials being carried out by the dockyard workmen.

On completion of her refit, *L52* was to join the 2nd Submarine Flotilla at Devonport; this of course suited me admirably as my home was there. Nevertheless it would be with a twinge of regret that I would leave the Portsmouth area. I had served a four and a half year apprenticeship aboard *HMS Fisgard*, which was moored in the harbour there. I had also enjoyed, and was still enjoying some fine rugby, and I often saw my younger brother who was now serving his apprenticeship. Apprentices received very little money, and I was pleased to be able to treat him to a Y.M.C.A. supper on the few occasions he was allowed ashore. When almost broke these apprentices were able to feast on one sausage and mashed potatoes, a round of bread and butter and a cup of tea for what is now less than 2p.

The last few weeks of any refit are inevitably hectic and extremely busy. It was during this period that we discovered what an extraordinary fellow 'Chinky' was. It was very difficult to guess his age because he wore a beard, he must have been between thirty-five and thirty-eight, but he looked much older. He spent most of his time under the influence of alcohol to a greater or lesser degree, and his eyes were almost always bloodshot and glazed. He was a bachelor, professing to have no time for the female gender, but he was passionately fond of classical and operatic music and a large quantity of his pay was spent on drink and gramophone records. 'Chinky' was a most polite and well-spoken fellow, but was seldom seen without half a cigarette poking from the scruffy beard, which he probably grew to hide his protruding teeth. Nevertheless he was a very kindly and likeable character, and the most extraordinary thing about him was that he could accomplish things whilst under the influence, in half the time that we lesser mortals could when stone cold sober. Crosswords and mathematical problems were child's play to him, and only those who had experience could appreciate his dexterity in adjusting the clearances of all exhaust, induction, fuel injection and air starting valves on a twelve-cylinder diesel engine in just two complete revolutions of the crankshaft.

If it alarmed 'Chinky' to have three E.R.A.s who were brand new conscripts to submarines as his messmates, he certainly didn't show it. Ted Burgess was a coppersmith and moulder, and I was an engine-smith, which couldn't have been very reassuring to 'Chinky', as 90% of the work done by E.R.A.s in a submarine is 'fitting'. However, the ten months of fitting and turning we did as apprentices stood us in good stead, as this was all I did for many years to come.

I was still eligible to play rugby for *Dolphin*, and really looked forward to my couple of games each week, working much overtime to compensate for the hour or two that I had to take off in order to play, and often swapping a Saturday duty for a Sunday, or even two weekdays. The E.R.A.'s team at Portsmouth was a very fine one, even better than *Dolphin's* team. There were probably only a couple of teams locally who could beat them.

Eventually *L52's* refit was complete, and we had to proceed to sea for main engine and diving trials. It was policy in those days to have a full power acceptance trial at the end of a refit, a policy that I did not entirely agree with, but it set a high standard to test the dockyard's workmanship. It was the crew that actually ran the engines, with the dockyard men and the depot ship representatives in attendance, the former to execute any repairs, and the latter to take statistical records.

We reached our billet in the Solent and gradually worked up to full power, which then had to be maintained for two hours. The engine room, indeed the whole boat seemed crammed full with officers and ratings, but although our engineer officer, W.O. Pat Waterson was there, together with Commander (E) and a lieutenant (E) from *Dolphin*, 'Chinky' Rice had already imposed his authority on the proceedings. He ordered Bernard Gavin to take the port engine, and me to take the starboard, and there we remained for the whole four hours, which included the working up period. Neither of us having been subjected to this nerve racking experience before, 'Chinky' kept giving us instructions on making any necessary fuel or timing adjustments, but this was a rather frustrating and almost impossible business, since it was difficult to interpret what he said at the best of times, but with 'Chinky' mumbling through his beard with the inevitable stub hanging from his mouth, and with the deafening roar of two twelve cylinder engines running at full power, it was well nigh impossible. Then there were all these bodies milling around, all it appeared, with a specific purpose. There was a moderate sea running, causing us to pitch and making it difficult to maintain accurate revolutions. When the bow plunged the propellers came near to the surface causing the engines to race, and then decelerating as the bows came up and the stern plunged downward.

We'd been at full power for about a half an hour when there was a sudden unearthly noise on my engine. Hoping I was doing the right thing, I eased the throttle immediately. I would have stopped the engine, but Pat Waterson signalled me not to. 'Chinky' who was busy taking fuel consumption readings behind me, tore past to reach the affected cylinder, having scant regard for anyone in his path. The noise was enough to have awakened the dead as one of the large exhaust valve springs had become detached and had run amok, almost decapitating one or two people before coming to rest at the back of the port engine. This spiral spring that normally returns the exhaust valve to its seat is about ten inches long, four inches in diameter and weighs about two lbs. The piston crashing onto the open exhaust valve each time it came to the top of its stroke made the noise.

Although I had reduced speed from 360 to 200 revolutions it amazed me to see 'Chinky' successfully re-secure this huge spring within five minutes, while the valve was still bobbing up and down. It seemed an incredible achievement to me at the time, although I soon learned to do it myself .It was quite a dangerous operation and one was jolly fortunate to get away with anything less than a blackened fingernail while performing it. These springs did not often become detached but we were constantly replacing them as the metal became fatigued and fractured.

The power trial continued with reasonable success, after which we passed the dockyard staff concerned with the main engines only, to a launch for return to the yard while we proceeded to our diving billet to the seaward side of the Isle of Wight. We each had about a quarter of an hour to devour some sandwiches, before we arrived at our station, where there was a destroyer awaiting us in case of mishap.

Here we did our first real dive following our refit, although L52 had already been partially submerged in the Dockyard basin in order to test the watertight integrity of the many hull valves that had been refitted, and to allow the First Lieutenant to work out a diving trim. I found it a little surprising that trimming the boat was the First Lieutenant's duty and not the engineer officer's, however, it all seemed to work very well, and it certainly ensured that before the First Lieutenant became a C.O. he was well acquainted with the layout and the general construction of the submarine.

We had no thrills on this dive as it was done in very slow time in only twenty fathoms of water. The First Lieutenant caught a good trim and we slid quietly to one hundred feet to give the hull glands and fittings a good test – 45 lb per sq inch. There were several minor leaks that were made good by either the dockyard staff or ourselves. The stern glands (where the propeller, or tail shafts passed through the pressure hull), were found to be leaking slightly, and as my 'diving station' was in the after ends, 'Chinky' sent word for me to tighten them up. This was a fairly straightforward operation even though the glands were awkward to get at. I knew that one must tighten up gradually all the way around the gland – in fact there was a rack on the gland to ensure this, but I was not experienced enough to know that by tightening the gland only the tiniest bit too much, the gland would overheat very quickly. However, I slackened off before there was any damage done to the gland packing.

Soon after this, the diving trials and the engine acceptance trials having gone completely satisfactorily, we returned to harbour, berthing alongside the jetty at Fort Blockhouse. And I, still filled with the curious mixture of anticipation and excitement that had been with me throughout the day, but now tempered with relief and an overwhelming tiredness, made my way inboard, thanking my lucky stars that I was not 'duty watch' on that evening. Now I was just looking forward to our move to Devonport.

Chapter Two

L52's C.O. was Lt Cdr D.M.Leathes, a reserved but extremely experienced and efficient officer. He had joined *L52* at the end of her refit and, together with the rest of us was still getting the feel of her. As we carried two 4-inch guns, our fourth officer was a commissioned Warrant Officer (gunner), Mr. Fryer. It was the privilege of all Warrant Officers to be addressed as Mister, although it was usual that the only Warrant Officers carried in submarines were engineers; Mr. Fryer was an exception. Our well seasoned E.O., Warrant Officer Mr. Pat Waterson, knew enough about submarines to allow 'Chinky' Rice to dictate policy in the engine room, and was tactful enough to turn a blind eye to his shortcomings.

On our arrival at Devonport, we berthed alongside the submarine tender *Adamant*, in which I had taken my first passage to Malta back in 1925. Although *Adamant* could not accommodate submarine crews, she was to be our parent ship for the next few months until *HMS Lucia* joined us, having herself completed a dockyard refit. This was no great hardship for those of us who had homes in Devonport or the Plymouth district, and we of course, went ashore whenever we had the opportunity.

It was small wonder that our No.1 suits did not last us for very long in those days. Even Chiefs and Petty Officers only had one small seat locker and one even smaller suitcase in which to store all our kit. The E.R.A.'s mess measured only seven feet by seven feet, and was just six feet high amidships. In this mess were four drop down bunks lying athwart ships in pairs one above the other, and one seat locker, which ran fore and aft against the hull, also serving as a bunk for our stoker mess man. The E.R.A.'s were entitled to a mess man, whose main duties were to clean the mess and to prepare the food. He was excused all other duties, except to operate valves within the vicinity of the mess while at 'Diving Stations' and to assist in the supply of ammunition while at 'Gun Action Stations', the latter because the magazine for the 4-inch shells was immediately below the E.R.A.'s mess. We were very lucky to have a good mess man, as it was often difficult to get stokers to volunteer for this job.

Each mess elected a 'caterer' who had to provide the food for all meals no matter how long we were at sea, without presenting his messmates with a heavy mess bill at the end of each month – this was no mean job! A monthly mess bill however, was inevitable. We were only allowed 1/11d (less than 6p) per man per day – even in those days it was impossible to live on that amount however meagre the fare. The caterer would normally deal with the 'pusser' (naval victualler) for about half his requirements, usually tea, sugar, condensed milk, meat and potatoes, and with a general dealer specialising in catering for ships companies for the remainder. It seemed impossible that these dealers could make any profit, but they must have because even in the United Kingdom, they clamoured for our custom. If the mess caterer could not rid himself of this office, that is, if none of his messmates would take a turn at the job, there was one sure way out of it, and that was to see that there was a mess bill of at least £3 or £4 to be paid at the end of each month.

We did however, have one big advantage over our general service counterparts. A kind benefactor had at some time left sufficient capital to provide submarine crews with a free issue of food after they had been at sea for longer than twenty-four hours. This was termed 'submarine comforts' and consisted mainly of tinned food, sardines, herrings, soup, cocoa, sausages and even bacon. These 'submarine comforts' helped a great deal in keeping our mess bills down.

If I have dwelt upon this eating and catering aspect a little long, that is because eating did form a very important part of our existence. When at sea there was little else to look forward to except the next meal, and getting ashore again. Also, since the basic pay for an acting 4th class E.R.A. was but 9/6d per day, even a mess bill of £2 at the end of the month was more than we wanted.

And what of the poor cook? Who wasn't a cook anyway! He was usually a seaman who either volunteered, or was pushed into the job. If the engineers and electrical experts thought they had problems, (and they very often had), my heart bled for the cook. Equipped with just a small electric cooker, hardly adequate for a large family, situated in a galley not even six feet square, this stout hearted chap would have to cook at least forty eight breakfasts, dinners and suppers each day, which sometimes included up to five or even six completely different menus, often with the boat pitching and rolling heavily, and with only the company of the thousands of cockroaches that thrived in the warm inaccessible niches behind the cooker, despite the repeated efforts of the First Lieutenant and his henchmen to exterminate them.

The cook had ample excuse for spoiling the odd meal, by either over or under cooking it, or by over salting, boiling dry etc. But this seldom happened. He often had to deal with electrical breakdowns caused by short circuits when pots over spilled on a particularly heavy roll, and sometimes there were storms that made it impossible to cook at all when the boat was on the surface. It was a blessing for us all, particularly the cook, when a form of 'general messing' was introduced a few years later.

Bread storage was always a problem, it was kept high up on racks in the torpedo stowage compartment, which usually doubled as the seamen's mess. Bread in those days went stale very quickly, and after just a few days in the humid atmosphere, a dirty green mould would develop and would permeate into the very centre of each loaf. A free issue of rock hard ship's biscuits would help out after four of five days at sea.

The subject of food should not be closed without a word on the one and only refrigerator. This fridge had a capacity of about sixteen cubic feet and served a crew of about forty-eight people, so all food had to be labelled as to whose mess it belonged, and the day that it would be required.

The 2nd Submarine Flotilla comprised L52, L53, L54, L56, L69 and L71. All were 'double gun' 'L' class with one 4-inch gun platform forward, and one aft of the bridge structure. They were also fitted with six 21-inch torpedo tubes in the bows. The two twelve cylinder diesel engines gave a surface speed of sixteen knots, and could be de-clutched allowing the main motors to give a maximum speed of nine knots underwater. This underwater speed could not be maintained for very long however, as the power to drive the main motors were supplied from three huge batteries, each of 110 cells. These batteries, situated under the control room and the accommodation space, would of course soon become discharged; the main engines driving the motors as generators carried out re-charging. A battery charge took anything between four to seven hours and this, of course had to be carried out while on the surface.

Each submarine spent about four days of each week at sea carrying out attacks, either gun or torpedo on the target provided, which more often than not, was *HMS Adamant*. If not doing this, we would be hunted by anti-submarine vessels, which were fitted, as we were, with very sensitive listening devices. Billeted in Cremyll Creek, it often took us over two hours to reach our allocated exercise area, which resulted in a very long day at sea.

At about this time a tall gangling young Sub Lieutenant joined us, Ben Bryant. It was always prudent to stand aside and give Ben his rein when he was stampeding through the narrow gangway on the way to his 'diving station' when the klaxon sounded. Over six feet in height he weighed thirteen stone, was a very useful rugby forward and nearly always wore leather sea boots. The sound of the klaxon, our call to 'diving stations', was alarming to say the least, and loud enough to wake the dead, but Ben in his sea boots and in full gallop was even more alarming. His 'diving station' was in the fore-ends, and mine close by at the forward blowing station. To avoid any physical injury I discreetly withdrew into the nearest mess until Ben flashed by. This young lad was yet another asset to *L52's* sporting capability, and as the C.O. of submarines *Sealion* and *Safari* was later to become one of our 'ace' submarine captains during World War Two. Later again, he became Rear Admiral 'Ben' Bryant C.B. D.S.O.** D.S.C.

Early in November 1927, *Lucia*, having completed her refit at Chatham Dockyard, rejoined our flotilla as the parent ship. Although this eased our living situation considerably as we could now eat and sleep aboard her when not at sea, no stretch of imagination could have regarded her as adequate accommodation for the crews of six submarines. She had reasonably good repair shops but the messes were very poor. The ships company E.R.A.'s and the submarine E.R.A.'s had separate messes, the latter being converted from what was originally a coalbunker. *Lucia*, except for the spring and summer cruises, rarely left her moorings in the Hamoaze almost opposite the little village of Cremyll on the Cornwall side.

When *Lucia* 'coaled ship' which thankfully due to her little time at sea, wasn't often, all submarines had to lie off. Not only until the coal lighter had departed and her bunkers had been trimmed, but until all her decks had been thoroughly scrubbed as well. Having been at sea all day, it could be 21:00 or later before the submarines were allowed back alongside to find, even with all the precautions taken, that a thick layer of coal dust had infiltrated our messes.

Casting off at 08:00 and securing alongside again at 18:00, does not appear to be an excessively long day, but it should be borne in mind that we went to 'stations for leaving harbour' well before 07:30, and when we returned there was often a battery charge to be carried out. The currents in that part of the Hamoaze could be very difficult for submarines securing alongside without damaging their rather frail main ballast tanks, which were of the 'saddle tank' type. Although the actual pressure hull was made from ¾ inch thick high quality steel, the saddle tank plating, which bore the brunt of any bumps when coming alongside, was only 3/16 inches thick. The slightest bump could cause rivets to spring, and subsequent leaks. It was infuriating, when having been at sea all day that it sometimes took over a half an hour of constant manoeuvring in order to secure alongside, all the time discharging our batteries even more.

On return from sea, besides recharging our batteries, there was often repair work to be carried out. The duty watch aboard, and the standby duty watch would share this, the rest of us could get cleaned and catch the next available liberty boat ashore. If a six-hour battery charge were required, then the standby watch would do the first two hours of this, to allow the duty watch to have supper before taking over. Unfortunately, by this time it was likely that the last liberty boat had gone, and unless there was an understanding and sympathetic Officer Of The Watch on the parent ship who would provide a special boat, it was too late to go ashore anyway. The duty watch of an E.R.A., one leading stoker, two stokers and one L.T.O. (leading torpedo operator, to attend to the electrics and to check the specific gravity of the battery acid) would then continue without a break until the early hours of the morning when the battery would again be fully charged. When the First Lieutenant, together with the duty P.O. did the rounds of the boat at 21:00 hours, it was customary for the duty E.R.A. to report 'Engineers rounds correct' even though the poor fellow hadn't had the opportunity to leave the engine room.

Depending on the submarine exercise requirements, each submarine would have a whole week in harbour every six weeks. This was to carry out any repair or routine examinations that could not normally be done in one day, or over one weekend. These 'maintenance weeks' were certainly no picnic for the crew, as firstly the engineer officer might have to seize this opportunity to change a couple of pistons or do some other heavy work which entailed pieces of dismantled machinery spread around the engine and motor rooms. Secondly the First Lieutenant would use this chance to open up the main battery tanks in order to take 'all round readings' (the density of each individual cell), and to top each cell up to the correct level with distilled water. It would be impossible for us to get into our messes during this operation. Thirdly the torpedo officer would have to disembark all torpedoes for overhaul in the parent ship, and then re-embark them. While this was happening the fore hatch would be out of use. And fourthly, at least one periscope would need to be changed, or at least its hoist wires renewed. In fact the whole boat would be in a completely chaotic state during this week, and quite uninhabitable. Indeed it was surprising that at the end of this self-refit, the boat became spick and span once more; and it was a great relief to get back to our normal routine and go to sea again.

My parents lived in St Budeaux, a suburb of Devonport, but my duty watches, a two and a half month spring cruise and exercises in the Mediterranean, and a similar period exercising in Scottish waters together with a Baltic cruise in the summer, meant that I saw very little of them. I did however; renew my acquaintance with my childhood sweetheart, Clare Polkinghorne – another reason for seeing so little of my parents

As *L52* was next due to refit in November 1928 in Devonport, Clare and I planned to get married then, with me hoping fervently that I would remain a member of the crew throughout the four or five month period of the refit. Having no money saved, I embarked on a stringent campaign of saving, remaining on board when on cruises, and doing 'subs' (substitutes) for my colleagues when they were duty. Although pay, even in submarines was still very meagre, I saved £150 in just over six months – a prodigious effort. My leisure time was occupied in writing long passionate love letters and rug making, and rather surprisingly I became quite proficient at both.

When in harbour, 'Chinky' Rice our enigmatic C.E.R.A. would return on board inebriated with monotonous regularity. Furthermore, whether in Devonport, Gibraltar, Valencia, Lisbon, Copenhagen or any of the Scottish ports, 'Chinky' would more often than not return on board with a bottle of either whisky or wine tucked into his trouser pocket. How he succeeded in getting away with this was amazing, as it was strictly forbidden to bring any alcohol on board.

Generous to the extreme, 'Chinky' would often take compassion on me and give me a bottle of Vermouth, thus making me an accessory, and sometimes even waking me up to do this. But it was very difficult to get cross with 'Chinky', and often after doing my stint charging batteries, or repair work, I'd return to the solitude of the mess to continue my letter writing or rug making, with a comforting glass of Vermouth beside me.

A great deal of our time while in harbour was spent on engine repairs or routine examinations in order to keep the machinery running efficiently. Much of this was hard, frustrating and, owing to inherent material or design weaknesses, often-repetitive work. With the vast experience of diesel engines, high pressure air compressors and telemotor (oil pressure operated) systems that Great Britain had at that time, it was surprising that we had so much trouble with this equipment. Air compressors, designed to charge the air bottle reservoirs to a pressure of 4000psi in about one and a half hours were the outside E.R.A.'s special nightmare, requiring to be fitted with new piston rings about every second time they were used. Three or four types of compressor were in use at that time, some a little better than others.

As far as the main engines were concerned, we were still experimenting with the use of various metals and alloys for our pistons and piston rings. And the vertical timing gear! - What an awkward job we had with that. Steel cylinder head bolts of nearly 1-½ inches diameter would snap like carrots. If we went to sea for a week it was usual to take about two hundred spare bolts. When these were used up, the cylinder heads were shored down from the hull with timber.

Despite this incessant grind the crews rarely grumbled, but one could well forgive them for having 'one over the eight' whenever they had the opportunity for a run ashore. Often they would return on board to find the duty watch still working, then, with a pang of conscience they would want to help with the job, even without changing out of their shore going apparel. This used to make me furious, but one had to be tactful as their intentions were good. Apart from the fact that they were in no condition to work anyway, most of the work involved the lifting and lowering of heavy machinery, where for safety reasons alone, great care had to be exercised. A piston and its connecting rod weighed nearly 3½ cwt.

Both our E.O. Pat Waterson, and our C.E.R.A. 'Chinky' Rice left L52 during 1928. The latter must have given the former many grey hairs; in fact 'Chinky' gave us all a few grey hairs. I t wouldn't have been so bad if he wasn't such a darned nice chap. Pat sent for me on one occasion and asked me if I was in the habit of giving the C.E.R.A. my tot of rum each day – which I hotly denied. We had been at sea for nearly a week and 'Chinky' was still 'under the influence'. The fact was that 'Chinky' had smuggled another bottle of whisky on board. This, together with his daily tot of rum (1/8 of a pint) and his already saturated condition when we sailed, had prevented him from regaining a sober state.

On another occasion, when we had just commenced a fortnight's docking in Devonport dockyard, 'Chinky' got himself knocked down by a car, receiving a really nasty leg wound. Someone helped him back to where he was temporarily accommodated, namely the cooking and washhouse alongside the dry dock, and although there was much work to be done in the boat, 'Chinky' did not appear for the whole period. His absence must have been noticed, at least by the E.O., but no questions were asked. We, his messmates, worked that little bit harder and strove to cover up for our chief, our mess man supplied him with food, and the Cox'n kept discreetly 'mum', a typical example of true submarine 'esprit de corps'.

As we were quite close to the R.N. Barracks, 'Chinky' would stagger into the sick bay each morning to get his wound dressed, and slowly it healed. It was surprising that the sick bay staff allowed him to leave - even they seemed to be intent on covering up for him, as indeed were the Dockyard Police. Each evening 'Chinky' would arise from his bed, stagger out of the dockyard gate and head into the nearest public house where he would stay until closing time. Nevertheless, at the end of our two weeks docking, he had more or less returned to normal, and was able to again take his rightful place as C.E.R.A. of the boat.

'Chinky' Rice was relieved by a pleasant and very experienced west-countryman, Sam Horne, who was as neatly turned out as 'Chinky' was untidy. Sam was a full-blown C.E.R.A. whereas 'Chinky' had never bothered to pass the exam. Actually the 'L' class were not entitled to a qualified C.E.R.A. as they were medium sized submarines and carried an engineer officer; our senior E.R.A. was referred to as the 'chief' but was unpaid. Only the larger submarines and those small 'H' class (which did not carry an E.O.) were entitled to a C.E.R.A.

There was another outstanding character in the crew of L52 that stands out in my memory, our Stoker Petty Officer, Tom Mudd. Tom was a delightful fellow, an ex pugilist, whether he had been a professional I do not know, but with two cauliflower ears and a broken nose, he certainly looked the part. We did carry a Chief Stoker but Tom was in charge of all the stokers who worked in the engine room, and was a tower of strength. Despite the playful but shrewd buffet administered for slackness in obeying his orders Tom enjoyed great popularity. He was always a cheerful optimist, and from time to time would go through the motions of shadow boxing. It was laughingly said that if we dived at the sound of a bell instead of the klaxon, Tom would come out of his corner fighting, instead of organizing his team to open or shut their respective valves and cocks

It was during this period in the 2nd Submarine Flotilla that I met a young Sub Lieutenant (E), Reginald Orlando Lockley, who was studying at the Royal Naval Engineering College at Devonport. He had commenced his naval career as an artificer apprentice, and was my brother's friend. After two years he, together with my brother, and another apprentice, had been summoned before a board in order to select one of them to be advanced to Sub Lieutenant. It was quite an achievement to be selected to appear before this annual promotion board, although one only would be selected for promotion from about two hundred apprentices, all of whom had already passed an extremely competitive examination from nationwide grammar and secondary schools. This brilliant young scholar from Kent was selected, and my brother arranged that he should be a welcome guest at our home whenever he wished. We became great friends, and he subsequently complicated our family tree by marrying my future wife's sister Violet, his nephew, Peter Lockley, marrying our only daughter.

In the late winter and early spring the flotilla took part in the combined fleet (Atlantic and Mediterranean) exercises, the two huge fleets meeting up at Gibraltar. As these two fleets comprised 75% of what was a very strong navy, this was a sight to behold – a magnificent spectacle indeed. The majority of the battleships and cruisers anchored in the bay between Gibraltar and the Spanish town of Algeciras, as there was scarcely room in the harbour to accommodate the flagships, destroyers and submarine parent ships.

The submarine flotillas (two parent ships and about sixteen submarines) were always given a berth in a sheltered spot to prevent too much bumping; the weather at that time of the year was usually foul. It was a tremendous advantage to be able to walk ashore from the parent ship rather than waiting for the liberty boat (ship's launch or motor boat), many of which had to travel a distance of up to two miles to the landing stage, which was not pleasant when there was a heavy sea running. It was an even greater advantage to be able to return on board at any time, instead of having to wait on the landing stage with crowds of 'well oiled' libertymen.

The total population of this huge fleet was in excess of fifty thousand men, of which perhaps a minimum of 20% would be ashore at any one time. Entry into Spanish territory (La Linea) was strictly forbidden, which meant that Gibraltar was literally saturated with naval personnel. This factor, apart from my ongoing endeavour to save, discouraged me from more than just an occasional 'run ashore'.

Before returning to our homeport, the flotilla invariably participated in a short 'showing the flag' cruise to one or two of the Spanish or Portuguese ports. I endeavoured to have one run ashore at each place but was not particularly enamoured with any of them; although this does not imply that some were not pleasant or interesting towns.

Without previous knowledge of these places one tended to just wander aimlessly around, unless there happened to be a tour organised by the local authorities. Sailors were landed in the dock area, where the majority were then inclined to migrate to the nearest drinking saloon, and stay there until it was time to return on board.

When embarking on these spring exercises, we almost invariably ran into a gale as soon as we left our home ports, the notorious Bay of Biscay, rarely in a pleasant mood at this time of the year, lived up to its reputation. On one occasion when the Atlantic Fleet used the ancient battleship *HMS Monarch* as a battle practice target, both for gunnery and torpedoes, it was so rough that the tug *St Jenny* turned turtle and sank with no survivors. During the summer exercises it was more usual to visit British and Scandinavian ports, which for me, was much more pleasant.

In the autumn of 1927 the 2nd submarine flotilla was ordered to Loch Ewe on the Scottish western seaboard, for extensive trials of the new Mk.8 torpedo. We were to spend two whole months there and any of the lads who had hoped to see the bright lights were to be very disappointed. Loch Ewe was a large well-sheltered anchorage, but miles away from a town of any size. The nearest small village that boasted a public house was Poolewe, five miles from the small wooden jetty where libertymen and recreational parties were landed. Foreseeing this bleak outlook, and realizing that there would be little to interest or entertain the submarine crews, Captain S/M had invited anyone owning a motorcycle to ship it aboard the parent ship before leaving Devonport. My *Rudge Whitworth* motorcycle was duly ridden into the dockyard, and lifted by crane onto *Lucia*.

The weather was pretty foul on our journey north, and the motor cycles, stowed in the waist of the ship and not under cover, were somewhat the worse for exposure to the salt sea air. There were about twenty of us who had brought our motorcycles, and we were instructed to land them as soon as we arrived. Four of us were fortunate enough to hire a small hut in the village of Poolewe, in which to keep them.

Whilst *Lucia, Adamant,* and the 2nd submarine flotilla were at Loch Ewe, the sports officer hired a flat field from the local farmer in order to provide a certain amount of recreational facility for the crews. There was a football knockout competition for the six submarines and various departments of the parent ship, which *L52* succeeded in winning – I have among my trophies a medal as a souvenir of the occasion.

As the roads in the area were poor and my cycle was not in good condition, this appeared to be a good opportunity to give the 'old bus' a refit. Unfortunately we were kept so busy with our exercises and urgent repairs to *L52* that, having taken the machine to pieces, I had little opportunity to reassemble it again. *L52*, like my motorcycle, was badly in need of, and due for refit. As the day for our departure from Loch Ewe drew near my cycle was still in bits strewn over the bench in the hut. I was granted a 'make and mend' (a half days leave) on the day before we left, and after having hastily reassembled my machine, and not having time for any adjustments, I was not surprised when the engine refused to start.

On the following morning prior to sailing, a motor launch was allocated to bring the cycles on board again. Needless to say I was 'in a pickle'. My motorcycle was at least five miles away from the jetty, and would not function at all. Hiring the one and only taxi in the area to tow me back along those winding and bumpy roads was one of the most alarming experiences I have ever had, and I was lucky to get back to the jetty in one piece. Last to arrive, my cycle was quickly heaved into the launch, and that was the last I saw of it until our arrival at Devonport four days later.

Whilst in the motor launch on the back to *Lucia* I was startled and dismayed to see the submarines casting off, two or three were headed for the harbour entrance and the others were laying off at about three hundred yards distant. Heavens! *L52* had sailed without me! Absent over leave! Ship under sailing orders! Perhaps it was hardly as bad as it seemed, after all, I had little or no control over the situation.

The busy Officer Of The Watch aboard *Lucia* impatiently listened to my tale of woe. 'Where is she?' he asked, and I miserably pointed to *L52*, now nearly half a mile away. Summoning the quartermaster, the O.O.W. immediately ordered the captain's motorboat away; this was a fast boat, soon catching up with *L52*, which was scarcely moving. Our C.O. ordered the motorboat to come alongside, and I scrambled up onto her casing, scaled the bridge structure and reported 'E.R.A. Blamey returning aboard sir', much to the amusement of those on duty on the bridge. It was a harrowing experience, and I felt very weary from my frantic efforts to get back aboard my submarine. I couldn't help thinking though, how much more comfortable it would have been on the parent ship for that journey south.

If my motorcycle was the worse for exposure on the journey north, it was even more so when we arrived back at Devonport. It had been transported on the quarterdeck of the tiny *Adamant* where there was very little freeboard. During the gale force winds the seas must have been literally breaking over her, and my poor motorcycle was now hardly recognizable. Pushing it out of the dockyard it was a relief to reach the nearest garage that transported it to my home where, by dint of hard work it eventually became a presentable and efficient machine once more.

Shortly after this, while carrying out a torpedo attack at sea, we had the misfortune to experience a 'hot run'. The engine on one of the torpedoes was accidentally started while still in its tube, and with the bow cap still shut. The exhaust gasses, mostly carbon monoxide, escaped into the torpedo compartment. It was a difficult situation, since to open the bow cap meant we would lose a very expensive torpedo, the propellers of which were now thrashing around in the tube and trying to drive the torpedo out at forty knots. The gasses soon started to overcome the torpedo men, and being on duty at the forward blowing station, I donned my gas mask in order to help drag these unconscious men out of the compartment.

In the meantime the boat had surfaced so that she could be ventilated. (It was a good job that this hadn't happened in wartime). The quickest way to get rid of the gasses was to start the main engines, and I dashed off to my post on the starboard main engine, only to collapse on arrival. We were not aware at that time that our gas masks afforded little protection against the gasses churned out by a faulty torpedo. However, I was not seriously gassed and soon came to again. In fact I did not actually lose consciousness, it was just that my legs would not support me. Returning to harbour immediately, the four victims were taken to the sick bay for treatment. Luckily there were no fatalities, and the casualties were back in harness within two or three days. Ben Bryant, our torpedo officer was one of them.

At last November 1928 arrived, and *L52* docked as arranged in Devonport dockyard, most of the crew including myself, remaining with her. My wedding day was fixed for Saturday the 10th of November, and I requested that I might have my two weeks Christmas leave advanced. The captain was pleased to grant this request as there was no provision for marriage leave in those days, and as well as a wedding present from the submarine crew, the wardroom officers also gave me one.

There were many good-humoured threats of sabotage by my messmates, who considered morning dress and topper an unsuitable rig for a submariner. I have often reflected on the motive that prompted me to get married in morning attire; heaven knows I could ill afford tailor made suits for my best man and myself. Lets hope it wasn't mere snobbishness, a trait I've always abhorred. I was very proud of my uniform and of the Royal Navy, but of course I could not provide my bride with a naval escort and swords, as that privilege was only accorded to officers. I was aware that many of the guests were to be West Country musical celebrities as my bride was regarded as the outstanding young pianist in the West Country. She had qualified at the age of seventeen as a performer (L.R.A.M.) and as a teacher (A.R.C.M.) and seemed to possess more gold, silver and bronze medals than an admiral.

The Royal Navy was well represented, as apart from my shipmates we both came from naval families. Clare's father, brother Bert and cousin Ernie Polkinhorne were, or had been artificers. My father had retired from the navy as a Lieutenant, brother Harold, known throughout the navy as 'Bill', was still an artificer apprentice, and my best man, cousin Jack Pellow, was a petty officer, (his father, my mother's only brother died whilst serving as a chief yeoman of signals). To complete the naval contingent, young Sub Lieutenant Reg Lockley was usher. Nearly all these young naval men were to have distinguished serving careers, either being decorated or mentioned in dispatches – quite a family record in fact – although only one had the audacity to record his experiences.

Being fortunate enough to procure a flat in the Stoke area of Plymouth, Clare and I looked forward to the remaining four months of L52's refit. Clare asked that I'd be agreeable if she could retain the cream of her pupils until we were forced to move away, which I was.

When the Christmas leave period came I was not entitled to any leave, but the captain was very sympathetic, especially as we were safely shored up in No.4. dry dock. It was discreetly suggested that I request for long weekend leave, which in the event stretched out to nearly ten days, for which needless to say I was most grateful.

Our captain was then relieved by a young South African Lieutenant, (Lt. Curry) who had just completed his 'perishers' course. The qualifying course for submarine C.O. was known as the 'perishers course', presumably because all who failed it had no option but to return to general service. We were very sorry to lose such a good C.O. as Lt Cdr Leathes, but he, being a pretty senior C.O. moved on to command the larger and ill fated submarine M2 which later sank with all hands in West Bay. She was the first British submarine to carry an aircraft, having a hanger fitted just forward of her bridge structure. Her small seaplane was launched from a catapult, and it was the malfunction of her hanger door while endeavouring to dive quickly after flying the aircraft off that caused this tragedy. There was always this need to cut down the time taken to dive, and rightly so, as we found in later years when war was again thrust on us. Then we were forced to take short cuts unheard of in peacetime.

Not long after completing five pleasant months of refitting in Devonport dockyard where our furnished flat was within three hundred yards of the dockyard gate, I was drafted back to *HMS Dolphin*, having completed my three compulsory years in the submarine service. Clare gave notice to her few remaining pupils, and we reluctantly left our comfortable apartment to look for something suitable in Southsea. This was the first of many such moves we were to experience. On the whole we were fairly fortunate but sometimes we paid more money than we could really afford for very poor accommodation.

As August the 13th drew near, the date that I was due to return to general service, the Commander (E) of the depot sent for me. He explained in a very charming manner that as the Admiralty had embarked on an extensive building program ('O', 'P' and 'R' classes), the service was badly in need of trained and experienced submariners. He then asked 'Would I volunteer for a further two years in the submarine service?'

I wasn't very enthusiastic, but in the event I signed on the dotted line of the form that was thrust in front of me. This done the Commander hastened to explain that the period of service for volunteers was five years, of which I had already served three. I was well aware that this was complete 'blarney' because several in *Dolphin* at that time had served for more than ten years; not that I had anything against submarines, even though it was a tough and uncompromising existence. But, apart from my period in *Valiant* I'd known little else - little did I know at that time that those five years were to become more than twenty-eight years!

It was pretty obvious to me that my next draft would be a foreign commission. As the submarine service, apart from Portland, Portsmouth and Devonport, had only flotillas in the Mediterranean and China, the chances were that it would be the latter.

Strangely it was not until the end of October that I was drafted, and then surprisingly, it was to the Malta flotilla. Clare and I spent a very pleasant summer in the Portsmouth area; the weather was glorious, and we indulged ourselves in much tennis. Also I had a fairly successful athletic season.

Clare was there on the *Dolphin* Gala day, and was for the first time, introduced to our ex- C.E.R.A 'Chinky' Rice. 'Chinky', never at ease with the ladies, and probably well primed despite the early hour, sprang to attention and saluted, remaining in this fixed position until I was finally tempted to say 'Stand at ease'.

Throughout this period in *Dolphin* I was a member of the trials party which, under the direction of Captain (E) Limpenny, proceeded to Messrs Vickers Armstrong at Barrow, Cammel Laird at Birkenhead, Scotts at Greenock, or the R.N.Dockyard at Chatham, depending where a completed submarine was ready for engine and diving trials. This wasn't a popular job, certainly not with me as it meant being away for anything up to six days at a time.

Besides the Captain, who was the chief engineer on the Admiral of Submarines staff, the party consisted of a Lieutenant (E), a C.E.R.A., and six E.R.A.'s.

We had quite a hectic time on these trials. On the captain's order, the E.R.A. detailed would dash off behind either the port or starboard engine, take a power card from each of the eight or twelve cylinders, and submit the set within fifteen minutes. This was no easy matter, due mainly to the heat and inaccessibility behind each engine, which resulted in burnt fingers and much swearing. Then again there was the inevitable problem of having too many bodies in too small a space.

The authorities were particularly mean with us on these trips providing us, (nearly all chief petty officers), with only enough money for the meanest of boarding houses, and just a few dry sandwiches for a train journey of up to ten hours. Nevertheless the stay at *Dolphin* was very pleasant, these trips away happening only about once a month. Tennis was ruled out for the latter part of our stay as Clare became pregnant. The local putting green then became the centre for our recreation. Apart from when with a trials party, it was very rare that I went to sea in a submarine. We were making the most of our young lives as it was expected that we would be parted for a period of at least two and a half years while I served on the China station, not a very bright outlook for a young married couple expecting their first baby. So when eventually the draft came through for the Malta flotilla we were both overjoyed.

Whereas no ratings and very few officers could afford to have their wives in China, many had their wives in Malta. Of course Clare would not be able to join me until the baby was born (another five or six months), so that when I left, Clare went back to her parents in Plymouth. I was given a working passage in a 'C' class cruiser of about three thousand tons, not as grim as my previous passage to Malta. For some reason we remained at Gibraltar for over three weeks, the longest period I have ever spent at Gibraltar at a stretch. Unlike my previous visit when the whole fleet was there, this time it was quite pleasant. At that time of the year (October/ November) the weather was good for swimming and tennis, neither did I have to 'subs' for all my messmates in order that I could go ashore.

On arrival at Malta we were immediately transferred to the submarine parent ship *HMS Cyclops* occupying the same billet in M'sida Creek as *Lucia* had five years earlier. *Cyclops* had most of her brood alongside, namely *L16, L18, L19, L21, L23* and *L26*. Two other submarines completed the flotilla, *K26*, now the last of the steam driven fleet submarines, and *X1*, the largest submarine in the world at that time.

We were to see very little of these two submarines. *K26* (always referred to as K two six) took part in a few of our exercises, normally a 'loner'; she did not berth alongside *Cyclops*, possibly because of her length. At three hundred and thirty eight feet she was almost half as long again as the *L* class. *X1* had a surface displacement 2780 tons, not huge by present day standards, but was armed with two 6-inch turrets as well as her main torpedo armament. *X1* suffered constant breakdowns, she rarely left the dockyard wall and was known as the 'wallflower'.

Cyclops, a converted merchantman, was certainly an improvement on *Lucia* but even so, could scarcely accommodate the crews of the six 'L' class boats. Although in truth she rarely had to, since usually at least one of the 'L' class was refitting in the dockyard.

Soon after my arrival I was drafted to *L21*, my messmates were, Alf Potter, the C.E.R.A, 'Doc' Cheney and George Etheridge. George was the only E.R.A. in *L21* to have his wife in Malta at that time, but I was hoping to have Clare out there with me as soon as possible after our baby was born.

The flotilla was kept busy, when not away from Malta on cruises, we were sent to sea on daily exercises four and sometimes five times a week. There was a magnificent fleet based at Malta, but as there was a need for great economy of fuel at the time, (1930/31) they rarely left their moorings in the Grand Harbour. Submarines being relatively economical to run, were continually at sea, whilst the surface craft were comfortably ensconced in harbour, If not exercising with sloops or destroyers, we would perform independent exercises. Captain S/M exercised his submarines as though they were M.T.B.s or Dive Bombers – full speed ahead, peeling off to dive in the shape of a fan etc. Though no fault could be found in bringing submarine crews to a high state of efficiency, these exercises seemed to be rather superfluous. It was our duty to be efficient and well prepared for war, and we were aware that there was room for improvement, but we were being used as toys, and to the extent that our crews were hard put to keep pace with the repair and maintenance work this caused. One assumes that it was owing to previous accidents and fatalities (We were accustomed to losing on average, one submarine a year) that we were forbidden to dive at night - such an essential requirement in time of war!

There were constant and recurring breakdowns on machinery. One continual snag on the 'L' class main engines was the vertical timing shaft, used to facilitate the advance and retarding of the fuel injection. It was a complicated design and could not stand up to the great strain imposed upon it. It was also a heavy and intricate piece of machinery to handle; one small mistake on reassembly could have disastrous consequences, not only to the engine but also to the career of the unfortunate E.R.A. responsible. There were also those inevitable cylinder head bolts (mentioned earlier) to contend with. It really was a nightmare experience to extract the stump of a broken bolt while the engine was still running, standing on small footrests holding a chisel bar against the offending bolt while the stoker on watch endeavoured to smite the other end with a heavy hammer. This was a precarious operation to say the least, with the engine running at 320 revolutions, and with the boat pitching and rolling. And then there was the seemingly eternal job of renewing the piston rings on the high-pressure air compressors (again mentioned previously). With all this recurring trouble it wasn't surprising that the submariners often regarded these exercises as somewhat frivolous.

Periodically Captain S/M would carry out a sea inspection of each of the submarines under his command. On one of these inspections he suggested that the engine room staff change a bottom end bearing (crank head bearing, weighing over one hundredweight) whilst at one hundred and fifty feet, after crash-diving when the temperature would be around one hundred and fifty degrees Fahrenheit (65C.), and with all the engine room staff wearing gas masks. Fortunately for us, this plan was changed to the replacement of an exhaust valve box, but under the same conditions. This was gruelling enough for the two or three of us who were doing the job, though probably not so tedious as for those waiting for us to finish. It was so hot that our gas masks were filling up with perspiration and we had to insert our fingers under the chin to allow it to run out. Two or three people not even working on the job were overcome by the heat.

About six months after joining *L21* there was a general reshuffle amongst the E.R.A.'s of the flotilla. George Etheridge and myself found ourselves transferred to *L16*. Our C.E.R.A. was 'Aggie' Branch, and the outside E.R.A. was 'Jan' Hewer, with George and I in the engine room. *L16's* commanding officer was Lt Cdr J.B.Mitford O.B.E., who later did so much to organize the training of submarine personnel in the use of D.S.E.A. equipment (Davis Submerged Escape Apparatus), and our E.O. was Warrant Engineer R. (Dick) Kemp.

My plans to get Clare out to Malta now suffered a setback. Clare had given birth to a bonny baby girl on the 25th of April 1930, but had had a particularly rough time during her confinement; in fact it later became clear that at one time I nearly lost the both of them. It was because of this that we decided not to risk any further additions to the family. It was a further six months before Clare was fit enough to take passage to Malta with our offspring. This was a very worrying time for me and at one time I was tempted, against my general principles, to request compassionate leave to see Clare and the baby. However she assured me that all was well and that this would not be necessary.

Before leaving Malta for a cruise, I procured a very nice flat at 15 Parallel Street. in Sliema, and hoped that we would return before Clare arrived. We were not really encouraged to have our families with us in those days, and the only grant was a pathetic £3 towards the wife's sea passage. Nor were there any such things as married quarters; the whole onus of having one's family living with them while abroad was on the husband. Clare procured a second-class passage on the *SS Balranald,* and my father accompanied her and the baby Joan to Southampton, from whence she sailed. I very much admired her courage as she had not been out of the country previously and was still not 100% fit. Moreover, there was this element of doubt as to whether or not our flotilla would have returned to Malta by the time of her arrival.

In the event there was a delay of several days in our return, and I did not arrive until two days after Clare. Luckily Clare's brother Bert, an electrical artificer serving on HMS *Devonshire*, had his wife in Malta, and I had arranged with her to meet Clare and escort her to the flat in the event that I was delayed. This she did, and I was most grateful, for when I did arrive, Clare and Joan were safely ensconced in the flat.

Clare soon made a complete recovery and we embarked upon a very pleasant period. *L16* was shortly due for a three months refit in Malta dockyard, which for me was an ideal situation. Having then been on the station for twelve months it was natural to anticipate a further eighteen months. The crew remained with the boat for the refit but there was little for us to do, and being detached from our parent ship, there was a good chance of the odd make and mend. The dockyard was situated several miles from where we lived, and we were docked at the furthermost end of the Dockyard Creek, beyond Vittoriosa and Senglea, almost abreast of Cospicua. However fares were very cheap, there were frequent ferries between Sliema and Valletta, also between Valleta (Grand Harbour) and Vittoriosa. Buses were even more frequent; one could travel the whole way on either bus or ferry. It was a pleasant trip by ferry from Sliema, out of Marsamxett harbour and around St Elmo's point into the Grand Harbour. Then taking another ferry from the Custom House steps to Senglea or Vittoriosa, the whole journey costing less than 21p in today's money.

Normally the E.R.A.'s were on board (duty watch) one night in four (thanks to our C.E.R.A. joining in to make our number up to four), but whilst in dry dock we did not even have to do this. When not in the dry dock, George and I were privileged to get the occasional sub, a favour which we would return when away from Malta.

Living was very cheap in Malta at that time. I paid a rental of only £4 per month for this very nice flat not more than a hundred yards from the sea front. At these prices we could afford a domestic help.

This was a period of much sporting activity. There was tennis, swimming and water polo in the summer, rugby and soccer in the winter. Clare was very patient with me during the rugger season, and rarely missed a match in which I was involved. She was very loyal and even pretended to be very interested in the 'great game' - it really is amazing what love can do! Often there was a game for the flotilla during the week (providing my submarine was not at sea) and a game on Sunday afternoon for the E.R.A.'s 1st team. The E.R.A.'s, of whom there were about five hundred on the station, boasted a very fine club in Floriana of which the whole branch was very proud. On my previous visit to Malta, the E.R.A.'s Club occupied very comfortable premises in the corner of Queens Square, which was formerly known as Victoria Square in Strada Reale. As this occupied a very valuable site in the centre of Valetta, the members were offered a new building in Floriana.

These new premises had marvellous facilities, including a large hall, lounge bar, billiard saloon, library and almost eighty small cabins, which members could hire on a long or short-term basis. The Commander in Chief performed the official opening ceremony. This club was extremely well conducted, the committee adhering strictly to the rules laid down, and its high reputation was jealously guarded. Ladies and other guests were welcome only on specific occasions and always on a Sunday evening when the committee arranged for a first class concert. It was a much sought after privilege to be invited to the club, even by senior officers who had their own club in Strada Reale. Our two senior stewards and barmen, Manoel and Tony were excellent fellows and had been employed by us for many years, having moved from the old premises.

Having much talent of all kinds at our disposal, we were in the forefront of many of the islands activities and competitions. We ran two excellent rugger fifteens, and were unbeaten for several seasons in Malta.

Water polo was often played in the summer, both for the flotilla and the submarine teams. *L21* had a particularly good team, having three of us that played for the flotilla, one of whom, Leading Seaman 'Lofty' Laker, was a full navy cap

Throughout the summer we bathed in the beautiful blue and crystal clear sea daily, changing at home and trotting down to the end of Parallel Street in our wraps. This period was one of the happiest in my life for not only was Joan a delightfully happy child, but Clare had made a compete recovery from her ordeal. Clare, Peggy Etheridge and Flo Rayner, airing their respective children along Tower Road toward St Julian's Bay, would often see our submarines diving and surfacing when we were on our daily exercises, sometimes within a mile of the Sliema promenade. We had become very friendly with Flo and Fred Rayner whilst we were there; Fred was the outside E.R.A. of *K26*.

Clare had not been in Malta for more than about six months when one of those tantalizing and frustrating situations arose with which we servicemen had often to contend. Almost without warning the whole flotilla, together with the parent ship, were ordered to return to the United Kingdom. This was most unexpected and very disappointing, as I was expecting at least another year of this blissful existence. It was quite a financial loss too, but there was nothing we could do about it. Naturally there was an unearthly scramble to book homeward passages for our families, and fortunately I was able to obtain a berth for Clare and the one-year-old Joan on the P & O liner *Kaiser-I-Hind* which was calling at Malta five days after we sailed. So that I was neither at Malta when my wife arrived, or when she departed.

Perhaps it was a good thing that Clare did not leave Malta at the same time as us, as we ran into a force 9 gale immediately on leaving harbour. I could never claim to be a good sailor, but by that time I had become accustomed to the pitching and rolling of a submarine in heavy weather. Not that it was anything but unpleasant and uncomfortable when on the surface where we spent most of our time. Everything one did seemed to be hard work; even lying in a bunk was exhausting. Sometimes the boat rolled so much that the bunk jumped out of its inner sockets, and together with its occupant would crash down upon the unfortunate person in the lower bunk. Eating was a precarious business – even if one felt like it. There was a raised lip built around the edge of the table, but it was wise to keep hold of your plate at all times; many times my meal has finished up in my lap.

On watch in the engine room in rough weather could be a thoroughly miserable experience, though no more so than the seaman's watch on the bridge. The E.R.A. of the watch was in a position of great responsibility, even if he did feel like dying. As for keeping accurate revolutions while station keeping, as well as attending to the odd repair job, this was a complete nightmare, since as the boat plunged her bows downward into the waves, her stern and therefore her propellers would be almost clear of the water, having practically no load, the engines would race madly, but then as the bows came up and the stern dug deep once more, the load came back on and the engines slowed down. This constant racing and slowing imposed a tremendous torque on the main shafts, with a subsequent strain on the engines. All the time the flotilla would be proceeding in single line ahead, trying to keep station on the parent ship and on one another.

After forty-eight hours of this battering our port engine came to a grinding halt. The E.R.A. of the watch diagnosed a seized bottom end (crank head) bearing. Obviously we had to fall out of line, and the whole flotilla eased speed to enquire the nature of our trouble. As fitting a spare bearing (which weighed almost one hundredweight) would take some time, and we could only make about six knots in these sea conditions, the flotilla left us to proceed as best we could and continued on to Gibraltar at twelve knots. I was given the job of removing the damaged bearing, not a pleasant one with one's legs dangling in the oily crank-pit, and the rancid smell of the overheated oil making one retch. This was no mean job even in a calm sea. The bearing had to be fitted with a maximum clearance of only ten thousandths of an inch, so the job entailed much scraping away of white metal

Having extracted the sick bearing from the crank-pit (engine sump) I discovered to my dismay that the cause of the seizure was that the 10-inch diameter crankpin on the main engine shaft, was fractured. The strain on the alternately racing and struggling engine had been too much. There was just nothing we could do, as this was a major refit job; the whole of the engine would have to be dismantled, and a new crankshaft weighing several tons fitted. Even the parent ship did not carry a spare crankshaft.

This job had taken almost three hours of heavy toil under very wretched conditions. Very dangerous too, as the boat was rolling up to thirty degrees each way, and it was impossible to communicate with my stoker assistant on the outboard side of the engine, owing to the roar of the other engine.

If I thought (and hoped), that having accepted that the port engine was now out of action until we reached the U.K., our engineer officer would call it a day, I was mistaken. Rightly or wrongly, he ordered the C.E.R.A. and one E.R.A to watch-keep turn and turn about on the starboard side, while Jan Hewer, the outside E.R.A and myself, worked turn and turn about slinging all the pistons and removing all the crank-head bearings in order to examine each crank pin for fracture or partial fracture. I thoroughly disliked this job, and honestly thought that it was ridiculous. Not only was it quite unnecessary, it was also very dangerous, as so much depended on the liaison between the E.R.A. and his stoker assistant at the back of the engine, also the chap operating the turning gear several yards away, which was very difficult with the din of the starboard engine. On reflection we were jolly fortunate not to have suffered a serious accident.

Whilst on the subject of hazardous jobs, it was always included in the engineer officers standing orders that main and crank-head bearings and piston skirts, be felt by hand for excess temperature by the E.R.A. on watch. This in my opinion was a ridiculous order, as (a) it was extremely unlikely that damage would be avoided, except perhaps on engine trials after all the bearings had been refitted. (b) It took the E.R.A. of the watch away from his proper place of duty where he should be alert between the engines and near to the controls, and (c) it exposed the E.R.A to a great physical hazard. I still shudder at the very thought of putting my whole arm through a 5 inch diameter hole into the crank-pit while whilst in a kneeling and very cramped position, with the engine running at three two zero revolutions and the boat lurching from side to side. Many fingers had been lost in this way, and I feel very thankful that I still have all my fingers and thumbs intact. Actually the greatest danger lay in getting too familiar; some people became almost blasé with this exercise, and that's when fingers were lost.

But to return to the present situation, *Cyclops* had sent the remaining submarines ahead and had remained with us, like a mother hen caring for its chicks. Thankfully the weather began to moderate, and it was most extraordinary to us, that on our arrival at Gibraltar three days later, *L16,* although only having one engine, was the only submarine fit to dive. The pounding the others had received had put their hydroplanes out of action.

We tarried at Gibraltar to lick our wounds for a day or so, but then continued our journey northward across the Bay of Biscay and on to the U.K. *Cyclops* led the flotilla, and *L16* was left to make her own way at the breakneck speed of six knots. The weather was now very fair; indeed it looked as though a steamroller had just been over the notorious bay.

One evening when we were almost abreast of Ushant, I received a message to report to the captain on the bridge, and naturally I wondered what this was in aid of - had I erred in any way? When I got to the bridge, I found that the *Kaiser-I – Hind* was overtaking us on the port quarter, and the captain, being aware that my wife was aboard her, thought that I would like to see her pass – maybe even wave. It was jolly decent of him to ask me if I'd like to send a greeting. The 'bunting tosser' (signalman) was sent for and a short message was flashed across on his Aldis lamp. It didn't take the *Kaiser-I- Hind* long to steam past our struggling little submarine, she was doing twenty-three knots to our six. I did wave but subsequently found that as it was early in the 'last dog', Clare had been tucking the baby in for the night. She did however receive my message a little later.

The liner berthed at Southampton the next day but we alas, ran into thick fog in the channel, and arrived at Fort Blockhouse much later. It was a most uncomfortable trip up channel; we could hear the hooting sirens of nearby ships in the busy sea-lanes, for nearly two days, we even heard the swish of their propellers at times. This of course, was in the days before Radar was invented, and a submarine on the surface was particularly vulnerable. Visibility was down to less than fifty yards at times. Our siren was sounded constantly, using up the 'outside wreckers' precious air. 'Wreckers' were notorious for being too conservative with their high-pressure air, but in this instance ours did not complain. Constantly peering into the gloom had been a frightful strain on the Captain, who remained on the bridge the whole time, with the Officer Of The Watch and the lookouts.

Normally in peacetime any of the crew not on watch were allowed up on to the bridge at the discretion of the O.O.W. (a maximum of six at a time) for a breath of fresh air. I often availed myself of this opportunity, and on this occasion I went up to the bridge several times, joining the lookouts in peering into the fog. It was a great relief when the fog eventually lifted and we could see the Isle of Wight. We then wended our way serenely past the Needles to finally arrive at Fort Blockhouse. On the whole it had not been a pleasant trip, and we were thankful to have arrived safely.

The first thing that happens when a ship arrives in the U.K. is that she is boarded by Customs and Excise officers to see if the crew have any contraband they wish to declare before proceeding ashore. These chaps are normally very reasonable and understanding, realizing that sailors, having spent a couple of years abroad, naturally wish to bring their wives and families a little present. But on this occasion we met up with a particularly small minded individual. On our meagre pay, we could not indulge in any large-scale purchases, and usually it was smuggling in the real sense that they were looking for, but this particular individual charged us more in duty, than the relatively small price we paid for our presents. Many, who hadn't the money to pay the duty asked, forfeited the articles they had bought. Not a very welcome homecoming!

Having only served twenty months abroad, it was expected that I would be due for another foreign commission very soon, and this time it would no doubt be in the China flotilla. As *L16* paid off, to be referred to the dockyard at Portsmouth, the crew were transferred to *HMS Dolphin*. After a short period I found myself, once again drafted to *L21*, which, with *Cyclops* and the rest of the flotilla were transferred to Devonport to become the 2nd Submarine Flotilla. This of course suited me admirably. Once more I found a flat in my hometown, this time in Ford Hill, and again our furniture came out of storage

The crew of *L21* had of course changed since our Malta days. Lt Cdr W.C. Thomas, a huge ginger haired navy rugby forward, was the C.O. and Lt. J.H. ('Jock') Forbes, not only a navy, but a Scottish international trial scrum half, was our First Lieutenant. 'Jock' was a very efficient and immensely popular First Lieutenant, and as I was a keen rugby player, we soon 'hit it off.'

The E.O. was the redoubtable Warrant Engineer Roy Demetrious Glenn, and my messmates were C.E.R.A. J. 'Buck' Buchanon, E.R.A. Bill French, and E.R.A. 'Jan' Hewer, all of whom were 'characters' in their own particular way.

Bill French, four or five years older than myself, having trained in *HMS Indus,* the artificers training establishment at Devonport, was a most extraordinary character. Very wayward at times and a little crude in his manner, he was nevertheless a very likeable fellow. Sharp in features, and in tongue when he minded to be, he had very broad shoulders and a wasp like waist. It was not too difficult to appreciate that he was a lightweight boxer of some calibre, or at least he had been – a little too much drink over the years had taken its toll. He was often under stoppage of leave, either having had too much to drink while ashore, or for being absent without leave.

Bill had been brought up in a rather tough part of old Plymouth, and at a very young age had boxed in the famous Cosmopolitan Gymnasium, the starting out point for many a famous west-country boxer. It was an ambition of all young boxers at that time, to box in the famous 'Cosmo'. Bill could easily have made a living at boxing, but chose instead to enter the navy as an artificer apprentice. It was said that he did box professionally while he was a naval apprentice, which was against orders, although this would not have worried Bill. He must have been even more skilful than the redoubtable Tom Mudd though, because he was completely unmarked. Eventually Bill's drinking habits and his inability to return on board at the correct time, led to his being drafted back to general service.

Generally messmates got along very well together, even though we all had our little faults and idiosyncrasies and were herded together for long periods, although occasionally there were quarrels, but these were soon forgotten. There was however, one occasion when things weren't patched up so quickly. Two of my messmates refused to speak to each other for about six months, which was very painful for all of us. They were placed in opposite watches so that they would not have to turn over the watch to each other. Being cooped up like sardines in a tin was not the best way to endure a prolonged squabble.

We were more often than not in four watches at sea, thanks to the C.E.R.A. joining in, but there was frequently a repair job to be done while off watch. If it were a big job, then the E.R.A. responsible would drop out of the watch bill. Moreover, no day passed, not even on passage, when the whole crew would not be closed up for either diving or gun action stations.

L21 had a most extraordinary crew for sport, winning most of the flotilla competitions in nearly all types of sport. Though work did not abate, I probably took part in more sport at that time than at any other time in my career, being included in any team from *L21* and most teams from the whole flotilla, as well as a number of representative sides, varying from swimming and water polo to rugby and athletics. This meant frequently returning aboard to work, in order not to laden my messmates with my share.

Eventually our First Lieutenant, Lt. 'Jock' Forbes, had to move on. 'Jock' was one of nature's gentlemen, quietly efficient in his duties, and seemingly a little above the 'rat race' for promotion yet destined for higher rank; he lost no dignity or respect by adopting a friendly attitude toward his crew. I was privileged to make friends with many officers of 'Jocks' calibre during my career, none of whom lost any respect or status by this friendly (but not patronizing) attitude. It was a big man who could command such respect and loyalty from his crew, without losing the 'common touch' as Kipling put it. 'Jock', as the C.O. of *Spearfish* died together with his whole crew, many of them friends of mine, when Spearfish was lost in August of 1940.

Another great character was our engineer officer, Warrant Engineer Roy Demetrious Glenn. Roy was a very competent engineer, but haughty and unapproachable, quite the reverse of 'Jock' Forbes. Roy as the engineer officer of the ill-fated *Thetis*, was to lose his life aboard her when she sank during sea trials early in the Second World War. The year was now 1932 and many of my shipmates and friends of this period were to lose their lives in the forthcoming struggle.

A spring cruise to Gibraltar and the western Mediterranean took us to Barcelona where a particular trip to the famous Mount Serrat, arranged for our benefit stands out in my mind. This would have been a very pleasant outing in normal circumstances – but continental bus drivers appear to me to have a built in death wish, and this one was no exception. Before we left the precincts of Barcelona we'd rammed and overturned a donkey cart laden with oranges and just drove madly on. The last I saw was the unfortunate Spaniard, surrounded in oranges and waving his fist at our fast receding coach. We hadn't gone more than a further few kilometres when, rounding a bend on the wrong side of the road we came face to face with the driver of a small car. This poor fellow had little choice but to swerve off the road, where he promptly overturned. This time our driver did stop, but as soon as his victim staggered bewildered out of his upturned car, he upbraided him for careless driving. A dozen lusty sailors put his car up the right way again to discover that it was not too badly damaged. Then our impatient driver signalled us to board the coach again, as he was anxious to be off, presumably before the other chap had recovered enough to take his number.

This driver scared the daylights out us as we climbed the winding road to within a few hundred yards of the summit. He was even worse on the descent, tearing into bends at break-neck speeds, looking back it's a wonder that we did not pitch him out of the widow and continue back without him. Most of these foreign drivers, at least, the ones that we seemed to get lumbered with, revelled in showing off.

Another memorable cruise that we did was through the Skagerrak and Kattegat to Copenhagen and Stockholm. What a marvellous approach to the latter! We wended our way through the hundreds of small islands, and were provided with a pilot aboard each submarine, whom we certainly needed in the maze of narrow channels. We appeared to be very popular there as an extravagant sporting programme was arranged. *Cyclops* and the 2nd submarine flotilla were in company with two large cruisers, *Exeter* and *York,* together with a whole flotilla of destroyers – a formidable squadron. On one festive afternoon, in the presence of the King of Sweden, we did battle with them at rugby, soccer, tug 'o war, and athletics in the big Olympic stadium. What a rare feast for the thousands of spectators. All this, and a magnificent display of counter marching by the combined Royal Marine bands of the two cruisers, which impressed their own country-men as much as the Swedes.

Stockholm was a beautiful and clean city, and the food was good and cheap. We remained there for about a week, returning home through the Kiel Canal. It was perhaps interesting to note that we were not greeted very enthusiastically while passing through the Kiel Canal, even though the Second World War was still more than six years away enough.

Returning home from the spring cruise on the following year, we ran into some pretty foul weather running up the coast of Portugal. On watch in the engine room while approaching Cape Finnisterre, I suddenly lost engine revolutions, particularly on the starboard engine. There did not appear to be any mechanical or fuel failure, but there was a peculiar knocking coming from outside the hull. It was difficult to know what to do, as we were keeping station line ahead. Actually the flotilla had broken into two columns and had increased the distance between each submarine on account of the weather. Nevertheless it presents a tricky situation when one boat suddenly loses speed.

Having stopped the starboard engine and informed the bridge, I was puzzling my head for a reason, when the engineer came into the engine room and told me the cause. He had been informed by the O.O.W. that the huge 3inch diameter after hydroplane actuating bar had fractured, not only dropping down onto the revolving starboard propeller, but allowing the after hydroplanes to drop into the vertical position, thereby acting as a 'Kitchen gear' on both propellers. The propellers forcing the water back onto this large vertical surface stopped the way on the boat almost immediately. The O.O.W. was very quick to take action, or we would have been rammed by the boat next astern.

As there was no chance in that sea of getting a party on to the after casing to try and get the planes into a midship (horizontal) position, we were very fortunate to even get a tow line away to the parent ship, and were then towed very slowly and carefully into the nearby Spanish port of Ferrol. It is a very difficult evolution to tow a submarine in heavy weather, so easy to part even a 2 inch steel cable, but we succeeded in reaching port without further mishap.

This incident would have been catastrophic had it happened in wartime, as we were completely immobilized, we couldn't even dive, as our main motors were of no more use to us than our main engines. The F.E.O. (Flotilla Engineer Officer), having arranged with the Spanish authorities for the welding of the actuating arm left us to it, and *Cyclops* departed to rejoin her brood.

To start with, the First Lieutenant trimmed down forward as much as he considered safe. Then with the fore hatch shut, he flooded numbers 1, 2, and 3 main ballast tanks. This brought the after hydroplanes almost clear of the water, and one blade of the propellers completely out. It was a comparatively easy job to disconnect each end of the broken arm which was then whisked off to the welding shop for repair, but I spent almost the rest of the night up to my knees in very cold water repairing, as well as possible under the circumstances, the damage to the blades of the starboard propeller. The tips of the blades were bent right over, and all that I could do to straighten them out was to clout them as hard as I could from a very uncomfortable position, with a 14lb hammer. Where chunks of the blade had been broken away, we had to grind or file the blade to try and make a leading edge. It was a nightmare of a job, especially on such a terribly cold night. The two of us E.R.A.'s working on this job with our stoker mates, only got a couple of hours rest at the end of the morning watch before the before the repaired hydroplane arm was returned to us ready for replacement.

The Spaniards had made a good job of the repair, our engineer officer having supervised the alignment, and it took us less than an hour to complete the job. How much this repair cost the Admiralty I have no idea; it would have lasted forever, but as soon as we arrived back at Devonport the dockyard fitted a new one. It was necessary however, to fit a new starboard propeller, and this we did in dry-dock; new tips being carefully moulded onto the old one so that it could be used as a spare.

My temporary repairs to our starboard propeller were effective enough for our trip across the Bay, but thank heavens we were not at war, as a competent hydrophone operator would have been able to detect the noise it made over twenty miles away. I was later to learn the importance of perfect leading edges on the blades of our propellers, the slightest 'nick' could cause a whistling noise that was easily detectable by he enemy.

Submarine losses by accident occurred almost annually, and this year (1929) was no exception. *L12 collided* with *H47* on the surface, ramming her forward of the conning tower and being dragged down by the rapidly sinking victim to a depth of nearly forty feet. The only survivors from *H47* were those on her bridge. *L12* was most fortunate to escape, as she was unable to properly shut her conning tower hatch, which was fouled by the lead of the signal lantern. I am not aware of the findings of the subsequent Courts Martial, but both submarines were on the surface in broad daylight. These accidents were most depressing to submarine personnel and meant the loss of many friends. I am unable to recollect who was lost on *H47*, but several, including the C.E.R.A. 'Ross' Hoggett of the *L12*, were my friends. 'Ross' survived but was later lost on *Tarpon*, together with my old friend George Etheridge.

Many Spanish and Scandinavian ports were visited while I was on *L21*, as well as many ports in the U.K. Belfast, Londonderry, Falmouth, Tobermory, Oban, Lamlash, Rosyth, Invergordon and Campbeltown were favourite ports of call.

We were leaving Campbeltown en route for Tobermory on one occasion, when the flotilla suffered another nasty accident. The six submarines were proceeding line ahead, rounding the Mull of Kintyre. We were led by *L19*, whose C.O. was the senior submarine officer. *L19* was followed by *L16, L21, L26, L23* and *L18*, each boat being two cables apart. I happened to be up on the bridge, and saw *L19* approaching a rather choppy patch of water. This was obviously a shallow patch, but amazingly she took no avoiding action. Luckily she only caught the edge of it, heeled over slightly and continued apparently undamaged. *L16* promptly went to starboard and *L21* to port. but *L26*, and she really had more time to assess the situation, continued on her course to become firmly fixed on the reef. There was little we could do without jeopardizing the safety of our own submarines. A signal from *Cyclops* ordered us to carry on to Tobermory while she went to *L26*'s assistance. It was low tide at the time and fortunately *L26* was able to clear herself six hours later on the high tide, whereupon both *L26* and *Cyclops* returned to Campbeltown in order to ascertain the damage.

Whilst awaiting divers to examine *L26*'s underbelly, her First Lieutenant ordered a battery charge, as she had expended a great deal of battery power in trying to clear herself off the reef. Unfortunately there had either been damage while grounding, or the battery ventilation system had not been opened up correctly, because soon after starting the charge they suffered a battery explosion. This explosion killed several of the crew, and injured several others. We did not hear of this catastrophe until we arrived in port.

Shortly after this we made a visit to Copenhagen, at which time I suffered a personal accident, although many would no doubt describe it as downright carelessness on my part. Myself and a couple of others had decided to go for a swim at a beautiful resort called Clampenborg. A long wooden jetty ran a hundred yards out into the bay from a delightful sandy beach. Walking out to the end of this jetty with a couple of chums I did what was for me, a spectacular 'jack-knife' dive. What I hadn't noticed was that the water was a mere three feet deep, and I very nearly broke my neck. Luckily it was a sandy bottom, but even so my face was very much in a mess when I 'blew all main ballast' to get to the surface. Barely conscious, the skin was removed from my nose, lips, and most painfully, my gums. My neck has never been quite the same since. The water around me was red with blood but I managed to regain what remained of my wits and composure, and endeavoured not to make a bigger fool of myself than I already had. This incident of course, went to prove that the old adage of 'look before you leap'. My main thoughts were to get myself looking presentable before we returned home, or Clare would think that I had been in some drunken brawl.

This was my second period in *L21*, the first, in Malta, was for about seven months, but this time it was over two and a half years, which included two dockyard refit periods of about four months each. There had been many changes in the crew during this time. Bill French had been relieved by 'Tubby' Stanbury who was a splendid and cheerful messmate. Bill Parford was another submarine conscript, who was with us for a while, but Bill never really adapted himself to this particular type of existence, moreover he used to get terribly seasick. Where some of us felt quite ill at times, poor Bill would be completely 'hors-de-combat'. At times, under the strain, he would vomit blood, but he had to suffer this agony for three years, before returning to general service. Even so the only ships suitable for Bill would be large battleships, as destroyers and sloops were worse than submarines in heavy weather. But Bill, a Cornishman, did not lack courage and determination; I can never once recall him missing his watch.

Two other young E.R.A.s who were in *L21* for a period were R. 'Kipper' Toombs and W.'Lofty'Evans. Both of whom alas, were lost together with their C.E.R.A 'Baron' Pickard when the submarine *Sterlet* was lost by enemy action in April of 1940.

We were very fortunate in having the amiable and very efficient stoker 'Lofty' Fenn as our mess man for a long period. 'Lofty' was an ideal chap for this post, A very pleasant messmate, and tactful in his approach, moreover he was very good at his own departmental job as a stoker. It was he, who during one of his brief spells as an engine room stoker was given the job of cleaning out the drain oil tank whilst in harbour. 'Lofty' was a big fellow, and this really was a small man's job. Apart from being filthy and uncomfortable, there were two or three small manholes to be negotiated inside the tank, and poor 'Lofty' became jammed in the manhole furthest from the tank entrance. The tank was under the main engines, with a maximum height of only two feet. I was sent in to assist him to remove some of his clothing in order to extricate himself, not that I could be of very great assistance under these circumstances owing to the limited space. I had been jammed up in these conditions on several occasions in the past, and one feels very much alone – certainly no place for one suffering from claustrophobia. The main thing is to keep calm; this is somewhat difficult if one is suffering from cramp, but a little more easy if there is someone there to talk to. However, much to everyone's relief, especially 'Lofty's', we eventually managed to get him out.

About this time *L21* underwent a long refit at Devonport dockyard, lasting nearly five months. This was quite a break for us as all the E.R.A.'s remained with her. Although there was plenty of work to do, we were not overworked, nor was there any overtime. For a part of this period we combined with another submarine, which was also refitting, so we were only duty about once a week, what a luxury!

This now was an ideal opportunity for me to take the examinations for my Charge Certificate and the higher educational exam. The former to qualify to take the examination for advancement to C.E.R.A, and the latter to qualify to take the Warrant Engineers professional exam, assuming that I wished to do so at a later date. This was a golden opportunity for me, as there was little chance to swot while at sea, and I surprised myself by gaining two first class passes, with a 95% pass in mathematics.

In the April of 1934 the inevitable draft arrived. This was to *Dolphin*, obviously to await a draft to the China station. The submarine service only had two flotilla's serving abroad, and I had already served in the Mediterranean.

Not knowing exactly when this would be, we decided that Clare and Joan would come to the Portsmouth area for as long as I was there. The thought of being parted for two and a half years weighed heavily on us. I certainly could not afford to have them in Hong Kong, very few officers could do that, this was a privilege only enjoyed by officers of senior rank or those who had a private income. Nowadays common sense has prevailed, and rarely are husbands parted from their wives for longer than one year. Free passages and married quarters are provided in many cases. Even now it seems that the seagoing sailor is at a disadvantage when compared to the sailor who seldom goes to sea. There has always been this minority who, for one reason or another, have managed to hog the depots and shore establishments, subsequently spending much longer with their families, but then, if they can get away with it, who can blame them? However, I could scarcely grumble as I had just spent two and a half years in home waters, and five months of that in refit. Furthermore, much to my surprise, I was to spend the next four or five months in *Dolphin*. This was another fine break as the summer was marvellous. I was 'spare crew', so rarely went to sea, and had Clare and Joan domiciled in good accommodation in Southsea.

We played much tennis, particularly with George and Peggy Etheridge, who had been our great friends in our Malta days. George, a large and very genial fellow, was good at most games. Sadly, he like many of my contemporaries was to lose his life in the forthcoming war.

My dreaded draft came early in October. Clare returned to Plymouth and I took passage to Hong Kong in the P& O liner *Ranpura*. Our little party consisted of C.E.R.A. 'Biff' Smith and five E.R.A.'s. Being fairly senior Chief Petty Officers we travelled second class, occupying two three berth cabins in a good position in the ship.

It was a pleasant voyage, no work to do and all of three weeks to do it in. We were the only servicemen aboard except one, and he was the future captain of the 4th Submarine Flotilla, Captain C.G.B. Coltart. C.V.O. who was travelling to Hong Kong, to take up his new appointment. This proved fortunate for us because, although we were all reasonably abstentious, after about two weeks we were rapidly running out of cash. So it was decided to draw lots to see who would approach our future captain with a view to procuring a 'rubber' (cash loan). 'Biff' Smith won this doubtful privilege, (he was senior anyway) and found Captain Coltart to be very sympathetic and generous.

We stopped at all the usual ports normally served by the P& O Line on the route through the Suez Canal to the Far East. This was my first passage through the Suez Canal and a most interesting one it was.

The only time that I landed during the voyage was when we called at Colombo. This was a golden opportunity to see my charming cousin Louise Smith, and her equally charming and hospitable husband Major Jack Smith. Having previously notified them of my passage on *Ranpura*, Jack was at the wharf as soon as we berthed, waiting to take me to their beautiful bungalow on the outskirts of the city to spend a few days with them before the ship continued on her way to Singapore.

Jack, previously a regular soldier in the British Army, had volunteered for transfer to the Ceylon Defence Force, where at the time, he held the rank of Major. Jack and Louise had spent many years in Ceylon, and remained there until after the Second World War, when he retired with the rank of Lieutenant Colonel.

When we arrived at Singapore we were nearly at the end of our journey, although we still had one thousand four hundred miles to go before reaching Hong Kong. A fairly large percentage of our passengers left the ship at Singapore, and a few more, bound for Hong Kong or Japan embarked. Although very low in cash at this juncture, I did have a run ashore in Singapore, having a little refreshment at the famous Raffles Hotel.

Finally, on our arrival at Hong Kong we found to our dismay that the parent ship, *HMS Medway* and her large brood of fifteen submarines was away on a cruise, and would not arrive back in Hong Kong for two weeks. This was rather shattering news for us, as by this time we were just about penniless. However, Captain Coltart again came to our rescue by arranging for us to draw a nominal weekly pay from the depot ship *HMS Tamar*. *Tamar*, an antiquated sloop moored in the dockyard, could not accommodate us, but arranged for us to be accommodated in a disused naval sanatorium right on the top of the Peak, over one thousand feet up. This saved the Admiralty quite a bit of money, and we were more than happy fending for ourselves. We were given a lodging allowance of 4/9d per day (24p), and the services of a sailor from *Tamar* as a mess man.

Travelling up and down on the Peak funicular railway, we seized this opportunity of exploring the city of Hong Kong, and of crossing the harbour on the frequent and very cheap ferries to Kowloon. It seemed very uncharacteristic of the authorities to let six E.R.A.'s have all this time free, we fully expected to be given work in the dockyard. Most mornings and afternoons were spent on a deck tennis court that we rigged up in a yard adjoining the sanatorium. All this was very pleasant, but it was natural that we were keen to get settled down, and to join our respective submarines.

HMS Medway duly arrived with her brood, which comprised six 'O' class, five 'P' class, (*Poseidon* having been sunk in collision, with great loss of life just before we left the U.K.), and four 'R' class. I was promptly drafted to *Oswald*.

Chapter Three

The 4th Submarine Flotilla was very large, but *Medway*, the first of the parent ships actually designed for the job, was able to cope fairly comfortably as it was seldom that there were more than twelve submarines alongside at one time. Almost always there were two or possibly three refitting, and one or two detached for special duties.

The submarine E.R.A.'s mess on *Medway* was a large one, but even with only twelve boats alongside this meant that seventy chiefs and E.R.A.'s were accommodated for meals, and many including myself, preferred to purchase a camp bed and sleep on the upper deck rather than slinging a hammock in this overcrowded mess.

On one occasion *Oswald* was sent to Singapore for three months in order to carry out intensive exercises to test defences. The 'O', 'P', and 'R' class submarines were fairly large ocean going boats, but living aboard the boat in Singapore during the summer was still not very pleasant, we had no effective air cooling or conditioning in those days.

Our Captain, who must have assumed command not long before my arrival, as he remained with us throughout the whole period that I was aboard, was Lt. Cdr. Mark T. Collyer, a man whom I would describe as taciturn and extremely efficient. The whole crew had a great regard for him although even the officers found him rather remote. Other officers were: First Lieutenant, Lt. Waters. Navigator, Lt 'Jumbo' Watkins, Torpedo and Gunnery Officer, Lt. Field. The Engineer Officer, Lt. (E) R.S. Hawkins, was to put me in the Captain's Report later in the commission, the first and only time in my career, an event that of course displeased me intensely.

While at sea and on watch in the engine room, it appeared that the Officer of the Watch on the bridge had decided to have a bit of a skylark at my expense. Engine manoeuvring orders were being relayed so quickly that it was impossible to comply with them all. In any case there was an inbuilt delay while the oil pressure operated camshaft moved from the ahead to the astern position. Exercising rapid changes of engine orders was essential, not least for reasons of 'man overboard', but it was obvious in this case that someone on the bridge was just trying to confuse the engine room staff. Eventually it had to happen! The port engine was momentarily started astern when the telegraph had been altered to ahead. As this was apparently what they had set out to accomplish, a reprimand from the engineer officer would have been sufficient. However, the Captain was very nice about it and dismissed the case without punishment, but my professional pride was injured. Lt. Hawkins was later to become a Vice Admiral, and the navy's Engineer in Chief.

We had a fine crew throughout that commission, although of course many were changed every six months when the relief's arrived from the U.K. We won our fair share of awards for gunnery, general efficiency and sport. The only sport we really excelled in was rugger, out of a crew of sixty we could raise a full XV, five of whom were picked for the flotilla, and three of us, Lt. (E) Hawkins (who later became one of the navy selectors), Lt. Watkins and myself to represent the navy in the far east. 'Blimp' or 'Jumbo' Watkins, as the crew affectionately knew him on account of his stature, was one of the hardest working and toughest forwards I'd ever played with. He was also one of the friendliest officers, and very popular with the whole crew. Alas his promising naval career was cut short when he lost his life as captain of the submarine *Triton*, in the Mediterranean in November 1940.

The submarine *Rainbow* took the lead in this flotilla as far as sport was concerned. This was mainly achieved by the efforts and enthusiasm of her First Lieutenant, Lt A.C. Miers. Tony Miers, affectionately known as 'Gamp', later attained the rank of Rear Admiral, he was 'well in' with the drafting staff and literally ruthless in the picking of his crew. A hard taskmaster, 'Gamp' would put his submarine, his service, his team, and his country before anything else. He fought the war as hard as he played his rugby, and was awarded the Victoria Cross and two D.S.O.'s for his daring exploits while in command of *Torbay*.

Not long after I joined her, *Oswald* went into Whampo dock on the Kowloon side, for a short refit. This was an experience to be sure. Not being very familiar with the Chinese at this time, they amazed me with their methods of getting a job done. They had many good craftsmen and, provided we kept close supervision, their finished product was very good. But it was quite unlike the naval dockyards in the U.K., where one could just sit back and let them get on with it. The foremen and inspectors were mainly European, and the charge men (referred to as No.1) and below, were Chinese.

We had our own allocation of work; although it was extremely hot working in the boat while it was in dry-dock. The crew, with the exception of the duty watch, who remained for supervision purposes, worked 'tropical routine', from 0700 to 1300, having a late lunch on returning to *Medway*.

This refit period also taught me how to converse with the Chinese, using 'pidgin' English; they seemed to understand this much better. Most amusing at first, but one soon came to speak it fluently. To the jinriksha 'boy' (probably aged at least sixty), 'Makee plenty quick' if one was in a hurry. To the little chesai (cheesi) boy, who was employed in the various Chief and Petty Officer's messes on board. 'What b'long Cheese-I? Meaning, 'What are you up to boy?' All R's became L's, and most words ended with 'ee'.

On completion of our refit the general programme for the flotilla was to cruise southward to Singapore, Java or Borneo in the winter, and northward to Wei-hai-wei on the small island of Lui-Kung-Tao, visiting ports en-route, in the summer. Most of the spring and autumn would be spent in or around Hong Kong. For some political reason, the Japanese had, at about this time come to dislike us very much, and as a consequence of this the normally pleasant cruise to Japan was cancelled. This dislike of the British intensified, and relations became very strained. Later, when a Japanese warship visited Hong Kong, her crew behaved in a blatantly arrogant and unfriendly way toward us. Not being politically minded at that time, I had no idea what it was all about.

To me Hong Kong was a fascinating place, although I would not care to spend a lengthy period there, especially in the summer when the weather is very hot and humid. Poverty abounded, especially in the depths of the Wanchei area to the east of Hong Kong. There were various cabarets and drinking saloons, naval clubs, NAAFI and seaman's institutes, but none of these interested me very much. There was a very handy C.P.O.'s club in the dockyard where one could assuage one's thirst with very reasonably priced English beer, and play a game of billiards. Eventually a friend of mine introduced me to a sports and social club, on the outskirts of Kowloon. This was the China Light and Power and Recreational Club, which accepted three or four C.P.O.'s as honorary members, and was situated about a mile from the ferry, off Nathan Road.

The club suited me very well as the members were mostly British, and all very friendly. The subscription was reasonable and there were two splendid tennis courts, also a badminton hall with table tennis and billiards. I purchased a badminton racquet at a sports shop in Hong Kong owned by a young Sikh, with whom I became very friendly. There were many Sikhs in Hong Kong and the New Territories, most of them found jobs as policemen. Returning to Hong Kong from the club, I often called on Rangit Singh for a chat, and was always made most welcome.

Right next to the China Light and Power Club was the German Club, and a more unfriendly and arrogant lot it would be difficult to find. Of course the time was 1934-35, and Germany was being a little unfriendly generally. The Nazis, led by the arch villain Hitler, were causing a stir. If we returned a tennis ball to them over a twelve-foot high netting, there would be a curt but unsmiling 'thank you'.

The submarines worked a rota policing Bias Bay against pirates, of which there were quite a few. This type of work was not very popular with the crews. It was a fortnight at sea, a sort of war patrol, which was generally uneventful. It was a job more suited to a small surface ship, of which there were very few in the eastern squadron. Apparently before these patrols were started, Bias Bay was rife with pirates hijacking and raiding the Chinese junks trading to the north of the busy port of Hong Kong.

It was good to get away from Hong Kong in the summer. The whole flotilla, in fact the whole China fleet, with the exception of the guard ships, those on the Bias patrol, and those refitting, sailed northward about thirteen hundred miles to Wei-hai-wei. Wei-hai-wei, on a ninety-nine year lease from the Chinese (long since expired), was almost on the same latitude as Malta, and enjoyed a wonderful summer climate. The flotilla would remain there, except for one or two short cruises to Dairen, Chefoo and Tsingtao for three months, the submarines going to sea for four days in each week for exercises.

There was very little to see at Wei-hai-wei, which boasted one hotel, almost wholly taken by those officers who could afford to have their wives with them. I would like to have had Clare in China, but it was beyond the pocket of all but a few officers who had a private income. On the borders of the extensive sports grounds there was a huge NAAFI canteen where sailors could quench their thirst after playing games. U.K. export beer was very cheap, and they must have had very large storage tanks. The food in the canteen restaurant was extremely good; an enormous meal of almost anything that could be purchased in Britain would cost about eighty cents (five new pence). Fruit was abundant on this small island, also very cheap. This gigantic canteen even housed about a half a dozen bowling alleys, where 'Jack' could work up an even greater thirst.

Most of the fleet and flotilla sporting competitions were held during this period, regattas, athletic and aquatic sports, football, hockey and tennis. It was a haven for those who liked sport, but not very popular with the 'lady lovers'. There was hardly a female to be seen; even the canteen staff were male.

It was rather surprising to us that the whole flotilla, (*Medway* and ten submarines) next paid a short visit to Dairen, as it was at that time in Japanese hands. A rugby match was arranged with the local inhabitants which, much to our surprise we lost. We had a strong side, but what we did not know at that time was that the wily Japs brought all their best players over from Japan, and that they had been training them for weeks.

Although the weather conditions throughout the summer in Wei-hai-wei were excellent, the anchorage was very exposed: it only needed a stiffish breeze for the boats, which formed a 'trot' of six either side of the *Medway*, to lay off at anchor in order to prevent the occurrence of damage to their saddle tanks. This was exasperating for us and caused much inconvenience. Quite frequently, no sooner had we arrived back alongside from a day's exercising at sea, secured up and started the battery charge, and retired inboard to the *Medway* for a bath and supper, then one third of the crew would be required back on the boat to take her out again in order to anchor, anything up to a mile away. These lads, who might, or might not have had their supper, would have to grab the personal gear they would need for tomorrow, and also some food for breakfast. If the charge was to be a long one, five or six hours, then a second E.R.A would be needed to share the burden of watch keeping, and to help with any other work that had to be completed before the boat sailed for sea the following day. The remainder of the crew, having enjoyed the comfort of *Medway* overnight, would return to the boat early next morning, bringing their breakfast and food for the day with them. They would also expect both main engines ready for sea before weighing anchor at 0800 hours.

Medway, beside her normal outfit of power boats, had two large launches which were used to deliver and collect men and supplies to the various submarines when they were laying off at anchor. These stoutly built launches could accommodate over a hundred men, nevertheless with ten submarines lying off, and two thirds of each crew waiting to go to or from the parent ship, this meant several trips and much wasted time. The fun came when it was really rough; the situation could then be highly dangerous. The huge launch, shaped like an overgrown cutter, would come alongside well forward to avoid damage to the tanks, with an eight foot swell running one had to seize the opportunity to jump from the fore-casing into the launch when its gunwales were almost level. This was rather a nerve-racking experience, as a misjudged jump could mean either getting very wet, or badly crushed between the launch and the submarine. Sometimes the launch would be so full of men that one had literally to jump on top of them. Miraculously there were very few casualties, and despite the danger and the discomfort of overcrowding, good humour usually prevailed. In these conditions it was such a tiresome procedure that I usually preferred to remain aboard the submarine as the duty E.R.A., at least I was on the spot when we had to up-anchor next morning.

Toward the end of September 1935, shortly before the flotilla was due to sail for Hong Kong, with a couple of courtesy visits planned en-route. We had returned from sea, two thirds of the crew were aboard *Medway*; the duty officer was 'Jumbo' Watkins and I was the duty E.R.A., when a motorboat arrived alongside bringing the First Lieutenant. We assumed that the swell had now abated sufficiently for us to return to *Medway*, but this was not the case: *Pandora, Phoenix, Osiris* and ourselves were recalled with orders to prepare for an unknown destination. We refuelled, stored, embarked torpedoes with real warheads (terribly exciting), charged our batteries, and headed south early next morning. It was not until then that we were told that our destination was the Mediterranean, where another little 'fascist' upstart was throwing his weight around, having already invaded the almost defenceless Abyssinia (now Ethiopia).

This did not entirely surprise us, as the political scene in Europe was becoming very agitated, thanks to Germany's Hitler and his 'goose-stepping' nazis who were trampling all those around him, and that grotesque little Italian called Mussolini, with his band of hysterical fascists. At the time of sailing it appeared to us very much like we were going to war, or at least to protect Britain's interest in the Mediterranean and North Africa. These two fanatical dictators were seeking to extend their respective empires, and to intimidate the rest of the world in general.

It was apparent to most, including myself, that war was sooner or later inevitable, and that it was just a matter of time before the 'balloon went up'. When these bullies got their lust for power their appetites became insatiable. Someone would have to have the courage to call 'stop', but who would it be? Both of these countries were building up a tremendous military might, and there were very few nations in a position to call a halt. Britain was pathetically weak, and we really had not recovered from World War One. For years now, defence had been very low on our priorities.

Much to our surprise we were ordered by a 'top priority' signal to put in to Hong Kong. This we discovered was to enable us to change our rather obsolete torpedoes for the Mk 8 type. The change being accomplished overnight, we sailed again early next morning without giving shore leave to any of the crews. As far as I can recollect our C.O., Cdr. Mark Collier was the senior submarine commander and thus led the way in *Oswald*. At Singapore we embarked more fuel and fresh provisions before pressing on to Aden.

The long passage across the Indian Ocean was uneventful and our main engines gave very little trouble. The weather on the whole was very good and consequently we were able to proceed most of the way with our fore hatch open. This was indeed a great asset in the tropics, as not only did it ventilate the boat, with the main engines drawing huge quantities of fresh air through the fore hatch, but also, those not on watch could bask in brilliant sunshine on the fore-casing. Of course when it came on to blow, and the waves came anywhere near the hatch, then the O.O.W. would order it to be shut – this was a very big (twenty-seven inch) hole in our hull!

Most of my time when not on watch was spent as far forward on the casing as possible, either writing or reading, or sometimes just sitting fascinated by the antics of the dolphins. Often there would be at least four or five of these delightful mammals keeping station on our bows, sometimes leaping right out of the sea, as if to get a better view of us, or to show us their prowess, or perhaps they just liked our company. We were travelling at over fifteen knots, and yet they had no trouble staying with us for mile after mile. Another thing that fascinated us was the antics of the flying fish. They would shoot out of the water and skim the surface for two or three hundred yards before disappearing again. Each morning we would discover three or four dead ones within or on the casing. In the darkness the surface of the sea glittered with phosphorescent light where it had been disturbed by our passage.

Another amenity we provided ourselves with was a salt-water shower and a four-foot square canvas tank on the fore casing. We didn't seem to be in any great hurry as fifteen knots was an economical speed, but we could not heave to for 'hands to bathe' for fear of the sharks. We had been swimming many times in harbour where sharks abounded, but then we had men posted on the conning tower to keep lookout. I must have broken many a freestyle record when the alarm was sounded.

We were in four watches for most of the way, which was pretty easy going, but most of the dogwatches were taken up with surface and dived exercises. The First Lieutenant liked to dive at least once a day in order to 'catch a trim'. We could of course calculate our loss of weight by the consumption of water and food, and our gain by the use of fuel that was automatically replaced by heavier seawater, but there was nothing like a dive to make sure, and to sharpen up the crew in their various jobs. During these dived exercises we practiced rapid changing of depth, lighting failures, (we were expected to be able to locate any valve or operating lever in the dark), dummy torpedo attacks etc, while on the surface we would practice gun actions and 'man overboard' routines. As far as we knew, we were likely to be engaged in war very soon! The four submarines would disperse for these exercises, to reform line ahead on completion, with *Oswald* in the lead.

On arrival at Aden we found a couple of 'L' class submarines already there without a parent ship. It must have been pretty grim for them, struggling in the heat of Aden without a parent ship. It was bad enough for us on our larger submarines, but we did have an upper deck galley situated in the bridge structure. This small oil fired galley was not popular with the cook as it involved humping food up and down the conning tower, but we were all pleased to use it in Aden.

Aden was in my opinion, a ghastly place. It had very little to offer except stifling heat, and we for some reason were kept there for three long weeks. Although it was a relief to get out of the boat, I landed only two or three times. The cruiser *HMS Norfolk* was also anchored there, and my brother Harold (Bill) was one of her engineer officers, he had recently been promoted to Warrant Engineer Officer. Although it wasn't 'the thing' to invite us into *Norfolk's* wardroom, Bill did all that he could for my four messmates and me. He sent a motor boat for us daily, in order that we might enjoy a bath aboard *Norfolk*; this was a great advantage, and we met up on the few occasions that I went ashore. It was very pleasant seeing my brother; we actually saw very little of one another during our service careers, but all the same; we were pleased when we finally left Aden. The two 'L' class submarines had to remain there, poor devils!

We'd had little news since leaving Wei-hai-wei, and such news that we gathered in Aden was not very reassuring. Mussolini continued with his conquest of Abyssinia, there was little to stop him. Where would he strike next? The Italians had had envious eyes on Malta for many years, and there were parts of the British Empire bordering on Abyssinia.

We passed through the Suez Canal with a canal pilot on each boat. This was rather a different situation to my last passage through the canal on *Ranpura*; I had to work for my living now. The E.R.A.'s were watch and watch about, as an E.R.A. was required on each engine during the canal passage. It surprised me that we were allowed to keep the forward hatch open in order to ventilate the boat, shutting it only when passing another ship. Those not on watch were allowed to laze on the fore casing, and it was most interesting to watch the passing ships, each of which gave way to our four submarines

It was as though we were almost home again when we reached Malta; having travelled nearly nine thousand miles since leaving Wei-hai-wei, we were now only two thousand miles from the U.K. *Cyclops* was there with her flotilla of 'L' class boats, forming the 1st Submarine Flotilla, moored at her usual billet at M'sida Creek. We were instructed to berth alongside in Lazaretto Creek, as *Cyclops* could not accommodate any of our crews, although she could offer us repair, storage, sick berth and bathing facilities. This did not worry us unduly, as we were used to living in the boat, and it was much cooler in Malta anyway. It was significant that, from the time of my joining *Oswald,* she only spent twenty-five per cent of her time alongside a parent ship.

Almost as soon as we arrived, we were ordered back to sea again in order to exercise diving at night. There is virtually no difference between diving during the night or the day but hitherto, because of peacetime submarine losses, diving during the hours of darkness was strictly forbidden. Probably night diving wasn't so much a danger to the submarine, as it was a hazard to merchant shipping. Although at first, night time diving appeared to us as quite a revolutionary step, it was really quite safe. Among the many safety precautions introduced at that time, was a very sensitive underwater listening set (HSD). Even so, this was considered to be inferior to the set used by the Germans, who were then building a formidable submarine fleet.

Night diving subsequently became commonplace, and at the time of leaving submarines I had dived as often at night as I had by day. The continuing improvements to the ASDIC underwater detection equipment made life much easier. Later, with the introduction of the snorkel, submarines could stay dived for much longer periods.

Another exercise we practiced even more was the 'crash dive', which up to then, had been the exception rather than the rule. Dives, up until that time had been very 'gentlemanly', the C.O. would order 'Stop both engines, out both engine clutches', in order to proceed on both main motors – 'Officer of the watch and lookouts below'. Then he would take a good look around before descending the conning tower and shutting the hatch himself. After shutting and clipping the lower hatch, he would then order, 'Group up - Half ahead both - Up periscope - Open main vents – Take her to thirty feet.'

'Q' (quick diving) tank would be blown, and the main vents shut early in the dive. With nothing less than a fully charged group of high pressure air bottles (4000 lbs per square inch), ready to blow main ballast, and the whole crew closed up at 'diving stations', with key men in key positions, this was a gradual and careful transition from surface running to dived running. It wasn't until war came, and submarines were harassed day and night by the enemy, that we really reduced the diving time to an absolute minimum, diving without warning, off the klaxon at any time of the day or night, with every second vital.

We were at last beginning to sit up and take notice of the threat of Italian and German military strength, particularly the latter, which were soon to intimidate many European countries by shaking the mailed fist and goose-stepping arrogantly on many toes.

We hadn't been in Malta for more than a week or two, when Stan Peel and I began to discuss the possibility and advisability of having our wives come out to join us. This wasn't encouraged, but there was no order actually forbidding it, and a state of emergency had not been introduced at that time.

In retrospect it was rather amusing that two E.R.A.'s should be summing up the political situation and deciding that, though far from being satisfactory, there was no suggestion of war for another two or three years. As it turned out, we were not very far from the truth; it was now November 1935, although things nearly 'blew up' in 1938, war was not declared until 1939.

Cables were dispatched to our respective wives with orders to 'drop everything' and come out to Malta as soon as they, were able. And they bless their respective hearts, did just that. Always resourceful, and like most naval wives, ready for any contingency, they booked passages, arranged inoculations, gave notice to landladies, stored furniture, packed personal belongings (including their husbands civilian attire), grabbed their children, and were in Malta before Christmas. Verily a tremendous feat – the Admiralty never recognized the treasure they had in naval personnel's wives.

Clare and Joan travelled to Malta tourist class on the *Largs Bay*, and yet again I was unable to meet them as *Oswald* had been sent to Alexandra for a couple of weeks. Before leaving I was very fortunate in discovering that both flats at 13 Parallel Street where we had lived previously, were vacant. The very pleasant Maltese lady who owned the premises was pleased to let the top flat to myself, and the ground flat to Stan Peel, both at a reasonable rental. Clare, her previous experience standing her in good stead, had little difficulty in getting settled in, and even helped Mrs. Peel to do the same before *Oswald* returned to Malta on Christmas Eve 1935. What a Christmas present this was. Joan was now five and a half years of age, and I hadn't seen them for fifteen months, I had fully expected it to be twice that period.

During the first six months that Clare was in Malta, *Oswald* spent two of these lengthy periods in Alexandria. To Stan Peel and me this was a dead loss. Having got our families out to Malta, it now seemed to be a policy at that time to keep one submarine in Alexandria. I disliked the place anyhow, and life with my family in Malta was so very pleasant. There was little that Britain, or for that matter, any peace loving nation, could do to prevent Mussolini from overrunning the unfortunate Abyssinia, but as time went on the political situation seemed to become a little more stable, which we felt justified our decision

Then once again came the crunch: After less than eight months away, our four submarines were ordered to return to China. Clare had been at Malta for less than seven months, during which time I had spent two and a half months in Alexandria.

So commenced our long voyage back to China, leaving behind my family and one of the happiest periods of my life. It was two very sad wives that travelled to the end of the breakwater at Grand Harbour to wave farewell. Neither Stan nor myself was able to wave in return as we were closed up at 'Harbour Stations' in the engine room. Perhaps this was just as well, else we may have been tempted to jump overboard and swim for it.

Lt Hawkins had left the boat by this time, and had been replaced by the redoubtable Warrant Engineer 'Alex' Lane. He was a volatile, tough and hot-tempered man, who had a vocabulary that would turn the air blue, but he was extremely popular, both with his seniors and his juniors. Very forthright, you might say that he 'called a spade a spade'. He was also a very efficient and capable engineer.

The return journey, on the surface all the way except for our daily trim dive, was quite uneventful. Our main engines caused us little trouble despite the enormous distance they covered. We only remained in Aden for one day, but seized the opportunity of a quick routine docking in Colombo.

These routine dockings (four days which usually extended to seven) not only gave the engineering staff the opportunity to examine all the underwater fitting and valves, but allowed the dock staff to paint all that part of the boat that was normally underwater, renew the zinc slabs that were fitted in their hundreds around hull fittings and inside external tanks to prevent corrosion, carry out any necessary repairs in these areas, and to exercise dropping the drop keel – a section of the keel, situated amidships and weighing ten tons, which could be quickly released in an emergency to increase the buoyancy of the boat.

Actually we were there nearly two weeks in total, which gave the captain the opportunity to give six days leave to each watch. Half the crew at a time were transported to the rest camp at Diyatalawa in the central highlands of Ceylon. This made a very welcome break for the crew, as it was really stifling in Colombo, especially in dry dock. Instead of travelling to Diyatalawa with my shipmates, permission was given for me to visit my cousin Jack Smith.. As Jack normally moved up to the hills for two months of the summer, I travelled up with him to the very comfortable bungalow allocated to him as a Major in the Ceylon Defence Forces. It was a very pleasant week and a welcome relief from the heat of Colombo.

Those unfortunates left behind, lived in a shed on the dockside, it was far too hot to live in the boat. They worked from 07:30 to 13:00 daily, working again in the evening when it was necessary to complete a job.

At the end of two weeks, we sailed for Singapore and Hong Kong, and on our arrival at Hong Kong we found that *Medway* had not yet left for Wei-hai-wei. It was now the summer of 1936 and very hot.

Before leaving for Wei-hai-wei it was decided that one submarine should be selected for an experiment to test the endurance of submarine crews in that zone, under war conditions. Very right and proper! And out of the fifteen submarines in the flotilla, who better for this than *Oswald*?

We sailed for the nearby Bias Bay where we dived, carrying out exercises and dummy attacks during each day, surfacing to charge our batteries at night. Only the normal seaman lookouts and the O.O.W. were allowed on the bridge at night, the remainder of us did not see daylight for over a fortnight.

At times the heat was almost unbearable, and one by one the whole crew became covered in a prickly heat rash. In addition to the normal work and watch-keeping routine, six of us were allocated to carry out a series of strenuous exercises before surfacing each night. The Surgeon Commander, who had been appointed to the submarine for this trip, carried out these tests with us and took our pulse and blood pressure at the end of each session. Although the general temperature was over one hundred and thirty degrees Fahrenheit, we were obliged to spend some time in the battery tank where the temperature was much higher, as part of each experiment. Taking part in strenuous exercise at the end of each day when the oxygen content in the boat was very low, and the CO2 content very high, was anything but funny.

However the whole exercise was somewhat of a novelty and a challenge, and in general good humour prevailed. I chaffed my shipmates as one by one they succumbed to the disagreeable and painful prickly heat rash, but at last it caught up with me, and when it did, it was a most severe attack. We were all covered, almost from head to foot with this angry looking rash which was most uncomfortable. The Surgeon Commander made light of our malady, but I would have thought it rather serious that most of the pores in our skin were not functioning correctly. The chosen six were also weighed, and samples of our perspiration and urine were analysed daily. Two weeks of this routine seemed like an eternity to us, although a few years later this sort of thing was quite commonplace.

At the conclusion of our two weeks penance we returned to Hong Kong dockyard where, before any of the crew were allowed to take a breather, we dived to the bottom of the basin for a further twenty-four hours. Here the whole crew were still kept busy operating the steering and hydroplanes in hand control. This was the longest period that any of us had spent dived, and owing to the physical and mental strain and the lack of oxygen, many of the crew had almost reached the limits of their endurance.

We were very relieved to surface and get into the parent ship. I know that I was sickened with the sight of the inside of the submarine. We all had a big pile of washing (dhobying) to do, as well as having a good bath. Water had been strictly rationed during this patrol.

The *Medway* did make a bit of a fuss of us in welcoming us back alongside, but the 'make and mend' we were accorded was largely taken up with extensive medical examinations in the sick bay. We all thought that a week's leave would have been more appropriate.

The whole flotilla, negative those refitting sailed for Wei-hai-wei and cooler climes a few days later. My rash remained with me for more than three weeks. This 'prickly heat' was common in the tropics, it was caused by the pores of the skin not being able to cope with the continual and excessive perspiration, which subsequently caused inflammation and irritation of the nerve terminals – a prickly sensation. But it did not prevent me from free swimming, though the sensation caused was similar to brushing ones skin against a hedgehog. Our discomfort would have lasted much longer had we remained in Hong Kong where the summer temperature is accompanied by a high degree of humidity.

An amusing incident while at Wei-hai-wei, involved our much respected engineer officer Alex Lane. A traditional part of the flotilla regatta was the E.O.'s motor dinghy race. Each submarine carried a small dinghy in it's casing, which could be propelled by a portable two stroke petrol engine. The conditions were that the E.O. had to start the engine, and then proceed around a marker buoy, and back to the parent ship, a distance of little over half a mile, as quickly as possible. This wasn't quite Alex's 'cup of tea', but he couldn't very well refuse, with Captain Submarines and all the other C.O.'s watching

Our dinghy engine was tuned to racing pitch by our outside E.R.A. (outside wrecker), and test started several times by Alex himself before the race – first crank every time. But alas, when the starting gun sounded, all that Alex could get out of her was a docile phut - phut!

We were watching from the foc'sle on the *Medway*, and could see Alex's normally ruddy complexion getting ruddier and ruddier; the air around *Oswald's* dinghy was literally 'blue' and I am sure that if that engine had not been bolted down, Alex would have thrown it into the sea.

Most of the others had finished the course when Alex finally gave up. The fact that he was not the only one left at the start was of little consolation to him. Back alongside, Stan Peel jumped down into the dinghy to find the cause of this calamity, and the engine started first time! We dare not let Alex see us laughing at his discomfort, but eventually he saw the humour of the situation.

After a few weeks in Hong Kong the *Medway* and the 4th Submarine Flotilla moved south to Singapore where we carried out exercises from the naval base at Seletar. The flotilla later split up in order to 'show the flag' to as many ports and islands as possible before returning to Hong Kong. *Oswald* was detailed to spend ten days at a small place in British North Borneo called Lahad Datu. It was little more than a village, with a small wooden pier situated in a beautiful bay on the northeast corner of Borneo. There seemed to be only about half a dozen white people there, and these were French.

At first our captain deemed it inadvisable to secure alongside the rickety pier, so we dropped anchor in the bay. This was most inconvenient as we were quite a distance from the pier, and only had our small dinghy with a very temperamental engine.

No sooner had we anchored in this beautiful tranquil bay than the First Lieutenant piped 'hands to bathe'. This was very acceptable as it was very hot, and excepting for the duty watch, most of immediately dived over the side. Within minutes there was a shout from the lookout on the bridge. 'Sharks on the port quarter'!

Swimming about a hundred yards off our port beam, I did a record dash to the saddle tanks, where I was quickly hauled aboard. Actually it wasn't sharks, it was swordfish, but as far as we were concerned we might as well have tangled with a shark as with a swordfish.

After a day or two, Mark Collier, having landed and examined the pier, decided that he could bring us alongside without carrying it away. It was a very tricky manoeuvre, but it did make our stay a little more pleasant. There was very little to entertain the crew, but the First Lieutenant organized a game of soccer with the locals. These young dark skinned lads who had little knowledge of the game, played in their bare feet, and could run like deer. It was an evening game but nevertheless boiling hot. At half time a couple of spectators shinned up the palms and threw down some coconuts, the milk of which was quickly drawn off to assuage our thirst.

There were beautiful sandy beaches lined with palm trees where we had picnics. The seawater was a little too warm at eighty-eight degrees to be very refreshing, it was fine while we were in the water, but the cooling effect was not lasting, and despite having lookouts, we did not venture far from the shore. Then, after these leisurely and balmy days, it was time to leave for Singapore once more.

On another occasion the *Medway* and flotilla visited Surabaya, in Dutch held Java. It was en-route to here that the flotilla split up in order that each submarine could carry out its own 'crossing the line' ceremony. The *Medway* had prepared a large canvas tank for each submarine, to be used for this traditional ceremony, and our crew had acquired all the paraphernalia for welcoming 'King Neptune' aboard.

Before performing the ceremony we indulged in a rather extravagant manoeuvre, seemingly quite out of character for our rather taciturn and serious minded captain. When 'Jumbo' Watkins informed him that we had 'crossed the line' (latitude zero degrees), the captain sounded the klaxon to dive. We then turned about on a reciprocal course and steamed north for about one mile, surfaced, and steamed south again, having as the captain put it, tied a knot in the line.

We then rigged and filled our canvas tank with water to await the regal visitation of none other than His Titanic Majesty King Neptune (in the person of our popular coxswain George Rose) and his entourage, who arrived on the casing via the fore hatch. As the ceremony progressed, all those of us who had not crossed the line previously were lathered and shaved with a big wooden razor, before being tipped backwards into the pool. The more unfortunate ones were obliged to chew on a bar of soap. The going was a little tougher than those crossing the line on a passenger liner, but after it was all over we were each presented with a certificate.

Having a small camera, I was asked to take most of the photographs of the ceremony.

Not that I had fancied myself as a photographer. Nothing daunted, I armed myself with this inexpensive camera and took photographs of the main cast, including some of the principals undergoing their ordeals. On arrival at Surabaya I dashed inboard to the parent ship where a Sick Berth Attendant indulged in a sideline of developing film. Returning to the sick bay two days later to collect the prints, the S.B.A. ruefully informed me that they were all blank. What could have gone wrong? On examining my camera I found that all the film was taken on 'exposure', and as they had been taken at midday on the equator, with the sun blistering our shoulders, they were rather over exposed.

It required a lot of courage to tell the lads that my photographic efforts had been completely abortive. His Titanic Majesty King Neptune in the person of coxswain Rose was sorely disappointed, however one or two others had taken snaps, so we were not entirely devoid of pictorial illustration of our well-arranged ceremony.

It was on our return trip to Singapore that we ran into a typhoon, at least the tail end of one. Our forward hydroplanes suffered serious damage in this terrific storm. The fore-planes in this class of submarine were completely out of the water when we were on the surface, and hydraulically housed in a vertical position against the fore casing to prevent damage in rough seas. This storm was so violent that it bent the actuating shaft.

My sympathies were with the bridge crew, seas were breaking right over the bridge and cascading down the conning tower 'green'. Even with the sheltered outboard induction valve open the seas restricted the engines air intake so much as to create a partial vacuum, which slowed down the engines. A stoutly built member of the crew ascending or descending through the conning tower would have the same effect, to a lesser degree. The storm lasted for two or three days, and if that was the fringe of a typhoon, then it was certainly not my wish to be in the middle of one.

The bent shaft that carried the fore-planes was removed when we arrived in harbour, and deemed by the parent ship irreparable. I wasn't the outside E.R.A., nor did I have any great working knowledge of the facilities in *Medway* but in retrospect I'd have thought that there was some solution to our problem, a difficult one perhaps, as this shaft was made of forged steel, six inches in diameter and six feet long, and there was no spare available.

Possibly it was because *Oswald* was due to return to the U.K. in eight months time that we were ordered to get on with our exercises without the use of fore-planes. Or maybe it was to test the long term handling of the submarine without the aid of the fore-planes. Naturally it was an enormous handicap when 'crash diving' or coming up for a gun action, but great credit must be paid to the First Lieutenant and the control room crew, in that we carried out all normal exercises as required for the remainder of the commission. Nevertheless we would not have lasted very long in wartime, as not only did it put thirty seconds on our diving time, but also the boat was very difficult to keep at periscope depth in a 'long' sea.

It was around about that time that one evening when I was duty watch on board, I went to do the E.R.A.'s rounds prior to reporting to the duty officer that engineer's rounds were 'correct'. My job was to see that the submarine was in good trim, main vents cottered and locked, run the L.P. blower on the main ballast tanks if necessary to achieve the correct trim, sight that all bilges were dry and check that all else on the engineers side was in proper order. This routine usually took about fifteen minutes and the report was made when the duty officer entered the boat with the duty P.O. at 21:00. The boat was quiet and deserted, the duty watch of seamen and stokers having cleaned up the boat ready for rounds, and then gone inboard to return on board at 22:00 to sleep.

When I arrived at the coxswain's office, there was the coxswain, slumped on the deck as drunk as a 'fiddlers bitch'. Now here was a fine 'to do!' It was only minutes before the duty officer did his rounds, when all mess curtains were pulled back so that the officer could see that the messes had been properly cleaned and in good order.

Of course I could have left George there to bear the brunt of his indiscretion, but we were all very fond of our coxswain – he was a good chap, and this was completely out of character. His position was equivalent to a Master At Arms in a big ship, and amongst his many other duties he was responsible for the rum ration. Something had obviously upset him as he had partaken of much rum. The rum locker was open and the keys were in the lock, a heinous crime, which if discovered would probably have resulted in him being reduced in rank. I had to decide what to do very quickly. He was a big fellow and it was all that I could do to drag him into his office and lay him out on the deck. Locking the rum locker and pocketing the key, I pulled the curtains across, and just kept my fingers crossed that the duty officer would not see fit to look into this office.

Reporting my rounds correct, I walked through the boat with the duty officer and the duty P.O. trying hard to engage them in conversation as we approached the coxswain's office. Fortunately, in the event all was well, but I did commit a serious offence in covering up the incident, and even so I was very worried as I had no idea of the quantity of rum the coxswain had consumed, he might well have been in need of medical attention. But at least with me sleeping in the boat, I was able to visit him several times during the night.

The poor Cox'n was in a terrible state when he came to early the next morning. Realizing what he had done, but not knowing who had covered up for him – if anybody. Worst of all, his precious keys were missing. He was very grateful to me when I returned them to him later. Of course one does not get any kudos for a job like that, but I think I did the whole boats crew a good turn – including the captain. Normally a Chief Petty Officer of very high integrity, something had caused our Cox'n to 'go haywire'. This easily happens in those rather exacting conditions we were under. The absence of mail from home was always a prime cause of worry, especially if there had been some domestic trouble. First class coxswains are worth their weight in gold, and we certainly didn't wish to lose George Rose over this 'one off' indiscretion. .

The value of the Chinese and the Hong Kong dollar fluctuated considerably, which meant that paying us our fortnightly pay became rather complicated. Not long before my arrival on the station it was decided to pay all naval personnel at a standard 1/3d dollar. This was good because the dollar did not fall as low while I was out there; at one time it reached a high level of 4/6d. Apparently before my arrival the dollar had risen to a value of 6/-, nearly five times the value the navy was paying at. This of course opened the way for all sorts of financial juggling, men quite legitimately, reduced allotment to wives to an absolute minimum, drawing practically the whole of their pay in the 1/3d dollar, then cashing it back into English currency through money changers ashore at say, 5/- a dollar, they quadrupled their pay, with the money changer still making a handsome profit. Later this situation was thwarted by an order that naval personnel were limited to drawing only 1/3 rd of their earnings in dollars valued at 1/3d. As this was about the average proportion spent, no one could make a huge profit.

A dollar was a lot of money to the average Chinese. A rickshaw boy could toil all day, running many miles for just one dollar. It is doubtful whether the women coolies, toiling all day in the hot sun would have made as much. What a hard working bunch they were; always dressed in the same garb, black cotton shirt and knee length pants, with wooden sandals and the traditional broad rimmed straw hats. They were reputed to take just two or three days off to give birth to a child, before resuming work with the poor little offspring strapped to their backs, head rolling from side to side as it's mother dug, shovelled or planted.

At this time most native women and many of the men wore the traditional waist length pigtail, and many women had their feet bound so that they grew only to half their normal size – these poor women could only hobble around.

A large proportion of the teeming population lived in sampans in the harbour. When these were under way the husband would sit comfortably in the stern smoking his pipe and steering, while his wife would propel the boat with a huge oar, and often with a baby strapped to her back. Each sampan carried half a dozen emaciated chickens, and often as many children.

It was quite a task avoiding these hundreds of sampans and junks when entering or leaving harbour. It only needed a typhoon to hit Hong Kong to wreak havoc among this floating population. Fortunately this catastrophe did not happen during my time in China.

Whilst the submarine *Perseus* was refitting in Taikoo dock on the eastern end of the island, I visited her to see a couple of my friends. To me she presented a most extraordinary and indeed precarious sight. If they had a conventional dry dock there, they were not using it to refit submarines. *Perseus* had literally been pulled up a slipway using a small tug or a lifeboat; a 'P' class submarine weighed fifteen hundred tons. I marvelled at the Admiralty accepting this method of docking, but the firm, of which many of the foremen were Europeans, had probably been docking vessels in this manner since the beginning of time, and considered it quite safe.

Many things appeared to run on a 'wing and a prayer'. Electric trams ran past the dockyard gates, both pairs of lines running in the centre of the wide road, which made it rather precarious to step out from the pavement to board a tram. The majority of drivers of private or public hire vehicles were anything but careful or considerate. Walking out to board a tram one day I was knocked down by a private car, fortunately escaping serious injury. The driver had been driving recklessly past the tram stop, and I staggered to my feet to remonstrate with him before continuing my journey in what had been a clean white suit, but was now rather dusty and bloody. This wasn't the only time that I'd been knocked down by a vehicle and escaped serious injury. My rugby training seemed to have taught me the correct way to fall.

At last the time came to leave the China station. There was an army troopship leaving Hong Kong with room enough to accommodate naval personnel due for relief. I was given the option to remain in *Oswald* and steam her home in about three months time, but declined. She was a good boat, with a happy crew, but I had been away from the U.K. for two and a half years, and there was always the chance that *Oswald's* departure might be delayed. She had travelled over forty thousand miles in those two and a half years, with comparatively few engine defects. I'd had an unexpected break to be with my family half way through, but this was largely due to my own enterprise, and at no small cost when our pay was so poor.

There were very few of the original crew remaining, the C.O., Mark Collier, and Stan Peel were two of them. They'd be steaming *Oswald* yet another nine thousand miles. Those that had joined *Oswald* recently would replace equivalent ranks and ratings due to return to the U.K., my relief for one. I'd liked to have returned with Stan Peel, but it was far more pleasant to travel by troopship, which in turn, was not so expensive as taking passage in a P and O liner.

Clare had left Malta with Joan in order to be home before me. Clare was comfortably ensconced by the time of my arrival at the end of May 1937.

I had put a few pounds by in order to purchase presents for those at home, but this was soon spent. I gave my badminton racquet to our No.1 Boy at the club, with whom I'd had so many enjoyable games. He was very grateful for it

Most of the passengers aboard the troopship *Lancashire* were naval ratings, about a hundred of whom were submariners, and there were quite a few army personnel with their families. A few of us endeavoured to organize some competitions, but had little response, in the end we gave up. They had been away for a long period and were only thinking about getting home. I was rather envious of the army chaps having their wives with them. Clare would have enjoyed this trip.

It was out of the question having Clare out in Hong Kong. For one thing it would have been more costly than we could afford, and not worth it for the time I'd spent in Hong Kong. Of the thirty-two months I'd spent away, only about eight had been spent in Hong Kong.

We docked at Southampton at the end of May 1937, the submariners being quickly hustled off and back to Fort Blockhouse as soon as we had cleared customs. A day or two later I was journeying homeward to Plymouth, to commence my Foreign Service leave, which was practically the whole of June and July.

Whilst I had been abroad my father had very generously had two houses built, one for my brother Harold and one for myself. Clare had already retrieved our furniture from storage and was settled into our new home, but there was much to be done in the garden; I busied myself levelling off an area in order to make a tennis lawn. This involved a tremendous amount of labour, but the weather was perfect, and the job was almost completed by the end of my leave.

Chapter Four

Naturally I was now beginning to wonder where my next move would be, and I fervently hoped that it would be to the flotilla based at Devonport. So I was rather disappointed when my draft eventually came through as C.E.R.A. of HM Submarine *Seahorse*, attached to Portland. I had not yet sat the C.E.R.A.'s exam, but as the 'S' class were only medium sized submarines and carried an engineer officer, an experienced E.R.A could be appointed as acting C.E.R.A.

When I arrived aboard *Seahorse* there was a strong buzz running that these 'S' class boats would shortly become the 2nd Submarine Flotilla at Devonport, which was in fact to happen a few months later. So for the time that we remained at Portland, and not wishing to disturb my family more than necessary by asking them to move again, I would dash off home to Devonport each weekend, or at least, as often as possible.

Our C.O. was Lt. Cdr. R.H. Dewhurst, who was later to become another very successful wartime submarine captain. He was one of the 'press on – go getter' types, blessed with unbounded energy. Our Engineer Officer was Commissioned Warrant Engineer 'Bill' Dinwoody, a very methodical and efficient engineer.

My new messmates were 'Jan' Hewer, the outside E.R.A. with whom I had been shipmates previously in *L.16*, and the two E.R.A's were Billy Packer and Archie Smith. These were two really fine young artificers, Billy a swarthy broad shouldered happy-go-lucky type, and Archie although quieter and more sedate, nevertheless full of fun and good humour. They were a most likeable pair, who had much in common and usually went ashore together.

Life aboard *Seahorse* wasn't exactly uneventful. Not long after my arrival, due to a mechanical failure, she took a nosedive to the seabed. The sea depth was fortunately no more than twenty-two fathoms, but she buried her nose deeply into the muddy bottom. It took us quite some time and much manoeuvring on the main motors to pull ourselves free, the suction of the mud around the bows holding us fiercely for more than an hour. Although in retrospect I suspect that an air shot from one of our torpedo tubes would have broken the vacuum. Fortunately there was no damage to the bows, but as we had called on all our reserves of electrical power, there was a very long battery charge needed when we returned to harbour.

On another occasion, when casting off from our sister boat *Swordfish* to proceed to sea, we succeeded in carving several slits into her main ballast tanks with our starboard propeller. Poor old *Swordfish* half flooded number three and four main ballast tanks on her port side, which caused her to lurch drunkenly twelve degrees to port, and this didn't improve the tips of our propeller either.

Almost as soon as we had transferred to Devonport, *Seahorse* went into the dockyard for a three-month refit. This suited me admirably, and gave me the chance to play for the Devonport Services Rugby Club, several times for the 1st XV, but mostly for the 2nd XV. But perhaps more importantly for me, with the pressure of work easing a little, I got the opportunity to sit my C.E.R.A.'s examination. This was a difficult examination for the submariners among us, as with the exception of one question on marine diesel engines, the remainder of the paper was wholly on the boiler and steam turbine aspect of marine engineering. Following the written examination was an oral one, where the examiner was none other than the Engineer Rear Admiral himself. I was very pleased to have passed this examination although up to about this time, the waiting period for advancement was between six to ten years. However, due to the serious political and international situation, and the consequent expansion of the fleet at this time, it was a mere eighteen months before I was advanced to acting C.E.R.A 2nd class, continuing in the same job of C.E.R.A. of *Seahorse,* but getting a little more pay for doing it.

Life continued much the same as it did in my *L21* days in the 2nd Submarine Flotilla. Our refit finished all too quickly and was followed by spring cruises to the Mediterranean, exercises with the Home Fleet, and independent exercises around the coast of Scotland. I didn't get ashore too often as I much appreciated substitutes for my duty watches when in Devonport, so it was only fair to 'sub' for the youngsters while in Scottish waters, and when visiting foreign ports.

At about this time our First Lieutenant was relieved by a young lieutenant named H. 'Rufus' Mackenzie, soon to become another of the most successful wartime submarine commanders, and one of the most popular members of the submarine service. I was later privileged to regard this man as a great friend.

Following summer leave in 1938 we departed from Devonport for the usual exercises around the Scottish coast. We called in at Lamlash, Oban, and Tobermory for a few days to give the crew a break. It was shortly after leaving Tobermory en-route for Lerwick in the Shetlands that we passed through some of the narrowest channels and most beautiful scenery I'd ever seen. One channel twixt Skye and the mainland, the Kyle of Lochalsh, seemed narrower than the Suez Canal. The weather was perfect, and I spent as much time as I was able, on the bridge. Even the notorious Pentland Firth was kind to us.

It was en-route from Lerwick to Invergordon that I met with one of the most alarming experiences. The international situation was very unsettled to say the least, with the German nazi jackboot descending on all and sundry. The Munich Crisis - they called it. To us war appeared inevitable. To get ourselves on a war footing we were taking part in a rather special exercise. The parent ship, *HMS Cyclops* was, (as she often did) representing an enemy convoy, but in this case was escorted by a whole flotilla of eight destroyers.

Our flotilla of submarines was spread out along the route so that we attacked the convoy one after another, *Seahorse* making the penultimate attack. There was quite a short sea running which helped us to remain undetected. Poor old *Cyclops* must have been belching along at full speed, twelve knots, and the destroyers were making speeds of twenty-five knots in order to screen the convoy.

Although sea conditions were favourable, it was a difficult attack to carry out without being detected by 'the enemies' ASDICS, aboard the eight destroyers. Our captain was working very hard to get *Seahorse* into an attacking position, and had already dived deep under one destroyer.

One has to have witnessed the activity in a submarine control room in order to appreciate the scene; the whole crew are at 'diving stations', the coxswain on the after hydroplanes, the 2nd coxswain on the foreplanes, a Petty Officer or a Leading Seaman on the wheel, outside E.R.A.on the blowing panel ready to make any adjustment to the trim, as ordered by the First Lieutenant, with his stoker mate raising and lowering the periscope at a flicker of the captain's eyelids. The captain himself was usually bathed in perspiration caused by both mental and physical exertion, the former by the effort to co-ordinate the information constantly being relayed to him by the navigator and the ASDIC operator, together with a seaman calling out the relative bearing on the periscope whenever the captain barked 'Now', and at the same time adjusting his speed, course and depth to every move made by the enemy, who was probably zigzagging. The physical effort was brought about by the need to constantly haul the heavy periscope crosshead around to various bearings, and the need to bob up and down with the constant raising and lowering of the periscope. Even if the First Lieutenant and his team were keeping the boat at a steady depth, the captain would follow the periscope eyepiece up from a stooping position so that he only allowed enough of the periscope to break surface to allow him to acquire all necessary target information, such as masthead height, target course and speed, and the type of vessel, in order to set the correct running depth on his torpedoes, the position and number of escorts etc. It was no easy feat, the whole object being to put *Seahorse* in the correct position for a successful attack without being detected.

Sometimes the captain would have to employ delaying tactics, taking a wide sweep, or even a complete circle in order that he did not overrun the target, and at other times having to run at full speed in order to get back within striking distance of the target. Even the best of attacks could be marred by a sudden alteration of course or speed by the enemy after the torpedoes had been fired, or, as often happened in those days, the malfunction of the torpedo itself.

A long-range attack gave a greater margin of error; it also increased the chances of the torpedo track being spotted. The track of a torpedo could be easily seen by a sharp-eyed lookout in a calm sea. On the other hand, getting too close to the target could obviously lead to problems of an equally, if not more serious nature. An attack range of somewhere between 1000 and 1500 yards seemed to be the ideal.

The monocular 'attack' periscope was seven inches in diameter, tapering to one and a half inches for the upper five feet so that the water disturbance was minimised when it was in the raised position. But this periscope only had one and a half times magnification. The 'search' periscope was bi-focal, and was nine inches in diameter tapering to three and a half inches at the top. This periscope could be switched between high or low magnification, and could be elevated to search the sky for aircraft, but it was not used in the later stages of an attack on account of the increased water disturbance, easily spotted from aircraft or by a good lookout in a surface ship.

If the depth keeping was poor, and good depth keeping was not always easy due to ground swell, variation in seawater density, or simply because the boat was in poor trim, the captain would be either standing on his toes, or in a kneeling position while making his attack. To get an overall appreciation of the situation, the captain would frequently make an 'all round sweep' through 360 degrees, which could be rather laborious if the periscope was scored and the hull gland tightened to prevent leaking.

Our captain was in the final stages of this attack when he decided to have one more 'all round sweep' before retuning to the main object of the attack. Suddenly he bellowed 'Flood Q. - Keep one hundred feet – Shut watertight doors!' and pressed the klaxon twice to rapidly change depth. In a trice the hydroplanes were 'hard to dive' and the main motors grouped up at full speed ahead. The flooding of 'Q' tank sited well forward, had allowed the rapid ingress of seven tons of seawater, which helped to get the boat down very quickly.

Obviously there was a sense of urgency, but what most of us did not know was that the captain had spotted a destroyer bearing down on us at a speed of over twenty knots and at a range of less than three hundred yards. But it was too late! The destroyer, which we later knew to be *Foxhound*, hit us. There was an almighty crash, and the boat heeled over with the impact. We were about fifteen degrees bow down and rapidly gaining depth.

Momentarily we were all completely stunned, incapable of thought or deed. The C.E.R.A.'s diving station being in the engine room, I was shut in together with Billy Packer, Archie Smith, and most of the engine room staff, and knew little of what was going on elsewhere, but the noise of the crash was telling us all we needed to know. 'This is it' I thought, and fully expected to see water pouring in from a gash in the pressure hull. But then, thank God – at least there was no water coming into the engine room, even though *Seahorse* was still in a steep downward plunge.

It was greatly to the credit of the First Lieut. 'Rufus' Mackenzie (who later described this incident in his book, The Sword of Damocles), the outside E.R.A. 'Jan' Hewer, and the planesmen, that they regained control of the boat at about two hundred and fifty feet, and that so little had to be done as regards pumping or flooding to regain a trim except for blowing the water out of 'Q' tank. It was obvious that we had not been holed, neither had the space between the upper and lower hatches of the conning tower flooded, as this would have made us at least seven tons heavy.

Something had obviously hit us with a resounding smack, and there were quite a few pale faces around, mine among them. I could almost feel the grey hair sprouting from my head. Our engineer officer seemed to be badly shaken as well, but then, much responsibility rested on his shoulders. Two faces that did not seem to register concern were those of that intrepid pair Billy Packer and Archie Smith, in fact the former was still wearing his usual ear-to-ear grin.

Soon the order came to open watertight doors, and I poked my head into the adjoining control room ostensibly to see if the outside E.R.A. had the situation in hand, but really to find out what in hell's name had happened.

We could not surface immediately on account of the heavy traffic overhead, nor was it safe to come to periscope depth until we had fired a couple of smoke signals. The underwater signal ejector (affectionately known as the 'mutton gun' throughout the submarine service) was situated at the after end of the engine room, and we soon had orders to fire a couple of yellow smoke candles with three minutes between each firing. This then, would indicate to those above that we wished to surface, as well as giving them an indication of our course and speed.

I could imagine the urgent exchange of signals between the destroyer concerned and our depot ship, assuming the former had not had her bottom ripped out, and was now lying at the bottom of the ocean; our periscope standards and bridge structure were very strongly constructed.

A couple of light explosive devices were dropped from above as a signal, and we came slowly to periscope depth, hoping to have a look around before surfacing. But our fears were soon realised; we were as blind as a bat! in fact the periscopes could not be operated at all.

An all round sweep on our hydrophones told us that the coast was clear, and the captain gave the order to surface, the First Lieutenant relaying this order to the outside E.R.A. in the form of 'Blow one!' (No. 1 main ballast tank), quickly followed by 'Blow two, three, four, and six.' The lower conning tower hatch was opened and the usual team ascended into the tower to await the order from the first Lieutenant when we had broken surface, to open the upper hatch. However, when this order came, the signalman found that the hatch would not budge. Instead, the captain and the bridge party returned to the control room and ascended through the gun tower hatch, slightly lower and forward of the conning tower.

And what a mess they saw! The destroyer had ploughed its way through the middle of the bridge structure, taking with it the top of both periscopes and standards, as well as the wireless mast, missing the conning tower hatch by about an inch.

Our damage was considerable, but we were very lucky to have attained sufficient depth in that short time, so that the destroyer did not hole our conning tower. I was never aware of the damage sustained by the *Foxhound*, but colliding with the standards through which both periscopes and the wireless mast passed must have caused some damage to her light steel plated hull.

81

We were ordered to follow our parent ship into Rosyth, where the depot ship staff hacked and burned (acetylene cutting) away some of the twisted metal, allowing access through the conning tower. They made us look a little more presentable, and rigged up a temporary wooden mast to carry the W/T aerial. Within twenty-four hours we were ordered to sail for Devonport where permanent repairs would be carried out.

All this of course, happened during the September 1938 international crisis, at the time when our dear old Prime Minister Neville Chamberlain, journeyed to Munich for a top level meeting with the then powerful and arrogant thug Hitler. There could have been no hope of a proper agreement, and Chamberlain must have known it, but being so woefully weak and unprepared against Germany's might, we were pleased to 'buy' a little time.

Most of us felt sorry for Chamberlain, a man of high integrity, when he returned from that meeting waving a piece of paper which was supposed to be an agreement with Hitler for 'peace in our time'. Only the most naïve would have believed that. But at least we were given a little grace whereby we could prepare ourselves for the inevitable onslaught.

The general political situation had been so critical that a wireless silence was imposed on us at that time, and although we had our temporary mast, we were not allowed to transmit unless ordered to do so. Consequently nothing was divulged to the press about our narrow escape, and we arrived at Plymouth unheralded a few days later. A coded message must have been sent to the dockyard staff so that they could prepare to receive us. My dear wife, who thought that I was up at Invergordon, was naturally very surprised when I walked in. Wishing not to alarm her in any way I explained that due to the crisis we were ordered back to Devonport in order that we could have new and more up to date periscopes fitted, which, in a way was true. She must have been wondering why still three weeks later, we were taking so long to change two periscopes, however, I unwittingly gave the game away when one morning at breakfast I inadvertently blurted out that they were 'holding a Court of Enquiry that day'.

'Enquiry into what?' she asked. So making as light of it as possible, I had to explain the real reason why we were enjoying these few unexpected weeks in Devonport.

The accident did not get beyond the Court of Enquiry stage, probably because of the crisis; there were no press reports and the whole affair was hushed up. Our captain was probably cautioned to use more care. It was as well that this matter went no further; as this same officer went on to accomplish some very useful work during World War Two, being awarded the D.S.O. on three occasions.

Much work had to be carried out reconstructing the bridge superstructure and realigning the periscope standards, by which time the whole flotilla had returned to Plymouth. When the repairs had been made good, exercises and cruises continued in the normal way.

Our 'chummy ship' at that time was *Starfish*. It was a strange but true fact that in a flotilla of small ships or submarines, or even a squadron of big ships, they almost inevitably paired themselves off into 'chummy ships'

My old friend Bert Pinch was the C.E.R.A. of *Starfish*. He was a year senior to me in the apprentices and joined submarines at about the same time as I did. Poor old *Starfish* was lost early in the war.

Another member of *Starfish's* crew that I was to come into contact with again in the future was her torpedo officer Sub Lieutenant L.W.A. 'Benny' Bennington. 'Benny' was older than the average sub lieutenant because he was promoted from the lower deck under the 'Mate' scheme. Not only was 'Benny' outstanding professionally, he was also quite a sportsman. Among his many athletic capabilities, he was a first class footballer, and had already been awarded a navy cap. *Seahorse* must have played *Starfish* at soccer dozens of times during this period, either in competition, or in friendly matches, and on one occasion I was delegated to mark the elusive 'Benny'. I had no great skill at soccer, being primarily a rugby player, but I was very fit and had a good turn of speed. It would have been of no avail trying to beat him at his own game, my role was to get in quickly and bowl him over – albeit fairly, as the rules governing physical contact were not quite as stringent in those days. Invariably we two had a great tussle, he was very patient with me which was perhaps just as well, for not only was he a top class soccer player, he was also a navy boxer, but perhaps more to the point, he was later to become my captain.

As the year 1939 drew on it became increasingly obvious to those of us who did not bury our heads in the sand that war was drawing nigh, and was now quite inevitable. This fact had been apparent to many of us for a number of years, mainly because no one would stand up and face the bullies of Europe, namely Adolf Hitler and his Nazi hordes in Germany, and Benito Mussolini and his fascist black-shirts in Italy. It seems that politicians will never learn even the most elementary lessons, and of course we the electorate, are not without blame; we like to hear the tune which is pleasant to our ears, and will not back the more courageous politicians who tell us the unpleasant truth.

Winston Churchill, soon to be First Lord of the Admiralty, had warned the nation, and indeed Europe, on many occasions, and had been scorned, and labelled a 'war-monger'. At last we were making frantic preparations to resist these 'bulldozers', but were sadly behind. Germany in particular was terrifically powerful, the 1918 treaties limiting her arms programme had long since been brazenly flaunted, and she flaunted her power both on land, sea and air.

We could not have had more than about forty-five submarines at that time, many of them obsolete. But we were building the new 'T' class, which were larger and had a powerful torpedo armament of eight tubes forward and four aft. *Thetis*, one of this class, was involved in a terrible tragedy. Her captain was Lt Cdr 'Sam' Bolus, and her E.O. was commissioned warrant officer Roy Demetrious Glen, who had been my engineer in *L21*. *Thetis* had just been completed by Cammel Lairds

Shipbuilders of Birkenhead, and was in the act of doing her acceptance trials. It was a normal routine, one that I had experienced many times. The crew were carrying out their trials duties together with the trials party from *Dolphin,* and the many Cammel Laird employees who had been responsible for the installation of her machinery.

They had successfully carried out the main engine full power trial, and with an accompanying vessel commenced the diving trials. Those not required for the latter had been transferred to another vessel, but there were still an excessive one hundred and three officers and men on board. It was to be a slow dive in order that the First Lieutenant could adjust the trim. Although having difficulty getting down, she appeared to be heavy forward. The torpedo crew was ordered to check the state of all the tubes. This was done by opening a small test cock on the rear door of each tube. As no water was forthcoming, it was assumed that the tubes were dry. Misunderstanding subsequent orders, the staff disastrously opened the rear door of No. 5 tube to verify this. Alas the small test cock had been blocked, and for some reason, although indicating shut, the bow cap on this tube was open. It was quite impossible for even four or five sturdy seamen to shut the rear door against the onrush of seawater from the 21" diameter tube.

By the time they realized that the torpedo compartment was going to be flooded it was too late to shut the watertight doors to the adjoining and much larger torpedo stowage compartment. In a flash two of the submarines six compartments were flooded, and *Thetis* was bows down on the seabed in about thirty fathoms of water.

The pathetic story of how the heroic crew struggled for hours under ghastly conditions to get fifteen feet of *Thetis's* stern above the water at an angle of forty degrees, of how the inept handling of the situation on the surface allowed her to slip back once again into the depths, and of how only two officers, a leading stoker and a civilian workman were able to escape with their lives through the after escape hatch, has since been vividly recounted by many writers. It is easy to be wise after the event, and it is not my intention to expound my theories on how most of that crew could have been saved - as I consider they could have been. Nor is it my intention to describe the terrible experiences suffered by those who were trapped, before finally and mercifully being rendered unconscious by the lack of oxygen and excessive CO_2. Indeed I would not have dwelt on this tragedy even to this extent had it not been that I was vaguely involved, and that many of my personal friends, not least Roy Glenn, struggled bravely for hours under insuperable odds to get the stern out of the water and keep it there, hoping that something could be done by the many craft that had assembled at the scene of the disaster.

At this time, *Seahorse* was at Portland. We had just completed a day's exercising at sea and, as was often the case, I was doing a 'sub' for the duty E.R.A. in order that the three young and single lads could have a run ashore. The duty E.R.A. had started the battery charge whilst I had my supper, and I wasn't exactly looking forward to the next four hours in the engine room. Billy Packer and Archie Smith were probably well on their way toward the Plymouth area by now, the latter had a 'crush' on a charming young damsel from down that way. (Archie's girlfriend in Ivybridge, I discovered many years after he had met his untimely end in dear old *Seahorse*, was none other than Queenie Dumble, a leading member of the N.A.D. musical comedy society of which Clare was the musical director for a number of years. She was a fine amateur actress, and had made herself known to me, as Archie had told her that I was doing a sub for him).

I hadn't been in the engine room for very long, when at about 19:00 the First Lieutenant appeared, and signalled that he wanted the charge broken. This seemed too good to be true, but we had only been charging for just over an hour, and the batteries needed at least a five hour charge if we were going to sea the next morning.

Having stopped the engines, we could now hear ourselves speak; he told me that a submarine had had a mishap in Liverpool Bay, and that the flotilla E.O. wished to see me immediately. The charge could not be re-started, as there was no one else available to keep watch.

The Flotilla Engineer Officer told me that the two large mine-laying submarines attached to the flotilla, *Porpoise* and *Cachalot*, were sailing for the scene of the disaster immediately, and that as the C.E.R.A. of *Porpoise* was on shore leave, I would have to take his place. I had about five minutes to explain what was happening, to my own First Lieutenant and my E.O., grab a towel and a toothbrush and dash down into the bowels of *Porpoise* before she cast off. Her own duty E.R.A and her E.O. had been busy preparing for sea, and her complement was made up by officers and ratings from the rest of the flotilla who did not happen to be ashore that evening.

I was not a great asset at this stage, not having seen these engines before; they were large eight cylinder reversible diesels. Luckily there was enough fuel in her tanks to cope with the situation; the chief stoker had hastily taken on some fresh water, whilst the coxswain had embarked as much provisions as possible in the short time allowed. Within fifteen minutes we had cast off and were heading down channel at full speed. Fifteen knots was the best speed we could make against a head sea.

What our role was to be once we arrived there, we had no idea. It was going to take us about thirty hours to get to the area, and already *Thetis* had been down for over eighteen hours. Unless we could do something positive when we arrived, it was unlikely that we could help in saving the lives of the crew. The more experienced of us were thinking of ways that we could be of assistance. Maybe they would use us to locate her, if they hadn't already done so, or perhaps use the two large submarines as 'camels'. At least we could make sure that we would be ready for anything, by having our batteries and air bottles charged to capacity.

Then to our great surprise, after nearly twenty-four hours steaming at full speed, *Porpoise* received a signal instructing her to go about and return to Portland. *Cachalot* continued on her way, but what role she played I do not know.

After all hope of saving the crew was lost, the salvage operation was put into the hands of a large salvage company who were still reclaiming the sunken German vessels of the previous war. It was not long before *Thetis* was raised and beached at Moelfre Bay, Anglesey, where ninety-nine bodies were removed. Later she was towed back to Cammel Lairds where new machinery was installed and she was re-named *Thunderbolt*.

Soon after war was declared, a volunteer crew whom I considered to be very plucky, commissioned *Thunderbolt*. Her E.O. was 'Jacky' Northwood, who remained with her until a few months before she was lost in action with all hands, after several successful war patrols.

The loss of *Thetis* had badly shaken us all. Submarine losses in peacetime had hitherto been about one per year until 1932, but this one entailed the greatest loss of life, and of course the public were kept in touch by press and radio during those tragic hours when Roy Glenn and his staff were putting up their tremendous struggle to raise her, although only a submariner could really appreciate the grim and unrewarding fight they put up.

Those lost included the E.O.'s of two other 'T' class submarines that were being built at Birkenhead, and had volunteered to accompany the trials in order to gain experience. My Brother-in-law, Reg Lockley, who was standing by the building of the battleship *Prince of Wales* as her senior engineer, was invited to attend the trials by his friend Lt. Jamieson, the E.O. of *Thetis's* sister ship. Fortunately for my Brother-in-Law, and for the *Prince of Wales,* Lt. Jamieson cancelled the invitation at the last minute because of the large number of people going to sea in her.

During my time on *Porpoise,* I didn't relish being in charge, and knowing less about the boat than my staff, but I had learned a lot more about her and her machinery by the time we arrived back in Portland. Her E.O., Lt George Gay, with whom I later became very friendly, was a tower of strength and a first class engineer. He insisted on keeping watch on the main engines until we strangers became a little more acquainted with them. All the same, it was a relief to get back to my own boat again; I certainly did not like these quick moves.

The whole flotilla returned to Devonport soon after this, and it was there when *Porpoise* was ordered into dry-dock several days before she was due. This put Lt (E) Gay in a bit of a fix, as he had arranged for fuel lighters to be alongside several days later, in order to discharge his diesel fuel. Orders were laid down that all fuel and ammunition must be discharged before a submarine enters a dry-dock. It was quite late in the afternoon, and liberty-men had gone ashore. My E.O. was ashore, and I was finishing off a job before proceeding ashore myself when Lt. Gay came over from *Porpoise* with a request that we took her fuel. Normally I would not concern myself with the quantity of fuel remaining in our tanks, that was the business of the

E.O. and the chief stoker. However, in the absence of these two worthies, and having ascertained that we could take all the fuel that *Porpoise* wished to discharge, I remained behind to supervise the transfer, hoping that my E.O. would approve of my decision in the morning.

George Gay was most grateful for my efforts, which enabled *Porpoise* to dock next morning. Taking fuel from another submarine was a tricky business as one could easily end up with half a tank of seawater instead of fuel, but all went well.

I had arrived home four hours late that day, but I had made a friend in George Gay who was one of nature's gentlemen, and who later went on to reach the exalted rank of Rear Admiral. This small incident had quite a bearing on my future, and indeed upon this story.

War by now was obviously very close, so close in fact that just a few in our service, (very few I am pleased to say) were beginning to develop tummy trouble, or resurrecting some other long forgotten ailment. It must have been in early June, and I was on my two weeks summer leave. Clare and I were enjoying a holiday in Perranporth, when I received a telegram instructing me to take a further ten days foreign service leave and on return I was to return to *Porpoise*, where I was to relieve their C.E.R.A. who had suddenly developed stomach ulcers, and had gone sick.

During our stay at Perranporth we had made friends with Mr. and Mrs. P.Mellors of Harrow, a friendship that lasted many years. Their son Geoffrey had a toy submarine, unfortunately broken, but which to the boy's delight I was able to repair.

Percy, who comes into my story again later, was one of the 'high ups' in the Post Office, and was later awarded the Imperial Service Order for his work during the London air raids.

Having received this telegram, we hastily returned to our home, where I used my additional leave to install an air-raid shelter in our garden. This was ideally situated, being protected by the elevated tennis court on the one side, and an old disused quarry on the other. It was about fifty yards from the house, and almost wholly underground. My father assisted me, and we made it very comfortable. We installed three bunks, although we hoped of course that we would never need to use them.

I was most thankful that I had made this effort, because the need to use it did eventually arise, when both Plymouth and Devonport were very heavily raided night after night. Clare, her sister Violet (Reg Lockley was away in the *Prince of Wales*), and Joan would spend most of their nights there for months on end.

Part Two - The War Years

Most of us had no doubt that we were on the side of right in this ghastly conflict, and we accepted the fact that sooner or later we would perish; it was the sort of show we'd make while perishing that concerned us.

Chapter Five

It was with great sorrow that I left *Seahorse* and her crew, but having been in her for nearly two years I suppose that I couldn't really grumble. All the same, a sudden switch like this to another boat, with no preparation or proper turnover (commonly known within the service as a pier-head jump), was most distasteful to me, moreover I certainly had no wish to serve overseas again at this time. *Porpoise* sailed for Portsmouth on the day after I joined her.

These mine laying submarines, which included, *Cachalot, Narwhal, Grampus, Rorqual* and *Seal,* apart from the conventional armament of six 21" torpedo tubes and a 4" gun, could carry fifty large mines in the casing, the conning tower, masts and periscopes being set to port in order to facilitate a straight run through the huge casing which surmounted the hull.

Arriving at Portsmouth we embarked six dummy mines from *HMS Vernon* and carried out a practice mine-laying operation in the Solent. These operations had been rare in the past, doubtless because it was rather an involved exercise and we had very few dummy mines. *HMS Vernon* would have to arrange to have them swept up after the exercise. There was no question of cutting the wires because the trolleys they were mounted upon, and which ultimately formed the anchor to secure them, were far more costly than the mine itself, and would have to be used again. Each trolley was linked to the next one in the mine casing and unhitched itself as one after the other the mines were toppled over the stern of the submarine.

The mines themselves were fearful looking objects, bristling with horns, the fracturing of any one of which would detonate seven hundred pounds of high explosive.

Each of these minelaying submarines carried a minelaying E.R.A. Just another E.R.A., but one who was responsible for the mechanical side of the mine trolleys, the minelaying equipment, and the flooding of the mine compensating tanks during a minelay.

I was never happy whilst we had a casing full of live mines, and was always extremely careful when I had to climb over mines in order to get at mechanisms external to the hull, even though there were safety devices to prevent an explosion before the mines were laid. The mine and trolley would sink to the ocean bed, and there remain until about twenty minutes later, when a mechanism would release the wire securing the mine to its trolley, thus allowing the mine to arise from its mooring to a predetermined depth. The important thing was that the mine should not break surface where it would be visible to the enemy.

Experts checked all the mine mechanisms before we loaded them on board. We then had to set each mine for the correct depth, connect each trolley to the next, and hope for the best. It was very disconcerting when, due to malfunction a mine broke surface, as this would indicate not only the presence of a minefield, but our own presence as well, particularly since we would be laying these mines right on the enemies doorstep.

As a mine and its trolley was heavier than its equal volume of seawater, about twenty gallons of water had to be flooded into the mine compensating tanks with each mine laid. This then would compensate for the weight loss of each mine, and therefore maintain the overall trim of the boat.

Minelaying was a hazardous operation, there were so many things that could go wrong, and I always breathed a sigh of relief when I heard the report 'All mines laid.' Even then we were never absolutely sure that they had all gone until we returned to harbour, or sent someone down into the casing to check when we surfaced at night to charge our batteries.

No sooner had we laid our six practice mines successfully than *Porpoise* was ordered to proceed on a two-week war patrol. It was mid-summer and very hot. Fourteen days seemed an eternity to us at that time, and it seemed such a wanton waste of those beautiful cloudless days. At least, the periscope watch-keeper said they were cloudless, many of us did not see daylight throughout the whole period. Very few submarines had done more than a week under war patrol conditions up to this time; it was hot, but at least not so hot and uncomfortable as my fortnight's patrol in *Oswald* in the tropics. Nearly all available submarines were undergoing the same ordeal, and *Porpoise's* billet was somewhere in the region of the Heligoland Bight, with submarines spread at intervals throughout the Skagerrak and Kattegat.

Watching through periscopes, charging batteries under the cover of darkness, listening on hydrophones and taking soundings with our 'echo sounder's, we were kept busy exercising, and carried out many dummy attacks on passing merchantmen.

Our captain was Commander G.W.G. 'Shrimp' Simpson. C.B.E. Lt. S.L.C. 'Lynch' Maydon had just relieved Lt. David Wanklyn as our First Lieutenant. (Wanklyn was later to become one of our most famous submarine commanders, as C.O. of the *Upholder* he was awarded the V.C. as well as the D.S.O. and Bar). Lt. (E) G. W. Gay was the engineer officer, Lt. A.R.Daniell, the torpedo and mine officer, and Lt. 'Basher' Coombs the navigating officer. Nearly all these officers and many of the crew were to perform distinguished service in submarines. Our C.O. 'Shrimp' Simpson was to become a Rear Admiral, and the tall, dedicated 'Lynch' Maydon was to be awarded the D.S.O. and Bar as C.O. of *Umbra*; George Gay was awarded the D.S.C. and later became a Rear Admiral (E). 'Tony' Daniell was awarded the D.S.O. and the D.S.C. before being severely wounded in action, and 'Basher' Coombs lost his life as C.O. of *Utmost* in 1942.

This class of submarine carried an engineering officer, a C.E.R.A. and no less than six E.R.A.'s. Our E.R.A.'s mess was like the 'League of Nations'. There was 'Mickey' Power, a southern Irishman in charge of the mine laying equipment. The outside E.R.A (outside wrecker) was 'Jumbo Jarvis, very soon to be advanced to C.E.R.A., with 'Tommy' Hargreaves, a Yorkshireman as his deputy. 'Jock' Forrest from Kilmarnock, 'Taff' Hughes from Swansea, 'Jock' West from Edinburgh, and myself, a real 'Cousin Jack' Cornishman in charge. They all appeared to be fine messmates, and none of them were afraid of work – which was just as well because they were to see plenty of it in the near future.

By the time we returned to Fort Blockhouse it was nearing the end of August, and within a day or two we had embarked fifty live mines, twelve torpedoes complete with warheads, a full quota of live armour piercing ammunition for our solitary 4"gun, and departed right away for an unknown destination. At least, it was supposed to be unknown, though most of the crew had decided (and rightly) that it was to be Malta.

I'd already bid my wife a fond farewell – a sad parting in view of the tense international situation, and the knowledge that wherever we went, Clare would be unable to join me.

Throughout our voyage down channel, across the Bay of Biscay, southward to Gibraltar and onwards to Malta, we carried out the wartime practice of remaining dived all day, and proceeding on the surface charging our batteries during the hours of darkness.

The weather had been perfect the whole way, and very hot when we arrived at Malta on the 29th of August. We secured alongside in French Creek, and rather surprisingly were accommodated in Fort St Angelo; this was probably because we were ordered to discharge our mines in the dockyard.

I'd never seen the inside of Fort St Angelo before, and although the accommodation that it offered could never be described as good, it was a relief to get out of the boat where we had been for the past month. We had been permitted to take only the bare necessities of kit with us when we left the U.K.; the bulk of our kit was packed into our kitbags and dispatched to Malta in a surface vessel. Luckily we all brought our No.1. Suits with us, as we never saw our kitbags again. What had happened to our kit we never did find out.

Those days seemed very tense and unreal; the political situation was coming to a climax. Air raid shelters, concrete pillboxes and gun emplacements were being constructed everywhere.

Our passage out to Malta had been fairly uneventful, except for a little main engine piston trouble. *Porpoise*, the first of her class, and had been in commission for a long time. Although her engines had been refitted fairly recently, there had been problems with the aluminium alloy with which the pistons were made. These pistons were 21" in diameter, and experiments were still being carried out to establish the best alloy with which to make them. Small portions of metal would flake off the head of the piston, getting between the piston and the cylinder, causing a whole or partial seizure. This was a very disturbing defect as there was little we could do to prevent it. We carried two spare pistons and two spare liners (cylinders), but it was many hours of hard and heavy work to change them. The cylinder cover itself weighed about six hundredweight, the piston and connecting rod about the same. Not so much the weight of these individual parts, but the extreme awkwardness, due to lack of space and headroom. A defective piston would be fared up, and new rings fitted ready for the next snag.

We hadn't been in Malta for more than three or four days when Commander Simpson cleared lower deck to read the articles of war, and to inform the whole of the ship's company that as from noon on that day, the 3rd of September 1939, a state of war existed between Great Britain and France on the one hand, and Germany on the other. It was almost with a sense of relief that this news reached our ears; we had been expecting it for many months. Nevertheless, it was still very difficult to fully appreciate the significance of it all.

I was fourteen years of age when the previous war had ended, and now, at the age of thirty-five, I had no misgivings of what was in store for us. For several years Clare had been suggesting that I had done more than my fair share of service in submarines – I'd now been in them for thirteen years, but my reply to this had always been along the lines of having now been fully trained and fully experienced as a submariner, if there was a war, they would have me back in submarines in less than no time anyway! I had always hoped that our weapons would never be used in anger, but now I knew that we were in it for real, and I felt that with Germany so very powerful, we were in for a very rough time. The previous war had been an awful blood bath and it was difficult to imagine that this one would be less so.

But still it all seemed so unreal. It was so peaceful, the weather beautiful, not a cloud to be seen in the clear blue sky - and yet we had just been informed that we were now at war. Hitler had shown over the past few years how cruel and ruthless the Nazis were; they had already massacred many thousands of innocent people, and had overrun central Europe. Now we had entered into hostilities in defence of Poland, with whom we had a treaty. I believed that it was a good thing that we were honouring this treaty, but on the other hand it all seemed rather farcical, as we could do very little to protect Poland more than to engage a little of Germany's armed might on the Northern Front. Several European countries had already been 'raped' and if someone did not make a stand, our turn would surely come.

Porpoise had obviously been sent out to the Mediterranean in case Italy decided to join the fracas right away - on Hitler's side of course. But much to our surprise, after only a few weeks we were ordered to return to the U.K. On the surface, steering a zigzag course to Gibraltar, we were in strict war routine, and we finally arrived at back Gosport having been escorted through the mine swept channel by a small craft, which flew the white ensign.

It was good to be back in the U.K. once more, but it seemed a strange world that we were in. There was a war on, though up to now (mid October), we had seen very little of it. Attached for the time to the *Dolphin* flotilla, *Porpoise* was now engaged in patrolling and minelaying in the Skagerrak and around the coast of

94

Denmark. This was not a pleasant period; firstly the war was not going well for us British, and secondly, we in *Porpoise* had not yet been 'blooded.' By that I mean that although we had been trained efficiently to do our job, we were not yet accustomed to the rigours of war, nor had we yet experienced depth-charging. Until we had, how could we be sure what our personal reactions would be? No matter how brave we felt, or how calm we thought we might be when stretched to the limit, we still could not be sure of conducting ourselves with calm and dignity when the crunch came - and come it must. Though we later became accustomed to depth-charging and all the many other types of unusual incidents, at the outset, these experiences were nerve shattering to say the least. Being the most senior rating in a crew of nearly sixty, and having a very responsible position, it was a matter of much concern to me that I would respond favourably under pressure. Though not regarding myself as deeply religious, I had been brought up to believe in God and in Christ, and in consequence offered up a little prayer each day, not so much asking for preferential treatment as regards my own personal safety, but for the safety of my family, and that I would face whatever came my way with resolution and courage.

It had always been my custom to attend church service whenever possible, and I continued to do this throughout the war years, although the opportunity did not afford itself very often. Most submarine parent ships carried a padre, who conducted a service, either in a small chapel set aside for this purpose, or in a broadside mess, temporarily vacated. Attending an evensong or a communion wasn't so easy, as I was in a tough school. The lads on the whole were not a particularly pious lot. However, I made no bones about my intentions, and I have to hand it to my shipmates that throughout the whole of my career I was never chided in this respect. There might have been the odd good humoured 'leg pull', but in fact on many occasions my messmates had carried on with work, to allow me to attend a service.

Our early war submarine losses were severe, and as *Porpoise* was a large, slow diving and rather cumbersome craft, when the enemy struck quickly, particularly from the air, it was fair to suppose that we would not last for very long. Surely if smaller and quicker diving submarines were being caught, it could only be a matter of time before we would succumb to aircraft attack, mines or anti-submarine vessels. Thankfully one did not seem to dwell on these thoughts for too long; in fact we were kept so busy and preoccupied that we had very little time to wonder about anything.

Within one month of the commencement of hostilities, *Oxley*, returning from patrol, was torpedoed and sunk by one of our own 'T' class submarines just proceeding on patrol. Both were on the surface, trimmed down to facilitate a quick dive and to present the smallest target possible, to the enemy. The 'T' class submarine *Triton* challenged *Oxley* to identify herself, and receiving no quick or satisfactory reply, promptly and quite properly fired a torpedo. *Oxley* paid a terrible price for apparently what was a slight delay in disentangling the Aldis (signalling) lamp lead that had been caught up in the conning tower, but as far as *Triton* was concerned, it was sink or be sunk! There were only two survivors, *Oxley's* captain (Lt. Cdr. Bowerman), and one rating.

Carrying out mine-laying operations was always unpleasant. We embarked fifty of these horrible horned devices alongside the jetty at Fort Blockhouse, and then laid them at strategic points either in the Skagerrak or around the Heligoland Bight, continuing on a war patrol afterwards. Surfacing at night to recharge the batteries was also a bit of a nightmare in these confined waters, and rarely did we fully charge the batteries without several interruptions, more often than not ending up by diving at dawn without the batteries being fully charged.

During the early months of the war many of our ships were lost or damaged by German aircraft dropping mines that were then detonated by the magnetic field generated naturally around the ship. At first the effects of this type of mine were disastrous, but in a trice our 'boffins' (back room boys) came up with the antidote. The magnetic field set up around a ship could be neutralized by an operation called 'degaussing'. So within a couple of months we were ordered to Chatham for this purpose.

It was whilst we were in Chatham dockyard that we witnessed the return of *Triumph* with her bows blown off by a contact mine. She had been on the surface at night, charging her batteries, when the O.O.W. (officer of the watch), who was none other than my old friend of the 2nd flotilla days Lt 'Benny' Bennington, sighted a mine in the darkness. Seeing that it was impossible to miss it, he altered course slightly to take it on the bows rather than the saddle tanks or pressure hull a little further aft, in which case she most certainly would have been lost. 'Benny' was awarded the D.S.C. for his prompt action. As it was, three months of intensive work in Chatham dockyard, and *'Triumph* was ready to continue her good work.

But soon there was to be a triple blow. *Seahorse, Starfish* and *Undine* (one of the new 'U' and 'V'class), were caught by the enemy while operating close inshore. *Starfish* and *Undine* were sunk, but the majority of the crews escaped to be taken prisoner; *Seahorse* was lost with all hands.

This was indeed a bitter pill for me to swallow, not only had I lost many of my friends, there but for the grace of God (and George Gay) would I have been. Most of *Seahorse's* crew were as when I left her, except that 'Billy' Packer (as young as he was) had relieved the E.R.A. who had relieved me, and 'Archie' Smith was now her outside E.R.A. 'Archie' had since become engaged to the fair damsel he had been courting in Ivybridge, whom I had never seen until I met her some thirty years later

War had now made itself manifest to me. It was difficult to analyse my reactions. Instead of feeling happy to escape their fate, I felt almost guilty that I wasn't still with them. One thing was abundantly clear, not only were we now fighting to guard our families and our country, but for our very lives.

There was little opportunity for relaxation. It was standard policy to allow submarine crews four days leave after two patrols, but only if they could be spared. Half the crew would have leave after one patrol, and the other half after the next. I managed to get home once before Christmas 1939. Not a pleasant journey, the trains ran late, were blacked out and crowded; by the time I arrived it was almost time to leave again.

Soon after our return from the Mediterranean, our C.O., Commander 'Shrimp' Simpson was relieved by Lt. Cdr. P.Q. Roberts. 'Shrimp', a very experienced submarine officer, was required for administrative duties. *Porpoise* had had very little tangible success during these early months, nothing really worthwhile, although of course there was very little information regarding the results of our minelaying missions.

In the late March of 1940 *Porpoise* was transferred to the nice new parent ship *HMS Forth* at Rosyth, whose flotilla comprised 'U' and 'S' classes, and two minelaying submarines.

It was on our first war patrol from Rosyth that we were allocated one of those precarious patrol areas in the mouth of the Skagerrak. These were relatively confined waters for a submarine of our size. To reduce both our diving time and our huge silhouette, we had 'Q' tank (quick diving tank), and almost 75% of our main ballast tanks flooded. But even though we had reduced our overall diving time by half since the pre-war days, we were still slow compared to the twenty-five second diving time of the smaller boats.

There were many small craft about in our patrol area, some of which purported to be fishing vessels, but most were anti submarine vessels looking and listening for 'the likes of us'. Rarely could we fully charge our batteries - small wonder, we weren't far from land, and with the Germans having the most sensitive hydrophones in the world, the noise of our main engines charging the batteries was enough to have 'awakened the dead'. We soon came to dislike calm weather and those beautiful moonlit nights.

On one particular night, three or four days before we were due to leave our billet, we were running slow ahead on the port engine to keep steerage way, and charging batteries at maximum output on the other. Already we had been forced to dive by a prowling anti-submarine vessel, and we were now cramming as much as we could into the batteries before dawn. Suddenly there came an urgent cry. 'Diving stations – Diving stations! Break the charge! Bring all tubes to the action state!' Followed by, as soon as we had engaged the starboard tail clutch, 'Full ahead both main motors! Hard aport! The boat heeled over to starboard, obviously on a tight turn.

Torpedo tubes were quickly reported 'Ready! Then came the order 'Fire one!' Followed by the five remaining tubes at three-second intervals. This must indeed be a very worthwhile target, to warrant six torpedoes!

As soon as the last torpedo was fired, our ears were filled with the unearthly screech of the klaxon, and the urgent call. 'Dive! - Dive! - Dive!' We forced the boat down to one hundred feet in what for us must have been a record time. The captain, O.O.W. and the lookouts had literally slithered down the tower. The captain was now anxiously looking at his stopwatch, counting the seconds and listening hopefully for the sound of one of our forty-knot torpedoes exploding on reaching its target. This we quickly learned was an enemy submarine at a range of about one mile, difficult to assess in this darkness. In spite of the distance and the darkness, our lookouts had sighted her silhouette swinging in to a surface attack. It could only be a German submarine, as there were no other British submarines patrolling in that area, or passing through.

We had just levelled off at one hundred feet when we heard the explosion we had been waiting for, just about the time that our torpedoes would have reached her. At last – success! There were no cheers, in fact I cannot remember anyone speaking, but we smiled our approval, after all this was our job, what we had been trained for. We certainly didn't smile however, when a few seconds later we heard the sound of her four torpedoes passing at regular intervals almost directly above us

There was much jubilation at our success, an enemy submarine was a big prize, and we, having had little success hitherto, were absolutely elated. Sinking this submarine before she ran amok amongst our convoys of merchantmen had probably saved many lives.

I did have a thought for her crew, all of who must have perished in a most terrible way; the chances of survival from a submarine in those circumstances were almost negligible. If we had remained on the surface we might possibly have rescued three or four of those who were on her bridge at the time, that is, if we had survived those four torpedoes.

Great credit was due to the lookout who had spotted her in the darkness, to the tubes crew who brought the tubes to the 'action' state in such a short time, and to the First Lieutenant and his staff, who had taken us down to a hundred feet so quickly – it must have been a very near thing for us. But of course, the major credit must go to the captain, whose timing was faultless.

One sound that we always feared, and one that we in *Porpoise* had heard on more than one occasion, was the scraping of a mine mooring wire against our saddle tanks. Even if intelligence did furnish us with reliable information regarding enemy minefields, there must have been hundreds of mines laid of which we had no knowledge. To look at a chart of the North Sea where minefields and potential minefields were marked in red was enough to make one's hair stand on end, it seemed impossible to miss them. But even then, there must have been many more that were unknown to our Intelligence Service, as well as those that had broken adrift from their moorings in heavy weather.

Nearing our own shores there were swept channels to which we had strictly to adhere, that is if it wasn't foggy, and assuming we already knew exactly where we were, and hoping that the enemy had not laid new mines in the meantime. As we neared home we had to proceed on the surface, often escorted, and diving only if attacked by enemy aircraft.

Returning to base after this patrol, feeling satisfied with our efforts and looking forward to a few days relaxation, we were met by our escort vessel a few miles out. The captain gave permission for a few of the engine room staff to go on to the bridge, two at a time, for a breath of fresh air. I seized this opportunity to see daylight for the first time in three weeks, and was having a quiet chat with the officer of the watch, on this occasion Lt. 'Basher' Coombs, a most likable and popular officer, who at that time was our navigator. He was elated by our success, and mentioned that some of our crew might get awards. At this I became righteously indignant, rebuking poor 'Basher' (just a young Lieutenant at the time) for even thinking of reward when we were merely doing our duty to a country that was fighting for its very existence. I have often since thought of that little chat, and of what an awful cheek I had, to chide him for his attitude.

Heaven knows why 'Basher' was so nicknamed. Tall, handsome and wearing a magnificent blond beard, he was certainly not wanting in true patriotism. Although I was much older (thirty-six years to his twenty-two), we were great friends, having played rugger together before the war. He looked so hurt at my rebuff that I wished that I had kept my council to myself.

Arriving at Rosyth we berthed alongside *HMS Forth,* where there was a devastating anti-climax in store for us. For some obscure reason the War Lords would not credit us with 'our kill'. 'P.Q.' was furious, and the whole crew felt completely 'browned off'. The outcome of this incident was that when the war was finally over (five and a half long years later), and German dossiers fell into our hands, it was definitely established that we had sunk the first German submarine of the war (*U1*). Our Captain was belatedly awarded the D.S.O., but at first caused quite a stir by refusing to accept this unless those of the crew who had contributed most to the success of the kill were also to receive recognition. I admired P.Q. for his stance, but as this was over five years after the event he had little success, and was finally cajoled into receiving his much deserved reward graciously. It is doubtful that more than a handful of his original crew had survived the war anyway.

It was from Rosyth that we now had our first experience of escorting convoys. There were precious iron ore shipments from Sweden to be protected against the marauding enemy, and it was thought that the presence of a submarine might at least present problems for enemy surface ships. In truth there was little we could do against enemy aircraft or submarines, in fact we would provide a fine slow moving target for them, but we could be very useful against a cruiser or pocket battleship.

This was a particularly unpleasant task, not only was summer approaching, when there would be literally no darkness in these northern regions, but we spent most of our time on the surface at a speed of eight knots, this being about the maximum speed of the convoys. We had no encounters with submarines, that is as far as we were aware, although we may well have been missed by torpedoes on several occasions, but we were very lucky to have dodged many attacks by aircraft that had been sent out specifically to deal with us. This was before the introduction of radar, and on a cloudy day an aircraft would suddenly appear out of nowhere, diving upon us and dropping bombs and depth charges, while we scrambled madly to get beneath the waves.

We had had extra holes cut in our mine casing, and this now enabled us to dive in under sixty seconds, but an aircraft could travel a long way in that time. While diving it was never a good thing to acquire more than a seven-degree bow down angle, as our propellers would then be thrashing away on the surface and achieving very little. With *Porpoise* at a bow down angle of twenty-five degrees, her bows could be at a depth of a hundred feet while her stern would still be out of the water, presenting an ideal target for a bomb.

We were learning the art of modern warfare fast, but sadly many boats were lost while taking lessons. We in *Porpoise* had many near misses, and the ships in the convoy suffered huge losses, both from the air and from submarine attack.

Early in June 1940 *Porpoise* was transferred to a newly formed base at Blyth. Here the submarine crews were accommodated in huts, and I was allocated a small cabin. Thinking that any patrol might be our last, I sent an urgent telegram to Clare asking her if she could come to Blyth. Although she had problems of her own in Plymouth, she caught the next train, and I had special permission to travel to Newcastle to meet her. It wasn't easy moving about in those days; there were certain restrictions regarding civilian movements to or from particular zones, trains were crowded, temporary ration cards had to be issued, and in Clare's case, she had to deposit Joan with my mother for an unknown duration.

Imagine my surprise when the train was reasonably on time, and that Clare had travelled this far with my sister-in-law Drecka, who was on her way even farther north to join my brother whose ship, the cruiser *HMS Birmingham* was having a short docking at Rosyth. Very resourceful people these naval wives, and full of courage.

Not being very flush with money in those days, I'd procured a modest couple of rooms with the use of the kitchen, in the small town of Blyth. This was a most distressing period in many respects, and I did appreciate Clare being with me, even if only for a short while. The military situation was appalling; General Petain of France had agreed to some form of capitulation with the Germans, and except for a few divisions of patriotic Frenchmen, the British Expeditionary Force was left without protection on its southern flank. The German Panzer divisions had quickly overrun Holland and Belgium who could offer only token resistance. The only alternative left to the B.E.F. was to attempt an evacuation from Dunkirk. With hundreds of thousands of our troops being harassed by overwhelming armoured forces, and without air cover, this seemed an impossible task. Nevertheless it was achieved by naval and civilian craft, and with relatively few casualties. Anything that could cross the channel was commandeered, but practically all our equipment was lost – guns, motor transport, stores, tanks and medical supplies. However, at least it gave our troops the chance to escape and fight again.

The big question was, having now overrun the rest of Europe, how long would it be before the Germans invaded our country? We had suffered a severe defeat, lost vast quantities of stores and arms, as well as most of the help from our allies. One would have thought that the Germans, having already experienced the grim tenacity of the British people, would have made an invasion of Britain their next priority. They were air raiding London and our coastal towns on a regular basis now. Blyth was not immune from this, and I witnessed many 'dogfights' in the desperate bid to protect our shores.

Returning from patrol it was difficult to undertake any big job that wasn't really vital, as at any time, we might be ordered to sea as a countermeasure to an invasion. We were kept at almost immediate notice for sea, and on several occasions we had to hurriedly re-assemble parts of machinery, having received an urgent signal to proceed to sea, and on two or three occasions Clare and I were awakened at night by the local policeman banging on the door of our furnished accommodation with orders for me to return on board immediately.

To embark mines, we had to proceed southward to Immingham, situated on the mouth of the Humber, and as these were very secret missions, there was no shore leave. Norway was being overrun by the Germans, their task made easy by the treachery of a minority section of its community nicknamed Quislings, after the principal collaborator. The occupation of Norway was an awful setback to us; the Germans were able to make things most difficult for the North Sea convoys and moreover, it brought them much nearer to our northern ports and harbours.

Porpoise and her sister ship *Narwhal* were employed in laying mines in strategic positions. On one occasion in mid July 1940, we were in Immingham together, and departed to lay our mines in different areas. On our return we learned that *Narwhal* was still absent, and considered overdue. She never did return. It wasn't a pleasant task entering our friend's cabins to pack up their personal belongings. *Narwhal* was the second of our six minelayers to be lost. *Grampus* having been presumed lost a couple of months earlier.

A day or two after the sad news about *Narwhal, Spearfish* was lost with her entire crew. Another particularly sad blow to me, as not only her captain, Lt 'Jock' Forbes, my friend and previous First Lieutenant, but also her C.E.R.A. was my great friend of *Oswald* days, Stan Peel. *Spearfish* had narrowly missed coming to grief earlier when, having suffered a heavy depth charging off the coast of Denmark, she escaped in a badly damaged condition, and as this was at that time the first occasion that one of our submarines had survived such a battering the Admiralty, anxious to analyse the results on the hull, machinery and crew, had ordered a huge surface escort to chaperone her back as she was unable to dive. She was subsequently repaired only to be lost a few months later.

So great was the possibility of our submarines getting sunk close inshore, with some of the crew being taken prisoner, that C.O.'s were instructed to advise their respective crews to devise some sort of a code with their wives in order that they could divulge on prisoner of war letters, information regarding the loss of their submarine,

Clare and I concocted some sort of understanding, which we thought would serve the purpose. Wives were expected to take letters thought to contain information, straight to the nearest naval authority. But there was no compulsion with this; it was left entirely up to the individual.

It was rumoured that if the Germans overran our country, and this seemed very likely at the time, we, the navy, and what was left of the army and air force, would 'fall back' (this sounds better than retreat) to Canada, to continue the fight from there. I abhorred the very thought of this, as there was no reason to believe that the Nazi hordes would treat our families differently from those of all the other countries they had overrun, such as Hungary, Poland, Austria, and Czechoslovakia, mostly sending them to the gas chambers, and committing many other appalling atrocities.

About this time, and completely out of the blue as far as I was concerned, a draft chit arrived, appointing me as C.E.R.A of *H31*. She was one of the old 'H' class submarines, based at Campbeltown on the west coast of Scotland, and employed solely for training purposes. A senior C.E.R.A. was required, as these submarines did not employ an engineer officer. I could hardly be termed a senior C.E.R.A. with only three years experience as a C.E.R.A. but with our heavy losses, the number of available C.E.R.A's had been severely reduced. One submarine was lost with no fewer than three C.E.R.A.'s on board, and by now many of the real old stagers were given depot ship jobs, where their experience could be put to good purpose in a training capacity.

This job would suit me very nicely for a while in order to lessen the pressure and to get myself back to normal. I had had a pretty tough time since joining *Porpoise*, no tougher than any of my contemporaries, but there had been much tension, and suddenly I had begun to feel very weary. One year of war could age one more than eight or ten years of peacetime, and I had had no decent leave. However, before the move could be operated, 'P.Q. Roberts had contacted *Dolphin* and had it quashed. 'Jumbo' Jarvis, who was our outside E.R.A. and had just been elevated to C.E.R.A., was to go in my stead.

It was very disappointing, and I was very angry - better that I had heard nothing in the first place. Not only did I have to soldier on in the same capacity, but also I had now lost a splendid outside E.R.A. and a very pleasant messmate. Tommy Hargreaves took over 'Jumbo's job and proved to be very efficient. Although *H31* did not get a very senior C.E.R.A., they got a jolly good one.

There was a very sad end to this story. *H31*, together with one or two other non-operational submarines was later sent out to cover the escape of *Scharnhorst*, which was at the time, sheltering at Brest. *H31* was not heard of again – followed the now familiar Admiralty statement, overdue, presumed lost.

Normally these very old submarines would not be sent out on operational patrol, but we had suffered heavy losses and it was important to keep *Scharnhorst* bottled up. Despite this shadowing *Scharnhorst* slipped out at night and made her way almost arrogantly up channel in company with *Gneisenau* and *Prinz Eugen* in February 1942, running a gauntlet of submarines, aircraft and surface craft.

What actually happened to *H31* nobody seems to know. Not having been claimed by the Germans, she was probably mined. In retrospect I realized that I had little to grumble about in remaining with *Porpoise.*

The Skagerrak position was getting very precarious. One unfortunate 'T' boat (*Tetrarch*), was hounded by anti-submarine vessels so persistently that she was forced to remain dived for a record period of forty-three hours. Apart from her batteries being flat, the crew also were just about flat; there could have been very little oxygen left in the boat, and the carbon dioxide content must have been bordering on the critical. Several of the crew were unconscious, before the captain finally allowed his First Lieutenant to surface the boat. Thankfully by that time all was clear. Sadly *Tetrarch* was later to be lost in the western Mediterranean.

On one occasion when we were about to leave our patrol and in an effort to get the main engines started quickly on surfacing, we had an awful mishap. It was one of those things that happen to everyone else, but this time it happened to me. As if we hadn't enough to worry us, we started the port main engine with the engine's turning gear in. I was on the starting levers, and did not check that the turning gear was disengaged before I pulled the huge levers into the starting position, I didn't get a chance afterwards as 'Taff' Hughes immediately opened the compressed air starting valve. I replaced the levers almost immediately, but – too late! The turning gear was strained to the extent of being jammed in the engaged position. This meant that temporarily, we had only the starboard engine to recharge the batteries, and to get us out of the patrol area quickly, before the next submarine came in.

For my sins, I spent the next most miserable and uncomfortable two or three hours lying on my back in the cold oily bilge disconnecting the whole contraption so that at least we could start the engine. I wouldn't let anyone else tackle the job for two reasons, firstly that I had let it happen, and secondly that being thin and wiry it seemed that I could do the job quicker, and speed was so essential.

There was scarcely any room under the huge engine clutch, and I had to 'surface' a couple of times for a breather and to avoid cramp. Eventually the debris was cleared, leaving us the problem of engaging the clutch without the aid of the motor operated turning gear. This could only be done by blowing the engines around as slowly as possible, using the starting air and hoping that it would stop in one of the twelve positions. This made no difference to the time it took to disengage the clutch when diving, just a little longer to engage the clutch on surfacing. There was nearly always haste to start the engines after surfacing, in fact we mostly started an engine before opening the conning tower hatch, this then would reduce the air pressure in the boat, which had slowly accumulated whilst dived. Opening the hatch with about four pounds of air pressure in the boat made for a risk of injury to the first man up. Normally, as the C.E.R.A, I would have supervised the starting of the engines on surfacing, having an E.R.A. on each engine.

Neither the captain nor the engineer officer 'blew their tops' at the time, which they could easily have done. Not that it would have improved the situation; our immediate concern was to get the port engine going as soon as possible. I fully expected to be 'carpeted' before the captain on our arrival in harbour, to explain what had happened, but he made no mention of the affair, which was jolly decent of him. George Gay had probably told him of the nauseating conditions that I had worked under to get it free; it was the most uncomfortable three hours I'd ever spent. It was a sharp lesson that I'd been taught, one had to be quick – but not too quick! Of the thousands of times that I'd started diesel engines, this was my first (and only) serious error.

During the latter part of 1940 *Porpoise* was transferred to the west coast of Scotland to carry out Bay of Biscay anti U boat patrols. We were billeted alongside the rather ancient parent ship *Titania* (known as 'The Tights' to submariners) in the Holy Loch. This at least, was a welcome change from our Norwegian and Skagerrak patrols, but certainly had its own particular hazards. We were in fact patrolling the western seaboard of France, which now in Nazi hands, was conveniently used as a base for the Atlantic marauding U boats.

We carried out several of these patrols with no success. With our huge silhouette we were hardly the right type of submarine for this work. Having to surface at night to charge our batteries, especially on a calm moonlit night, even though we were trimmed down as low in the water as we dared we were jolly fortunate not to have been sighted and torpedoed.

Trimmed down to almost neutral buoyancy, with the mine casing almost awash always created problems in the engine room. There was so much backpressure on the engine exhaust that the valve springs weren't powerful enough to shut the exhaust valves with a snap. On several occasions our engines became partially flooded with seawater, a situation that would bring tears to any C.E.R.A.'s eyes. It really was heartbreaking not to be able to run the engines in an efficient manner. To make matters worse, there was seldom an opportunity to warm our engines up gradually, the C.O. would surface and require full power immediately, this produced terrible stresses and strains on our large, relatively slow speed diesel engines.

Relatively few executive officers appreciated the limitations of running machinery, or the need for careful and sympathetic attention. The engineers duty was to keep the machinery running efficiently – most C.O.'s knew what speed and power could be attained, but this data was derived from trials that were carried out in ideal conditions – full buoyancy, clean bottom, calm waters, selected fuel, and at least two hours working up to full power. I was always very much in favour of giving the captain what he needed, but it was also my duty to nurse the machinery as much as possible so that it was in good condition when most urgently required.

Some executive officers appetites for more revolutions was insatiable, they always wanted more speed, a higher charging rate for the batteries, and the H.P. air bottles fully charged in record time. This of course was understandable, as it was their prime concern to get the submarine into position, to have everything ready to make an attack, and to be ready to cope with the expected counter attack. On the other hand, many of them knew little about the mechanics, or the problems which beset the engineering staff.

Being the C.E.R.A., and having six E.R.A.'s under me, it was not necessary for me to keep watch on the main engines, but it was my duty to be present when starting, and I always insisted that I kept the first two hours after surfacing each evening, in the engine room. This was the most vital period as far as the engines were concerned, as they were cold, and would immediately have a load put on them. Moreover, as invariably it was barely dark when we would surface, there was every likelihood of us having to dive again - in a hurry!

Allowing as much load (mostly electrical), on the engines as I considered safe, I would get them properly warmed up and settled down before calling for a relief and returning to my mess to enjoy a much needed tot of rum and breakfast at about 2100. Not long afterwards, at about midnight, we would have our main meal of the day. Sometimes, if we were harassed on surfacing, a late breakfast would be followed by dinner less than one or two hours later. All cooking had to be completed, and the boat cooled down and ventilated before dawn. At around about noon, during the long period of daylight hours when we were dived, we would have a cold meal with a cup of tea.

There was an efficient battery ventilating system fitted, which discharged battery gasses into the atmosphere while we were on the surface. But as this involved opening another huge valve, that had to be shut very quickly on diving, more often than not, battery gasses were directed by fans into the forward end of the engine room, where the main engine intakes swallowed them up. Nevertheless the stench of this gas did permeate throughout the boat, and of course, when dived we just had to live with it. It was a very astute (and lucky) First Lieutenant who was able to get his batteries fully charged while on patrol.

There were few minefields in our area, nor did we encounter many anti-submarine vessels. But there was always the uncomfortable feeling that one of the many fishing vessels might be an armed German, so we spent a great deal of our time dodging them. Only once did we see a U boat, but unfortunately we could not get into a favourable position to attack. However, two of our submarines were successful in sinking U boats in this area. At this period in 1940, the U boat menace was at its worst. In one period of five weeks 460,000 tons of our shipping was lost, all of them bringing much needed provisions and vital war materials to Britain

Clare had returned to Plymouth from Blyth, but thinking that we were to be operating from Holy Loch for a longer period, I sent her a telegram asking her to again come north. I managed to get a couple of furnished rooms a mile or so from Dunoon. This at least allowed me to spend a little time ashore with my wife between patrols. It was rather a nerve racking time for Clare, she would see *Porpoise* pass our abode proceeding on patrol, and knew that within twenty-six to twenty-eight days she should see her returning – and what a relief that would be. On one occasion an indiscreet wife of one of the depot ships staff ventured to say to her 'Isn't it time that *Porpoise* returned from patrol?' Actually it was about time that *Porpoise* returned, and we proceeded up past our lodgings the very next day.

In the event this chance remark caused Clare much anxiety as she thought that this lady had heard a rumour that *Porpoise* was overdue. I was furious with the person concerned, and let it be known My poor dear wife had more than her share of worry, without these thoughtless remarks.

After four or five months of these patrols off the west coast of France, *Porpoise* was once more recalled to Blyth where we were sent off on what seemed a rather special mine laying operation. Calling at Immingham to embark our fifty mines, we were joined by a Norwegian naval officer who was to act as pilot. We proceeded as usual, dived by day and surfaced by night, to the mouth of a Norwegian fjord that was used by the Germans to transport troops and war materials. This fjord apparently bypassed nearly a hundred miles of the North Sea, and aircraft and anti-submarine vessels frequently patrolled the entrance(s).

We were to lay our mines in a position nearly fifty miles inside the entrance, and it was of course most important that the many aircraft and vessels lurking about the entrance did not observe us. With batteries fully charged and at periscope depth, we entered the fjord soon after dawn, wending our way slowly inland. These fjords were usually very deep, and with towering cliffs on each side, this one averaged about one thousand two hundred yards in width.

We turned at a position carefully selected by the Norwegian pilot, and commenced laying the first leg of seventeen mines. Suddenly the whole boat shuddered and we came to a grinding halt with a 'bow up' angle. Of all the bad luck! We had grounded on an uncharted sandbank with the top of our periscope standards well above the surface.

The unfortunate Norwegian pilot looked very surprised and embarrassed, as well he might. But we were in a most awful predicament, about thirty miles into enemy occupied country, and aground on a sandbank with three feet of our periscope standards sticking out of the water, and seventeen of our own mines astern of us. Moreover, within eight hundred yards to westward, on the north bank was a lighthouse or beacon. It seemed certain that this structure must be manned either by Germans, or that treacherous body of people referred to as 5th columnists (Quislings). Surely they could not help but spot us, and would quickly flash the news that an enemy submarine was in the fjord, then even if we could get ourselves clear of this sandbank, our escape route to seaward would be closed. What a situation to be in! Desperately we tried to wriggle ourselves free, having to increase our buoyancy a little, but not daring to surface completely as we were still not sure that we had been spotted. The suspense was awful, we could either be spotted and blown out of the water by the enemy, or we could take a similar punishment from our own mines! Eventually we chose to risk the latter, and cleared the bank by going full speed astern on our motors and executing a perfect stern dive. Our main concern now was that we were backing on to the minefield that we had just laid. True the mines were designed to sink with the trolley, and programmed not to be released to come to their pre-determined depth until some time later, but we could not bank on this. If we came up prematurely, our propellers would entangle the wire securing the seven hundred pounds of T.N.T. to its trolley, drawing the mine into ourselves. All this concern was of course enhanced by the likelihood of further, and possibly more serious grounding.

But fortune was with us, we found deeper water and we settled once more at periscope depth where we proceeded to lay seventeen more mines across to the south bank, and the remaining sixteen diagonally across to the north bank. We then had nearly a six-hour run to the south in order to get clear by nightfall. Our greatest headache now, was whether we'd been spotted, and if we had, was it by friend or foe? If it were the latter, then we knew we were in for a load of trouble on the way out.

We were surprised and greatly relieved when we were paid no particular attention on reaching the mouth of the fjord. Rarely did we learn the results of our mine laying efforts, but we did hear later that this had been a highly successful mission. The margin between a successful mission and an unsuccessful one was very slender, and however skilful the captain, it had to be attended by a little good fortune. One wrong person to have seen this commotion taking place under their very noses, and not only would our costly minelay have been abortive, but we'd have been very lucky to have escaped with our lives. To this day it seems incredible that we weren't spotted in that fjord; I can only think that if anyone did see us, it was a loyal Norwegian. The vast majority of Norwegians understandably hated the occupation of their country, and many found the means to escape to Britain in order to carry on the fight, as indeed did our present pilot.

At about this time, the *Porpoise* class of submarine suffered yet another loss. First *Grampus*, then *Narwhal*, and now we learned that *Seal* had been badly damaged either by aircraft, or mine. She was on the surface in enemy waters and could neither steer nor dive. Utterly at the mercy of the enemy, her unfortunate Captain (Lt Cdr. R.P. Lonsdale) was given the ghastly alternative of either surrendering his ship, or that none of his crew would be saved. For an officer of his integrity this was a terrible choice. Destroying all confidential matter, he chose the former, and after four and a half years in a German prison, faced a court martial on his release. There wasn't a submariner in the country that did not feel in some way involved in this court martial. Many must have searched their consciences asking themselves what they would have done under similar circumstances.

On his decision had depended the lives of sixty of his crew. On the other hand he had allowed his ship to fall into the hands of the enemy. It was a great relief to all of us when the court, having probed deeply into all the circumstances, saw fit to acquit him. Lt. Cdr. Lonsdale, having lived with this nightmare for four and a half years in captivity, and then enduring his lengthy court martial with great dignity (the radio and press having squeezed every ounce of blood out of both him and the case), requested to retire from the Royal Navy. Always a pious man, he went into the ministry. The last time I saw him was as Rector of a small village church, looking far older than his years and rather sad. He did not recognize me, nor did I make myself known to him, I think that to have done so would have stirred up unpleasant memories and disturbed that peaceful village setting. Those four and a half years of captivity must have been a living hell for him.

One of *Seal's* E.R.A.'s Don Lister, together with another submariner prisoner of war, 'Wally' Hammond, contrived to escape from captivity. A typical pair of submarine E.R.A.'s were these two, full of resourcefulness, enterprise and courage. The Germans probably heaved a sigh of relief when they finally managed to escape. Don had made two previous abortive attempts at escape, one from the notorious Colditz, for which he suffered weeks of solitary confinement on being caught.

At the end of August 1940 after being at war for almost one year, *Porpoise* was once more ordered around to the west coast of Scotland to join *Forth*, who had moved from Rosyth around to the Holy Loch in the Clyde estuary. This time we were required for a quite different purpose. The Atlantic convoys were our very bloodstream; the losses from submarine attacks were great, but added to this was the deadly peril of a breakaway German battleship, pocket battleship or cruiser wreaking havoc among a convoy inadequately protected by surface craft.

A tremendously strong fleet had to remain in our Scottish waters to cope with a German fleet attack, or if possible, bottle them up. Apart from other worldwide commitments, the escorting of many Atlantic convoys stretched our sea power to its limits. In some cases, convoys of forty merchantmen with an average speed of sometimes less than ten knots, were given the protection of an almost obsolete battleship, or a couple of armed merchantmen (auxiliary cruisers), together with a couple of destroyers, until they came within striking distance of the German U boats, when they were then relieved by eight or ten anti-submarine vessels.

It was considered that the presence of a submarine for the western part of this voyage might deter an attack by a German surface warship. So, for a period of more than six months, mostly during the stormy 1940/41 winter, it fell to us to escort convoys from Canada to longitude 20 degrees west, then pick up a returning convoy and return to Halifax Nova Scotia - a peculiar role for a mine-laying submarine to play.

Before leaving the Holy Loch for this mission, our captain, Lt Cdr. P.Q. Roberts was relieved by Lt Cdr J. Hopkins. I had always regarded P.Q. as a good wartime captain and was sorry to see him go. He demanded his 'pound of flesh' from his crew, who on the whole, gave it unstintingly, and I was grateful to him, not only for quashing my draft to *H31*, but also for not making a fuss over the 'turning gear' incident. 'Lynch' Maydon, and 'Basher' Coombs had left us before this time, to take the Commanding Officers Qualifying ('Perisher') Course. I think that Lt Daniell took over as First Lieutenant until he too, was relieved by a more junior Lieutenant in order to take the 'Perisher' course. These young lieutenants all went on to make their marks as submarine C.O.'s.

Within one year of the outbreak of war, the majority of the original crew had left *Porpoise* to form the trained nucleus of crews for the new submarines, which were being churned out. Officers and ratings that had just completed a brief submarine training course, the majority of whom had been called up for the duration of the war only, replaced them. The E.R.A.'s were no exception, although I did have one very senior and experienced E.R.A. join. He was Bert Shute, a contemporary of mine in the apprentices, who had been in the submarine service for nearly as long as I had. Bert was quite a character, like my old friend 'Chinky' Rice, he had not passed the professional examination for C.E.R.A., and was more than a little fond of his liquor, a weakness that was to cause me many a headache in the future.

Another original member of the crew that we were very sorry to lose was my own boss, Lt. George Gay, a charming, brave and very knowledgeable officer, who was moved on to the *Clyde*, one of the three 'River' class, and now our largest submarines. George was to have his fair amount of thrills in *Clyde*, and was awarded the D.S.C. before joining a parent ship as Senior Engineer. I was to see much more of George Gay in the post-war years.

George Gay was relieved by Lt E. 'Jerry' Kirkby, who was at that time, not a very experienced submarine officer. Jerry was a 'bit of a lad', and excelled at most games, especially rugby, at which he was a regular member of the navy XV, and was very near to international standard. Unfortunately we seldom had the opportunity to play games in those war years, in fact submariners were forbidden to play rugby in case of injury.

Prior to commencing our escort duties we were sent to the small seaport of Ardrossan to undergo a fourteen-day dry-docking period; we were almost due for a longer refit, but this would have to suffice, as the general situation was rather desperate. Ardrossan had no experience at all in dealing with submarines; so most of the responsibility fell on our shoulders, in fact my chaps did most of the work. Nevertheless it was a welcome break from war patrols, and most of the crew were given a few days leave. I was too busy to take my four days leave, but sent for Clare to join me instead. Procuring food was becoming difficult when living ashore as most items were strictly rationed, and as we were unknown in the area there was very little in the way of 'extras'. But I was happy enough just to be able to have Clare with me

Having finished our docking, Clare returned to Plymouth and *Porpoise* joined up with a huge convoy of near empty ships, which were congregating inside the boom at the mouth of the Clyde. We sailed late one night for Halifax Nova Scotia, as part of a convoy.

Taking orders from the commodore of the convoy, we were not permitted to dive, and had to zigzag with the others. The convoy speed of eight knots was very slow for us, but our speed was governed by the slowest vessel. A signal to the commodore requesting permission to carry out a 'trim dive' was granted, but otherwise we were to remain on the surface; it appeared that at that time, due to our proximity to the Western Approaches, we were considered to be a bit of a liability rather than an asset.

On account of the fuel and stores we carried, and the varying density of the seawater, the First Lieutenant was keen to adjust the trim of the boat daily. But until we reached longitude 20 west, when most of our escort of frigates and destroyers left us to escort an incoming convoy, the commodore would not authorize this. Even then, we were ordered to detach ourselves to port or starboard, dive and catch a trim, carry out a few exercises for the benefit of the 'rookies' aboard, and then catch up with the convoy, again taking up position, usually on the port or starboard quarter.

In all it was a very tiring and tedious task, quite different from the fiercely hectic work we had been carrying out. Nevertheless it had its moments. During the period October 1940 to April 1941 we met up with some appalling weather, one particular storm was as bad as I'd ever experienced, including the typhoon that *Oswald* had met in the China Seas.

From the Clyde it took us about sixteen days to reach Halifax, the convoy splitting up into smaller groups before we reached there. On arrival we tied up alongside the old auxiliary cruiser *Alaunia,* and waited for the next British bound convoy to assemble, forty-four merchantmen laden with vital foodstuff and much needed war materials. It really was a marvellous sight, to see this armada set out in four lines ahead, each line comprising eleven ships, and led at this time by the old battleship *Royal Sovereign,* flying the commodores flag (probably a retired rear admiral, recalled for war service).

As the German U boats were not operating as far east at that time, it would be two or three days out of Halifax before the whole convoy would commence 'zigzagging'. These convoys were invariably very slow, never making more than seven or eight knots.

At night we would move a little further away to reduce the chances of a collision, as the whole convoy would be 'blacked out'. Moreover, some of these old ships were none to reliable about keeping station – an engine would break down, or a steering gear would jam. This would cause a certain amount of chaos at night, and that ship's staff would work frantically to repair the defect so as not to get left behind. It was dangerous policy to wait about for a straggler. Having reached longitude 25 west, we would then depart from that convoy to rendezvous with a western bound convoy, repeating the dose! Our stay's in Halifax was rarely longer than ten days.

It amazed me to see the number of submarines in Halifax harbour, most of which rarely went to sea. We were the only British submarine, and we were kept very busy, probably because most of the others were rather antiquated boats owned by our allies. The huge French *Surcouf* was one of these. She was very powerfully armed – two 8 inch guns in a turret – and would have fulfilled our role excellently, except that they had a little domestic trouble aboard her. Apparently the crew that had rescued her from falling into the hands of the Germans had a few dissenters among them. Before she left Britain for Halifax there had been a real rumpus aboard her, in which I understand two or three were killed.

Much to our disgust, *Surcouf* and two or three other submarines were taking up good space alongside *Alaunia*, and each time we returned with a convoy we had to be accommodated elsewhere. *Surcouf* was still there when, six months later, we terminated this job, but apparently she departed on a mission shortly after we left, and was never heard of again. What happened to her I do not know, but her crew were certainly not getting enough sea training to deal with such a huge submarine in wartime.

Though several allied submarines did most valuable work during the war, those in Halifax at that time appeared to be more of a liability. I personally, found this period rather depressing despite being relatively safe. We were fulfilling an important role but it wasn't a pleasant one. Our home towns, particularly Plymouth were being savaged by German bombers, the weather in the north Atlantic was bitterly cold and stormy. Our duties were monotonous and uninspiring, and *Porpoise* was becoming sorely in need of a refit.

The route taken by the convoys varied, sometimes we took a very northerly route, where it was not uncommon to sight icebergs or to get mixed up with large chunks of drift ice. It was very disturbing down below to hear these large pieces of ice colliding with our hull and saddle tanks. Although we were not travelling at any great speed these chunks could have easily split our frail tanks, or cause rivets to spring and leak.

Our accommodation in Halifax, sometimes in an old cargo vessel, was really most unsatisfactory. Once we arrived back from a tiring three weeks at sea and all they could offer the E.R.A.'s was an old shack on the upper deck. I hadn't seen it before my chaps came back to the submarine to tell me that it was entirely unacceptable. I went inboard right away to inspect this shack, and I too was quite disgusted. I sought out my E.O., the First Lieutenant, and subsequently the captain, to complain. This was rather embarrassing as I was on good terms with all three, but

I was very angry that my staff should be offered such a pokey hole in which to live, after we had spent so long at sea in such appalling conditions.

Our captain, 'Happy Jack' Hopkins, informed me that he had already voiced his opinion to the Base officer, regarding this very unsatisfactory accommodation, and the reply had been that no other accommodation was available, and that shore accommodation was out of the question. Having been informed by my messmates that they would prefer to live aboard the boat, I conveyed this startling disclosure to the captain who was pleased to grant us permission, as a way out of this uncompromising situation. It wasn't good to be living aboard the submarine while alongside, but at least we weren't being pitched about, as we were at sea. Moreover our sympathetic captain declared that as no adequate accommodation was available, he would authorize payment of 'hard laying' money (1/3d per day), which we received every twenty-four hours spent at sea, from the time we left the U.K. This was small compensation, but it was all that he could do.

As I have mentioned previously, on one convoy in February 1941 we ran into the worst storm I have ever experienced at sea. We had turned, and were escorting the westward bound convoy when the weather deteriorated so badly that all we could do was to try and keep our head into these seas. We lost touch with the convoy, and I would think that they lost touch with one another. For nearly five days we kept our nose into the storm, hardly making any progress. It was impossible to dive in this, and even if we were able to, our batteries would only have lasted for twenty-four hours. A large canvas bath (the 'bird bath') was rigged beneath the conning tower hatch to catch the torrents of seawater that flooding constantly down the tower. This 'bird bath' was continually being pumped out by the ballast pump.

It was also fun and games trying to 'ditch gash' each evening. Although we were endeavouring to keep our bows into the sea, we were rolling considerably as well as pitching, making it very difficult for the chap on the bridge to hoist an almost full bucket of semi fluid refuse up through the conning tower on the end of a long line without losing half of its contents over the unfortunates standing beneath in the control room. The buckets were then emptied over the side, with all the empty tins being punctured and flattened so that they would sink and not be detected by the enemy. This whole 'gash ditching' operation was always supervised by an officer or a senior petty officer.

After two days of this storm I was informed that the forward part of the protective bridge structure was being stove in by the huge waves. The captain wished to know if it was possible for me to rig timber shores, so there was nothing for me to do but to fight my way up on to the bridge to weigh up the situation, and to take measurements.

Sometimes on my belly and sometimes on my back, but always clinging grimly to the brass ladder, I finally reached the bridge and beheld a most alarming sight. Looking upward to where the sky should be there was a mountainous sea just about to break over us. A lookout yelled at me to hold tight, and it was as well he did, for I would have been most certainly washed overboard. The lookouts, poor devils, were reduced to the O.O.W. and two seamen, as one leading seaman had already had a miraculous escape, even though lashed to the handrail he had been washed overboard, but then mercifully, washed back again.

The intense fury of this gale (it must have been of hurricane force) had whipped up sixty feet high foam capped waves, and it was with the greatest difficulty that I was able to take measurements. It was bad enough down below, but up here it was really frightening, when down in a trough the waves were nearly forty feet above the lookouts on the bridge. The most dangerous time for those on the bridge was the short time when they were changing over watches, and they had to unlash themselves. If a lookout was washed overboard he was a 'goner', as the boat could not have successfully turned about. I prayed that the main engines and the steering gear would not fail, they were taking an awful pounding.

We looked so puny and inadequate in this cauldron; heaven knows how some of the more antiquated ships were faring. We had one consolation though; there was no fear of an enemy attack in this weather. I had often envied the seamen their spell of lookout duty on the bridge, when we of the engine room branch were confined to the smelly atmosphere of the engine room. But never again, - two hours on the bridge in these conditions must have seemed an eternity.

There was no doubt about the bridge cab being stove in. This slightly hooded portion of the fore part of the bridge, designed to give some protection for the O.O.W.'s charts, and a measure of protection for the O.O.W. and lookouts, was definitely showing signs of damage. The gigantic waves were hitting it with such force that there were distinct signs of an imminent collapse, in which case there would have been no protection for the bridge staff and the bridge would be virtually untenable.

Armed with my measurements I descended once more into the bowels of the submarine, where I cut three lengths of the 4inch diameter timber that I kept for any emergency, then having found a heavy sledge hammer and some large wooden wedges, I detailed off a sturdy stoker to accompany me, and again set off up to the bridge. It was difficult climbing up to the bridge with our heavy lengths of timber, but even more difficult shoring up the bridge cab from the more stable and robust periscope standards. The three large wooden shores proved to be just what was needed, even though they restricted the space on the bridge. The young stoker held the timber while I drove home the large wedges. This was certainly working under extreme difficulty, not only were we lashed to the bridge, but the boat, besides pitching violently, was rolling through an arc of over eighty degrees, and to add to our problems, our hands soon became completely numb with the cold.

At last, having successfully completed this operation, I was very thankful to get below once more. Wet through and freezing cold, I was pleased that I had a tot of rum tucked away in my locker, which I shared with the young stoker. Any of the

113

E.R.A's could have done that job, but, probably to their disgust, I was one of those bosses who, though not thinking others incapable, still preferred to do the awkward jobs himself.

During this storm, the conditions within the submarine were so bad that the poor cook was unable to indulge in the culinary arts despite the fittings on the cooker to prevent pots and pans sliding off. It wasn't that the cook was seasick; in fact strangely enough very few of the crew were seasick, but such food as we had was straight out of a tin. After about three days of this semi-starvation, 'Mickey' Power, our mining E.R.A. and a native of Southern Ireland, declared that he couldn't stand life without a potato any longer. He then went for'd and unearthed several large potatoes from a sack in the fore-ends, and baked them in their jackets. I really can't remember tasting anything nicer, but our troubles were anything but over, as the storm still raged.

Much of the steel plating that formed our fore casing was torn away, our solitary 4" gun was swinging from port to starboard as the teeth on its training rack were stripped by the fury of the seas; no one could get to the fore casing to secure it. In the torpedo stowage compartment, where many of the seamen messed and slung their hammocks, the metal securing bands on a torpedo fractured, allowing this one and a half ton monster to career from side to side. Luckily there were no casualties, but as this was also the storage space for bags of potatoes, onions, carrots, and crates of eggs etc. it can easily be imagined what this compartment resembled in a very short space of time. These precious commodities were pulped to resemble an 'Irish Stew'. No more baked potatoes for 'Mickey' Power. But the destruction of our fresh vegetables was a minor consideration, this torpedo, with nearly seven hundred pounds of explosive in its nose was a real danger to machinery and pipe systems, with the boat rolling forty-five degrees each way at times.

Four very gallant sailors, ably led by a leading seaman, volunteered to go into the compartment to secure it. Armed with ropes and wires, they finally succeeded in securing the 'rogue' torpedo without a casualty. To these seamen we were very grateful. It had appeared to be impossible to enter this compartment without being pulped with the remainder of the 'Irish stew'.

The storm blew itself out after five days, although the seas were still very high. At last our lives became almost normal again. We even had cooked food, though without fresh vegetables. It was good to be back on cooked food once more, as winter in the north Atlantic is perishing cold. Even wearing the warmest of clothes, I have been three weeks without getting warm on these trips. When we joined submarines we were issued with thick woollen sweaters and even thicker woollen drawers (long johns). I had often worn the sweaters but had always regarded the long johns as being rather ludicrous. Now I was pleased to use them – they fitted very snugly around the ankles and under the armpits. During the storm I had rigged a plumb line to measure the roll. This recorded forty-five degrees each way in the worst instances. The captain also took readings and stated that it was in excess of forty-seven degrees. What was worrying about this is that forty-five degrees was nearing the angle where the acid in the main batteries would start to spill over; it was also nearing our critical roll angle. When rolling badly the boat would continually lose buoyancy, due to the air in the main ballast tanks escaping from the free flood holes in the bottom of the tanks, a situation known as 'cross venting'. This necessitated running the low-pressure blower as often as every fifteen minutes.

The Commodore endeavoured to re-assemble his convoy after the storm, but what success he had I do not know. This must have been the worst storm that many of these ships had encountered, and bearing in mind that some of them were in a very decrepit state, they could well have foundered. In peacetime this would have made abundant news for the press; in wartime nothing more was heard about it.

The seamen were very pleased when the weather abated. When shipping seas like these, the very efficient 'Ursula' suits were a Godsend, since the standard foul weather rig was quite incapable of keeping seawater out. Designed early in the war by Commander G.C. Phillips, who at the time was commanding the submarine *Ursula*, these suits really were a vast improvement. They were excellent even in the roughest weather. Lightweight and easy to put on, they gave a freedom of action, which did not hinder travel through the conning tower; many of our chaps were quite large, and the hatch very small. Often I assisted watch keepers out of these suits after spending a two-hour watch on the bridge in bad weather conditions. Sometimes these people were frozen nearly solid, with beards and even eyelids coated with frost, and although it was a little against the grain, we engine room personnel felt obliged to take pity on these seamen and let them drape their saturated garments over the non moving parts of our clean and polished bright-work. The stokers took pride in the appearance of the engines, and when not greasing or lubricating the moving parts, spent much of their time on watch polishing – it took only a few minutes draped in salt water saturated garments to undo this good work.

On our arrival in Halifax, and looking a very sorry sight, we were immediately invaded by a host of workmen striving to repair casing and bridge damage before the next convoy was due to leave. Plating lost overboard was replaced, the damaged gun-rack repaired, the bridge cab strengthened and my invaluable pit props taken out and stowed behind the engines, ready for the next emergency. Strangely our forward hydroplanes, regarded as being particularly vulnerable in heavy weather, had suffered no damage at all. The weather in Halifax was bitterly cold, ten to fifteen degrees Fahrenheit below freezing, but it was sunny and crisp. I went ashore for a breather and a little exercise whenever I had the chance.

Each convoy escort duty usually lasted about three weeks per round trip, and we rarely had it calm. When it wasn't too rough, or when not on watch or at dogwatch exercises, we would spend most of the time playing cards. Mostly we played Pontoon or Brag for minimal stakes – usually for matches, or for dried peas.

'Happy Jack' Hopkins, our C.O., and our engineer officer Lt. Jerry Kirkby were keen bridge players, and as they were unable to make a four in the wardroom, quite frequently invited myself and one of my E.R.A.'s, (usually Bert Pinch) in for a rubber of bridge

'Bert', unfortunately was often a cause of slight embarrassment to me. Whilst in harbour I was constantly covering up for the likeable 'Bert', so that he would not be in the captains report due to his drinking; rather a peculiar situation all round. I was always prepared to cover up for any of my staff providing they were worth it, and most of them were, but 'Bert' and I had this added bond of having spent four and a half years together during our apprenticeship. He was a fine and skilled tradesman, and never grumbled at the amount of overtime (unpaid) that he was required to do. This covering up could only be done in the case of minor indiscretions, and then as such to avoid wasting the captains or the First Lieutenant's time, and of course to save the dignity of a senior petty or chief petty officer. Mostly it was done with the connivance of the coxswain, with whom I am pleased to say, I was mostly on good terms with.

'Bert' tried me sorely at times, but a little patience and forbearance were amply rewarded. Often he would arrive back on board having had 'one over the eight' to discover that we were still working to complete some repair job. The difficulty then, was to prevent 'Bert' from getting stuck into the job, still dressed in his No.1 suit. Apart from anything else, this could be dangerous, as often parts of the machinery that we were handling or lowering into position weighed several hundredweights. Often we would struggle against the clock to finish a job before the liberty-men returned; after all they had gone ashore to forget about the war and the work for a few hours, and that was good for them. We did not often get all night leave away from our parent ship, but if we did 'Bert' would probably be adrift the next morning, albeit only by a few minutes, in which case I'd eat my breakfast quickly, discreetly entreat the coxswain to defer reporting 'All hands on board' for five or ten minutes, then dash up to the bridge to see if 'Bert' was in sight. All very involved, because the First Lieutenant had in turn, to report to the C.O. It was always with a sigh of relief when I spotted the slim figure of 'Bert' staggering along the jetty carrying a monumental hangover.

From the time we left harbour to the time we returned, our state of preparedness never relaxed. At any time we might have to dive to carry out an attack. 'Non quam non paratus' was *Porpoise's* motto, and prepared we had to be. But now after six months of this convoy work, *Porpoise* was sorely in need of a major refit, and I kept my fingers crossed that we would not be refitting on this side of the Atlantic. Assuming that we would soon be returning to the U.K. the whole ships company availed themselves of the abundance of commodities that were in the shops but could not be obtained at home. Our personal locker space in the boat was very limited, especially as, in the absence of the parent ship we had all our kit on board, but I still found room for my purchases of tinned food, silk stockings etc.

Later, when it became known that on our next trip we were going the whole way, and not just to 25 degrees west, I purchased as much as I could, including a whole smoked ham, and then prevailed upon my old friend the 2nd coxswain to sew me a large canvas bag, wherein to put my precious stores.

On one of my rare appearances on the bridge during this last crossing, I saw between forty and fifty tankers and cargo ships of all shapes and sizes ploughing through the waves at seven and a half knots in four lines ahead, headed by the old battleship *Resolution* (the '*Resso*', as she was affectionately named was a sister ship to *the Royal Oak,* on which I did practically my first sea trip). The weather was good, it was now the end of April, and all looked peaceful. This was the 'calm before the storm' because these ships were to have a 'helluva' time of it later. Only about half of them would reach port, the other half falling prey to the dreaded U boat attacks. The German U boats were hunting in packs and would get in among the convoy at night, where it was almost impossible to miss with either torpedo or gun, and then they would make their escape in the general shambles that resulted from their attacks. Later, with the advent of radar, and more sophisticated methods of dealing with the U boat packs, our losses decreased, and the U boat losses in turn became very heavy. But this was still the early part of 1941, and our losses were devastating.

By late 1943 early 1944 German submarines were already being fitted with the snorkel device, which allowed the submarine to remain dived practically the whole time. The snorkel mast, which could be lowered when not in use, allowed the main engines to be used while at periscope depth. It consisted basically of a mast carrying twin pipes which when raised protruded just above the surface, the engine air intake descending through one large pipe, and the exhaust being pushed up the other pipe to vent into the sea just below the water. So the submarine was now able to recharge its batteries while dived, the self-closing valve at the top of the mast would automatically shut if the boat inadvertently went below periscope depth, or if a heavy sea came over.

What we asked ourselves had the future in store for us? We were badly in need of a refit, but where? Of course, I hoped that it would be in Devonport. But this became more and more unlikely, as we received news that Devonport was the subject of heavy air raids. This news itself was enough to dampen my spirits.

At longitude 25 degrees west, we detached ourselves from the convoy when the anti- submarine escorts took over. It was just after this that a signal was issued by the Admiralty stating that Plymouth (and Devonport) had been raided on two or three consecutive nights but, although there had been much damage, casualties among service personnel's families were light. For the Admiralty to have issued such a signal to all ships at sea, it seemed to us that these raids must have been very severe and, as we had had no mail for several weeks, hardly reassuring.

Then we were told that the Clyde was to be our destination, and that each watch was to get one weeks leave, I asked that I might be considered for the first leave, on account of that signal.

117

Chapter Six

Escorted for the last lap into the Clyde, we finally secured alongside the parent ship *Titania* (which had now replaced *Forth*), in the Holy Loch.

But if any of us had thoughts of proceeding on leave straight away, we were in for a disappointment. The Clyde had just suffered one of its few air-raids, and there had been severe damage to the electricity generating supply, rendering the famous shipbuilding firm of 'Scotts' at Greenock inoperative. *Porpoise* having just arrived, and not being available for war patrol, was a heaven sent blessing to them. Secured up alongside at Scotts, her two huge diesel engines could easily provide enough electricity to keep production going, and so we had just time to clean ourselves up after our Atlantic crossing when we were ordered to cast off from *Titania* and make our way across to Greenock. There, after connecting up our charging leads to the firm's electricity supply, we became a generating station.

Having with the engineer officer already made the necessary arrangements for this operation, which was expected to last for three weeks, I hastened to catch the train to Plymouth, carrying with me all my precious supplies and presents. It was a very long and tiresome journey south, not made easier by my personal anxiety. I had not received any mail for a month, and I couldn't help wondering if my house, or indeed my family, still existed. All train journeys at this time were difficult. There were hold-ups because of air-raids (troop trains and goods trains were rightly given priority), trains and stations were blacked out, and the staff sadly depleted. The journey seemed endless, but eventually I arrived at North Road station, and, grabbing the only taxi, I sadly surveyed the almost unbelievable scenes of destruction on the journey out to Church Way. It was difficult to describe my feelings when I found that all was well with Clare and Joan. Incendiary bombs had damaged the house. Thanks largely to my wife's courage and resourcefulness, (I later learned that on at least two occasions, and at great personal risk, she left our air-raid shelter at the height of the raid to extinguish fires caused by incendiaries both in and around the house). Several items of our furniture were damaged, but temporary repairs to the roof had now been made.

The raids on Plymouth had been devastating, large areas of the city had been completely flattened. As we were close to the large military targets (the R.N Barracks, the dockyard, and the oil tanks across the river Tamar), our area, St Budeaux, had its fair share of both high explosive and firebombs. Clare, Joan and, Sister in Law Violet (Reg Lockley was at war in the *Prince of Wales*), had slept in the air-raid shelter for weeks on end. Joan had turned down the suggestion that she be evacuated, saying that she preferred to stay and 'face the music' with her mother.

Nevertheless she was later prevailed upon to be evacuated to Callington, returning home at weekends.

Although our work at Greenock was expected to last two or three weeks, I received a telegram before my week's leave was up, saying that *Porpoise* was moving to Troon for her refit, and that I was to return to her there. My mother was pleased to care for Joan so that Clare was able to return to Troon with me, as our refit was expected to last for about ten weeks.

As we were unable to obtain accommodation in Troon, we contacted our friends in Ardrossan, fifteen miles up the coast where we had had a short docking earlier. Our friends were happy to accommodate us.

Troon was a delightful little town that had not been troubled by air attacks. In fact apart from food rationing and blackouts at night, the townsfolk seemed quite unaware that there was a desperate war being fought. But this relaxed and 'away from it all' environment had its repercussions for us, because with the summer coming along, most house owners with spare accommodation wanted the holidaymakers from Glasgow in preference to ourselves. Now, as so much of my time was being wasted travelling to and from Ardrossan, Clare and I (whenever I had the time) desperately tried to get 'digs' in Troon, but to no avail. Catching the workman's special to from Ardrossan to Troon at 07:30 each morning – it was often after 19:30 before I returned. Although I was not exactly satisfied with this situation, I considered that I had little to grumble about after all those months at sea.

Porpoise was the very first submarine to be refitted in Troon, and they had no experience of working on large diesel engines. Furthermore, there appeared to be little sense of urgency. The shipyard workers would not work on Saturday afternoon, but would work at double pay for the whole of Sunday, which meant that I had to be there. This I accepted, as all dockyards and firms throughout the country were working overtime to keep pace with the level of production required.

Our engine room staff had quite a lot of work to do during this refit, but my job was to maintain a liaison with the shipyard staff and to ensure that all work completed was up to the high standard required for submarines, as both our lives and our potential as a fighting unit depended upon this.

The experienced staffs of the Royal Naval Dockyards normally carry out tests and trials in peacetime to a standard ready for the examination and satisfaction of the crew, and now in wartime, the importance of achieving these required standards was even greater. This small shipyard had no previous experience of refitting submarines, although on the whole the general standard of craftsmanship and skill was high. But the fact still remained that as this work was new to them, and they were without submarine 'know-how', it was difficult for them to appreciate how one piece of machinery or one valve was so important. Also although most of these workers were in reserved occupations and therefore exempt from joining the services, the shipyard had obviously lost many young tradesmen who had insisted upon leaving to enlist. So to a degree, they would be short of expertise. Not having been in air raids, it was difficult for many of these workers to appreciate that the country was at war, and that at this time we weren't winning.

These matters came to a bit of a climax one day when I found four of these shipyard men seated down in our dingy little auxiliary machinery space playing cards. Without consulting my engineer officer, or the yard foreman, I ordered them off the boat. There was 'hell to pay' for this. The senior foreman of the yard immediately sent me a message demanding my presence in his office. My reply wasn't very courteous either; I said that if he wished to interview me, then he would have to do it through my engineer officer and the captain. But he didn't appear to be too keen to do things through official channels - after all it was his workmen who were playing cards when they should have been working, and in wartime too, with the boat working to a very tight schedule.   This bowler-hatted gentleman subsequently came to see me, and politely asked me if I would like to come to his office to discuss matters. After half an hour's honest talking we parted the best of friends, and remained so for the rest of the refit. He appreciated my difficulties, and the strains that we were subjected to, and of course I realized that he was not without his own problems. Actually, things seemed to run much more smoothly after that incident. Of course, I knew that I had overstepped my authority, but I had one aim in mind, and that was to get *Porpoise* into good shape for the job that would inevitably be in store for us. I think, and hope, that the chaps realized this, and in the end I became almost popular.

After the cards incident, I would often visit my bowler-hatted friend in his office, to discuss 'ways and means', invariably over a glass of ale. He was as useful to me as I to him. If it hadn't been for the cards incident, I might never have come into contact with him. Because of our good relationship there were certainly many jobs taken in hand by the yard that were not on the original defect list, and much extra work was carried out merely on a promise from myself that it would be put on a supplementary defect list.

Our captain 'Happy Jack' Hopkins, and my boss 'Jerry' Kirkby were still with us, but most of our other officers came and went, there being very little for them to do whilst we were refitting. Crew changes were not confined to officers; many of our engine room staff were replaced by those new to submarines. This was both worrying and frustrating, since it seemed that as soon as we had trained a 'rookie', getting him to open and shut the correct valves and in the right order etc, then he would be whisked away from us. Our very lives depended on the proper training of even the most junior rating; a badly trained one could strip a gear wheel, bend a connecting rod, ruin an attack, or even send us to the bottom.

Among the newcomers at this time was a tall, handsome young Sub-Lieutenant, Ian McIntosh, who straightaway was thirsting for knowledge. We were halfway through our refit and poor old *Porpoise* was a shambles, when Ian asked me if I could spare the time to show him over what was left of the boat, and explain the purpose of all the various items of machinery, valves and piping systems. Although very busy, I was pleased to help him. This was his first submarine, although he had passed his submarine training course nearly six months previously. He did not explain this gap, but I discovered later that he had been on his way out to join a submarine in the eastern Mediterranean, via the Cape, when his transport was sunk nearly six hundred miles off the West African coast. Eighty-two men had scrambled into one of the few available lifeboats that were designed to carry fifty-six. With no mechanical propulsion, adverse winds prevented them from making the west African coast, and their alternative was to make for the one thousand six hundred mile distant south American coast. The senior officer in the boat was a rather inexperienced R.N.V.R. Lieutenant, who appointed the young McIntosh to navigate. Eighty-two men had to share rations designed to last fifty-six men for fourteen days.

This story of survival has already been told, and it is not for me to relate, but they did not all survive the very fierce tropical heat, nearly sixty of them perished before they made landfall in Brazil twenty-three days later. Those who did last out the voyage were in a pretty poor state. At the age of twenty, young Ian McIntosh was awarded the MBE for his brave effort. He finally returned to the U.K. by devious routes, and was then given a few weeks to recover from his ordeal before joining *Porpoise*. He was still quite gaunt and thin when he joined us.

Ian McIntosh wasn't with us for many months, but we became great friends. Of Australian stock, he was very clever and soon picked up the job before being whisked away again to take up the post of 1st Lt. in another submarine, finally getting his own command at the ripe old age of twenty-two. Ian had a very distinguished war record, and eventually became Vice Admiral Sir Ian McIntosh KBE. DSO. DSC. I was to see much of him later, when as a Commander; he was in charge of the Submarine Commanding Officers Qualifying Courses. Ian was yet another of the extraordinary characters turned out by the submarine service.

Toward the end of the refit our C.O. suggested that in my interest and in the interest of *Porpoise* it might be advisable for me to find accommodation in Troon. I explained the difficulty that I had found when we had first arrived, and that the situation would be even more acute now (six weeks later), when the holidaymakers were arriving. He replied that he would see what he could do, and within two days I was informed that accommodation was available, and Clare and I moved down to Troon. The captain had certainly acted quickly, this move saved me much valuable time as well as bus fares. Our new digs were jolly good and very cheap, almost in fact, a nominal rent. The owners were a young couple who were friends of our captain.

These new lodgings made things much easier for me, as I had to be available on board at very short notice. Now the shipyard was working all night, as apparently *Porpoise* was needed in a hurry. Weird contraptions began to arrive on the dockside, addressed for us. Among these were twelve one thousand gallon oil containers, which were fitted with wheels and could be stored on the rails in the mine casing. These could be connected together by siphon pipes to form one long fuel tank. It required little imagination to guess what they would be used for. Malta at this time was in a very serious plight, having been besieged for several months. Convoys endeavouring to get through were suffering very heavy losses, as the enemy dominated the air from both north and south, practically the whole of the North African coast being in their hands.

Apart from all the other paraphernalia we were taking, we embarked in our already well laden mine casing, eight 4000lb bombs, each in a separate watertight container, doubtless to be off loaded at Malta. These would be a further headache for our First Lieutenant when setting the trim.

The tail end of this relatively short refit was even more hectic than normal, especially as we had to embark our new fuel tanks before doing main engine and diving trials. Inexperienced dockyard workmen, and our own new people didn't help matters, but the trials were successful, and we crossed to the Holy Loch, to embark stores, fuel, torpedoes and ammunition from *Titania.*

No sooner had we arrived alongside *Titania* than we had yet another change of C.O.'s. 'Happy Jack' Hopkins was relieved by Commander E.F. Pizey, who had already been awarded a DSO for his exploits as C.O. of *Oberon*. Tall and handsome, he was a fine and experienced captain.

I suggested to Clare that she came over to Dunoon for the few days before we left. The lady who had boarded us previously was fully booked but she let us have a small cottage back in the hills behind Hunters Quay, it was a delightful little cottage set entirely in woodlands, and away from it all, so completely peaceful, with birds and squirrels all around us. I felt as though I would like to spend the rest of my life there.

It was as well that Clare had stayed on, because in the event, those two or three extra days that we expected to be together, turned out to be ten days. We did not count the extra cost, life was at a very low premium in the Mediterranean, and that apparently, was where we were going.

We had a few days at sea to 'shake down' the practically all-new crew, diving and exercising in a protected area. Some of these lads were new to the navy, let alone submarines. When a boat was commissioned, either when new or after a refit, there would normally be a 'working up period' of two to three weeks, followed by a patrol somewhere where it wasn't 'too hot'. But we were now immediately required for the real thing – it was the Mediterranean for us!

Came the day to sail I bid a fond but very sad farewell to Clare. What a terribly worrying time it was for her. We didn't discuss it very much but she had a pretty shrewd idea of what my chances were. The poor girl was left to settle our bill for the cottage then find her way to Glasgow where she would catch the next uncomfortable and blacked out train to London, and thence to Plymouth where my mother was looking after Joan.

We sailed with an escort, and remained on the surface through the Irish Sea. . The weather was perfect, the sky was cloudless, and it was difficult to realize that we were at war – was this the calm before the storm perhaps? When we reached the north Cornish coast, just abreast of Perranporth where I'd spent part of my honeymoon, we signalled our escort for permission to carry out a diving exercise before we finally parted company. This we then did, with our escort standing by ready to inform any approaching aircraft that we were a friendly submarine.

We took her down on a 'crash dive', and the results were anything but reassuring. The dive was repeated two or three time, but I knew that if we didn't improve our performance, then we certainly wouldn't last very long in the Mediterranean.

Bidding farewell to our escort – I think that in peacetime she was the Duke of Westminster's private yacht, her captain flashed us a signal of good luck and then we were on our own. We surfaced at night and dived by day, the usual wartime routine, changing night into day for mealtimes, 'up spirits' being at about six bells in the First Watch, with dinner at about midnight.

The interior of any submarine is very complex, with it's maze of pipe systems and valves, and so much machinery crowded into such a small space, but even so, some of our new people seemed to me to be taking an awfully long time to master their own particular jobs. On several occasions the wrong valves were opened or shut in error. I became so concerned for our safety that I forsook my bunk and slept on a mattress on the forward plates of the engine room – that is, at the very few times that I had a chance to sleep during the next couple of months – making just brief visits to the mess for meals, and the chance to get away from the infernal din of the engines for a while.

Porpoise had always been awkward to handle at periscope depth in a long following sea. Presumably this was a characteristic of her class due to her large mine casing. Whenever she came to periscope depth, unless drastic counter action was quickly taken it was a pretty safe bet that she would try to continue her upward trend until the periscope standards were awash. 'Q' tank had to be flooded, and main motors 'grouped up' to increase her speed. These following sea conditions existed as we crossed the Bay of Biscay, and the captain gave orders that if the boat came to twenty-seven feet, 'Q' tank was to be flooded and main motors were to be run 'grouped up' at full ahead in order to regain thirty-two feet as quickly as possible.

A spurious upward movement had to be arrested several times during each day, the extra ten tons of seawater in 'Q' tank being quickly blown with high-pressure air as soon as periscope depth was again reached. But on one particular occasion it was unfortunate that the officer of the 1st dog watch belatedly flooded 'Q' when *Porpoise* was already on her way down, with motors grouped up at full speed ahead and planes set to hard to dive. Consequently with a bow down angle, and now being ten tons heavy, we continued our decent to a depth far greater than that intended.

I don't think that I've ever seen anyone move quite as quickly as our captain did at that time. He had reached the control room in a flash, issuing a stream of orders to halt this descent and to get us back on depth. One learnt to get out of the way of these chaps when they were in 'full cry'. When the captain unceremoniously pushed the O.O.W. aside in the control room, the depth gauge needle was passing one hundred feet, and we still had a bow down angle of over ten degrees. The captain barked out orders. 'Blow 'Q'. - Stop together. - Blow number 1 main ballast.' We were now passing two hundred feet and still going down – two hundred and fifty feet was our maximum safe depth. Despite the fact that there is usually a temperature layer, where water is colder (and consequently denser) between two hundred and two hundred and fifty feet, we still continued our plunge, until we finally acquired a bow up angle when our stern was at three hundred and fifty feet.

It was as well that our downward trend was arrested at this depth, where the pressure on our ¾ inch high tensile steel hull was one hundred and fifty five lbs per square inch, *Porpoise's* working depth was limited to two hundred and fifty feet (pressure 110 lbs per square inch) due to a class weakness. By design, the after part of the pressure hull on this class of boat was slightly elliptical instead of circular, this was in order to accommodate the mine casing, and was later modified on the remainder of the class, but not *Porpoise*. On later examination we found that the three hundred and fifty feet that we had reached was indeed too deep, as the four 4 inch steel supports fitted aft to counteract this weakness, were all badly bent.

On our arrival at Gibraltar the dockyard staff cut away these bent stanchions and fitted new ones. In doing this it was discovered that the hull had collapsed by nearly ½ an inch. This of course, further weakened us, and subsequently we were ordered not to exceed a depth of two hundred feet.

This was a very bad start to our period of work in the Mediterranean; two hundred feet was no great depth and gave us little scope to 'go deep' when evasive action was required. Moreover, my previous experience in these clear waters told me that on a calm day, it was possible to see a submarine at nearly that depth. The whole affair had left me with the uncomfortable feeling that *Porpoise* was now seriously handicapped by this structural weakness. At that time the Germans had submarines that were capable of depths up to one thousand feet, and after calculating that with our control room at two hundred feet and a bow up angle set at twenty degrees, with *Porpoise's* overall length of two hundred and eighty five feet, her stern would be at two hundred and fifty feet anyway, I felt even more uncomfortable!

Our main propulsion shaft alignment was also affected to some degree, but there were no noticeable problems such as overheating bearings, thrust blocks or stern glands, nor did it appear that the alignment of the mine rails was seriously affected. These rails were to be used extensively during the next eighteen months, either for laying mines, or for our newly fitted fuel tanks.

Having had our four support stanchions renewed, we discharged all but eighty tons of our own diesel fuel, this being sufficient to take us to Malta and onward to Alexandria. We then embarked over one hundred and twenty tons of aviation spirit, which would be discharged when we reached Malta. Every nook and cranny aboard us was filled with foodstuffs and other vital supplies for the beleaguered island. There were hundreds of boxes of ammunition for the use of the very few aircraft (Hurricanes) that helped to protect the island, and for the anti-aircraft guns. Much of this ammunition was stowed behind the main engines, making access almost impossible. Normally this impediment to the access of moving machinery would be intolerable to an engineer officer and would never be permitted, he would insist, 'not without orders in writing', but this was an urgent requirement, and as such had to be accepted.

We were in Gibraltar for several days, and much to my surprise were given shore leave. Although the Gibraltarians themselves were very loyal and patriotic, by the very nature of its geographical position Gibraltar must have been infested with spies. Spain could see and almost hear, everything that went on in or around 'Gib', certainly all arrivals and departures. Spain though neutral, was at that time very sympathetic to the Nazis, and to fascist Italy, and was a hotbed of international intrigue. It would not have surprised me if the enemy knew exactly our mission as soon as we arrived at 'Gib', but we did hope that they would not know of our time of departure.

We had very little trouble with the behaviour of our crew while at Gibraltar, except that one chap, and I regret to say that he was a junior engine room rating, tried to 'jump ship'. In fact we did sail one man short, but he was soon found ashore and bundled on the next submarine leaving for Malta. I was pleased that he did not rejoin *Porpoise.*

Carrying out a trim dive in the basin before leaving, we found that owing to all this additional weight, our internal trim and compensating tanks were practically empty, leaving the First Lieutenant very little scope for the adjustment of his trim. Fuel oil used during the trip would automatically be replaced by seawater, thus making us a little heavier, but the Chief Stoker still gave the First Lieutenant twelve hourly fuel consumption figures and the density of the seawater (which could vary considerably), so that he could make the trim adjustments. The greater density of the seawater in the 'Med' was compensated for largely by the temperature, warmer water being less dense. One factor in our favour was that the hundred and twenty tons of aviation spirit was a little lighter than the equal quantity of diesel oil fuel that we would otherwise have been carrying.

Malta was at that time in a very precarious position, having the enemy occupied territories of France, Italy and Sicily (and later Greece), to the north of her, and North Africa to the south of her. She was constantly under heavy bombing attacks and had only a few Hurricane fighters to defend her. The approach channels between Pantellaria and Sicily were mined, and enemy aircraft and submarines were lying in wait for blockade-runners like ourselves. Several heavily escorted convoys from each end of the 'Med' had been badly mauled while endeavouring to run the gauntlet of these blockades, one or two attempts ending in near annihilation. On one occasion just one solitary tanker got through, and even she was very badly damaged. Great damage and losses were also suffered by the escorting warships.

Two or three larger submarines, including *Olympus* and our sister ship *Cachalot* had already broken through, laden as we were, but the contribution they carried, although vitally important, was minute when compared to the overall needs of the Island.

W e proceeded toward Malta using the usual routine of diving by day and surfacing at night until we neared the highly dangerous passage between Sicily and Pantellaria where we were ordered to remain dived for twenty-four hours. With fully charged batteries, and at a speed of three to four knots we could cover about ninety miles in twenty-four hours. This would take us reasonably clear of the danger area and within a hundred miles of Malta. But by then we would have very flat batteries, and we would then have to surface during the early hours in order to put on a charge.

Malta had to be approached very carefully through swept channels, as the approaches to the harbour were heavily mined, not only by us but also by the enemy. There was certainly no room here for navigational errors. As far as I can remember we weren't given an escort, probably because there wasn't one available. These approaches through sanctuaries or swept channels, both to Malta and Alexandria, were quite nerve racking. I hope that I didn't betray to the crew the awful suspense that I felt, but they probably felt the same, especially those who had a more intimate appreciation of the situation.

However we arrived safely and finally made our way into the Grand Harbour, securing alongside in Marsa Creek in preparation for the discharge of our precious cargo. This wasn't exactly a straightforward task because we had several interruptions with air raids, and having now been spotted by the enemy we knew that we would get no respite from our work until this highly inflammable cargo was safely offloaded. It was going to be a long and difficult job, because we dare not show any lights. Then we had trouble with the fuel connections, the adaptors provided for us had a different type of screw thread than the shore connection. Eventually we were ordered to slip and leave Grand Harbour, to proceed to a billet just outside the harbour where we could dive and sit on the seabed at about a hundred and twenty feet, while the dockyard manufactured a new adaptor. It took us nearly three nights to discharge all our cargo, then without any shore leave we departed Malta and headed for Alexandria, where we were to embark a similar cargo.

Any diesel fuel except that required for the nine hundred and fifty mile trip to 'Alex' was left behind for the hard pressed 10th flotilla which were operating from

Malta, performing the vital task of attacking enemy convoys which were supplying Rommel's armies in North Africa.

I would very much have liked to have had just one run ashore in Malta, if only to see whether our old familiar landmarks were still there. However, a run ashore would have to wait. At least it was good to know that we were able to help Malta in her hour of need.

Our meagre fuel allowance left us very little scope to attack any enemy shipping that we might see on our way to 'Alex'. Rigid economy was the order of the day, and this tight fuel situation was to cause the engine room staff quite a few headaches in the coming days, and not a few grey hairs. Now that we had discharged our cargo at Malta, we did have permission to attack selected targets, but we were not able to stray very far from our main course or we would never have made it back to 'Alex'.

We duly reached 'Alex, where *HMS Medway* was the parent ship to a large mixed 1st Submarine Flotilla, which was commanded by Captain 'Sammy' Raw, later relieved by Captain P. Ruck-Keene. *Medway* had left China for the 'Med' in 1940, bringing with her fifteen 'chicks'. Alas these were the rather large and cumbersome ocean going 'O', 'P' and 'R' classes, which were ill fitted for the closed waters of the Mediterranean. Within a few weeks of their arrival *Odin*, *Orpheus* and *Phoenix* had been lost, and just before we arrived, my old boat *Oswald* was added to this list, as well as *Regulus* and *Rainbow*. My friend 'Fred' Bussey with whom I had fought many a losing battle over fifty and a hundred yards, was the C.E.R.A. of *Rainbow*.

The 1st Submarine Flotilla now in the main comprised 'T' class boats, of which *Turbulent* was one; her C.O. was the popular 'Tubby' Linton who was later posthumously awarded a V.C. for his distinguished record in the 'Med', being credited with nearly a hundred and fifty thousand tons of enemy shipping before *Turbulent* was lost.

Actually *Medway* had more submarines than she could really accommodate, at least as far as personnel were concerned, and once again *Porpoise's* E.R.A.'s, indeed most of her crew, found themselves living aboard the boat.

We were kept so busy that there was little opportunity to absorb any news from the other theatres of war. I knew that Germany had declared war on Russia, if indeed 'declared war' was the correct term; Germany it seems, merely overran a country, with little sense of reason. Of Russia's military strength I had no idea, but I did know that they had many millions of men, and vaguely thought that the move to invade Russia wasn't a very shrewd one from Germany's point of view. However, as nothing seemed to prevent Hitler's progress into the very heart of Russia, the move could perhaps be justified.

Other unpleasant news was that Crete had now been invaded by the Germans, and that our garrison there appeared to be fighting a losing battle. Within a few weeks we were forced to evacuate the Island, suffering severe losses in doing so, not only in personnel and equipment, but also in warships while trying to get the troops away. Our 'K' class destroyers bore the brunt, *HMS Kelly* whose captain was the Earl Mountbatten, was among the ships sunk. *HMS Kendaher* was also lost, her C.E.R.A , my friend 'Ginger' Symons, being a survivor. 'Ginger' had a pretty tough time, and I was later able to visit him in hospital in 'Alex'. He subsequently recovered, to be promoted to Temporary Warrant Engineer, but I didn't see him again until after the war, when Clare and I were his guests at a ships dance in *HMS Defiance*.

Rommel, after a couple of minor setbacks, was in full cry along the North African front, and getting mighty close to 'Alex'. Tobruk was besieged, and Malta was taking a terrible pounding. The 10th Submarine Flotilla, although doing splendid work harassing the enemy supply lines, were themselves suffering heavy losses.

If we had cause to feel miserable in 1940, then 1941 afforded no relief. In fact the chain of events during that year were catastrophic. I have no intention to chronicle these events, but merely to give some idea of the 'backs to the wall' situation that we were in.

German submarines sank the aircraft carrier *Ark Royal*, and the battleship *Barham*, each with a heavy loss of life. The battleships *Queen Elizabeth* and my old ship the *Valiant* had both been badly damaged by a brilliant Italian midget submarine attack in Alexandria harbour. *HMS Hood*, my father's old ship and the pride of the British navy, had been sunk in an encounter with Germany's most modern battleship *Bismark*. The odds had seemed pretty even when *Hood* and our latest battleship *Prince of Wales* met up with *Bismark* and the large cruiser *Prinz Eugen*, but almost as soon as the action commenced, a 15" salvo from *Bismark* penetrated *Hood's* magazine. There was an almighty explosion and *Hood* simply disappeared, with a terrible loss of life. Only three out of nearly two thousand men survived. The sinking of the fast moving *Hood*, thought to be the last thing in battle cruisers, was a tremendous loss, but the effect on the countries morale was equally devastating.

The *Prince of Wales*, which was then barely beyond her working up period, was ordered to break off the engagement in order to shadow the enemy. *Bismark* had to be sunk at all costs, or she would wreak complete havoc on our North Atlantic convoys. And sink her we did, although it took nearly the whole of the Home Fleet to round her up.

Toward the end of 1941 the Japanese carried out a surprise attack on the U.S. Pacific Fleet at Pearl Harbour, and almost annihilated it. Now a state of war existed between Japan and the United States. As Germany and Italy sided with Japan, we were now 'all in the soup' together, and the well prepared Japanese forces lost no time in pursuing their initial successes, accordingly they commenced an invasion of all U.S., British, French and Dutch colonies and possessions in the Far East. Hong Kong soon fell, and Japan continued a rapid advance through French and Indo-China toward Singapore.

Prince of Wales and *Repulse* were dispatched to augment the Far Eastern fleet. They hadn't been there much more than a 'dog-watch' when a further calamity occurred. These two large and fast warships were proceeding on an easterly direction together with three escorting destroyers, when they were caught by wave upon wave of Japanese dive bombers and sunk. This was indeed a terrible loss, especially as more than eight hundred of their crew perished. The destroyers, themselves being attacked but presenting much more difficult targets, picked up many of the survivors who were then taken back to Singapore. My brother-in-law Reg Lockley, was the Senior Engineer of *Prince of Wales*, and had remained in her engine room until it became untenable due to escaping super-heated steam. Bringing the last of his stalwarts to the upper deck, the bomb that then blew him overboard, killed most of the party who had kept the engines going until the last possible minute.

Badly burned, wounded by shell splinters and practically unconscious, Reg was picked out of the water by one of the destroyers, and taken with the other survivors to Singapore. Luckily for him, he was flown out of Singapore before it fell to the Japanese hordes, when most of the other survivors were taken prisoner, consequently enduring much hardship and ill treatment at the hands of their captors.

Reg Lockley never spoke much of this disastrous action, nor of his personal experiences, but much later I overheard a conversation between two Petty Officers, one of whom was a survivor from the last party of men to leave the engine room. Apparently Reg had been heroic in his efforts to keep the engines running. There were no decorations awarded to either crew because the ships were lost, but there must have been many brave acts in the fight to stave off those Japanese dive-bombers. Four of the crew of the *Prince of Wales* were mentioned in dispatches, and Reg was one of them.

These many reverses in our fortunes had of course, a very demoralizing effect upon all of us, there was no doubt that we were well and truly on the receiving end. Even so, I can't say that I ever gave up hope, although it did seem that only a miracle could save us at that time. There was however one ray of hope - in that the country was being led by that extraordinary man, Winston Churchill. He was a constant tower of strength, and quite refused to admit defeat. I am sure that there was no other man at that time who could have inspired us to continue our tasks when all looked so black and hopeless.

If I have painted a pretty dismal picture of the general situation from Britain's standpoint in 1941, it was as most of us saw it, although perhaps it was as well that we had little time to reflect upon it. The German jackboot was grinding us to destruction; the whole 'free world' was in deadly peril. But timely encouraging words from our intrepid Prime Minister, who refused to be cowed by these onslaughts and reverses, gave us heart to fight on.

Porpoise was very soon making the return trip to Malta, laden once more with a precious cargo of fuel (mostly aviation high octane spirit), ammunition and food. I was pleased to leave Alexandria as I neither cared for the city nor felt at home with its inhabitants.

With the exception of special missions to Malta, or any 'cloak and dagger' operations, submarines of the flotilla usually patrolled for about twenty-one days, returning to base for eight to ten days between each patrol in order to carry out repairs and maintenance in preparation for the next one. For us it was normal patrol routine en-route, except that whilst heavily laden with cargo we were forbidden to make attacks unless we received specific orders to do so. The passage after leaving 'Alex' was fairly humdrum everyday routine; it was the approach to Malta that worried us. We had to time ourselves so that we didn't arrive during the hours of darkness (on account of the boom defences). On the other hand we didn't wish to get caught by aircraft while on the surface in the swept channel. Channels had to be swept daily because the enemy was constantly dropping mines. It wasn't very amusing to have to dive in a hurry in order to escape enemy bombs when we knew that there were mines not very far to port or starboard. Added to this of course, was the knowledge that we had these tanks up above us in the mine casing, carrying ten thousand gallons of high-octane spirit, we were in essence a floating bomb, a factor which one could hardly forget. In some circumstances we would make our approach dived, almost to the harbour entrance, constantly taking periscope bearings of known points on the island to assure ourselves that we were still in the swept channel. This again was very tricky because we did not wish to be taken for an enemy submarine. It was always a tremendous relief to get secured up alongside, even though, as we rarely discharged our cargo at the same place, we were constantly harassed with different fuel connections, and the problems of almost always having to carry out the discharge operation during the hours of darkness.

This time I did get ashore and visited the E.R.A.'s club. I found that it was still functioning, but under great difficulty. Obviously we were unable to get any food there, nor for that matter, could we get much to drink. Our faithful and popular Maltese stewards Tony and Manuel, were still there, and were delighted to see us, and it was a great credit to those concerned that the club continued to function financially as there was very little trade. But still the rent, and the small numbers of staff had to be paid.

It was really heartrending to witness the devastation of Malta, and the state of its inhabitants; they really were very hungry. The few dogs that I saw were merely skin and bones. I understood that our E.R.A.'s Club was the only club on the island still functioning. The R.N. Officers Club in Strada Reale and the R.N. Writers Club in Sliema, the White Ensign in Valetta and the R.N. Canteen at Corradina were all wrecked by air raids, and so I think that the E.R.A.'s Club extended its hospitality to most senior ratings and officers.

131

Knowing that no food could be obtained ashore, we took the precaution of taking sandwiches ashore with us. Needless to say we did not partake of these ourselves, it was a great pleasure to give them to those who needed them much more than we did. Tony and Manuel had their share of course.

As a result of this visit we brought a lot more than a few sandwiches when we next visited Malta. Chocolate, cigarettes, tins of food, and even potatoes were stowed in our private lockers to dispense when we arrived at Malta. Most was purchased at our NAAFI canteen in *Medway*, but we augmented the supply by eating sparingly en-route, for let me point out that we rarely went short of good food in submarines. The food might not have been of the fresh variety, but there was always an ample supply of tinned and dried food. Strictly speaking we were not allowed to give our own rations away, but under these circumstances the normal rules were relaxed, or at least, 'blind eyes were turned', and even the odd tot of rum (saved from our daily rations), was taken ashore.

With regard to the cigarettes, chocolates and other luxuries purchased at the canteen, this was a heavy financial drain on our pockets, and so they were mostly sold for the price that we paid for them. Although there was no food ashore and very little to drink, it was still good to get off the boat at night and sleep in a comfortable bed. We were given the occasional night leave, the duty watch and selected members of the crew then having to cope with the unloading of the cargo.

It was rarely that I saw any of my friends of the 10th flotilla, although my old friend Les Honeywill, and many others were out there. The C.O. of the 10th flotilla was none other than *Porpoise's* C.O. at the outbreak of war, Captain 'Shrimp' Simpson. We did not forget these people either, when we brought our luxuries out from 'Alex'.

We mostly discharged our cargo either in Grand Harbour, or at Marsa Sirocco on the southeast corner of the island. During the day we were allocated a 'bottoming billet' outside the harbour in about a hundred and twenty feet of water. This was tedious, but at least it gave us a good period of sleep, ready for our busy time at night. But even then, while lying on the bottom we were not immune, and were constantly disturbed by all kinds of peculiar noises. It seemed that the enemy knew what was happening, and had adopted the practice of dropping a few random depth charges in the hope of getting us.

Before we went to lie on the bottom I would dash ashore to find out what type of fuel connection was to be used, so that whilst we were lying doggo during the day, the dockyard or submarine base staff would manufacture the required adaptor ready to connect up after surfacing at night.

The reason for these 'bottoming' precautions was that several boats had been damaged and two or three lost during air attacks, most of our fighters being grounded through shortage of fuel. *Pandora* was dive-bombed and sunk while alongside in Dockyard Creek; most of her crew escaped, but my friend C.E.R.A. Jim Colborne was killed while making an attempt to save the boat from sinking. *P36* was also sunk in harbour, and it was the survivors of these two boats who then lost their lives in *Olympus,* which was subsequently lost on the way back to the U.K. The Greek submarine *Glenkes was* also sunk in Dockyard Creek, we could see her conning tower still above the water, while we were discharging our cargo. Another interesting sight in Malta dockyard at that time, was the two halves of the destroyer *Havoc* in dry-dock. She had either been torpedoed or mined, and the dockyard was now in the throes of welding the two halves together again. It had been a truly magnificent achievement to get the two halves of the ship back into harbour, and great credit was due to her crew.

Whilst we were in the dockyard I seized the opportunity to rescue my spare gear (pistons, cylinder heads etc.) from the badly blitzed storehouses. The authorities were extremely pleased to get rid of it, and the extra weight helped us with our trim on the return trip to 'Alex'. When we reached 'Alex' we transferred this spare gear to the *Medway's* store. None of the gear was suitable for the 10th flotilla, but much of it was applicable to the 'O', 'P' and 'R' classes.

Despite our recent refit at Troon, we were still having a lot of piston trouble with the main engines. This was the same old snag – metal fatigue, but there was little that we could do about it, as any replacements from the depot ship seemed to suffer with the same problem. Many times we had to sling a piston at sea. This entailed bringing a defective piston to the top of its stroke, disconnecting and removing the huge crank head bearing, securing the piston and connecting rod, and then running the engine on seven cylinders only. It was a tricky job, especially in any sort of sea, but as we were always in a hurry, it was quicker than changing a piston complete.

The 'slinging' of a piston also meant that when the engine was restarted, it would be running out of balance. Not only were we firing on just seven cylinders, but also the crankshaft would be five or six hundredweight out of balance. The vibration caused by this was quite alarming, and both the engine and the shaft were subjected to all kinds of strain. This recurring engine fault meant that besides all other jobs carried out when we returned to harbour there was inevitably a piston or a cylinder liner to be changed.

If I did go ashore with the lads, I could still never be sure of being free from trouble. There were six E.R.A.'s in our mess, and both they and myself were a hardworking lot, but with so much time spent at sea, we were probably getting a little touchy. After a few drinks, 'Jock' Forrest and 'Taff' Hughes would invariably 'set to' thumping one another. This might have been great fun for them, getting it off their chests as it were, but it was a pain in the neck for me. To start with, it could be a very precarious operation separating them. But I had had much experience of these situations over the years, and with the help of a couple of messmates we would bundle them into two separate horse drawn vehicles, and set them off shipwards – in opposite directions. Next morning, despite the odd black eye or swollen lip, they'd be the best of friends. 'Bert' Shute had left us before we sailed from the U.K. so at least there was one less problem that I had to worry about.

As *Medway* was unable to provide the aviation spirit that we needed for our Malta run, we most always had to proceed to Haifa, or sometimes to Port Said first. Just in harbour long enough to fuel and store, there would be no shore leave, primarily because of the secrecy of our mission. On one occasion we even shipped a destroyer's propeller shaft in the after end of our mine casing. This weighed several tons, and it was very tricky to load through the mine doors without damaging our intricate mine-laying equipment.

This high-octane spirit was terrible stuff to have in our fuel tanks. Glands and joints that would not normally leak with diesel fuel, now leaked profusely, and had either to be tightened or the joint renewed with more suitable packing. There was a perpetual smell of this spirit in the engine room, which then permeated throughout the whole boat, particularly after we had discharged our cargo. One could come off watch feeling quite intoxicated, and our engines ran as though they were supercharged, which of course they were. I considered this situation to be highly dangerous, and strictly forbade smoking in the engine room. After discharging aviation spirit, we flooded the tanks three times with seawater to clean them and to get rid of any residual vapour. We would then leave these tanks flooded.

Later, in an effort to make more room for stores, it was decided to remove the whole of one of our main batteries, which weighed about fifty tons. This of course helped with the trimming problem on the outward journey when we were in ballast, but not after we had discharged our cargo. It also of course, restricted our electrical reserves and our dived speed. We weren't a great deal of use for attacking enemy shipping with only two batteries, but it appeared that our most important role was blockade running, and so that was our priority. However we did carry out a few patrols in the Aegean Sea prior to having one battery removed.

It was during one of these patrols that we sighted two large enemy merchantmen escorted by three anti-submarine vessels. They were in a position and travelling at a speed that prevented us from getting within a three-mile range, so this was going to have to be a long-range attack with the likelihood of a hit rather remote, especially as they were zigzagging. Our captain unleashed four torpedoes, and we went deep. Within the prescribed period of about four and a half minutes we heard an explosion which must have been a hit on one of the vessels, but prior to that we heard what any submariner dreads, the sound of one of our own torpedoes running amok; first it passed close to our bows, and then passed almost directly above us before finally receding into the distance astern of us. I had had this experience previously, but that was in peacetime when there wasn't seven hundred pounds of high explosive in the nose of the torpedo.

Although the torpedo was set to run at eight feet below the surface the steering had obviously gone awry, and there was no guarantee that the depth mechanism wasn't faulty as well, so the torpedo might well be running at a hundred feet, about the same depth as we were at. This was a petrifying experience, certainly just as terrifying as hearing an enemy torpedo running overhead. It was as well that we weren't using the acoustic or magnetic torpedoes that the Germans had already developed.

Having registered our hit on the enemy, the resultant counter attack was very feeble. The remaining merchantman scuttled away very quickly, leaving the escorts to pick up any survivors. We often found that after we had carried out a successful attack, the enemy was so concerned with their own troubles that we escaped 'scott free'. Dropping depth charges within six hundred yards of survivors in the water would probably kill them. Moreover, it was much more difficult to detect us when a ship was sinking and making all sorts of underwater noises such as boiler explosions and watertight bulkheads creaking and collapsing. But on the other hand if we missed, then we knew that we were in for a hiding, as the tracks of the torpedo would invariably give away our position.

After three or four of these blockade-running trips to Malta, Commander 'Bert' Pizey was relieved by Lieutenant L.W.S. 'Benny' Bennington DSC. This seemed a big downgrading of seniority for such a large submarine, but owing to heavy losses many senior submarine officers were required for administrative duties. We were sorry to lose Cdr Pizey, a most efficient and experienced C.O. who inspired confidence, a valuable asset at this juncture. However, with our new captain being 'Benny' Bennington, of the old 2nd submarine flotilla days, we had no reason for concern. 'Benny had a wealth of experience. Our other officers were Lt. E.A. Hobson as First Lieutenant, Lt. 'Johnny' Pope, Torpedo Officer. Lt. Chris Thurlow. RNR. Navigator. Lt. J.M. 'Steady Boy' Steadman RNR, in charge of mine lying, and Lt (E). 'Jerry' Kirkby, my boss. A good team! The whole crew was now settling down and becoming very efficient.

We had a fair degree of success on the few war patrols that we did carry out, mostly on our return passages from Malta. 'Benny's ice cool brain and extraordinary judgment accounted for several enemy ships. I have previously pointed out the difficulties of achieving a successful attack, especially when the enemy, protected by several shallow draft anti-submarine vessels, is zigzagging. Also it didn't help matters that in those days the submarine itself had to be pointing in the right direction for the torpedoes to be fired. Enemy and own ship information given out by the control room calculator ('fruit machine'), and by the hydrophone operator, was continuously relayed to the captain. ASDICS were rarely used during an attack, as in the active (pinging) mode these could be detected by the enemy who, even suspecting the presence of a submarine would constantly change course while heading away.

'Benny' seemed to rely largely on his own superb judgment, and in one inspired period scored three hits on three separate enemy ships out of four torpedoes fired. Normally a 25% score was deemed to be good. If a ship were considered worth it, the captain would fire a spread of three, four or even six torpedoes in the hope of getting one or two hits, each torpedo being fired at an interval of about three seconds.

However, our main purpose was still to provide supplies to Malta. Malta was in a pretty bad way by now, with most of the population living much of their time underground. Large areas of the island were completely demolished by bombing, especially around the area of Grand Harbour, and it was a continuous struggle to keep the two airfields open so that our own aircraft could use them.

On one return passage we were ordered to carry out a short patrol. The Italian fleet had ventured out and had been sighted off the Italian coast. As we had nothing near at hand to engage them, *Porpoise* was ordered toward them. Steering in a north-easterly direction on the surface and at full speed, it wasn't long before we were spotted by enemy aircraft and had to dive quickly as that type of aircraft were known to carry three or four depth charges. When the planes had vanished we surfaced and continued at full speed toward the enemy fleet (barely making fifteen knots, as we were due for a docking). This diving and surfacing due to enemy aircraft was repeated many times in broad daylight until the Italians were probably under the impression that a whole flotilla of submarines was heading toward them. But we didn't even get a glimpse of their smoke before darkness fell. Possibly our chase had been a ruse to head them off toward our own ships, although there were precious few of those around. Later we received a signal instructing us to leave the chase and continue on our way to Alexandria.

Having the responsibility of maintaining the engines to the level that would give the captain full power whenever he required it, I loathed this full power – crash dive succession, inevitable though it was. We were already having piston and liner trouble, and this full power to stop, and then back to full power again was not conducive to efficient running and maintaining steady temperatures. Although there was a system provided to circulate engine-cooling water when dived, this could not usually be used, as more often than not we would immediately shut off for depth charging after diving. Consequently after about three or four of these 'crash dives' the engine cooling water was just about boiling, and the temperature in the engine room almost unbearable. However, in wartime there was scant respect paid to the economical and careful running of the engines, it was up to those responsible to nurse them as much as possible.

Wise and sympathetic C.O.'s would only order full speed when it was really necessary, realizing that it was futile to 'kill the golden goose'. A good E.O. on the other hand, would see that his C.O. was given all the speed that he required, at the same time endeavouring not to put too much of a prolonged strain on the engines. One E.O. friend of mine gave his unsympathetic C.O. more revolutions than he should and seized all the pistons on one engine, which then put them in an extremely dangerous position, but more about that later.

This particular return trip to 'Alex' involved more than this emergency call; we were next instructed to patrol around the southern coast of Italy, a patrol which

HMSM *L52*. A double-gun L-Class. The author's first submarine

The 2nd Submarine Flotilla leaving Loch Ewe after extensive torpedo exercises

HMSM *Oswald* crossing the line ceremony south of Borneo

HMSM *Oswald* surfacing in Hong Kong harbour after an uncomfortable 24 hours on the seabed. The temperature inside the submarine was 150 deg F. with no air conditioning

The result of a heavy Italian air attack on Senglea, Malta. British forces could only make limited resistance, due to a lack of fighter aircraft, fuel and ammunition.

HMSM *Porpoise* sinks an enemy supply ship by gunfire. She fired several shells alarmingly close to the submarine, before her gun was silenced.

HMSM *Porpoise's* Captain Lt. W.L.A. Bennington presses home his attack. An old friend of the author, 'Benny' was unerring with his torpedoes.

The '*Porpoise* Carrier Service' - Thousands of tons of fuel, food and ammunition for the relief of Malta.

'Benny' brings *Porpoise* safely back to Britain.

Porpoise's CERA, his seven stalwart ERA's and our messman. They were Irish, Scots, Welsh, English and Cornish.

HMSM *Strongbow* L to R. C.O. Lt. J.A.R. Troup, S/Lt. McAlpine RNVR, E.O. J.C.E. Blamey (author), S/Lt. J. Annear RNVR, Lt. P.H.B. Minchiner and RN, Lt. E. Harding RNR. This photo was taken after a severe depth charging while on patrol in the Malacca Straits.

Captain 'Jacky' Slaughter's departing present with *Montclare's* craftsmen who made it. CERA 'Bill' Burdon is on the extreme right.

HMSM *Sidon* on sonar buoy exercises off Falmouth, Cornwall.

The author and his wife, Clare Blamey on their way to the HMS *Raleigh* annual ball, just before he left submarines in 1954.

eventually proved to be the longest period I'd spent at sea up to this time. It was thirty-five days from the time we left Malta to the time we arrived alongside *Medway*. This was five whole weeks without seeing daylight for some of us. We had given the 10th flotilla all the diesel fuel we could spare, but had since travelled a long way off course, much of it at an uneconomical full speed, and we were now desperately short of fuel. We were more than a hundred miles from 'Alex' when our very reliable chief stoker gave us the warning.

This was very worrying indeed; we would have been in a 'right mess' if we were stranded on the surface unable to dive because our batteries were flat, especially as the enemy were known to have submarines patrolling the approaches to Alexandria; we really would have been a sitting duck.

We changed from one oil fuel tank to another, getting the last dregs of fuel out of each, and then even took a suction on the engine room bilges in order to retrieve the few extra gallons that would have leaked from the fuel pumps since we had left Malta. Normally we would have remained dived by day until we were close to the sanctuary, but that would not have been economical. We even ceased to zigzag, in order to cover the distance more quickly. We would have been a fine target for any lurking enemy U-boat. But again we lived to tell the tale.

On our return journeys from Malta we often carried several passengers who were due to leave the island, this helped to compensate for the loss of weight. On one occasion an R.N. lay reader was billeted in the E.R.A.'s mess, a Mr. Gracey, and a very fine chap he was. I hope that our language didn't shock him too much. He was going to take up an appointment at the Seaman's Mission in Alexandria. These trips must have been terribly uncomfortable and very nerve racking for passengers who were not accustomed to the conditions. However, they had all already had a pretty hectic time of it in Malta, and only had to endure our mode of existence for eight or nine days. Most of the passengers were accommodated in the empty battery tank, which was pretty grim, although one could at least stand almost upright in this huge tank, and there was adequate ventilation, the same air being circulated when dived as for the rest of us.

When carrying a V.I.P. our mess man would have to doss down wherever he could, usually on a camp bed under the table. So if the klaxon sounded we'd have to be very careful where we landed when we jumped out of our bunks, especially as the lighting was dimmed - usually just one red bulb.

Toward the end of April 1942 the situation in Malta became so grave that it became untenable for the 10th Submarine Flotilla, and they were ordered to Alexandria. The crews were getting no rest at all; returning after three or four weeks of nerve racking patrol, often damaged by depth charges, they'd either have to spend most of the short spell before the next patrol underground or on the bottom of Lazaretto Creek dodging air raids. *Porpoise* had discharged yet another cargo, and had departed from Malta at the same time. We did not contact any of the 10th flotilla en route as they were probably ordered to do a short patrol before proceeding to 'Alex'. However all of them arrived in 'Alex' at about the same time, except the unfortunate *Urge*, (C.O. Lt. Cdr. Tomlinson D.S.O. and whose C.E.R.A. was 'Tommo' Toms D.S.M..). *Medway* now had a few more chicks to care for.

I think the crews must have been accommodated ashore, as they could not live aboard their boats as we did; the 'U' and 'V' classes were only about 650 tons. However, this did not work out very satisfactorily; they were very far from the area's to be patrolled, and had very limited fuel capacity. Within less than four months they returned to the Malta base. If our conditions were unenviable, theirs were even worse.

Porpoise continued with her blockade running trips, and on one of our return trips we received a signal ordering us to stand by with a small boarding party, one of whom was to be the C.E.R.A. Apparently one of our aircraft had damaged an Italian submarine and she was unable to dive. It was possible that we might be able to tow her back to port with us.

I'd had a go at many jobs in various places and situations, but I wasn't looking forward to this mission one little bit. The 'buzz' was that we were to be transferred by flying boat. Frankly I was scared stiff! There was so much we didn't know. How badly was she damaged? How many of her crew was aboard? Where would we have to take her? Would her own engineers co-operate? Inevitably there would be a language problem. In fact I could foresee a number of problems, heaven knows if I would ever return to dear old *Porpoise* again. However, after nearly twenty-four hours of sweating it out, with my toilet gear packed and ready to go, we received a signal cancelling the whole thing. I have no idea what had happened to change the plans, but it was rumoured that the Italian boat had sunk. Needless to say I for one was very relieved. I had not got a very comfortable job, but I would not willingly have swapped it for a damaged Italian submarine.

On another return trip we suffered damage to our outboard induction valve. This large valve supplied air to the main engines from a fairly sheltered spot on the bridge, and was used in very rough weather instead of using the conning tower hatch. As this valve was leaking very badly when the boat was dived, it was necessary for an E.R.A. to go up on to the bridge when the weather had eased, squeeze through a small hatch in the after end of the bridge, and on to the outside of the pressure hull inside the mine casing. As I was very familiar with the construction of this 'mushroom' shaped valve I undertook to do the job myself. Not that any of our E.R.A.'s could not have done the job equally as well, or equally as quickly, but speed was of the utmost importance. Never have I felt so lonely. The captain forbade me to put the valve completely out of action so that he could not dive if the need arose, and gave me to understand, quite rightly, that if we were spotted on the surface he could give me a few seconds only to get back to the conning tower hatch. This wasn't a great distance 'as the crow flies' but in the dark and very cramped conditions up there it would be an arduous and dangerous dash.

Working with the aid of one small torch, and with water lapping around my feet, I removed the inspection cover of the valve and found that my diagnosis of the fault had been correct. I was able to complete the job in fifty minutes. It was rather cold, but working furiously under these circumstances the sweat was pouring off me. Having finished the job I couldn't get back into the boat quickly enough, and swallowed the tot of neat rum that they offered me in one gulp.

On another occasion we carried out a landing party exercise – real 'cloak and dagger' stuff. We embarked some six or eight soldiers with two small inflatable boats, and landed them on the enemy occupied coast. Under the leadership of a very youthful army Captain, they accomplished their mission and all returned unharmed when we came close inshore for them twenty-four hours later. They had created havoc on a railway and some bridges. These were very hazardous exercises for them, and for that matter, us as well. Close inshore in about seven fathoms of water was hardly the place for a large mine laying submarine. Many of these missions went awry, with either the unfortunate raiding party, or the rescuing submarine, for one reason or another being unable to make the rendezvous on time.

In the early summer of 1942 we were ordered to proceed straight to Port Said after one of our cargo carrying missions, for a two day dry-docking, primarily to dispose of the weed building up on our bottom; this weed could make a difference of nearly two knots to our speed. On our arrival I was rather surprised to see what I thought was one of our 'King George V'-Class battleships, but closer inspection revealed her to be the obsolete battleship *Centurion*. Her formidable forward turret of four 16" guns was made of wood!

Seizing the opportunity of being in dock, I naturally undertook to do several small jobs that could only be attempted under these conditions and in this short time. The telemotor operated flood valve on our quick diving 'Q' tank was leaking badly, also the high-octane aviation spirit had literally destroyed several of our hull valves. Our propellers needed 'fairing up' to prevent whistling noises which could easily be detected by the enemy, and our propeller stern gland packings needed renewal. This would keep us very busy. The atmosphere in the boat was stifling as the sun poured down upon our exposed hull.

As two of the valves to be worked on were on tanks that had been carrying aviation spirit, I took the precaution of displaying 'no smoking' notices in the engine room. These notices were always kept at hand because they were also displayed during the last three hours of a battery charge when potentially explosive battery gasses were given off. It wasn't that I considered that there was any real danger, as these tanks were always flooded with seawater after discharging this spirit, and then emptied three times as a further precautionary measure.

Having instructed the E.R.A.'s in the requirements, I proceeded out of the boat to examine some external fittings. While making my way over the brow there was a terrific bang. The whole boat shook, and it seemed that the wooden shores holding her upright in the dock would collapse. Dashing back into the boat to see what was wrong, I could see a thick blue haze coming from the engine room. There had been an explosion in an external fuel tank due to the removal of a hull valve, which had allowed air to form an explosive mixture enhanced by the extreme heat of the sun on the side of the tank. It was very fortunate that no one was hurt as the complete valve shot past the E.R.A.like a shell.

Though there was no interior damage to the boat, except of course to the valve itself, the damage to the tank had been considerable. The explosion had blown the base off the fuel tank and into the main ballast tank below, ripping the metal plating apart like paper. It was fortunate that the huge Kingston valves on the bottom of No.5 main ballast tank were open or the damage to the whole saddle tank would have been much worse. As it was, it was bad enough. As the damage to the fuel tank could not be repaired in the time available, we cut away the debris, blanked off all the fittings and made the whole into one large ballast tank. This meant that ten tons less fuel could be carried on each subsequent trip to Malta. It also meant that when on the surface, we had ten tons more buoyancy on the port side, thus giving us a list to starboard. Once dived of course, we resumed an even keel. Adapting our fuel system to cut out this fuel tank was quite an involved business, and being away from the parent ship we had no technical advise from the flotilla engineer officer and his staff. Not being experienced in submarine work, the staff at Port Said carried out the work asked of them, but could offer us little technical advice. The Suez Canal Docking Co. as it was known, was run by the French; all foremen, constructors and inspectors were French, but most of the rank and file, including the craftsmen fitters and charge-men were Egyptian. Actually the work produced by this Company was of a high standard, although of course they had to rely upon our advice regarding the submarines.

Instead of being at Port Said for two days our stay stretched into ten days, and consequently accommodation had to be found for the crew. It was impossible to endure the conditions in the boat for more than two days. We were on the north bank of the canal with the desert stretching away to the north. Port Said itself being on the south bank. At first we were billeted in tents on the blazing hot sand with just a few mosquito nets between us, and this didn't please our captain very much. After being told that this was all the available accommodation, 'Benny' rushed around interviewing consuls, senior army officers and diplomats. He must have impressed someone, for very soon we were whisked off to Port Said itself, where we were, except for the officers, accommodated in a very nice theatre. A portable cooking range was installed, the chiefs and P.O.'s were given the dressing rooms, and the lads had camp beds in the stalls. Being the senior chief, I was appointed to the stars dressing room, with the coxswain in the room next door. All this was rather comic opera stuff, but we were very comfortable and it was certainly good to get away from the boat for a bit. Certainly I was nicely fixed, having a delightful room all to myself. As we hadn't much money I organized bridge parties in my spacious room and imported some of the local brew. This not only saved money, but prevented those two worthies 'Jock' Forrest and 'Taff' Hughes from knocking seven bells out of each other in the city.

The only snag was that we (except for the duty watch) had to cross the canal by boat each morning and evening. Having no boat of our own we had to hire an Arab motorboat. These were very unreliable, and didn't appear to be particularly anxious to stop for us. It was infuriating to be left stranded after a days work. On one occasion the rather impetuous 'Steady Boy' (Lt. Steadman) opened fire with his revolver on a passing motor launch that had refused to pick us up – we had been waiting for nearly an hour, and several passing boats had ignored us. I don't think 'Steady boy' had intended any harm, but there would have been 'hell to pay' if he had wounded any of the Egyptians – they appeared to have little enough affection for us as it was.

This short interlude at Port Said was soon over and, repairs having been carried out, we returned to Alexandria and to our parent ship where we stayed for a few days to attend a court of enquiry regarding our explosion. The court of enquiry was conducted aboard the *Queen Elizabeth*, which together with my other old ship *Valiant* was in Alexandria at that time. This explosion could be a very serious business as far as our E.O. Gerry Kirkwood and myself were concerned. If negligence was thought to have been involved, it could well have been the prelude to a Court Martial. It was certainly just as well that we had taken the precaution of displaying the 'No Smoking' boards in the engine room. I was confident that the order had been observed, having drummed into the staff the dangers involved with this high-octane spirit.

The enquiry was conducted by the *Q.E.'s* captain, and was attended by several fairly high-ranking officers. Several of the crew, particularly the engine room staff, were called one at a time to be questioned. I felt pretty miserable about the whole business, not that it was my fault, but for the fact that our useful carrying capacity had been reduced. If we had to do this cargo carrying to relieve Malta, then I was all for carrying as much as we could.

One of the principle witnesses was a high-ranking Dutch chemist who was attached to one of the big oil companies. His evidence was that small quantities of the spirit could have been retained in the rust on the walls of the tank. These would gasify due to the heat of the sun, to cause a spontaneous combustion when mixed with air on opening up the tank. This explanation was accepted by the court, and we were exonerated from all blame.

Within a day or two we were on our way to Malta with another load. It was on our return journey from this trip that we were again ordered to do another short patrol. Rommel's 'Africa Korps' was doing pretty well at that time; they were obviously getting fuel and stores through from Europe. On one morning the captain was called to the periscope to identify what appeared to be a small tanker heading for the African coast. Her sole armament appeared to be one small gun mounted on her foc'sle, perhaps not quite as big as ours, but still very useful. She was only about one thousand tons and, as torpedoes were very precious at the time 'Benny' decided to engage her with our gun. This was the first time that we had engaged an armed vessel with our gun, and I felt a little uncomfortable about it. I wasn't qualified in armaments or ordnance but I had been called in on many occasions when we were exercising our gun because it had a habit of failing to recoil after firing, and sitting back on its haunches like a stubborn mule refusing to budge. The reason for this was that its air/oil recoil cylinder would lose its pressure after firing. I would then get blocks and tackles and haul the offending barrel back into position, recharge the cylinders, get a smile of thanks from the frustrated gun layer and the gunnery officer, and depart back down to the bowels of the submarine once more. Little did I consider that we would use this antiquated weapon in anger, when *Porpoise* was fulfilling so many other useful roles.

But here we were in broad daylight, about to throw shells at a vessel that presumably had equal if not more firepower than ourselves. She would only have to hit our hull once to put us completely out of action. I trusted Benny's judgment implicitly, but he hadn't been with us long enough to be familiar with our old gun. At best we wouldn't get our first round away in less than twenty-five seconds, and she was bound to spot us as we surfaced.

'Stand by gun action!' came the order, and the crew rushed to their stations, guns crew ready crouching in the gun tower and the conning tower, waiting for the cascade of water that was inevitably to come as the hatches were opened. 'Full ahead! – Group up! Keep sixty feet! –Down periscope!' followed a succession of precise orders. 'Blow No.1 main ballast! - Surface- Blow all main ballast! –Half ahead together – Stop port! – In port engine clutch! – Half ahead port!' – by which time the boat was careering rapidly upwards. When the depth gauge showed fifteen feet the First Lieutenant blew his whistle and the hatches were opened, the guns crew dashing to their respective stations. 'Target bearing green ten, range one thousand two hundred yards! Open fire!'

Of course I could hear none of this, but I'd heard it all before when I'd had the job of outside E.R.A. Having got both engines started, we in the engine room anxiously awaited the welcome sound of the first round firing, over the roar of the engines. Sure enough, about twenty-five seconds after the whistle had been blown (which to us, seemed an eternity); we heard the resounding clap of our first round. This I thought, would probably also be our last round, and the next order would be 'Dive! Dive! Dive!', especially as we heard one or two ominous noises of shells striking the water uncomfortably close. But no! Shot after shot rang out. It seemed that at last that our old cannon was relenting from its previous bad behaviour.

With a slight correction in range, leading seaman Barker, our gun layer, was soon registering direct hits, first putting her gun out of action (none too soon), and then setting fire to her. We had fired thirty-five rounds without a hitch – unheard of!

As an explosion of her highly inflammable cargo was now imminent, the tanker crew commenced abandoning ship. We must have destroyed her boats because only one small boat got clear before she sank.

We were not very far from the North African coast, and were keeping a good all round lookouts for enemy planes, but it was our policy to take prisoners whenever we got the chance, in order to get as much information on the enemy disposition as possible. To this end we signalled the small boat containing what appeared to be the only survivors to come alongside. There were eight of them, including the wounded chief engineer. The captain had gone down with his ship.

Some of our crew were ordered to the casing to help get the survivors aboard as quickly as possible. Priority was given to the wounded man, and it took a little time to get him on to the conning tower and down the hatch. This had no sooner been done than our lookout spotted an enemy plane coming in to attack. The order was immediately given 'Dive! Dive! Dive!' We were in a very vulnerable situation, and we only succeeded in getting one other prisoner aboard and down the hatch before we were at a hundred feet. It was fortunate for us that this aircraft did not hit us with the bomb she dropped, but she did riddle our casing with cannon fire. It was also rather sad that when we came to periscope depth again there was no trace of the remainder of the survivors, or their boat. We had to assume that they were destroyed by their own aircraft.

The wounded engineer who had made a very unceremonious and hurried descent of the conning tower, was strapped to a stretcher, still conscious and obviously in a pretty serious condition. The captain and our coxswain examined and dressed his wounds, and he was made as comfortable as possible on one of the wardroom bunks. There was little else that could be done for him and certainly no question of cutting our patrol; it was several days before we were due back in 'Alex'. The situation at that time was so desperate that we couldn't have returned to base if one of our own crew was wounded. If this appears callous, then let me point out that we were in a war to the death through no fault of our own, and that any relaxation of a war patrol might mean the death of some of our own gallant men; the lives of our soldiers fighting in the North African desert depended desperately on our successful blockades.

The other prisoner was a seaman, who assisted in nursing his wounded comrade. They were Italians, but surprisingly had no affection for the Germans despite the fact that at that time, they appeared to be batting on a 'good wicket.' The general condition of the wounded man deteriorated during the next few days, hardly surprising, as a submarine on war patrol in the height of summer is not the best place for a sick man, and we were also on the receiving end of a few more depth charges before we reached the end of that patrol.

As soon as we got alongside, the Italian engineer was whisked away to hospital in 'Alex'. The other prisoner was taken away to army HQ to see if he could divulge any vital information.

It was after another trip that we returned to our parent ship with one of our own crew desperately ill. He had been very poorly for a few days but there was little that we could do for him. He was a wireless operator, and a grand young fellow. It was tragic that he died a few days later, as he had only been married shortly before we left the U.K.

Our coxswain, as was customary, organized a sale of his personal effects. This turned out to be the most extraordinary auction sale I'd ever attended. It was held in the torpedo stowage compartment, with only our own crew present. All items of his kit were sold, some three or four times over as purchasers handed articles back in to be sold again. Back in the days when our pay was so very meagre, over £250 was raised in a very short time (the present day equivalent would be about eight times that figure). I recollect that 'Benny' purchased a vest for £15 and a cap ribbon for nearly £20, which I then paid a further £5 at the resale. Our poor coxswain was left with almost a complete kit when the bidding ended; whether he disposed of this in the parent ship later I do not know, but the whole of the proceeds were sent home to the young fellows widow.

The 10th flotilla base was *HMS Talbot*, the old quarantine quarters on the Lazaretto Creek side of Manoel Island. Because of its vulnerability to air attack it was honeycombed with underground passages and dugouts. The whole of the sick bay was underground. My only visit there was when I arrived back off one of our patrols with a terribly soar throat. In the interest of the health of the rest of the crew, the First Lieutenant suggested that I reported to the sick bay for diagnosis and treatment. It was diagnosed as a severe attack of quinsy, and the doctor wished me to remain there in bed for a few days. Although I was feeling very poorly, I hastily talked him out of that one. Firstly I did not wish to miss my boat, and secondly I couldn't see myself getting better in those conditions anyway, with it being deep in the bowels of the earth and with the atmosphere so damp and musty. *Porpoise's* E.R.A.'s mess was no palace, with the gun tower above it, the magazine below it, and the Chiefs and P.O.'s heads immediately opposite, it certainly wasn't all that could be desired, but at least I had a decent bunk, and it was preferable to remaining here. The only redeeming feature of that sick bay was that it was safe from air raids.

My sympathies were with the chaps of the 10th flotilla; it must have been absolute hell for them. Apart from short spells between patrols when half the crew could be sent to an inland camp where they had reasonably good food, ultra violet ray treatment and a good rest, they spent their lives either at sea in one of the small 'U' or 'V' class submarines, or either at the bottom of the harbour or in those damp musty underground tunnels.

So I took my quinsy away with me, thanking the sick bay staff for their attention and the dope that I'd been given. I had a pretty miserable trip back to 'Alex' but my throat was better by the time we arrived there.

Chapter Seven

In the early summer of 1942 our engineer officer 'Jerry' Kirkby left us. I was sorry to see him go as we had always got along very well together; he had left the running of the department largely in my hands with a minimum of interference, and had always backed me up when required to do so, a situation which had suited me admirably. 'Jerry' had been with us since the redoubtable George Gay left us. Where he went afterwards I do not know, but he was relieved by Temporary Acting Engineer Officer Joe Chaimberlain. Joe was a contemporary of mine whilst serving our apprenticeship, and was a year older than me. He had been promoted almost right away, and I had been recommended nearly two years previously. Fortunately Joe adopted the same procedure as 'Jerry' Kirkby had, and allowed me a free rein with the department. It was not that he didn't know the job – he had been in the submarine service for many years.

Another one who now left us was our coxswain, the popular and very likable 'Chopper' Vaughan; he was relieved by an equally nice fellow, C.P.O. 'Ginger' Ridley with whom I also got along famously.

I used to cut hair and trim beards throughout our period in the Mediterranean, and enjoyed doing it. Of course I did not charge for my service, it was something that I had a natural aptitude for, and it kept the lads and the officers looking clean and tidy about the head. This haircutting led to an amusing incident before 'Chopper' Vaughan left us. He asked me if I could spare a few moments to trim his hair one night after we had surfaced while on patrol. Commencing the operation in the passageway outside his mess, our TGM, C.P.O. Joe Brighton jokingly quipped, 'Cut a piece of his ear off Joe, and you shall have a tincture of my tot.' With the boat now rolling quite a bit at that time, this is precisely what I did. It was but a very small piece out of his lobe, but 'Chopper' screamed and bled as though I'd severed a main artery. He certainly couldn't see the funny side, because he was running around holding his ear and calling us every bad name in his very extensive vocabulary. He repeated all this performance again when I later looked into his mess for the tincture of rum that the now very dubious Joe Brighton had promised me.

Whilst we were in the 'Med' the 'Daily Mirror' had a brainwave. Obviously we didn't see a newspaper for weeks on end, and even when we did, they were weeks old. So the Mirror produced a newspaper especially for submariners, with as much topical news as was available, plus several strip cartoons, pictures of ravishing blondes and brunettes, and personal letters from those at home. This paper, named 'Good Morning' was numbered but undated. If we expected to be on patrol for twenty-eight days, we would be issued with a copy for each mess of twenty-eight consecutive numbers. This continued until the end of the war, it was a really marvellous idea, and very much appreciated by the submariners. Together with our meals, it was the highlight of our day.

The 'Daily Mirror' lavishly entertained three hundred submariners of all ranks at the 'Savoy' in London after the war, and I was fortunately included; all expenses were paid, including hotel accommodation for the night.

There was one passenger billeted in the E.R.A.'s mess on one of our return trips from Malta who was in no way concerned with what was going on. He was another of those extraordinary characters that one so often came across in the submarine service. 'Ginger' Sayers, had been carrying out C.E.R.A.'s duties in one of the 10th flotilla boats until he was injured while returning to his boat, which was in Malta dockyard, after a run ashore. Ginger, being in a slightly inebriated condition (only 'Ginger' could have found enough liquor in Malta to become inebriated in those days), had fallen from the top to the bottom of a huge dry-dock. This was a very long way down, and if he hadn't been 'tin hats', and his fall hadn't been broken three or four times by the steps in the dock, he would doubtless have been killed. As it was, he had several fractured bones, including his pelvis. Apparently he was still conscious when the Surgeon Commander who had been called to the scene was deliberating on the best way to get him to the top, and 'Ginger had yelled out, 'Flood the dock sir, and bloody well float me up.'

'Ginger was a long time in Bighi Hospital laying flat on his back with his legs kept apart, which must have been purgatory for him. In the meantime his boat had left for 'Alex'. Now pronounced fit enough to join her, although he still had difficulty in walking, he insisted on helping my hard-pressed E.R.A.'s by keeping a watch in the engine room. 'Ginger was a typical example of the breed of submarine E.R.A., dexterous with his tools, hard working, hard drinking, tough and fearless. We had many like him; they got into trouble with the authorities occasionally, but were indispensable, especially in wartime.

Arriving in Malta on one of our trips we learned that *Olympus*, one of our old China flotilla boats had hit a mine just after leaving Malta en route for the U.K. She had done her stint in the 'Med' and was due for refit. In addition to her own crew she was carrying over thirty other submariners who were due for relief, many of whom were already survivors from submarines sunk in and around Malta. She sank slowly, about five miles north of Malta, and nearly all were able to don life jackets or D.S.E.A. sets, and get into the sea. Apparently she was unable to raise the alarm either by wireless or visual signal. As submarines carried no form of life raft, the officers organized the crew to remain together for the long swim ahead of them. Although there were several hours of daylight remaining, and the seawater temperature in May was seventy degrees with no adverse currents, this was still a huge task, even for strong swimmers.

The amazing thing about this concerted effort was that the majority succeeded in getting to within a half a mile of the shore. Then disaster! Perhaps that final effort, when land seemed so near, was just too much in their exhausted state. Maybe some had shed the lifejackets, which had hampered their movement through the water, but the fact remains that only about ten very exhausted and semi-conscious men reached the land. What a tragedy! And to think that these chaps had been on their way to be reunited with their families. C.E.R.A. Bill Guest was among the many of my friends who perished. Another friend, 'Shiner' Wright, later promoted to Temporary Warrant Engineer, and awarded the D.S.M. and B.E.M. was one who succeeded in scrambling onto the shore on a sandy beach near St Paul's Bay.

On our return trip we received a signal telling us to 'heave to' in the sanctuary off Alexandria, where we had to loiter on the surface for over an hour before entering the swept channel. It wasn't the first time we had had to do this, and I loathed this hanging about on the surface. True we were relatively safe from air attack by the enemy, or our own forces, safe also from mines (provided that the enemy hadn't dropped a few more), but I wasn't so sure about submarine attack. It was as calm as a millpond, and we would have been a sitting target for an enemy submarine venturing that far in. They would not have known where our minefields were, but it would have been worth the risk – we had done this with success in the German approaches, and so had they, a fact which we knew to our cost. I think my nerves always became a little edgy just before entering harbour. My feeling was that we had been subjected to so many hazards that it would be pathetic to be hit in the belly by a torpedo or mine just as we felt that we had good reason to lift some of the tension.

However, we again arrived safely and tied up alongside *Medway* where we could have a good bath and a comfortable meal. It was good news to learn that the whole of the starboard watch were to have four days leave in Cairo. Whether that should have included me, or whether the port watch were due to go after the others returned I cannot remember. I wasn't fussed about going to Cairo but it was a long time since I'd had any respite. Unfortunately we had had piston trouble on both engines, and so I decided to remain behind to supervise the repair job. The flotilla E.O. suggested that since half of our crew were away, we commence work on both engines, and was prepared to delegate six E.R.A.'s in order to expedite this work. I was reluctant to adopt this measure, and put the case strongly to my E.O. that we should only put one engine out of action at a time.

There was much excitement with the lads going to Cairo, accommodation had been reserved in a hotel, and they could forget the war for a few days. But I was in no way envious, I had no ambition to visit Cairo and the Egyptians didn't appear to welcome us too heartily anyway. On the other hand, the only alternative was to be steeped in hard work; there was always an urgency to complete repairs, and even more so now that we had suffered heavy set-backs in North Africa. Rommel's Afrika Korps was not much more than sixty miles distant; in fact it surprised us that leave was granted at all.

Away the lads went, and I was left to get on with the work with a reduced staff, augmented by two or three E.R.A.'s from the spare crew. I'd hoped to complete one engine in two days, and the other one by the time the leave party returned. But this was not to be; no sooner had our leave party arrived in Cairo than a recall signal was sent. Rommel had made another attack, and was now less than sixty miles from 'Alex', not quite within shelling range, but certainly within bombing range. The C. in C (Admiral. Sir Andrew Cunningham) decided that all naval ships that were able, should leave port. There weren't a large number of naval ships in 'Alex' at that time, but some, such as *Porpoise*, with one engine out of action, weren't able to leave immediately. My old ship (*HMS Valiant*) was sitting ignominiously on the bottom, having been badly damaged by Italian frogmen; she was certainly not going anywhere.

This order to evacuate Alexandra caused a bit of a stir, as *Medway* was to leave almost immediately. All submarines alongside including those undergoing repairs, two of these having just returned from a twenty-eight day patrol, had to lie off at anchor after embarking fuel and provisions. Heads of departments had to see that any items of their machinery undergoing repair inboard, was returned to their boats right away, and I had to call for a couple of volunteers to work through the night (they had already worked through the day), to bring the starboard engine to a state of readiness.

Medway, together with the remainder of the flotilla, negative *Porpoise*, left at dawn the following day. The submarines were left to make their own way, and *Medway* was screened by anti-submarine vessels. I think they were making for Port Said, a mere one hundred and twenty miles almost due east.

Not wishing to be caught by Rommel in 'Alex', I was working frantically with as many men as we could usefully employ to get the engine ready. There was no time to brood over the situation; the mere fact that the Royal Navy was evacuating the port was a grim prospect. The harbour seemed very empty, just us and the mighty *Valiant*; she was holed and sitting on the harbour bed, but at least her eight 15" guns were capable of firing, besides which she had twelve 6" guns and a vast number of anti-aircraft guns (Bofors etc.).

Our holidaymakers arrived back from Cairo at about tot time (11:30) bitterly disappointed and disgruntled, but ready to work as required. This was not necessary however, as we were ready for sea in all respects by the last 'dog-watch (16:00 to 18:00). We actually left 'Alex' at dawn the following day, the 30th of June 1942. Twenty-four hours after *Medway*.

Then – horror of horrors – we received a signal saying that *Medway* had been torpedoed and sunk by an enemy submarine. This was a true catastrophe. It was impossible at the time to appreciate the magnitude of this loss. Here was a whole, and very precious flotilla of submarines, without a parent ship. Apart from accommodation, there was the loss of all the stores and spare gear for electrical and mechanical machinery, spare periscopes, hundreds of spare torpedoes and other ammunition. Although I later learned that about two hundred of *Medway's* spare torpedoes had been dispatched overland as a precautionary step.

Medway had taken nearly twenty minutes to disappear beneath the waves, which allowed all the crew and submarine staff to be rescued by destroyer escorts. Those aboard her included three or four WREN officers who were being evacuated from 'Alex', one of whom displayed extraordinary courage by assisting non-swimmers and those who were wounded; she was subsequently decorated for her efforts.

It was difficult to understand how a submarine could get into an attacking position when there was a strong anti-submarine escort present, using ASDIC. I was later given a graphic account of the *Medway's* sinking by my old friend Phil King, who was serving as the spare crew C.E.R.A. aboard her. He said that he had felt no shock at all, even though she was hit by no fewer than five torpedoes. Phil, who was in the water waiting to be picked up, stated that she went down stern first, with one solitary rating sitting on her bow when she finally disappeared. Maybe this fellow could not swim, as he would most assuredly have been sucked under with her.

For the second time in the war most of my personal belongings went to the bottom of the sea!

Porpoise proceeded to Port Said, where our crew were once again accommodated in an army camp on the fringe of the desert north of Suez, whilst the flotilla collected its wits, and the 'big boys' (Captain Ruck-Keene and his staff), dashed about in an effort to make more permanent arrangements.

It didn't take the C. in C. and Captain Ruck-Keene too long to decide that Beirut was the most suitable available base, and as far as I can recollect, *Porpoise* proceeded on one of her missions from Port Said while these arrangements were being made, and returned to Beirut about a month later.

The spare crews, depot ship staff, and submarine crews were accommodated in an old French army barracks. Probably because we were the last of the flotilla to arrive, we continued to live in the boat – nothing new to us. In fact throughout the four or five months we were based at Beirut I did not even see the barracks.

Presumably there were workshops at these barracks, but neither these nor the accommodation could be compared with Medway, which was designed to care for more than twelve large submarines. If life had been tedious for the submarine crews hitherto, it was even more so now. Gone were all those marvellously equipped workshops, the huge submarine spare gear store, the periscope, torpedoes and electrical fitting workshops, the submarine battery charging facilities (not that we were encouraged to use these very often, only if both engines were out of action), the sick bay and the dental surgery etc.

With the deteriorating situation in the Mediterranean it was even more important that the submarines continued their patrols, and for *Porpoise* to carry vital stores to Malta. We were still having problems with metal fatigue in our pistons. Any spare pistons or cylinder liners carried in *Medway* were now at the bottom of the sea. We normally carried two spare pistons and liners, and had to make do with them.

Leaving Beirut early in August, laden with stores of every description, we had a relatively uneventful trip to Malta, but the return journey was not quite so uneventful.

We had received a signal ordering us to carry out a patrol off the North African coast in order to intercept enemy convoys that were bent on doing the same for Rommel as we had just done for Malta.

We were patrolling west of Benghazi with orders not to get nearer to the coast than forty miles as the enemy had several direction finding devices sited along that coast which could easily detect us within that range, particularly if we were on the surface charging batteries at night. We had had no success during this patrol, but with a batch of signals received just before midnight, we were ordered to a position from which we could intercept a convoy. Aircraft had reported its position, course and speed, and the indications were, that it would be relatively easy for us to be in position before daybreak.

Having been on an interception course for nearly three hours, we received another urgent signal correcting the enemy position. This put the enemy much further away, in another direction. To be in an attacking position we now had to cease charging batteries and proceed at full speed. It also involved getting closer to the coast, not very desirable for us, as we were belching away at fifteen and a half knots. It was a pity about the batteries as, anticipating a busy day, we really needed them to be fully charged, however, they were two thirds charged, and this would have to do.

Enemy convoys always appeared to have adequate anti-submarine escort at this time, which promised us a pretty rough time after the attack. Dawn was approaching and we still had some distance to make; once dived our speed would be much reduced.

Suddenly the whole crew were alerted and summoned to diving stations. We below did not know the cause of the alarm, but apparently an enemy destroyer was sighted, almost directly in our path and very near.

We had obviously been located from ashore, and this warship had either been diverted from the convoy, or sent out to intercept us. She must have heard us for some time, or might even have made the original detection. Had we been fitted with Radar, then we would of course have been alerted. As it was we were not operating ASDICS or our listening devices as we were making such a din ourselves, and fortunately the captain was already on the bridge; he'd been there nearly all night.

At first she attempted to ram us, and of course had a wonderful opportunity to do this, but thanks to the captain's superb handling of our boat, the destroyer narrowly missed our stern. It was not until then that 'Benny' gave the order 'Dive! Dive! Dive!' This was a very astute move because a submarine is anything but manoeuvrable whilst she is in the act of diving, and would most certainly have been a 'sitting duck'. We dived in what must have been a record time, and we had already more than halved our diving time since the beginning of the war.

The enemy, knowing our exact position and diving course, was back over us before we had a chance to alter course or to go into 'silent routine'. We had shut off from depth charging, and were hastening to control the dive by blowing out the additional ten tons of water in 'Q' tank. It was very necessary to arrest our downward plunge before we reached our meagre maximum safe depth of just two hundred feet.

'Silent routine' meant keeping as quiet as possible, proceeding along very slowly on one motor, just keeping enough way on the boat to provide sufficient rudder and hydroplane control, these being operated in hand control in order to eliminate the noise of the operating motors. Operating hydroplanes and steering in hand control was hard work, especially if the boat has been dived for some time, and the oxygen content is getting low.

Whilst we were still in the throes of controlling our dive the destroyer passed right overhead, and, as expected, dropped her first pattern of depth charges, six or eight of them. This caused an unholy commotion, as they were very close and shook the boat from stem to stern. Fuses blew and we were plunged into sudden darkness, always an un-nerving experience. The First Lieutenant and his staff did well to maintain a steady depth, and the L.T.O's soon restored the lighting – by now we were well practiced in dealing with these eventualities, but this time we knew that there would be more to come. We weren't disappointed in this, for she soon returned to the attack.

By this time we were properly in 'silent routine' and the captain was altering course; this at least would now make it more difficult for the enemy who, although not yet having developed ASDIC, had some of the very finest listening devices.

Proceeding very slowly on one motor made altering course a slow business, so that we had not moved very far from our diving position when a further pattern of charges fell around us. Very near again, but perhaps not quite as bad as the first attack – or were we getting used to it? Again we had the same trouble with the lights, and several of our gauges were now out of action, although our depth gauges had quickly been shut off to protect them against depth charging; it was a severe shaking up that they were now getting, rather than excessive pressure caused by the depth charging.

Lighting was again quickly restored, but keeping the boat at a constant depth was becoming increasingly difficult. The tremendous shaking that she was taking was causing many water, oil and high-pressure air leaks. These of course, had to be attended to as quickly as possible, and as quietly as possible, a difficult task in itself, as it involved using large heavy spanners in very restricted spaces, some almost inaccessible.

We could plainly hear the destroyer's propellers as she closed for each subsequent attack, and could tell almost exactly when to expect the next explosion of depth charges.

The captain was taking such evasive action as he was able, but he was unable to change course or depth quickly at this speed, there being little response to either the rudder or the hydroplanes. He did speed up and change course with each pattern of depth charges – the enemy would be unable to hear until the noise from these charges subsided. It would have helped considerably if we could have gone to three hundred feet where it would have been harder to detect us.

We were not using our ASDIC set as its impulses would disclose our position, although this destroyer appeared to have a pretty good idea of that already, and I recollect that our listening apparatus was already out of action. Perhaps this was just as well, as our operator George Backman, would have just about had his eardrums shattered had he been listening when these depth charges exploded.

We endured these attacks for about the next two hours. Some of the patterns of depth charges were closer and did more damage than others, but as time went on the destroyer seemed to be drawing away from us and losing contact. Some of these attacks had been so severe; the whole boat had shaken as if it were about to break in half. I had experienced many depth charges previously but this was by far the worst up to now!

It was a very tense and nerve racking time for the crew, but they had stood up to it magnificently. It must be remembered as well, that many of the crew were very young, and some of them having recently joined *Porpoise* were now having their baptism. One phlegmatic sailor, A.B. Stan Hawkey, who was later awarded the D.S.M., stated that he had counted eighty depth charges in all.

The E.R.A's and myself were now kept busy tightening up all the leaking joints, and for this job I was grateful. It was more nerve racking for the majority of the crew who had to stay at their posts keeping absolutely quiet. I well remember my baptism – and the relief that I had felt afterwards. I think I had been in one blue funk wondering what it would really be like until that day in the Skagerrak. Nothing is quite like being in a submarine plastered with depth charges, and until one has had to endure this discomforting experience, one cannot be really sure of how one will react

Most of us had no doubt that we were on the side of right in this ghastly conflict, and accepted the fact that sooner or later we would probably perish; but it was the sort of show that we'd make while perishing that concerned us more. If I had to go, then I hoped that it would be quick, and I loathed the thought of being taken prisoner.

What my exact reactions were at this time is rather vague, but strangely one of the things that I do remember was someone wishing our torpedo officer ('Johnny' Pope) many happy returns of the day. It was his birthday, the 19th of August 1942, probably his 21st, I'm not sure. I must have been in the torpedo compartment stopping an HP air or a telemotor leak, and I remember that it all seemed rather ironical to me at the time, as there was some doubt as to whether he would get another birthday, but in any case they were certainly getting the red carpet out for him. One joker asked us to imagine the amazement on the face of the enemy sound detector operator when he heard the strains of 'Happy birthday to you...........' coming up from the depths.

I remember well the 'enfants terrible' Lt Chris Thurlow, and 3rd Officer Lt.'Steady boy' Steadman, nothing appeared to shake them. Our coxswain, 'Ginger' Ridley who had operated our after planes throughout the action was a grand fellow. Then there was big 'Ginger' Facer, our yeoman of signals, Joe Brightman our TGM, George Backman our hydrophone operator, as well as those of the engine room department, Tommy Hargrieves (outside E.R.A.) and his mate, leading stoker Draper. 'Jock' Forrest and 'Taff' Hughes (the engine room E.R.A's), and stokers W.F. Illesley and 'Jock' Harrison, to mention but a few of those imperturbable characters who set such a fine example to the young 'uns on that day.

After a few of these salvoes it became increasingly obvious that our batteries were becoming damaged. We had had our third battery restored to us by now, and there were one hundred and twelve cells in each battery, with each cell weighing over eight hundredweight (about 400 Kilos). The cells rested on wooden slats in the battery tanks, each cell was wedged tightly together. Owing to the nature of the electrolyte (dilute sulphuric acid), the tanks were covered with a thick coating of bitumastic, and there was a small sump positioned at the end of each tank to collect any spillage, which could then be tested, and the sump dried out. A quick analysis of the liquid taken from each sump revealed that some of the cells must have cracked, causing them to leak. We carried a strong alkali to neutralize the acid in the sumps.

Quite suddenly the attacks ceased, and all was quiet. Whether the destroyer had exhausted her supply of depth charges, or had concluded that she had finished us off, we didn't know. She would doubtless continue to patrol the area for many hours as a precautionary measure; at least, that is what our own anti-submarine vessels would have done. The great Admiral Max Horton's orders were to 'Sit on the target for forty-eight hours'.

For us, time was running out. We were not sure what other damage had been caused, but we did know that we had suffered considerable electrical damage – just how bad, we were later to discover.

Much acid had leaked from the battery cells, but thankfully this had not yet come into contact with any salt water, which would then by chemical action, produce the deadly chlorine gas. We were fast exhausting our supply of neutralizing agent, and furthermore, as the level of the electrolyte in many of the badly damaged cells became low, any electrical load placed on them caused very unpleasant fumes. There was a great urgency to eliminate these cells from the electrical circuits. More and more cells needed isolating ('cutting out'), and we only carried a few short lengths of 'cutting out' leads with which to do this job. But we did possess a long main charging lead (about 2″ diameter), which we cut into shorter lengths.

Our captain, who was kept in constant touch on the state of our electrical and mechanical machinery by his technical staff, was the very acme of what we could hope and indeed expect a captain to be under such circumstances – cool, calm, and efficient. But above all, encouraging.

I had known 'Benny' for many years, and had a great admiration for him. We had been in 'the trade' (the submarine service) for a long period, and although until now we had never been shipmates, we had served in the same flotilla on several occasions. It was with him that I had battled on the football field on so many occasions in the past, and who had taken my robust tactics so sportingly. Promoted from the lower deck, he was popular with all ranks and was one of the most imperturbable and courageous men that I have ever served with, and I say that after many years in a service bristling with that type, both officers and ratings.

Although this is not supposed to be a personal tribute to 'Benny' it did surprise me that at some time during his distinguished wartime record that he was not awarded the Victoria Cross. His wartime memoirs would make fine reading indeed, but alas, as none but he could write them (and his modesty would forbid that) it is doubtful that they will ever be recorded.

But to return to our present predicament, the engineering staff had made good most of the leaks, but we still couldn't tell whether the engines would start or not, nor at this depth, the state of the periscopes. We had dived before 06:00, and it was now well past 10:30 and nearly two hours since we had last heard from our 'friend' up top. There was now a pressure of nearly 5psi. in the boat, due to the many HP air leaks and, though we'd been dived for less than five hours, the atmosphere was very murky.

In normal conditions we could remain dived for over twenty-four hours provided the battery lasted, even though we were not fitted with air conditioning or oxygen generating plants. But the main limiting factor was now the state of our batteries. We thought that we had been moving away from the scene, but not being able to locate the enemy, we were not sure whether we were drawing away or closing with her. But we did know that the batteries were in a bad state, and we would not be able to remain dived for very much longer.

The captain ordered 'Periscope depth' (thirty-two feet), only to discover that both periscopes had been damaged, and little could be seen. The high-powered periscope was totally out of action, and the attack periscope (thin at the top so as not to cause water disturbance) was not much better. A certain amount of water must have leaked into them during the depth charging, and if nothing more serious, both badly needed desiccating (drying out), and we did not have the equipment to do this. This was a bitter blow because our sound detector was out of action as well. So we were virtually blind.

As the enemy did not appear to be too close to hand, (a metal rod held against the hull and put to the ear would pick up sound up to about a half a mile) the captain decided to surface and if necessary fight it out. It was doubtful that we would be able to use our torpedoes because of the time that it would have probably taken to get ourselves lined up on a firing course with the enemy, and to have engaged a destroyer with our gun would have been a pretty hopeless task at the best of times. She would be bristling with guns, and we had one unreliable 4" and one 1" Oerlikon, primarily for use against aircraft.

However, whichever way one looked at it we had little to lose, we certainly could not remain dived any longer, and it was almost a sense of relief when the captain ordered. 'Gun action – Stand by main engines.'

Only once before had we done this in anger, but we had practised the drill many times, always endeavouring to cut down on the time, because usually the only real point in this exercise is the element of surprise.

It was not likely that there would be much of an element of surprise this time, as the enemy knew our whereabouts, and probably also knew that we would be wounded. We did not know the enemies range or bearing, and we would be surfacing slowly as we couldn't even muster half speed on the motors, so - if there was a stick up there, then we were surely going to be on the receiving end of it. It would be particularly unfortunate if we surfaced stern on to the target, as this would mean altering our course before we could fire, since being fitted forward of the bridge, the gun could not be brought to bear abaft of Red 145 and Green 145.

We in the engine room were having our problems as well, and were praying that the badly shaken engines would start at the first attempt. We knew that we would receive the order to start one engine just before the hatches were opened, firstly to reduce the pressure that had built up in the boat (very dangerous to those first opening the hatch), secondly in order to get a little more speed and manoeuvrability, thirdly, to induce some clean air into the boat. The odds lay heavily against us; there would be no room for mistakes of any kind. Let's hope that the old gun would behave herself!

At last, we in the engine room heard the hiss of air going into the main ballast tanks, followed by 'Full ahead port engine', the sharp bow up angle, and the First Lieutenant's whistle signal to open the hatch. Luckily the port engine started right away, followed soon after by the starboard. What a shambles! They sounded like a bag of old bones clattering.

 Now we were anxiously awaiting the sound of our gun, which could normally be heard against the roar of the engines. I had a feeling that if we found ourselves close to the enemy 'Benny' would try to ram her, that would probably be more effective than our old gun.

Seconds ticked by! Surely the enemy would have opened fire before now. We were a long time getting our first round away; it would be unfortunate indeed if the old gun decided to sit back on its haunches this time. We in the engine room were so preoccupied that no one recorded the time we surfaced, not accurately anyway, but it could only have been a few seconds after the port engine had started. Something should have happened before this! The tension was terrible.

Then after almost three minutes on the surface, the engine telegraphs rang to 'Half Ahead both'. This relieved the tension a little and I took the liberty of sending one of the stokers into the control room to find out what had happened. He quickly returned with the news that when we had surfaced the enemy was nowhere in sight. We could not even see his smoke on the horizon.

This was quite incredible news, as less than two hours earlier we had every reason to know that he was there. The only possible explanation was that having been sure that he'd sunk us; he had departed at full speed to catch up with the convoy and to celebrate their 'kill'.

What an incredible 'let off!' But we soon realized that our troubles were far from over. It was manifestly clear that, with the rapid deterioration of our main batteries, we would be unable to dive again. Also that enemy aircraft would almost certainly be sent out to check on us. It would have helped considerably if we could have dived, even just for short periods to avoid aircraft. We had sighted enemy aircraft through our periscopes every day throughout this short patrol, so it was a pretty safe bet that there would be more sighted soon. Our recent attacker was no doubt making his action report, and very soon there would be a reconnaissance plane sent out.

Breaking W/T silence, signals were hastily coded and sent to base. We reported that we were badly damaged and unable to dive, and quickly received permission to vacate our patrol area and return to base, with the consoling additional information that assistance would be forthcoming.

We were very much on our own. Nearly seven hundred miles from base and just thirty miles from an enemy coast, with a pair of decidedly dicey engines that even with careful nursing would only churn out fourteen knots. And we were unable to dive! – A real sitting duck! But now at last we were drawing away from land in a northeasterly direction, if only we could make nightfall without being spotted. The chances of our detection would be much less at night.

In the meantime we were all working very hard, not only nursing our engines, but making necessary repairs to auxiliary machinery, and assisting the First Lieutenant's staff to restore some order with the batteries. They were 'cutting out' all the damaged cells, which, although reducing the available voltage, might make it possible for us to dive for short periods to avoid detection. Cutting up and soldering the ends of those huge 'cutting out leads' was no mean task and, as it became clear that many more cells than we had thought were damaged, it became a tiring and despairing one. However, this work did keep us from brooding over our unenviable plight.

The captain ordered all possible speed, and left the engine room staff to get on with it. There were six or seven hours left to nightfall, and we were squeezing every ounce out of our poor old 'donkeys'. Two or three of us were crawling through the bilges, taking up the slack in the engine holding down bolts – a 'devilish' job when the engines were running. A careful watch was kept on all bearings, especially the thrust blocks situated just forward of the stern glands. One of these did get uncomfortably hot, but not quite hot enough to melt the white metal thrust pads.

At long last darkness fell affording us a welcome respite, although our problems were by no means over. Dawn might even find us with an escort, but this was most unlikely.

A tot of rum and a hot meal did a lot to make us more cheerful, and we snatched what sleep we could. But dawn came again all too quickly, and with it that awful feeling of nakedness. At first there was nothing in sight, but as the morning wore on our lookouts spotted two very low flying aircraft. They were on a reciprocal course and closing rapidly. Our meagre armament was quickly brought to bear, as it seemed very likely that the enemy had found us, but at last one of them gave the recognition signal of the day. They were a couple of Beau-fighters, and had been sent out to escort us. Although this gave us a tremendous boost, and we almost felt like cheering – we knew that these two would have been most inadequate protection for us had the enemy spotted us.

Still about five hundred miles from base, they were unable to remain with us long. They flew very low over the water in order not to attract attention, and withdrew after just a couple of hours to be relieved by another pair, which arrived an hour later. This went on until darkness fell, and it seemed incredible to us that we saw nothing more of the enemy. By this time we could not have been more than twenty hours out of Beirut, only about half of that in daylight, and now considerably further from the enemy occupied coastline. Rommel had been halted within fifty miles of 'Alex'.

When dawn broke again, our previous day's escorts were replaced more practically, by two 'Hunt' class destroyers, whose presence lifted the tension considerably. They remained with us all day, one on our port bow and the other off to starboard. During the night we received a signal to alter course to Port Said where there were better facilities for replacing our batteries. I think that by this time our batteries were virtually useless, and all the electricity demand was being maintained by the floating charge we had on our engines; if we had stopped our engines I doubt that we would have ever got them started again.

With our two escorts, we had now indulged in the luxury of zigzagging as an anti-submarine precaution. Previously we had kept a straight course in order to cover distance as quickly as possible, but now as we approached our base, the threat of submarine attack became more likely.

Our batteries were in a shocking condition and were kept as far as possible in a dormant state, with no electricity being put in and none taken out. Having exhausted our supply of battery acid neutralizing agent, the electrolyte now leaking from the cells and into the battery tanks was further neutralized by our limited supply of fresh water before being pumped to sea via the bilge pump. I wondered what effect all that acid would have on the bilge pump impellors, but the main objective was to reach port, and there was little point in worrying about something that I could do nothing about. A worse thought was that if the depth charging had broken the bitumastic lining of the tanks then the neat acid could be having a very serious corrosive effect on our pressure hull.

It was comforting to have the two destroyers with us, at least we felt reasonably safe from air, or even surface attack. Our meagre fourteen knots was almost slow speed for them. A few friendly visual signals were exchanged; these were usually very witty, often referring the recipient to a biblical passage.

Nearing Port Said our escorts left us. Our captain sent an appropriate 'Thank you' signal. On arrival we had the difficult task of manoeuvring alongside with two decidedly shaky main engines, instead of the more usual practice of using main motors.

It had been arranged for our repairs to be carried out by the French owned Suez Canal Company, and we were docked right away on the north bank, as we were when we had our previous fuel tank explosion. Accommodation had to be found for us immediately as we could not live aboard while they were replacing the batteries. The set up was much the same as before, first they put us under canvas (a prey for all the mosquito's in the Near East) until our captain chased around to procure more suitable accommodation for us.

We were now able to make an appraisal of the damage sustained, and commenced to make both semi-permanent and temporary repairs. The task was a big one, and not made easier by language problems. Although many of the work force spoke reasonably good English there were of course many technical terms pertinent only to submarines, which made things difficult. The military situation was still very acute and, as the value of submarines in the Mediterranean was now at a premium, our repairs had to be carried out with all speed.

The crew, although not having access to machines and welding equipment, did much work under difficult conditions. The heat whilst we were in the dry dock was terrific, and again we had this business of arranging transport across to the other side of the canal in time for the evening meal for those of the crew who weren't required to keep watch during the night.

Removing the main batteries was a most difficult and hazardous operation. Damage to the cells was even more extensive than we had thought. About one third of all the cells were either broken or cracked, with many spilling out sulphuric acid. Great care was required to transport each cell through the boat to the gun tower hatch where a crane lifted them out to the dockside. The shock of the depth charging, (some of the charges would have exploded beneath us), had cracked the bitumastic lining away from the hull, and allowed the acid to eat away large patches, some of these up to 3/8 inch deep – half the total thickness of the hull. It was left to the Suez Canal Company to fill these cavities with expert welding, before relining the tank with bitumastic.

As I have said, this was the worst depth charging I had experienced up until this time. I remember that my reaction at the time of the attack had not been so much one of fear, but more one of anger and frustration at not being able to hit back. We would spend weeks at sea seeking the enemy, sometimes a whole patrol would elapse with not a single enemy ship sighted, and even when we did, it was often impossible to get ourselves into the right position in time to carry out an attack. As I have explained before there are many prerequisites to be taken into consideration prior to a submarine attack on a surface enemy, and if the attack is to be successful and the submarine is to be given a chance of survival after making its attack, then all of these prerequisites should be met, at least to the best possible set of levels under the prevailing circumstances. I kept thinking back to that attack, and I found myself growing increasingly belligerent. I had dearly wanted to see our tormentor destroyed, together with all her crew. Surely, I kept asking myself, there should have been some way that we could have responded in a situation like that? Some way of retaliating?

After giving this matter much thought, I conceived what I thought at that time to be a very bright idea, and even made rough drawings to show our captain. It would take a relatively small charge; say 20 or 30 pounds of explosive to tear a hole in a ships bottom. These charges would have little effect upon ourselves, as the charges the enemy would be dropping would be at least ten times that powerful. But what if a submarine caught in similar circumstances as we were, had the capability of releasing four small mines of say 30 lbs, each attached by a wire to her bridge structure so that they could be checked at about ten feet below the surface, and then let the attacker run on to them? I was sure that this would have the desired effect. Hitting one of these small mines would almost certainly put something like a destroyer out of action, if not sink her. And the danger to us? Very little in my opinion. After all in situations like that, where we were being systematically broken up, we had everything to gain and nothing to lose! What would this be compared to the very heavy explosions raining down on us by courtesy of the enemy above? There were snags of course, which would have to be overcome. International convention ruled that mines could not be laid or released indiscriminately. Even torpedoes had to be designed so that they sank on reaching the end of their run (approximately 5 miles). All this protocol was supposed to be observed, in spite of the fact that the Germans appeared to pay scant respect to any of these conventions or treaties.

Having the devices secured to the bridge presented problems in that, having come to periscope depth, the securing wire necessary to keep the mine at the prescribed depth, would foul our screws, and possibly wind the mine on to ourselves. There would have to be a method of winding the mine in, taking up the slack. I thought that these difficulties could be overcome, and certainly that a degree of hazard must under the circumstances, be acceptable. In retrospect, had that destroyer executed her job efficiently she would without a shadow of doubt destroyed us, in spite of 'Benny's' superb handling. But at least we could have raised a finger, or a mine, in protest.

The introduction of such a weapon would have to be considered in all aspects by the 'back room boys' – most of whom had never been to sea. Many bright ideas evolved during the war, the large majority of them proving impractical – including mine. I expounded my theory to 'Benny' who listened patiently and sympathetically, but I heard no more about it. Probably someone had come up with this idea before me, it may have already been considered and turned down.

There is no doubt that the effect of our hammering left me in a very belligerent mood, quite out of character really, as I'd never considered myself a warlike individual. My job in life was to keep the boat's machinery working efficiently, and to this end I worked very hard.

This period of nearly four weeks refitting in Port Said was very exhausting, not that we had to work particularly hard, but the heat was stifling, especially when we were in the dry-dock. I worked in close liaison with one or two of the firm's foremen who were grateful to get advice on points pertaining to submarines.

The repair work was almost completed and we were lying off at a buoy, when the cooling water-jacketing around one section of our port exhaust pipe sprang a leak. This was a common defect and it was sometimes possible to effect a temporary repair by making up a metal band to hold a rubber patch over the leak, but as we were still in the hands of the repair yard, I decided to remove this weighty section (about two hundredweight) in order to do a more permanent repair by welding.

This was an unwieldy piece of equipment, and difficult to get out of the engine room hatch into a boat. The patching and testing was duly carried out by the firm, but while hoisting it back aboard with our small derrick, it became detached, bounced off the saddle tank, and disappeared into the murky depths of the canal. It was as well that it did not fall into the small boat, as it would certainly have gone straight through the bottom, and we would have followed it down there.

Now we were faced with a tricky problem. This piece of gear had to be recovered, as there was no spare. It was lying on the bottom in about thirty feet of very murky water just abreast of the engine room hatch, on the starboard side. To enlist the services of a diver would create a stir, and probably prove costly. The simplest solution would be to send someone down in a DSEA set, so I volunteered myself. I really didn't relish the thought of diving into the unknown; heaven knows what I'd see down there – that's if I could see at all. There was little or no tide to change the water in this part of the canal.

Donning a DSEA set I slid down a weighted rope into the area where the exhaust pipe was known to be, it was almost dark when I reached the bottom at about twenty-five feet. It was as well that I was wearing shoes, as the bottom was littered with hundreds of years of debris, broken bottles, cans, and whatever other junk that ships in harbour had chosen to throw over the side. My quarry wasn't as easy to locate as I had imagined, and I walked about the seabed using the weight on the end of my line to keep me down, otherwise my oxygen bag would have taken me back up to the surface. At last having located it, I secured a stout line around it, in order that those above me might pull it up and haul it back aboard.

Diving with the aid of a DSEA set was not strange to me as I'd previously cleared our propeller shafts of wires and ropes etc on several occasions, but needless to say, it wasn't nearly as pleasant in those murky depths as it had been in a clear blue open sea.

To create a little diversity and exercise for the crew while we were in Port Said, I organized aquatic sports. We had several good swimmers in our crew, including Lieutenant 'Steady Boy' Steadman who had been a junior champion. These competitions usually developed into friendly rivalry between the seaman and the engine room branches. 'Steady boy' had no difficulty in swimming the fifty and one hundred yard events, but as he was not quite as fit as he would have liked to have been, I had him trailing behind in the four forty yards, in fact he was not even third. A rare bit of fun was the obstacle race, where I introduced a number of non-swimming (non-Olympic) obstacles such as climbing on to our stern to thread a needle.

The crew seemed to enjoy this little water gala, and I recollect that 'Benny' gave all the prizes. He did not participate, as swimming was one of the few forms of sport at which he did not excel.

Permanent and temporary repairs having finally been completed, we departed for Beirut to store ship and carry on with our cargo carrying patrols.

On return from our next mission a few of us were given four days recuperation leave in Jerusalem. I rarely submitted my name for this sort of trip, but not only did I feel needful of a change of environment – I'd lived in *Porpoise* for practically twelve months without respite, and after all, this was a chance to see the famous city of Jerusalem.

The trip was arranged for us by the Palestine Police Force, who were nearly all British, and were to be our hosts. Even then I don't suppose that I would have gone without having been loaned a spare crew C.E.R.A. and two E.R.A.'s. to see to any repairs and maintenance in our absence. And whom should it be but my old friend and shipmate Phil King who advised me to make the most of this golden opportunity. I had no compunction about leaving my job in his experienced and capable hands.

I had seen very little of Beirut, and was not very impressed with the little I had seen – maybe it was because I wasn't in the mood to be impressed. However, this was different, a chance to be away from the boat for a few days, and to visit this very historical city. Quite how we got there I am unable to remember, but when we arrived we received a most cordial reception from the police officers. We were each given comfortable sleeping quarters with mosquito nets, and dined with the police officers in their communal dining hall. Of course they had a job of work to do, but they arranged experienced guides to conduct us on our tours of the city. Sadly these four days were over far too quickly and we were back in *Porpoise* once more. I would have liked to have spent two or three weeks there.

The only other rest period I'd had since we left the U.K. was three days as a guest of a Haifa advocate named Keiser whilst we were in port embarking fuel for Malta. He had a beautiful residence on the hill Mount Carmel, just outside the town; he and his wife were most hospitable. Many of our crew were guests of other residents, and quite why they were so kind and considerate, I do not know, because they did not seem to be involved in the conflict. They were Palestinians, and Palestine, later to become Israel, was their home.

On our return to *Porpoise* from Jerusalem, Phil King and his men had my engines ready for sea, and it was only a day later that we were on our way to Malta once more.

Two or three more of these cargo-carrying trips brought us to December 1942, and *Porpoise* had been in this theatre of war for almost eighteen months. Latterly it had been a ceaseless struggle to keep our main engines in shape. *Porpoise* was the oldest of the mine-laying class of submarines, having been completed in August 1932. and it wasn't only her main engines that needed a complete overhaul, especially after our severe depth charging. I'd now been in the boat for over three years of wartime patrols and was feeling pretty well worn out myself, though I wouldn't admit it at the time. Even when we returned to harbour from a patrol, we spent most of our time working, preparing for the next one.

Whenever we were in Beirut on a Sunday (which wasn't all that often), I insisted on attending evensong at a little Anglican church I'd discovered on the outskirts of the town. It was rather significant that almost every port we visited had a little Anglican church tucked away somewhere, and I generally made a point of attending evensong.

This was a pleasant little church, and I always felt refreshed after attending a service. Some kind person provided a cup of coffee in the church hall after the service, but mostly I had to dash back to the boat to finish a job, or to let one of the E.R.A.'s get ashore. Phil King seemed to have gotten himself nicely attached to us whenever we were in harbour and it was a great comfort to have someone to stand in for me, not that two or three of our own E.R.A.'s couldn't have done so, but they also needed the break.

Lieutenant Bennington had not been in *Porpoise* for very long when he sent for me to inform me that a certificate, together with the personal recommendation of one of my previous commanding officers for my advancement to Temporary Warrant Engineer had been mislaid. He informed me that this paperwork should have been submitted eighteen months previously. To rectify this, he would forward it immediately, adding his own report on my personal and technical qualifications. I remember that Lt. Cdr 'Happy Jack' Hopkins had asked me if I would be willing to accept this promotion if it was ratified, and replying that I would, but in the flurry of war and work since that time, I had completely forgotten. The Navy was now so short of Warrant Engineer Officers that the Admiralty was selecting the most senior and recommended C.E.R.A.'s for this work, promoting them almost immediately. This indicated that I ought to have been promoted almost a year previously, and had already lost a year's seniority. As it was, it was unlikely that I would now be promoted until *Porpoise* returned to the U.K.

Early in December 1942 *Porpoise* received a signal stating that after her next cargo carrying patrol she was to proceed onwards to undergo an extensive refit. This was welcome news indeed to all the crew, but there was a snag! We were scheduled to proceed straight across the Atlantic from Gibraltar to refit in Philadelphia U.S.A. Ugh! The very thought of this was nauseating to most of us. It wasn't that we had anything against Philadelphia; it was just that we were expecting to return to the U.K. As it was, most of our crew would spend the next five or six months in the United Sates. True this would have certain advantages; there would be no air raids and no food rationing, but our families had to endure these dangers, hardships and privations at home.

Eighteen months of gruelling warfare in the 'Med' had taken a toll; not only on the crew, but also on the main engines, and the engineer officer and I considered they were not in a fit state to cross the Atlantic at this time of the year. At least – that was our story! We put it to the captain that should we meet up with a storm such as we had encountered in the winter of 1940, then we would indeed be in trouble.

We seemed to meet with very little opposition in our efforts to convince the higher authorities that it would be much more beneficial to refit *Porpoise* in the U.K. especially if in a naval dockyard. In retrospect this was rather selfish, but we must have had a strong case as we learned, even before we reached Malta for the last time, that we were now to proceed to Portsmouth where we would most likely be taken in hand for refit. Needless to say there was much jubilation amongst the crew at this news.

This last trip to Malta was without particular incident, and we discharged our cargo of fuel, ammunition and food, before embarking half a dozen naval personnel who were long overdue for return to the U.K. We were keeping our fingers crossed that we would not be required for an extra patrol from Malta – so many boats had been lost doing that one extra patrol. 'Tubby' Linton had been asked to embark on one extra patrol in *Turbulent*, David Wanklyn an extra patrol in *Upholder* before returning to the U.K. Each had done more than their share of successful patrols, and both were then lost with all hands while doing this 'extra one'. The military situation had at least improved a little. Rommel's advance in North Africa had been arrested (in fact he was soon to be driven back).

We bade farewell to our colleagues in Malta, and set out to run the Pantellaria gauntlet once more. It was only natural that we should remember *Olympus's* fate at this time, and we prayed that we would get through unscathed. It was the same routine as on our outward journey only in reverse, except that now we had a highly trained and very experienced crew. We reached 'Gib' safely, but even then our worries were not over, as we were very much at war in the Atlantic.

We arrived at Portsmouth not long before Christmas 1942, and what a day (and night) that was! *Dolphin's* lower deck had been cleared, and the sailors manned the walls and jetties to cheer us alongside. Our forward periscope was raised and the signalman, 'Ginger' Facer proudly hoisted our 'jolly roger' depicting our successes as well as our 'Porpoise Carrier Services' pennant thereon. It was a fairly impressive display, six large ships sunk by torpedo, one smaller ship by gunfire, several mine laying expeditions (result of these unknown) two or three cloak and dagger exploits, and nine cargo carrying trips to Malta. Not as spectacular as half a dozen other submarines, but nevertheless highly praised. The daily papers had been given our story, and they gave us a tremendous 'write up'.

Porpoise had, excepting the relatively short periods of refitting, been on operational duty for over three years, and apart from this list of successes had laid over five hundred mines, sunk a German U boat (not confirmed until the end of the war) and escorted many convoys, both in the Atlantic and the North Sea.

We arrived in Gosport in the late forenoon, and had our mid-day meal in the boat for the last time. Our refitting venue was still in the balance until the Engineer Captain on the Admiral's staff, the Engineer Commander of *HMS Dolphin*, the Senior Engineer, and several others came down to *Porpoise* during that afternoon to see and hear her main engines running. I had to make several demonstrations. They all agreed that *Porpoise* should if possible, refit in a naval yard.

With one thing and another it was quite a tiring day for the crew, there were the Customs officers, the press wanting their stories, and the senior technical officers carrying out investigations.

In the evening when most of the excitement had died down, the captain and officers entertained the Chiefs and Petty Officers in the wardroom of *Porpoise* – rather an unusual occurrence in those days. It was quite a party! Several of the lads had been to the canteen and as the evening wore on, quite unashamedly, two or three bottles of neat rum were produced from hiding places. By the time we had poured out our drinks and our troubles to one another we were all in various states of inebriation - some more than others. I well remember one tough nut actually crying on my shoulder, but the whole of the crew conducted themselves extremely well; it must be remembered that we'd been through a very harrowing time together and we appreciated the good fortune of having returned, moreover half the crew were proceeding on a fortnights leave the next morning, and of course, it was Christmas time. 'Benny' had joined in all the celebrations, remaining unruffled and dignified as ever; he was the complete master of these situations. How some of those lads caught their respective trains the next morning is a mystery, in fact I believe that many of them missed their first trains.

Within the next few weeks, sometime in the February I think, the London Gazette announced that our captain had been awarded the D.S.O., the First Lieutenant and the E.O. the D.S.C., and four of us the D.S.M. I regret to say that I did not obtain a copy of the Gazette and cannot remember the individual citations. Despite what I had said to dear old 'Basher' Coombes, I felt very honoured and proud when I was summoned to attend an investiture at Buckingham Palace.

I can honestly state that the thought of receiving a decoration had not entered my head, it was not that most of these awards were not well earned or deserved. Dear old *Porpoise* had done well and our country appreciated it, but as far as I was concerned we were merely doing the job that we'd been trained to do, and for a country that was, and despite a little chaos, still is, very dear to us. As regards the courage which was mentioned in the citation – there were times when I was scared stiff – the only relief was that we hadn't time to think about it until afterwards, and then it was with a feeling of nausea more than anything else.

It was some time in March that we were summoned to receive our awards. We were allowed two guests, and free travel warrants. There was now a very embarrassing decision for me to take, were my Palace guests to be Clare and Joan (now twelve years old), or Clare and my mother? I decided that my mother should accompany us, and that Joan should travel as far as Buckingham Palace gates with our friends Elsie and Percy Mellors, who had kindly offered to accommodate us for two or three days. Joan was very philosophical about this (bless her heart) and was quite content to play second fiddle to her Grandma, which was an enormous relief to me, although my mother fully appreciated my dilemma.

Percy Mellors drove us to the Palace, and with Elsie and Joan awaited our return. On arrival our invitations were examined and we were ushered into the Palace. Clare and my mother were directed to the Great Hall, where the presentations were to be made – and from whence came strains of orchestral music, and those to be presented to King George V1 to a large and beautiful adjoining room full of works of art and tapestries.

Here we were relieved of our hats, coats and gas masks. There were people from each of the services, about fifty all told, and I sat by my *Porpoise* shipmates. We were then instructed on the procedure, and how to address his Majesty. Next we were arranged in the order we were to be summoned. About midway along the line when it was nearly time to be summoned I was able to see into this magnificent reception hall where his Majesty King George V1 stood erectly in his uniform of Admiral of the Fleet, pinning on a medal and having a word with each man in turn.

There sat the audience - two guests for each recipient, with perhaps an additional chosen few, all looking thoroughly absorbed in the proceedings. Behind and beside the King stood Admirals, Generals and Court Officials, many of them in spectacular attire. On a background balcony an orchestra played soft and suitable music.

It was an awesome experience, but one which I would not have missed. I felt as nervous as a kitten until my name was called (mustn't let the side down at this stage), but then walked smartly up to the dais, turned left and saluted, bowed my head slightly and shook hands with His Majesty. Hanging the medal on the clasp, which had already been secured to my tunic, he enquired how long I had served on *Porpoise*. He probably had been given this information previously, but when I answered 'Almost three and a half years your Majesty' he raised his eyebrows and said, 'That is a long time to be in one submarine.' How right he was, especially in wartime. Then I saluted, turned right and marched to another door where another official relieved me of the temporary clasp, handed me a jewellers box wherein to keep my silver medal, and led me through a heavily carpeted corridor to the original room, where my belongings were duly returned. There we awaited the end of the presentations and investitures.

Although unable to witness any more of the proceedings, I was pleased that Clare and my mother could enjoy this wonderfully organized and spectacular ceremonial.

Then we heard strains of the National Anthem, and were out of the Palace again within two hours of entering. My general impression was that the whole affair was so minutely organized that, short of one of the principles becoming completely overcome by the occasion, nothing could really go wrong. Even then I think that the attendants would be at his side, and he would probably come to with his medal pinned to his chest just the same.

At the Palace gates we were met, not only by Joan and our hosts, but also by a whole host of reporters and photographers. Here I was able to include Elsie and Percy into our little group to have our photographs taken. I found it very embarrassing talking to reporters about previous happenings, but they had all done their homework and knew of the Gazette citations.

On my return to Plymouth for a few days leave, a reporter from the Western Morning News was sent to my home, and yet another photograph, this time of me digging in my garden, found its way into the local press. Also the Plymouth Co-operative Society had quickly cottoned on to the flag we had flown on our arrival home, namely 'The Porpoise Carrier Service' (P.C.S.), and displayed it in the local paper together with a suitable caption.

I felt a little coy about the whole thing really. Whereas there was a genuine feeling of pride at being singled out, one felt very humble when one remembered the friends and shipmates who had lost their lives with very little recognition of the stalwart and unflinching service they had given.

In the meantime *Porpoise* had commenced her refit in Portsmouth dockyard, and I stood by her until my promotion to Temporary Acting Warrant Engineer Officer came through in April. 'Benny' had assured me that I would not have to wait long, and had given me a copy of the signal he had sent to F.O. Submarines. This stated that I had been duly recommended for promotion eighteen months previously, and then paid glowing tribute to the way that I had carried out my duties under very exacting conditions – 'My example had been of the highest order and an inspiration to my staff'. This was high praise indeed, from an officer for whom I in turn, had the highest regard.

Most of the crew, including 'Benny' had left the boat within two or three weeks of its return to home waters. Submarine ace 'Benny', still only a lieutenant, was appointed command of the almost completed submarine *Tally Ho*, and took more than half of *Porpoise's* crew with him. He had previously expressed a wish that I should go with him, but *Tally Ho* already had a very capable and experienced engineer officer. Lt (E) P. D. (David) Scott Maxwell D.S.C. had been standing by her for several months.

I would have liked to have served with 'Benny' again, indeed I would have liked to have served with the *Porpoise* crew again – they were a grand lot who were welded into an extremely efficient team. But on the other hand, I was utterly worn out and badly in need of a break after three and a half years of physical and mental strain.

Well this was the break – over three months standing by *Porpoise* while they literally tore her apart. Actually it was well over twelve months before she was ready for sea again; the old girl had taken quite a bit of punishment.

Chapter Eight

I then left *Porpoise* to undergo one or two short courses on promotion. They actually found time to give me a week's 'square bashing' on the barracks parade ground (termed a disciplinary course). I was then given two weeks leave to get 'kitted up' with a new uniform, and returned to the Warrant Officers mess at *HMS Dolphin*.

Clare returned to Gosport with me, as we wanted to seize every opportunity of being together. Joan had by this time been evacuated to Callington. She had not been keen to move from Plymouth despite the hammering the city had taken, but her school was moved to a safer area.

The weather was good, and we made the most of this short spell. Nevertheless I was kept fairly busy learning the art of being a naval officer. There were several duties that I would now have to perform that I had not hitherto been involved with. I had experience with most of the technical paperwork, but I would now be required to assess the character and ability of the whole of the engine room department of a submarine, as well as representing wrongdoers as defending or prosecuting officer.

My transfer to the Warrant Officers mess in Maidstone block went smoothly and on my arrival in the mess I was given a very cordial reception. After all, many of my new messmates were old friends. I had served with several of them previously.

Needless to say I wondered what appointment was in store for me, and I hadn't long to wait. Early in May of 1943 I was appointed as E.O. to the submarine *Shalimar* which was being built at HM Dockyard Chatham, and still a long way from completion. The C.E.R.A., the outside E.R.A., five stokers and three or four key ratings were already standing by. A few more would be drafted as they became available; The C.O., First Lieutenant, and the other officers would not be joining until the boat was almost completed.

Shalimar was afloat at this stage, but was really not much more than a shell, no engines, no main motors, and the date of completion was somewhere toward the beginning of 1943. Nevertheless there was plenty to do, every one of her many tanks and compartments had yet to be tested, and this was a great opportunity for me to compose my 'engineer officers note book', trace all pipe systems and examine every piece of new machinery that was fitted into the boat.

Clare came up to Chatham with me, as I was not overworked at this juncture, and it was another splendid opportunity for us to be together for a while, we found furnished accommodation on the outskirts of Gillingham. This wasn't exactly a quiet spot, although it was rather surprising that the Germans didn't concentrate their raids more on the naval barracks and dockyards. Most of our bombing troubles seemed to stem from the enemy aircrafts habit of jettisoning their left over bombs after the London raids.

I was briefed before leaving Blockhouse that crews, or part crews of submarines building were administered from *HMS Dolphin*. I would be the only officer on site for several months and would therefore have to deal with any of the crew's personal problems. My C.E.R.A. seemed a very capable fellow, although like most standing by, he had very little experience. I kept my fingers crossed that this 'stand by' crew would be a well-behaved lot as there was little for them to do at this stage. For me the awful tension of being on a war patrol was gone, but this was the warship that would ultimately be taking me back on patrol, and in consequence my interest was to see that all work carried out on her was to be of a very high standard.

Shalimar's main engines were being built at the works of Davey Paxman Ltd of Colchester, necessitating several visits to the factory with the C.E.R.A., especially when they carried out the final performance tests.

Then something happened that I did not bargain for. We had at some time previously captured a German submarine intact, *U570* a relatively small boat of some five hundred tons. She was renamed *HMSM Graph,* and commissioned with a British crew before being sent on patrol. On this patrol *Graph* received such damage that she was unable to dive. She suffered 90% damage to her main battery containers, even worse than the 60% damage suffered to *Porpoise's* battery in the summer of 1942. Once repaired she was taken to sea once more on patrol. Her C.O being Lt. Cdr P.B. Marriott DSO, with Lt Peter Langley Smith as his First Lieutenant. She was purported to have sunk a German submarine on this patrol, but this was later discounted.

Having completed several war patrols for us, it was then decided to scrap *Graph*. She was again taken to Chatham dockyard, and the crew, except the C.E.R.A. and seven other key ratings returning to *Dolphin*. I was detailed to be in sole charge of her until she was finally scrapped, or that *Shalimar* departed from Chatham, whichever was earlier.

Naval Intelligence were still very interested in *Graph*, and we had many visits from officers of that department of the Admiralty, and after welcoming them, I would turn these people over to *Graph's* very capable C.E.R.A. Preece, who was far more capable of showing them what they wished to see than I was. Unfortunately it was not possible for me to have entertained them as I would have wished; we had no liquor and very few rations.

We were continuously receiving signals from the Director of Naval Intelligence seeking information on her construction and machinery, and *Graph's* skeleton crew were kept busy dismantling machinery for examination. All this seemed an awful lot of unnecessary fuss to me, although I did appreciate that it might well be of more importance than it appeared, and rendered all the assistance that I could. *Shalimar,* the boat that I'd have to take to war was my prime interest. This lasted for three months and then *Graph* was transferred wholly to the RN dockyard staff. But these

Admiralty boffins were very grateful for the help given, as few of them seemed to know much about submarines. I subsequently received a very complimentary letter from Captain, 1st Submarine flotilla at *Dolphin*, which enclosed a copy of a signal to him from the Director of Naval Intelligence thanking him for all the assistance they had received regarding *Graph*, and mentioning me by name. I was congratulated for my efforts.

This was all very unexpected and very pleasing to one who was so newly promoted. I often wondered what was behind it all; certainly more than a passing interest in the way that the Germans built and ran their submarines. But I was pleased now to relinquish my responsibilities with *Graph* and concentrate on *Shalimar*, which was now really beginning to take shape. A huge section of her hull had now been removed in order to embark her two main motors (there had been a delay in receiving these), and her main engines, which had arrived from Colchester. They were laid on their respective beds and the hull section welded back into place.

There was also a 'T' class submarine, *Trenchant,* building in Chatham at that time. *Trenchant* was ahead of *Shalimar* and for several months the only two officers in the building group were myself and *Trenchant's* E.O, Lt. (E) Mike Chambers. New to submarines, and new to the Navy, Mike had recently left university with a first class degree in engineering. We became great friends, and although lacking the academic qualifications, I was able to pass on the benefit of my long experience to him.

Unfortunately, Clare was not able to remain with me during this period, as she had to return to Plymouth to nurse her very sick mother. But in Clare's absence I was able to teach Mike a little about the ancient game of darts in the little pub just outside the dockyard gate, called the 'Royal Marine.'

1943 was a momentous year for the allies. It commenced very badly, particularly in the Atlantic where our losses had reached calamitous proportions during March 627,000 tons of shipping lost without one single U boat being sunk. But then with the aid of new devices, especially the fitting of Radar into Catalina and other patrolling aircraft, the tide began to turn. Losses of shipping reduced, and numbers of U boats destroyed increased until in July there was a loss of 123,000 tons of shipping set against a loss of thirteen U boats, a crippling loss for the Germans. This then, was the turning point in the grim struggle for the supremacy of the Atlantic. Furthermore, the 'Battle of Britain' in the air had prevented the Germans subjecting us to any large-scale air attack.

I state these facts because, although the war was far from over, at least there was something to be cheerful about, which was a very welcome factor. The winter of 1943/44 was bleak and bitterly cold, there was very little coal for the home fires.

Eventually, toward the end of January 1944 *Shalimar* was given her full complement of officers and men. Our captain was Lt W.G.Meeke DSC, who had had war patrol experience before helping to pioneer, and instruct the crews of a newly formed midget submarine flotilla. He was quite senior to be in command of an S class submarine The First Lieutenant was Lt A.R.C. Jenks, this being his first job as No.1.

Trenchant in the meantime had been completed, and had carried out her trials. Her C.O was Lt Cdr A.R. Hezlett DSC. He later went on to carry out very successful patrols in the Far East, and to attain the rank of Vice Admiral before retiring. Before leaving Chatham to carry out their 'working up period' in Scottish waters, *Trenchant's* officers gave the appropriate farewell party to the dockyard officers who had in any way been connected with her, and of course, the officers of *Shalimar* were also invited, together with their wives.

Then toward the end of February, it was *Shalimar's* turn to carry out diving trials, followed by power trials. We also had a farewell party on board, as well as a commissioning party ashore for the whole ships company and their wives and girl friends.

Before leaving Chatham I was informed by the captain that my duties would also include the censuring of all outgoing mail (a job that I loathed), and that I would also be the cipher officer. To this end I attended a two-day course of instruction at the Code and Cipher Office in barracks. Little did I realize at that time how this job was to cause me so many headaches in the future. This cipher job, I found to be rather complex, especially as I had my mind on so many other matters at that time, but I struggled hard to make myself acquainted with the procedures.

On leaving Chatham we were escorted on the surface to Portsmouth where we embarked fuel and stores, before sailing, again under escort for the Scottish areas where we were to carry out our three-month 'work up' period. This was a considerably longer period than submarine crews had been given earlier, because at this stage, having sustained such heavy losses in our submarine force, at least 80% of any new crew would be completely inexperienced men. Not only did we have to see that each man knew his job, but at the same time of course there were the many inevitable teething problems to contend with. Apparently this valuable lesson of the need to extend the 'work up' time had at last been learned by the Admiralty. Many a submarine had been lost even before her crew had properly 'shaken down'. I had suffered many nerve racking experiences in *Porpoise* while we were working with an 80% inexperienced crew after a refit.

Shalimar arrived alongside the parent ship in the Holy Loch at about the middle of March 1944, nearly three months later than she was originally due. Refitting and building programmers rarely managed to adhere to original dates, and neither *Shalimar* nor *Trenchant* were exceptions. All sorts of snags had cropped up, over which we the crew had absolutely no control. To start with our main engines had been late in arriving, and so our main motors were subsequently channelled off to another boat in a more advanced stage of build than *Shalimar*. This was understandable as firms had great difficulty in keeping to delivery dates. Not only was there an acute shortage of materials, but also many of their skilled and semi-skilled workforces had been conscripted into the services. Heavy air attacks had

180

taken their effect on buildings, plant and machinery, not to mention the destruction of finished products and the time wasted while work staff sheltered during raids.

Nevertheless, at this time the military situation was much brighter. We had almost pushed the enemy out of North Africa, and already landings had been made in Italy and Sicily. The U.S.A. had come in actively on our side, and the combined air forces were pounding both military and industrial targets.

We kept hard at it, during this 'working up' period; engine trials over the measured mile, noise trials in Loch Goil, torpedo trials in Loch Long, and diving exercises off Inchmarnock Sound, where we had a full fifty fathoms of water. Our maximum working depth was three hundred and fifty feet, and we had to find a deep spot within our protected waters where we could test dive to this depth. This we did, and all went well.

We understood that before proceeding on a war patrol we would first carry out a two-week patrol in an area off the north east of Orkney that was considered to be 'not a dangerous area.' The idea was to give the crew experience of prolonged living in the boat. After this we were to have a weeks leave for each watch, before proceeding to foreign waters. Where we were destined was a secret, but we all accepted the fact that it would be the Far East. Clare of course, had not been with me at this time as we were mostly at sea, and so I was really looking forward to a week of leave.

We were three of four days in Loch Goil carrying out our noise trials. This was a very tedious business, passing up and down the loch at periscope depth and various speeds, while running each piece of auxiliary machinery in turn while the resultant noise was recorded by underwater devices and relayed to a small hut on the loch side. This was to be very valuable information when enemy anti-submarine vessels hunted us. Much of our machinery was mounted on rubber pads, and there were bonded rubber connections set in any pipe system that would be in use while dived. Seawater systems used to cool bearings and main motors were subject to full diving pressure. The captain was afterwards given a full list of the noise, quoted in decibels, made by both on board machinery, and the propellers at various speeds.

On one afternoon when we had no trials to do, we had secured alongside the small jetty, and I was contemplating a quiet and restful afternoon. During lunch 'Willy' Meeke our captain said. 'It's a fine afternoon chief!' The engineer officer was always referred to as 'Chief'. 'I would appreciate it if you and the Sub Lieutenant would join me in climbing the Cobbler.'

This shook me a little as I'd never before indulged in the precarious sport of climbing. Moreover I knew little about the Cobbler except that it was one of the highest peaks in that part of Scotland, and lay between the head of Loch Goil and Loch Long. A quick glimpse at the navigators chart revealed that it was nearly 2900 feet high. Without proper climbing equipment or even footwear, this seemed a frightening prospect, especially to one so completely uninitiated to climbing, like myself. But then, one didn't say 'no' to one's captain when he was inviting you out for a quiet afternoon's sport. The young Sub Lieutenant seemed much more keen than I, but then, he was twenty years younger.

Donning submarine sweaters and rubber half boots we set off, and within a few hundred yards came upon snow. The three of us were pretty fit men, though it was quite some time since any of us had taken part in strenuous exercise, but Willy was bursting with enthusiasm.

There was nothing very hazardous on the way up, which suited the 'sub' and I very nicely. It was a bit of a sweat, but we reached the summit after one or two scrambles, and Willy then produced a bar of chocolate for each of us, and we sat down to enjoy a most welcome rest. It was a clear day, and the view was magnificent. Then Willy suggested that we took a more difficult route back down. To this I put my foot down. 'Not on your life, sir!' I said, and 'sub' somewhat more tactfully, also declined. It was clear to me that descent, even by the same route, would be more difficult than the ascent, especially in the footwear we were using.

So snorting at us contemptuously, Willy set off along the ridge, whilst we commenced to retrace our steps downward, hoping to meet up with our C.O. about half way down. We hadn't descended more than four hundred feet when we heard a loud cry from somewhere above us. Looking upward and to our right, we caught a glimpse of Willy making a rather undignified descent on his belly, having lost his foothold.

It looked to us like the end of Willy, as there was a sheer drop of over a hundred feet just below where he was. Fortunately he managed to grab a rock just above a narrow ledge. From this he was able to drop down on to the ledge and start making his way toward the route we had taken, but a crevasse prevented further progress, and he was stuck. 'Sub' and I had in the meantime started to scramble upwards toward him.

To get our captain back onto 'terra firma' once more, I had to hold 'sub' at arms length whilst he leaned precariously over the crevasse and grabbed Willy's arms, the latter having lowered himself as far as possible. At the order 'Now', I heaved 'sub', who in turn heaved Willy, who pushed as hard as he could toward us, at the same time letting go his hold. All three of us then rolled back from the crevasse, safe, but in a very undignified manner.

My initial action when I had picked myself up was one of anger, and, rather disrespectfully I'm afraid, I burst out with. 'I hope that will teach you a b..... lesson!' But Willy was quite unperturbed; he just grinned and thanked us, as though it had been some small and inconsequential happening. Actually he'd come very near to losing his life. Whatever sort of a captain he would turn out to be, I didn't know – but he certainly didn't lack courage. The episode had scared the life out of me, and I felt quite tired and worn out by the time we arrived back on board. I remarked to the First Lieutenant that we almost had to start looking for a new captain.

We had almost finished our 'working up' and were due to start our fortnight's patrol, then a spot of leave. *Trenchant* and *Strongbow* (the latter having been competed by Scotts at Greenock) were three weeks ahead of us and having had their weeks leave, were soon to depart.

Returning from a days exercises in Inchmarnock water one evening, after a trying and tiring day, and having just enjoyed a welcome bath before my meal, a messenger informed me that the flotilla engineer officer wished to see me immediately. Hastily donning my clothes, I dashed up to his office, wondering the cause of this urgent summons.

The summons was indeed urgent. He informed me that as *Strongbow's* E.O. had just 'gone sick' and as she was sailing the next day (for the Far East, although this was supposed to have been a secret). I was to transfer from *Shalimar* to *Strongbow* that evening.

I was stunned! To leave the boat that I had watched grow, and the staff I had trained was bad enough, but to be pushed off for more war service without my leave was just too much, and I didn't take kindly to the idea at all. I raised all kinds of objection, made myself a damned nuisance in fact, and appealed to my new captain Lt J.A.R.Troup DSC. and to the flotilla E.O. for at least a days exercise in *Strongbow*, telling them that this would be as much in their interest as it would be in mine. I could not believe that there wasn't another E.O. available; after all, someone would have to relieve me in *Shalimar*. My own captain pleaded, but to no avail. It seemed that I was destined to get another one of those very undesirable 'pier-head jumps'.

The result of my appeal was a delay in the boat's sailing, and one day of exercises for my benefit. And so early the next morning *Strongbow* left harbour for Inchmarnock Water where we spent the whole day in strenuous exercises in order that I could satisfy myself with the performance of her main and auxiliary machinery.

The result of this day at sea was that I was not at all satisfied with *Strongbow*, and I requested a written order to take over unless she could be delayed to allow the parent ship to do some urgent work (on the high pressure air compressors in particular). This all created quite a stir, and I wasn't very popular with the parent ship technical staff, nor for that matter, with my new captain, who was very young and enthusiastic, and eager to get at the enemy. A delay in sailing was not an unimportant matter, as it meant missing the convoy with whom we were due to sail, and of course, what we were not aware of at the time, was that it was nearing the time for D day, an operation that was currently demanding all the organizing ability of the 'top brass'. My new captain was very disturbed by the disclosure that it was not only my opinion that several pieces of on board machinery, particularly the vital air compressors, needed examination before *Strongbow* was fit to sail, and that I would submit my reasons in writing. As my predecessor did not appear to have taken sufficient care in the overseeing and setting to work of *Strongbow's* machinery, and had left it to the very last day before going sick, I was in no mood to accept this shoddy workmanship.

It was decided to delay our sailing, primarily for one week. Examinations and tests soon justified my complaints and the depot ships staff of engineers threw themselves into the task of getting the machinery into the most efficient state possible.

Since we would not be ready for sea for at least a week, I sent Clare a telegram asking her to come to Glasgow. Soon I received a telegram in reply, telling me that she would arrive at a certain time (actually the times of the trains in those days was anything but certain). I met her at Glasgow and we journeyed together to Dunoon, and thence to Ardenadum where I had booked a rather expensive hotel for the week.

Our C.O., Lt. J.A.R. Troup, who had previously been awarded the DSC for his work as First Lieutenant to the famous 'Tubby' Linton VC in *Turbulent*, could hardly be described as a patient man. He must have been quite a bright boy, being made a C.O. at the ripe old age of twenty-two, and in retrospect I also realized that he had been very tolerant with me at that time. I know that I was like a bear with a sore head, having been torn away so suddenly and rudely from the boat that I had so carefully nursed and prepared for war. However, Lt. Troup subsequently proved himself to be a splendid captain, and I think that he really did appreciate the fact that I was endeavouring to give him a boat that was as mechanically sound as possible with which to go to war.

Our First Lieutenant was Lt. 'Buck' Ryan. The navigator was Lt. E.R. 'Ted' Harding who was a highly qualified Merchant Navy officer, and the torpedo officer was Lt. Geoff Annear RNVR. – all very young, and with very little experience.

My C.E.R.A. was an excellent fellow who had been awarded the DSM on two previous occasions. The submarine service abounded with C.E.R.A.'s extraordinary, and 'Rob Roy' McCurrach was such a one. He was not one of the typically tough types, though tough he must have been, to have endured almost thirty war patrols – almost a record at that time. Not only was he a skilled craftsman (fitter and turner) with a wealth of experience and knowledge of submarines on war patrol, he was an accomplished musician, an artist of no mean calibre, and a writer who had had several of his articles accepted by periodicals. Moreover, he looked the part, tall, with a distinguished bearing and a very refined manner. If I had been able to pick my C.E.R.A. then I couldn't have picked a better one. If there was one fault that I could find with him, it was that he did far more of his share of the work, even though the E.R.A.'s were perfectly competent. This was a common trait among many of the chief and senior E.R.A.'s brought about partly because of the importance of the work, and often the limitations on the time in which the work had to be completed. It was not because they lacked faith in their juniors.

Despite the hard work carried out by the depot ship and our own crew, it was two weeks before *Strongbow* was ready for sea. I was pleased that I had sent for Clare, and that we had made the most of the break, even though it was often after 19:00 before I would arrive back at the hotel each night. Even the proprietor's heart softened enough to reduce the tariff for the second week. Clare deserved the extra week as she had been taken completely unawares, as indeed I had been; she had been expecting to have me home within a month. This was a big upheaval for her for such a short period, and very expensive for us, but I was going to the big eastern theatre of war, and there was a very distinct possibility that we would not see each other again.

We seemed to be very far away from the war here, the food at the hotel was good, and there didn't appear to be a shortage, despite being on short rations for four years. We had dishes here that it would be impossible to procure in the south; I was paying full board, but only had an evening meal at the hotel.

Those two weeks passed very quickly, and then it was time to sail. We said our fond farewells and Clare watched *Strongbow* slide away down the Clyde past Dunoon, through the boom defences and begin her journey to Trincomalee, and war with the Japanese. It was a sad parting, and I felt thoroughly miserable, I'd scarcely had time to become acquainted with the captain, my wardroom messmates, or the crew. This very sudden switch of submarines had upset me. Furthermore, unlike most of the crew, I had a fair idea of what was in store for us. For the past sixteen months my life had not been too hazardous or uncomfortable, Clare and I had been together for most of that time. Now for me, life in the raw was about to start again.

Chapter Nine

We joined a large convoy of merchantmen heading southwards, and stayed with them until we were almost abreast of Gibraltar. We had to get permission from the Commodore of the convoy to carry out a trim dive each day, otherwise we were ordered to remain on the surface in the middle of the convoy.

Three frigate type warships, and a small carrier, which carried three of four reconnaissance aircraft, escorted the convoy. During the hours of daylight one or two of these small planes would take off and fly ahead of the convoy on the lookout for enemy submarines, and on their return the carrier would then alter course ready for the aircraft to land into the wind.

Whilst we were keeping station, and zigzagging with the convoy, permission was given for three at a time on the bridge for fresh air. On one of these occasions I was very interested to watch one of these planes coming in to land on the carrier. The carrier was very close to us, travelling at high speed on a reciprocal course as we had a following wind. The aircraft came in to land just as the carrier was abreast of us, then much to my amazement I could see that the aircraft was about three or four feet too low when she reached the carrier, I expected to see her veer off and come around for a second attempt, but with a sickening crash she flew straight into the stern of the carrier. The occupants of the plane must surely have been killed outright, if not they must have been drowned as the buckled aircraft dropped like a stone straight down into the carriers wake. The convoy was ordered to continue on course, but two of the escorts were detached to look for possible survivors. It had all seemed so unreal, the whole affair was over in a 'jiffy' and left me wondering whether I had actually witnessed this tragedy, which had happened within one thousand yards (five cables) of *Strongbow*.

Our daily dogwatch trim dive was not popular with the convoy Commodore. This was understandable; he had enough on his plate just keeping his convoy in order, without having a submarine diving in the midst of it. On the other hand, it was reasonable that our captain, with a new submarine and a crew to train, would make this request.

I was getting settled into the boat by this time and was getting to know my messmates and the crew. The captain was very young and very efficient. He came from a naval family, and had been brought up in true naval tradition.

Geoff Annear, our young torpedo and gunnery officer had rather an intriguing background. An RNVR Lieutenant, he was very well educated, speaking several languages, and had enlisted as a Petty Officer for special duties, being promoted to Sub Lieutenant before transferring to the submarine service. He did not speak of his clandestine exploits, but I gathered that he had been landed in occupied France several times on secret missions fraught with hazard. It was rumoured that he had earned a decoration for this, but he didn't wear a ribbon. Perhaps he was still waiting to receive it, as his missions were obviously very secret. Though we were quite friendly, I did not question him on this point.

Having rounded Finistere, we were blowing around on our main ballast tanks one morning after a trim dive, using the low-pressure blower (L.P. blower), when the machine came to a sudden grinding halt. On examination I found that a large steel nut had been trapped in the intake. The workmen installing the machine must have left this there, and it had now finally been drawn right into the machine, damaging it beyond repair. This was a great setback, as our captain was very keen to get into action. It was quickly established that there were no spares for this machine, either at Gibraltar or Malta, but a signal instructed us to proceed onward to Malta, and the spares would be flown out. In the meantime we would have to blow our tanks with high-pressure air only.

We were detached from the convoy when abreast of the Straits of Gibraltar, and proceeded alone in an easterly direction toward the 'Rock'. By now we were a little out of touch with the happenings in Europe. We did receive a signal stating that landings had been made, but fortunes had fluctuated so much over the past few years that it was difficult to get very excited. We were on our way to do battle with the Japanese, a bitter and cruel foe against whom up to now, we hadn't been doing so well.

Strongbow remained in 'Gib' for a few days, before proceeding on the surface and unaccompanied to Malta, not even indulging in the luxury of zigzagging. The whole of North Africa was now in allied hands, and we were desperately fighting our way up through Italy.

It was good to see Malta again, the siege had been lifted, though food (and drink) was still scarce, and there had been much devastation. Our replacement L.P. air compressor had not yet arrived, and the delay did not please our captain. Heaven knows I wasn't relishing the idea of being back on war patrol, but I didn't relish delay on this account.

Our machine arrived nearly a week later, and it didn't take us long to install it. Not surprisingly, *Trenchant* arrived several days before we left, and leaving Malta at the same time we proceeded independently, arriving at Port Said, and at Aden, again at the same time. This of course was an excuse for a little party, *Trenchant's* wardroom, indeed all her messes, seemed huge when compared with ours, and her captain had his own separate little cabin, true it was only the size of a pillbox, but at least he had a little privacy.

Two additional officers joined us before leaving Malta. RNVR Lieutenants who had been trained in the art of operating midget submarines, probably trained by 'Willie' Meeke. They were on their way to the Far East to put their training into practice. One of these was a huge blonde haired fellow called Heinmarsh; I wondered however he was able to stow himself into a two man submarine. They made our tiny wardroom seem very crowded, especially at night when they slept on camp beds under the table. However, they did help out our three watch-keeping officers.

We entertained *Trenchant's* officers at Aden, and needless to say our little mess was full to overflowing, she also, had two of these midget submarine officers taking passage in her. It was quite a party, with much liquor consumed, despite the fact that it was stifling hot. Incidentally, I had now been elected *Strongbow's* wine caterer, a post that most small ship E.O's seemed to end up with. On our arrival at Trincomalee on the eastern seaboard of Ceylon (now Sri-Lanka), we found that there were three submarine flotillas, each with its own parent ship. *Adamant* with the 4th flotilla. *Maidstone* with the 1st flotilla, and *Wolfe* with the 2nd flotilla. We became part of the eight 'S' class submarines comprising the 2nd flotilla. The other two had been constructed as submarine parent ships, but *Wolfe* had been converted from the old Canadian Pacific liner *Montcalm*.

Captain S/M2 was none other than my old friend and shipmate of *Valiant* days, Captain J.E. Slaughter DSO. ('Jacky' to all – except when he was within earshot). He, together with another Sub Lieutenant, from *Valiant's* gunroom, Captain H.C. Browne DSO, and myself had joined the submarine service at about the same time in 1926.

My captain raised his eyebrows when 'Jacky' greeted me 'Hallo Joe you old b...d!' This was one of 'Jacky's' terms of endearment, but I knew better than to take advantage of his familiarity, and he, quite rightly always wanted his pound of flesh from every officer and rating, whether he knew them or not. Also I knew that 'Jacky' could be anything but friendly to anyone he thought might be shirking his duty or transgressing in any other way.

'Trinco' was a fine harbour, and had for many years provided an anchorage for ships of the British Navy. I had not been there previously and the first thing that I noticed when I went up top for a look around, was the top of a huge floating dock, which was apparently lying on the bottom. On enquiry I discovered that not long before our arrival, my old ship *Valiant*, which I'd last seen in a severely damaged condition in 'Alex' was being dry-docked for repair when this huge dock just broke in halves, dumping poor old *Valiant* back into the sea again. It was fortunate that *Valiant's* watertight integrity had been preserved, and that she wasn't capsized. Obviously someone had blundered badly, either in the weight distribution (*Valiant* had a displacement of 27000 tons), or in the pumping out of the dock's tanks in order to raise the battleship out of the water. Not only was this a very costly error, but one, which put this invaluable dock completely out of action for the remainder of the war. I had been in several small floating docks in the past and had learned from the dock masters that the pumping out of the tanks to give the dock full buoyancy was a very delicate operation.

Strongbow was very soon on war patrol in the Malacca Straits, endeavouring to stop any supplies and reinforcements getting up the coast to Burma, where a desperate warfare was being fought in the jungle, and where for the first time, British and colonial troops were driving the Japanese back.

If we at sea in submarines were having a trying time in the excessive heat, it must have been hell for the soldiers in the jungle, where the heat and humidity were intense, the mosquito's abounded, and having to contend against swamps and thick undergrowth in their relentless fight against the enemy. We were also on the lookout for enemy submarines returning to their bases after attacking our shipping in the Indian Ocean, or supply ships (many of which were large Chinese junks) taking supplies and equipment to the Japanese occupational forces in Sumatra.

We commenced our patrol around the Andaman Islands, moving southwards to the Nicobar Islands then down the Malaysian coast to the Port Swettanham area. There were many large junks about, some obviously carrying war supplies. As it would have been difficult to torpedo these craft, even if they had been worth it (a torpedo was valued at £3000), we either had to sink them by gunfire or make fast alongside so that a boarding party could fix a scuttling charge. I always regarded the latter method as a hazardous operation as the Japanese were a very cunning race, and we could have easily fallen into a trap. Nevertheless, these craft had to be dispatched as they carried cargo that was very valuable to the enemy.

It was always a relief when the boarding parties returned and we were safely at periscope depth again. – this did not take long, as we rarely came to full buoyancy. We were extremely vulnerable in this condition and it would have been very easy to have used a junk as a decoy, perhaps with a Japanese submarine lurking nearby, or it would have been easy to toss a bomb aboard us as we came alongside. However, we sank many heavily laden junks in this manner.

I think it was on our initial patrol in the Malacca Straits that we had a most unpleasant experience. We considered it rare and indeed lucky if our nightly battery charge was not interrupted or cut short by the enemy, and we would often have to get our charge on as and when we could. Under these conditions the batteries were probably generating a lot more gas than they should have been, and as a precautionary measure I forbade smoking in the engine room while the batteries were ventilating. This battery gas was evil smelling and dangerous, but at least it was diluted by the huge quantities of air sucked through by the main engines. In harbour these gasses would be discharged to the atmosphere through a huge valve built into the bridge structure, but obviously it would be dangerous to use this system when we were trimmed down and standing by to dive at a moments notice. It was also very unpleasant for the engine room watch keepers, especially the E.R.A.'s, who hardly dared to move from the control platform and therefore caught the brunt of this gaseous discharge. When the charge was in its final phase, 'no smoking' would be ordered though out the boat, in order to avoid the risk of an explosion.

On this particular day, we had dived at dawn after completing a hectic night of stopping and starting battery charges, and settled down to 'watch diving' stations in the hope of spotting any enemy vessels that we could attack. Very soon some of the crew were complaining of severe headaches, and soon many were stating to vomit. I myself had such a chronic headache that I could scarcely think rationally – I'd never before experienced such a pain in my head. The captain, himself a victim, had wisely withdrawn to seaward, dispatching a signal to base explaining the situation. It was my duty to decipher signals, but under the circumstances it was very difficult to concentrate. However, within a short time we received a reply giving us permission to withdraw from the patrol area for twenty-four hours.

As soon as we were able to surface and ventilate the boat the situation improved, although it was several hours before we were rid of our headaches. It was fortunate for us that there were no enemy patrol vessels in the vicinity, as the crew would have found it very difficult to carry out their duties efficiently. We would have had to surface in broad daylight, with not even a guns crew fit enough to put up a fight. Within twelve hours we were back on the job once more, even though many of us still had headaches for the next twenty-four hours or so.

The First Lieutenant was relieved before the next patrol, and in his stead came a very young Lieutenant of the regular Navy, one Peter Minchiner, who was not yet twenty years of age. It was his first appointment as First Lieutenant, and he obviously could not have had much experience in submarines. He had had a short period as 3rd officer under Lt J.P. (Johnny} Fyfe in *Unruly* in the Mediterranean, and as 'Johnny' Fyfe was one of that submarine ace 'Tubby' Linton's prodigies (as was Tony Troup), his training would have been first class. They were to prove worthy pupils of the master.

From the start we got along famously, which was a great relief to me. Me, the battle worn veteran of many patrols and Peter, the young enthusiast. He was sympathetic to my department and my problems, and I was pleased to help him to the utmost of my ability.

As the war had progressed there was a steady flow of new devices available to us. Some of them, in my opinion more of a liability than an asset. We had an evaporator (water making machine) installed, which created more noise, much heat (in an already tropical climate), and very little water.

Our air conditioning plant, necessary in these conditions, was very elementary and not very effective. We mostly wore just a pair of shorts and either a vest or a shirt. Even these soon became saturated with perspiration, and as there was not enough water to indulge in even the very minimum of dhobying (laundering), these garments were discarded in a communal small locker in a corner of the mess, the door being shut tight to prevent the smell from permeating. The mere thought of emptying this locker at the end of a patrol still nauseates me.

But we did have several items of fine and helpful new equipment. We had been fitted with radar for some time, and now we also had an echo sounding (depth recording) machine as well as a bathy-thermograph which recorded the temperature of the seawater. It had been established that normally there were distinct

191

temperature layers at various depths – usually one at around the two hundred feet mark. With a sudden drop in sea temperature there would naturally be an increase in the density, which of course would have the effect of making the submarine lighter, making it possible, with the aid of a good trim to literally stop the motors and sit on this layer. It was a great advantage for a hunted submarine to be able to lie doggo, but the big asset was that when the boat dived below this layer it became increasingly difficult for the enemy to track her either with Asdic or hydrophones. Unfortunately this had little advantage in most of the Malacca Strait areas as more often than not we were operating in depths of less than two hundred feet.

Our second patrol in this area was relatively uneventful, the usual quota of large junks, one small freighter (the *Torso Mari* of eight hundred tons) and an abortive attack on a really valuable quarry, a Japanese submarine proceeding on the surface. This was a difficult attack as she was so far off that we could not get ourselves into an attacking position. We missed with two valuable torpedoes.

The duration of these patrols was usually three weeks on the billet and three or four days each way from 'Trinco' making about twenty-nine days in all.

It was good to be back alongside *Wolfe*, and we had then twelve days or so to catch up with the work that needed doing, sleep, good food (and drink) and catch up with some healthy exercise.

We had a very fine Warrant Officers mess on *Wolfe*, its members consisting of fifteen warrant and commissioned warrant officers from the depot ship, and one warrant engineer from each of the attached submarines. Of course, about two thirds of the submarine engineers were at sea at any one time. They were a splendid and very jolly crowd, and captain S/M ('Jacky' Slaughter) just loved being our guest, be it for a formal dinner or an evening of 'liar dice' (at which he was an expert).

We in our mess were able to have some fine singsongs, as apart from several good voices we had Warrant Engineer A.E.J. 'Shorty' Hodge, the E.O. of *Shakespeare* who was an excellent pianist. 'Shorty', like me was at sea for two thirds of his time, but fortunately for me *Shakespeare* proceeded on patrol just three or four days before *Strongbow*. I enjoyed those singsongs, sometimes they became a little raucous, but generally they were quite melodious and well conducted.

Among the submarine E.O.'s I had several old friends, particularly Bert Pinch who was the E.O. of *Statesman* and Fred Raynor the E.O. of *Strategem*. Bert had been *in L21* with me in the early days, and we'd been in several flotillas together, he'd already been awarded the DSM. Clare and I had been great friends with Fred and Mrs. Raynor in the 1930's when Fred was in *K26* – the last of the steam driven submarines of the First World War.

To keep the submarine crews in a reasonable physical and mental condition, it was Captain S/M's policy to keep them at sea for twenty-eight or twenty-nine days, allowing twelve to fourteen days between patrols. Depot ship assistance was given during the period in harbour to help the crews with repair and maintenance work, and to allow them an opportunity to get a little fresh air and sunshine. There were plenty of good beaches nearby and picnic parties were organized. As far as it could be arranged, half the crew was allowed four days leave every other harbour period. (About once every three months).

Despite the work that had to be carried out between patrols I endeavoured to avail myself of this privilege as often as I could, not only did I need to rest away from it all, but my cousins in Colombo expressed a wish that I visited them as often as I could.

Visiting Jack and Louise Smith was always pleasant, and it gave me a complete rest. They had spent many years in Ceylon, lived in a beautiful bungalow and were excellent hosts. Jack, now a major, had been transferred from the British army to the Ceylon Defence Force. By virtue of his rank he was also allocated a bungalow up in the hills near Dijatelawa where many of the defence forces were sent for exercises and a period of rest during the hot season.

For most of the crew the four days leave meant a coach trip to the naval camp near Dijatlawa, although it was sometimes arranged for small private parties to visit the homes of the tea or rubber planters, who were very helpful and hospitable. For me it was a flight across Ceylon in a small RAF transport plane, a U.S. built Beach craft which carried about eight passengers. This was a daily return trip, and Jacky Slaughter's secretary arranged my passage

Before we proceeded on patrol, Captain S/M would carry out an inspection of the boat, in order to satisfy himself that the crew had no complaints, and that the boat was in all respects, ready for sea. On the whole this was merely a formality, as it would have been too late to change very much so soon before leaving anyway.

On one of these occasions I awaited Jacky Slaughter and his retinue, (usually a senior officer from each branch) in the control room, there to follow Captain S/M as he went through into the engine room. I was about to do this when the Commander S/M, Cdr H.F. 'Boggy' Bone DSO* DSC* tapped me on the shoulder saying 'What is there to prevent some lunatic stoker from opening No. 5 Main Ballast Kingston valve?' Feeling rather cross that he should have picked on a stoker, one of my staff – I rather disrespectfully replied, 'Nothing sir, except that we have no lunatic stokers!' And hastily followed Jacky Slaughter into the engine room, but not before I caught an approving wink from the flotilla engineer officer Cdr (E) 'W.A.'Gussy' Stewart OBE.

Actually 'Boggy' Bone's question was quite a pertinent one (if only he had not picked on a stoker); as No. 5 Main Ballast tank was fitted to carry diesel fuel in order to increase our range on patrol. Inadvertently opening its Kingston valve while on patrol could have been catastrophic. 'Boggy' was now grounded, but had been a very successful submarine captain in his time. He had a reputation for being blunt and taciturn, and had been ruthless in combat. Nevertheless he was also scrupulously fair, and I imagine that he would have chuckled to himself at being ticked off by a junior officer. I became quite friendly with him later, he was very keen on contract bridge, and I was always included in his four whenever I was in harbour.

Whenever I could spare myself from the endless work that went on while in harbour, it was very pleasant and invigorating to join in a picnic party and swim on one of the wonderful beaches, or to accept an invitation, usually extended by my C.O. to join the more senior officers in water skiing. I wasn't very clever at water skiing, but it was grand fun, and it was certainly a very good thing to get as much fresh air and exercise as possible to make up for those long weeks at sea, when I rarely even caught a glimpse of the sun.

I didn't really get to know 'Trinco' at all; on the very few occasions that I did land, there seemed to be little other than a small dockyard, a large canteen, an officers club, a small naval hospital, and few people other than service personnel. As there was very limited food and drink, it seemed that we were better off on board, where even there, there were times when the drinks were rationed. This did not affect me particularly as my rations were saved during the long periods we were at sea; I was even able to distribute my 'wealth' at times between my harbour locked messmates.

On our next patrol we narrowly missed adding another submarine to our list of sinkings. Enemy submarines were very high on the list of targets, as I suppose we were to the enemy. At about this time, something a little more personal crept in. There was a most notorious Japanese submarine captain who was nicknamed 'The Butcher'. Apparently he had earned this name as he stood out amongst a generally ruthless enemy as being a cruel and callous fiend. He was a very successful captain, who had sunk a number of our ships, but he took no prisoners, at least for only long enough to strip them of all their pride, and torture them before casting them back into the shark infested seas, whether living or dead.

Without detracting from the very important work and orders issued to them, any of our submarine commanders would have given anything to account for the submarine commanded by this unscrupulous fiend. We received some pretty accurate information from naval intelligence, and several of our chaps at one time or another, had almost ended the 'Butchers' reign of fear. But a submarine was not an easy target, and the 'Butcher' seemed to have a charmed life, which he probably did not value anyway.

On this patrol, when we were well into the Malacca Straits, the O.O.W spotted through the periscope what appeared to be a submarine on the surface proceeding on a northwesterly direction. She was a long distance away, and although the captain commenced an attack immediately, the effort was abortive and we couldn't get near enough to fire our torpedoes. She was travelling at speed and zigzagging. This was very disappointing, as it could well have been the 'Butcher'.

Really worthwhile targets were scarce, but on the 12th of October 1944, we sank a merchantman that was worth at least a couple of torpedoes. We later learned that this was the *Menryo Maru*, a vessel of about sixteen hundred tons.

Later on this patrol we had orders to rendezvous with a couple of agents off the Sumatran coast. This was a delicate piece of work for our navigator, Ted Harding. Not only did we have to locate this tiny bay in a tremendous coastline, but we also had to get pretty close inshore whilst dived. I thought that to find these two men was like looking for a needle in a haystack, but sure enough they were there – at least, we hoped it was them - two natives paddling around in a small catamaran about a mile off shore.

It was still daylight and we were not due to rendezvous until dark, for their safety as well as our own; Sumatra was still wholly occupied by Japanese troops. These fellows certainly led very precarious lives, and the strictest secrecy had to be maintained at all costs.

Before leaving *Wolfe*, our captain had been given a top-secret message in a sealed envelope, which either had to be handed to these two agents, or if this was not possible then it had to be destroyed. These agents were living under the very noses of the Japanese invaders.

When they spotted our periscope they became very excited and began to paddle quickly in an effort to keep with us. To prevent them wearing themselves out we discharged a message in a bottle ejected from our submerged signal ejector ('mutton gun'. as we called it). This was to tell them that we would keep them in our sights, and would surface near to them at nightfall.

This we did, and the captain invited them down into the wardroom. They looked like a couple of Sumatrans. In fact one was a native, the other being American. They were very thrilled to be asked aboard and remained with us for about half an hour. When they departed in their quaint craft, it was with several tins of food and a couple of bottles of Scotch – they to continue their furtive and precarious existence, while we retired seaward to continue our vigil. I've often wondered whether they managed to sweat it out to the end, but I do not doubt that they would have rather taken their own lives than fall into the hands of the Japanese.

It might have been on this patrol that we had a little trouble with McAlpine's tooth. 'Mac' had been appointed to us as a fourth hand, partly to relieve our three officers of a little watch keeping, and partly to gain experience. He had been a medical student before being conscripted into the service as an RNVR Sub Lieutenant, and unfortunately for him, he had now developed a very severe toothache. Tony Troup had not the wherewithal to extract the molar, but enlisted my help to stuff the tooth with a crushed M& B tablet; this seemed better than tying string around the tooth and dropping 'Mac' down the magazine hatch. Quite miraculously this seemed to do the trick, and eased the situation considerably while 'Mac' waited for professional treatment from the flotilla dental officer on our return to 'Trinco'.

We had very little success on this patrol, just one small freighter. The boat's machinery was behaving itself pretty well, and my main duty, apart from deciphering innumerable signals, was to engage the captain in many games of cribbage, in order to keep him alert at night.

About a week before the end of this patrol I developed an irritating rash at the base of my spine, which was also rather painful. Seeking out the flotilla medical officer on our return to *Wolfe*, he immediately diagnosed shingles. This didn't mean very much to me as I had no idea what shingles were. I vaguely associated it with the female sex, and was naturally rather concerned. The 'Doc' explained that it was an inflammation of the nerve terminals, brought about by my being in a 'run down' condition. My favourite past times of swimming and water skiing were banned and even then it seemed unlikely that I would be fit enough for *Strongbow's* next patrol in about two weeks time. This left me rather shaken, not being able to swim was a bitter blow, and although I can think of little that is more uncomfortable than a submarine on patrol in tropical heat, I was not in favour of anyone else taking over my job. 'Doc' told me that it was a mild attack, and if I was careful it might not develop further. I hoped that he would be right, as it was damned uncomfortable, not to mention painful. Tony Troup was concerned, as he had no wish to break up what he now considered to be a very good team. Moreover, a new E.O. however good he might be at his job may not be a good cribbage player – and that would be a very severe setback indeed to the allied war effort!

As it neared the time for *Strongbow* to sail, which on this occasion was a little later than we had anticipated, my blisters were drying up. Nevertheless the doctor was still quite concerned, and reluctant to give me medical clearance so that I could take my place in *Strongbow* again. He was an awfully nice fellow, and I could well understand his reluctance, as I would get no professional attention once we left harbour. Moreover, there was that constant perspiration for a whole month, not to mention the nervous strain, which was the apparent cause of the malady.

I knew that there were a couple of excellent E.O.'s in the spare crew who were just itching to have a go at my job. But there was this bond that existed between most of us, one felt to be a part of the submarine. Basically I suppose it was a selfish attitude, and I set about pulling one or two small strings. I knew that the 'boss man' 'Jacky' Slaughter would help me if he felt it justifiable – after all, being old shipmates did count for something.

So I did sail with *Strongbow* on her next patrol, armed to the teeth with all sorts of dope that the 'Doc' had provided. Poor 'Doc'! I did feel sorry for him, as I was after all, his responsibility. But I consoled myself that it had almost cleared up, and by the time we had reached our billet in the Malacca Straits it had almost gone. Anyone would think I had been pleading for my life instead of throwing away a chance of a nice peaceful month aboard *Wolfe* while *Strongbow* was away fighting a war. I did have ample time to meditate on my insistence though, and in retrospect realized that it probably wasn't in the best interest of *Strongbow*. But it does emphasize this attachment that one develops for one's boat.

We received news that the war in Europe was progressing favourably for us; and this gave us heart. This was the first time since 1939 that we really were getting on top of the enemy, and even victory seemed not too much to hope for. The allies were carrying out devastating bombing raids on Germany's industrial towns, and preventing them from doing the same to us. In the Pacific, the Americans were giving the Japanese a taste of their own medicine as well.

Early in this patrol we did have bad news. We had not lost a submarine in this theatre of war for some time, but now *Stratagem* had failed to return from patrol. There were the usual signals requesting her to give her position, and when these had been repeated several times it seemed apparent that the boat was lost. This was particularly sad for us in our small wardroom, firstly her captain, Lt. 'Pat' Pelly was Tony Troup's cousin, and secondly, with her went my dear old friend Fred Raynor, her E.O. *Stratagem* had left for her final patrol nearly two weeks before us and I remember Fred being very depressed; it was almost as if he could sense the impending disaster.

It was later revealed that she was sunk by depth charges close inshore in only about thirty fathoms of water Her fore ends and tube space were flooded but nevertheless one officer and two ratings succeeded in escaping with the aid of DSEA. I was rather baffled about this, as we had had orders that all DSEA hatches were to be secured from the outside to avoid the rubber sealing joint being dislodged during depth charging. However, it was a magnificent effort to have made the surface from that depth. They were taken prisoner, and were very cruelly treated by the Japanese. Lt. D.C. Douglas, the torpedo officer who made the escape, was normally a very athletic twelve stone, but he weighed in at less than seven stone when rescued a year later.

It was on this patrol that we started to play 'Monopoly' in the wardroom. I wasn't particularly keen on the game, but played to make up the numbers. The youngsters (all in their early twenties – myself almost forty), amused themselves by ganging up on me, and normally I took this in good part, but on one occasion they ribbed me so much that I took the board complete with thousands of pounds of paper money, and threw the whole thing sky high, scattering the paper money in all directions and bursting out. 'Don't ever ask me to play this bloody game again!' It was a stupid thing to do, and I felt very ashamed of my outburst, especially as the captain was playing. Nothing more was said, and they proceeded to clear up the mess. I think that they were really surprised that I had lost my calm – and really, I could have killed any of them at the time. Ten minutes later I humbly apologized for my ungentlemanly behaviour, and we all had a good laugh, but I have never played that game since.

Normally with these fine young men, it was I who poured oil on troubled waters, being the one who had weathered the storm and who knew that after a couple of weeks in these conditions one became very touchy, and if there was to be any sort of life at all, allowances had to be made. That affair rather frightened me, the fact that I had lost my calm over such a completely trivial matter, but no mention was made of this incident ever again.

It was while we were on our way back from this patrol that Ted Harding, an excellent navigator, retorted jokingly when I made some obscure remark about our position, 'Chief! What in Hell's name do you know about navigation?'

'More than you think' I replied, and then added. 'I don't suppose that there's anyone among you who could box the "cobblers compass"!'

Now here was a chance for me to show off for a bit. When I was a boy, and a member of the RN Barracks Boys Brigade (a sort of sea cadet), my father who was himself a fine navigator, taught me to box the "Cobblers Compass". Nothing to it really, as all one had to do was to substitute "Nail, sole, eel and welt" for "North, South, East and West". The only snag was could I remember it? I hadn't recited this one for years.

Much to their astonishment (and mine), I ran through it perfectly - Nail by 'eel. Nail Nail 'eel. Nail 'eel by nail. Nail 'eel. Nail 'eel by "eel............. etc. Etc. though all the thirty-two points of the compass. Their mouths gaped in utter surprise, it was a pretty useless thing, this "Cobblers Compass", but to me at that moment, it was well worth remembering as I had, for over thirty years. I have seen Ted quite recently; he is now one of the senior Trinity House Pilots with the rank of Captain RNR. I forgot to ask him though, whether they had taught him to box the "Cobblers Compass".

When we returned to 'Trinco', there was much excited talk about *Severn's* torpedo hit. *Severn* was one of the original three large 'River' class submarines. (*Thames*, one of her sisters, had already been sunk with the crippling loss of several of our most experienced Chiefs and E.R.A.'s.

Apparently *Severn's* T.I. had been carrying out routines on his torpedo tubes, which were loaded, when by some mischance No. 1 tube was fired. The bow cap was open as well. I would not have considered it possible, with all the safety precautions relating to a primed torpedo in the tube, but fire it did, and it scored a perfect hit amidships on a large, but fortunately empty freighter, almost a mile away on the other side of Trincomalee harbour. There was then 'all hell' let loose, as everyone thought, quite understandably in the circumstances, that an enemy submarine had penetrated the harbour defences, and was about to strike again. Though why she should have picked that freighter, when there were three large submarine depot ships there for the taking, should have been hard to imagine.

I don't think that *Severn* was in a hurry to add this freighter to her 'Jolly Roger'. There must have been a court of inquiry after the incident, or even a court martial, but I am unable to remember any results of these.

It was now my turn for another four days leave. (I worked opposite my C.E.R.A.) and was offered accommodation with a Mr. Wilkins, a tea planter whose large plantation was on the eastern slopes en-route for Neuralia. Geoff Anneer had asked me to accompany him, and it made a change from Colombo, although I really would have preferred four days with my cousins Dick and Louise Smith.

Dick Wilkins was a grand fellow, whose wife had been evacuated to Australia when there was fear of a Japanese invasion. He lived in a large bungalow, tended by three or four servants. Dick was most hospitable, and we had a very pleasant and restful four days. Restful that is, when we weren't blasting away at targets with the service .45 revolver that Geoff had brought along with him. Why he should have brought this gun and several hundred rounds of ammunition on leave with him, I could not quite understand. However, he got Dick and myself out firing with him, which was really a bit of fun. Dick proved himself to be a crack shot! I knew from past experience that I was fairly adept, but it was poor young Geoff who could scarcely get on to the target. We ragged him terribly over this.

On returning to *Wolfe*, I was invited by 'Benny' (now Lt Cdr Bennington DSO DSC & Bar), the C.O. of *Tally Ho*, to a concert on board *Maidstone*. Our sister mess (Warrant Officers mess in *Maidstone* was the proud possessor of two members of the magic circle. One of these was their commissioned Gunner, the other their commissioned warrant shipwright, and they were really excellent.

I was also invited to witness an evening's boxing aboard *Maidstone*. One of those taking part was none other than my old *Porpoise* shipmate, and now the 3rd officer in *Tally Ho*, 'Steady Boy' Steadman. I had known that 'Steady Boy' was an excellent swimmer, but this was a potential that I was not aware of. He obviously had at one time been very good, but understandably at this time was not very fit, even so, he did last the full three rounds very well.

Tally Ho and her crew had now been in this theatre of war for nearly two years, and were due to return home to the U.K. for refit. 'Benny' had enjoyed an outstanding success with *Tally Ho*, even having the audacity to sink a Japanese cruiser. On the other hand, *Tally Ho* herself had had several narrow shaves, nothing narrower than being rammed by an enemy warship, which holed all but two of her main ballast tanks on the port side. Only 'Benny's' superb handling (as in *Triumph* and *Porpoise*) saved her from destruction. He could certainly handle a boat in a tight corner. After the ramming, and even while she was still leaning over at a frightening angle of fifteen degrees, he dived her, which of course then put her back in an upright position as all of her tanks flooded. Everything possible was done to lighten the port side on their laborious fifteen hundred mile journey back to 'Trinco', including moving torpedoes and spare gear, even so she still entered 'Trinco' harbour with a twelve degree list, but both *Tally Ho* and 'Benny' lived to fight another day.

Our 'chummy' ship *Trenchant*, and her C.O. Cdr 'Baldy' Hezlet, were also playing hell with the enemy, working part of the time as a pair with *Tally Ho*.

On return from one of our patrols I had a rather shattering setback. Our C.E.R.A. 'Rob Roy' McCurragh came to my cabin and asked if he could speak to me privately. I had a great regard for this young man, who was a fine workman, and of very high integrity, he also ran the department very well, and was as far as I was concerned, an absolute 'tower of strength'. Normally a cheerful person, McCurragh was now looking very serious and worried.

'What is it Chief?' I enquired.

'I just can't do any more of this sir' he blurted out, and I thought that he was going to break down.

'Any more of what chief?' I asked, truly nonplussed.

'Any more war patrols sir!' He replied. 'I'm truly sorry to spring this on you sir, but really I've reached the end of my tether.'

I tried to hide my feelings. This was a heavy blow for me. So I then suggested that he go away and sleep on it, and that he would possibly feel differently about it all after a few days in harbour.

Of course, it wasn't for my Chief E.R.A. to decide that he wasn't going to do any more war patrols, even for a short period; that decision would only be taken by the flotilla medical officer. But knowing McCurragh, I knew firstly that he would have given the matter a great deal of thought, and secondly, he would not have come to me if he hadn't been genuine. He had been in operational submarines almost continuously since the beginning of the war, and had been on more operational patrols than almost anyone else, and he had twice been awarded the DSM for his outstanding work and courage. Knowing him as a man of absolute integrity, it was clear to me that he had reached the end of his tether and was in fact now bordering on a nervous breakdown. Having had quite a bellyful myself (that is why I had contracted shingles earlier on), I did feel sympathetic – it must have taken a great deal of courage, just to come and talk to me about this. I knew that he had had a tougher passage than most, and although there was still much fighting to be done yet, at least at this time we seemed to be getting the upper hand. The end even seemed to be more or less in sight.

I couldn't help feeling sorry for myself too. I'd had rather an unsettling start with my sudden and unexpected appointment to *Strongbow*. But at least I had a splendid C.E.R.A., congenial wardroom messmates, and a good engine room staff.

I spoke to the captain, who then asked me to bring the C.E.R.A. along to his cabin. He in turn then consulted Captain S/M2 ('Jacky' Slaughter) who, in spite of his rough exterior, was a considerate and kindly man. Even so, I think that it was my strong recommendation that C.E.R.A. McCuragh should be relieved of his seagoing duties, and given at least a spell in the depot ship, that turned the scales.

The chief was promptly relieved by the only available senior E.R.A. in the spare crew who was eligible to take on the duties of a C.E.R.A., one 'Tiger' Jones. I had not met up with this tough character previously, but when I examined his papers I could well imagine why he'd been nicknamed 'Tiger' He had been in trouble with the authorities in one way or another ever since he'd been out there, and it was understandable that no submarine E.O. was keen to have him. Although there was no fault to be found with him professionally, it was his custom to go ashore (whenever he wasn't already under stoppage of leave), to get thoroughly pickled, and then feel it his duty to do battle with someone – often the naval police patrol – not considered the most tactful thing to do. He was under stoppage of shore leave when he joined *Strongbow*.

Sending for him immediately, I explained to him that we had trouble enough on our hands without beating up the naval patrols. I told him that as far as I was concerned the past was history, and that if he used a little discretion when ashore, and kept out of trouble, then we would get along nicely. There was a job of work to do, and only we could do it.

In his gruff and curt manner, he agreed to try, and I in turn prayed that he would succeed, as the C.E.R.A. of a submarine is a very important and vital member of the crew. Rather than have any domestic trouble in the department, which was now running very smoothly, I'd have been happier without him, at least I could do his job.

However, succeed he did, and during the period that *Strongbow* was patrolling the Far East we had no further trouble. It must have been a tremendous effort on his part, and I gave him full points. He was quite a skilled worker, but without perhaps, the finesse of his predecessor.

Poor young 'Rob McCurragh, who had done so well for *Strongbow*, was drafted to the spare crew in *HMS Wolfe* and remained there for a long time. The 'high-ups' did not seem to appreciate his predicament. Maybe he should have waited until he broke down completely.

Meanwhile my old boat, *Shalimar* (C.O. Lt. Cdr. W.G. Meeke DSC.), was having problems. Having stood by her whilst building, I was pleased to see that she was mechanically sound, but the main motors that were supplied to her in lieu of the ones scheduled, left much to be desired, and after a couple of patrols she was sent to Colombo for considerable repair to her main motor insulation. She was there for nearly five months in all, which didn't please 'Willy' Meeke. I was not aware until *Shalimar* had arrived at 'Trinco', that the E.O. who had taken my place aboard her was Warrant Engineer R.V. 'Dicky' Myhill.

Our next patrol was a tedious and boring one, there was a distinct dearth of worthwhile targets. We sank the usual few large junks that were carrying food and materials to the Japanese in Burma, and we returned with one Chinese junk skipper. Presumably this was to seek information regarding the movement of junks and stores. He was a pleasant little fellow, and had no love for his Japanese masters who had confiscated his junk.

We were in harbour for Christmas day 1944, a very tame affair, but much better than being on patrol. It was generally my misfortune to be duty on Christmas day. Whether or not I was on duty on this particular day I cannot remember, but I'm quite certain that I did not go ashore. I recollect that our flotilla padre had a small carol service back in the officers cabin flat. Our flotilla only carried an Anglican clergyman, the Rev Rhodes RNVR, and a fine fellow he was. He was referred to as 'the Bish' by the irreverent ones. In many ways it was a tough job being a flotilla padre, and although most of the officers had the greatest respect for him, alas not many attended the voluntary church services. One of his duties was to be the censor officer for the depot ship crew, with the unenviable task of reading every private letter before it could be posted. I had been lumbered with this job on occasions, and I loathed it. It was however, a very necessary job, as some fellows inadvertently disclosed information which ought to have been withheld, but at the same time, I found it most embarrassing. There was a certain technique that could be developed in reading these letters, they could be read in a very abstract way, so that one could blue pencil a passage that might give some information to an enemy, but at the same time be oblivious to the actual text of the letter.

The most unenviable of the Padre's tasks was to contact the mothers, wives and next of kin of those lost, or very much overdue. – a task which this young clergyman did with much sympathy and understanding.

It was about this time that *Adamant* and *Maidstone* departed Trincomalee with their respective flotillas and headed for Australia, where they were to operate from Perth. This was obviously because there were becoming fewer targets to the north west of Singapore. Most of the heavy fighting was taking place on and around the islands previously captured by the Japanese. The Japanese were either taking troops and stores to reinforce the garrisons, which were now being heavily attacked by the Americans, or evacuating the islands where there was no further hope.

So *Wolfe* and the 2nd submarine flotilla were left alone at 'Trinco' to do what there was to be done in the East Indian Ocean and the Malacca Straits. The huge harbour seemed quite empty without the other two flotillas, as there were very few other ships there. The war was moving away eastward, and we were driving the Japanese back through the jungles of Burma

Strongbow again proceeded on patrol on the 29th of December 1944, and arrived off the Nicobar Islands coast early on the 1st of January. We nosed around a bit to see if there were any worthwhile targets, before moving down into the Malacca Straits, and our designated patrol area 'H'. This was the most southerly area in the Straits, the one that *Tally Ho* and *Trenchant* had been running amok in before moving on to Australia. Being both shallow and narrow this was really a very unsuitable area for the larger 'T' class, However those two boats had been very successful working as a team, and had met with little resistance in the way of anti-submarine vessels and escorts.

Whilst proceeding to our billet, our C.O. Tony Troup, suggested that to relieve the monotony experienced on our last patrol, we (six officers) should draw dates out of a hat, (this would give us about five days each) and we would be accredited, or blamed, for anything that transpired on those days. When on the 8th of January we chased and sank a tug and an oil lighter proceeding out of the Panei River along the coast, Geoff Anneer was credited for this as it happened on 'his days'. In retrospect

202

this sounds rather childish, but at that time it created a diversion. 'Good old Geoff' we said.

The next day, the 9th of January we sighted a four thousand ton vessel that was escorted by two anti-submarine vessels, but not being able to get into an attacking position in time, we missed our chance. Not much credit given to Ted Harding, our navigator. Although of course it was not his fault – but it was one of his days! .

Targets of this size being very scarce at this time, our C.O. sent a signal to base giving the enemies course and speed, they were drawing away from us in a north by north west direction, and we were hoping that one of our submarines in a more northerly area might be able to intercept.

My old boat *Porpoise*, now commanded by Lt. H.B. 'Mossy' Turner DSO had recently arrived after her extensive refit, and was now patrolling the adjacent area to the north, while *Stygian* was also on patrol nearby.

We had been encountering heavy thunderstorms and rain all day and night; in fact it was in the early hours of the morning following a radar pickup, that we sighted this vessel in a lightning flash. The next day we sank a fifty ton junk off Penang, not much of a catch compared with yesterdays target, but at least it prevented another thirty or forty tons of supplies from reaching the Japanese army in Burma.

Later in the day we were contacted and attacked by a 'Wakataki' class destroyer, which appeared to be operating some form of ASDICS. However we suffered no damage and she soon lost contact. It was at least bearable to be depth charged after having sunk an enemy ship, but to be hammered for nothing seemed a little unfair.

The 11th of January was one of Peter Minchiner's days, but all he succeeded in getting was a rather severe attack of malaria, which apparently he was prone to from time to time. Young Peter really was poorly according to the coxswain (our medical man); he had a temperature of 104. Peter himself remarked that this wasn't untoward for him, and that he'd just have to take some quinine and sweat it out for three or four days.

Although I was able to step in and keep periscope watch when dived, (my sight wasn't A1. I'd worn glasses for years – but the captain was never far distant). I was not qualified in any way to keep watch on the surface at night. However, it wasn't too arduous for the others, we had the extra young officer (McAlpine) to make them in three watches, with Tony available at a moments notice.

Chapter Ten

Early on the 13th of January (a Friday, and one of my days), we dived at about 05:30, having fully charged our batteries and our H.P. air bottle groups. At about 06:00 the O.O.W looking through the high-powered periscope sighted what appeared to be four anti-submarine vessels (two of them frigates), heading toward us. It was soon apparent that they were equipped with some form of ASDIC, and had located us. One would have expected a squadron of this strength to be escorting a very important convoy. It was unfortunate that they were not, because we might have been able to divert their attention by sinking a couple of their charges. As it was, their whole attention was centred on us, and we, who had been operating in the extreme southeast corner of our area, were in very shallow water.

We had quickly gone into 'silent routine', and had shut off from depth charging. As 'silent routine' allowed us to proceed only slowly on one motor, and we were in barely two hundred feet of water, it afforded us small opportunity to take evasive action. Although sound did not affect ASDIC impulses, they were doubtless using this in conjunction with H.E. (hydrophone effects). There was no possibility of us being below a temperature level, which would normally be a little over two hundred feet. Our Bathythermograph could detect these temperature layers, below which the temperature of the seawater was several degrees lower, and consequently denser. This layer was likely to sever the impulse echoes, and gave a submarine the chance to sever the contact.

Our C.O. had ordered a depth of eighty feet and our A/S operator, Leading Seaman Ridge, was using his H.E. to keep him informed of the relative bearings of the vessels. At about 06:40 Ridge reported that one of the vessels was closing to attack, and soon we could hear the approaching swish of her propellers with our naked ears, followed by the inevitable 'Whoomp!' of three depth charges which shook the boat from stem to stern. She seemed to pass just astern of us, not too close, although close enough to give poor old *Strongbow* a good shaking up. There was a slight interval before a second vessel came in to the attack. ' Whoomp!' 'Whooomp!' 'Whooomp!' Another three charges went off, again near enough to be very uncomfortable, but causing very little damage. Very methodical and patient, these 'Japs', and certainly very aggressive.

Our First Lieutenant, still quite poorly and weak, and still with a temperature of 103 degrees, decided that he wasn't going to remain in his bunk while we were being pounded by enemy depth charges, so he crept into the control room where he insisted on taking up his normal 'Diving station', in charge of the trim. I don't think that our C.O. was too keen about this, for Peter's sake, although he must have been pleased to have the right people in the right jobs at a time like this. The captain had altered course and had ordered a change of depth, but we were severely handicapped by our slow speed and the meagre depth of water.

By about 08:00 it seemed quiet up above, so we decided to come to periscope depth to take a look at our tormentors. We appeared to have shaken them off, as they were now a considerable distance away on our starboard beam. We altered course again, away from them. But alas, at about 08:30 they made positive contact again and altered course in our direction.

We were trying to find deeper water, but were still in only thirty fathoms (180 feet). The captain ordered one hundred and twenty-five feet, and we had hardly got down there before we heard the ominous sounds of approaching propellers. 'Whooomp!' 'Whooomp!' 'Whooomp!' 'Whooomp!' Four this time, now they were getting extravagant – and a little too close for comfort! Fuses blew, lights went out, and a load of corking showered off the pressure hull. However, the damage was slight, there were a few air leaks and a few telemotor (hydraulic oil) leaks which my staff quickly made good, and the L.T.O.'s soon restored a lot of the lighting, even though many bulbs were broken.

'Phew!' It was becoming stiflingly hot in the boat. The fans, which normally circulated the small amount of air around the boat, had now been stopped for three hours, and the surrounding seawater was at a temperature of over eighty-eight degrees F. Moreover, the circulating water to the main motors and bearings (cooling) had been shut off when we had dived and gone into 'silent running', and had shut off from depth charging.

Many of us were drinking more than our normal share of fresh water, as the sweat was running off us and literally squelching in our shoes. I found comfort in drinking the cold tea left on the wardroom table after the snack that we were having when we had dived four hours ago.

After another interval during which our captain made further efforts to elude them, there was further activity topsides. Leading Seaman Ridge reported that another vessel was closing for attack. It seemed unlikely that these hounds had ever completely lost contact with us. Two of them stood off, pinpointing our position for the other two to pass over us and pound us with their depth charges.

This time we received a pattern of five, which again shook us very badly, though at the time it did not appear to cause major damage. Lights were again extinguished and there were more leaks to be repaired. We maintained our trim at one hundred and twenty feet, but by this stage we were having serious problems with our listening device, no doubt caused by the heavy depth charging. This was a severe handicap for us, as it made it even more difficult to take evasive action. Even if we could not shake them off entirely, our captain could alter course to port or to starboard, but this depended on Ridge giving him the bearing of the attacking vessel soon enough.

As the forenoon wore on the atmosphere inside the boat was becoming more and more unpleasant, not only was it very hot and humid, but the pressure was rising due to all the air leaks, and with many electrical fuses having blown it was becoming very smelly.

During the course of my travels through the boat to check for damage (I was the only one with the captain's permission to move about, and even then, very stealthily), I found that the temperature aft of the control room was almost unbearable. I could only sympathize with the lads in the engine room and after ends. This extremely high temperature was mainly due to fact that having met up with the 'Japs' so soon after diving, the main engines had not had their customary cooling period, and without cooling water circulation the main motor radiators had just about reached boiling point.

The situation generally was a very tense and thirsty one, and unfortunately the ready use fresh water tanks were now empty. To replenish these tanks from the main fresh water this tank would have to be pressurized to allow the water to be blown across, and this of course would cause noise. The captain would not permit this at this juncture.

It was very disconcerting that we could not shake these blighters off. We had by this time, been dived for over eight hours, still in very shallow water, and still maintaining the strictest of silence.

Soon after 14:00 we heard another attack developing, but with his defective equipment Leading Seaman Ridge had difficulty in deciding from which direction. I wondered what would happen to his eardrums if he were still listening when the depth charges exploded. Actually he could hear the charges enter the water, and then he would remove his earphones until the explosions were over.

When we received this particular pattern we received it good and proper! We could hear her screws approaching but it was too late to take evasive action. She seemed to be coming in from our port quarter Whooomp! Whooomp! Whooomp!. It was difficult to say whether there were four or five charges. The whole boat seemed to jump a couple of feet. A cup on the wardroom table appeared to leap up and disintegrate in mid air, the lights were once more extinguished, and then for no apparent reason the boat suddenly assumed a steep bow down angle. We had been at one hundred and twenty feet, but now we hit the bottom at one hundred and seventy feet, and remained there. I think we would still have hit the bottom had there been one thousand seven hundred feet of water, except of course that our hull would have been crushed long before we reached that depth.

The captain again ordered me to make an examination of the boat and to give him a report of the damage. I needed little bidding as, apart from anything else, the engine room had reported that the hatch had lifted, allowing a quantity of seawater into the boat This was difficult to understand, as the hatch, contrary to peacetime practice, was secure from the outside before leaving harbour. But lift it did! This was no figment of the imagination on the part of the engine room staff. There was the seawater to prove it. The only explanation I could offer was that such was the terrific pressure created by the depth charges, the joint rubber had compressed such that the reactionary movement, equal and opposite, temporarily dislodged the joint ring from its recess. If this were the case, then we were extremely fortunate that the that the ring had re-seated itself, if it had not, then the sea would have continued to pour in, and at that depth there would have been nothing that we could have done about it.

We were now lying on the ocean bed, and my first concern was to see if we were taking in any more seawater. There were several severe air and telemotor leaks to be stemmed as quickly as possible – the pressure in the boat was already high, and the loss of telemotor oil would reduce the efficiency of our power operated machinery.

Commencing my inspection from aft, I was not in the least surprised to find that both propeller stern glands were leaking badly, the 'whip' in the shafts due to the sudden shocks would have caused this. As we were shipping water pretty badly through these glands, we lost no time in tightening them up. This was a very awkward job, due to the inaccessibility of these glands, and the fact that they had to be tightened very carefully and evenly while the shaft was rotating. Over tightening or uneven tightening would soon produce serious overheating which in turn would rapidly deteriorate the stern gland packing. We managed to stop the leaks, but we would have to remember to slacken the glands off again, when (and if) we got under way again.

There were also numerous air and oil leaks that had to be stopped. My E.R.A.'s were soon busy, and with the help of the stokers, battled away often in very inaccessible places to arrest these leaks. Everything had to be done with the minimum of noise, we were still speaking in whispers. E.R.A. Holmes, our 'outside wrecker' was having great difficulty with one particular H.P. air leak behind the chart table. There was little room to move, and his two huge spanners, measuring four inches across the jaws and each weighing at least ten lbs had to be handled with great care, as the least noise would be picked up by our tormentors, and they would undoubtedly return for the kill.

I was not convinced that an intake of seawater was the cause of our sudden plunge, the amount that we had taken in did not warrant this, especially as most of the flooding had been back aft, which would have tended to drop our stern and not our bow. As soon as the lighting had been restored I discovered the cause. Due to the shock of what must have been almost a direct hit, our after hydroplanes had jumped fifteen degrees out of phase with their indicator.

The after planes operator (the coxswain at diving stations), was in no way to blame, and putting this back in order was relatively easy, but there was an even more serious defect on the steering mechanism. This was a little more difficult as part of the 'hunting gear' was fractured, and it took us some time to affect a temporary repair.

These were two very important items of machinery, and it was very fortunate for us that they could be made serviceable again, at least I hoped they were, as there was no means of testing them at the time.

At this stage, with the enemy above about to give us another pasting, it was difficult to know what other damage we had sustained until we could test run the machinery, and this we could not do. It was also very important that we did not over exert ourselves more than necessary until we could get more oxygen into the boat, and heaven knows when that would be as we were now stationary on the seabed and unable to take any evasive action whatsoever.

After having completed my report to the captain, he decided against pumping out any tanks for the time being – we must have been at least a couple of tons heavy at that time. Keep very quiet and very still was the order, and I was the only one permitted to move about. Throughout the boat we had members of the engine room staff either coping with defects themselves, or assisting me, and of course, the other departments also had defects to cope with, the electrical department in particular having more than its fair share.

I was very glad to be able to keep occupied; it must have been very distressing for those unable to play a useful part. The majority of the crew had little or nothing to do as we lay doggo on the bottom. This was perhaps just as well, as by now the heat was unbearable and breathing was becoming very laboured.

Peter Minchiner, sitting on a stool in the control room beside the coxswain and 2nd coxswain, was looking thoroughly worn out but refused to leave the control room. Ted Harding, having no navigational commitments was now laying, apparently quite unconcernedly on a seat locker in the wardroom, and when there was nothing else to do, I too, was pleased to sit wearily in the wardroom.

The C.E.R.A. moving silently around the engine room looking for defects, reported that the main engine holding down bolts were slack. This did not surprise me as I had had a similar experience in *Porpoise*. There were about sixty of these high tensile fitted steel bolts securing our main engines to their bases, which in turn, were built up through internal oil fuel tanks from the hull. As each engine weighed about fifty tons, any shock, especially the sort of shocks that we had been experiencing, would tend to stretch these securing bolts. It would have been an impossible task to tighten them all properly under these conditions, especially without making a noise. We tightened a few bolts on each engine, though not too tightly as I was concerned about the general alignment of the engines, main motors, propeller shafts and clutches. It was possible that tightening might even cause further misalignment. This would probably have been the case as subsequent inspection revealed that these sturdy bolts had been bent by as much as an 1/8 of an inch. Heaven knows what problems we were going to have with this misalignment when we tried to get ourselves off the bottom!

The C.E.R.A. also discovered that three or four feet of the low-pressure air compressor line in the after ends was fractured. This did not appear to be a vital problem provided that our H.P. air compressor lines were in order and we had plenty of air at four thousand psi in reserve. However we set to and secured the fractured casting with huge boiler clamps. It was as well that we did, because I was later to discover that the shocks had bent the H.P. air compressor shafts so much that one of them was completely out of action, and the other one nearly as bad.

In the meantime we knew that our Sperry gyro compass was out of action, and that our magnetic compass (Faithful Freddie) was extremely 'dicey', also our ASDIC and listening devices were now very unreliable (the latter would only operate in a clockwise direction since early morning).

It was getting late in the afternoon, we had been dived for ten hours. Normally this would not have been regarded as an over long period, but due to the excessive air pressure and the overpowering heat, conditions were very poor and many of the crew were in a distressed state. The shortage of drinking water had of course contributed to this, and with the captain's sanction, I had during the attack, put some air into the fresh water tank and blown some precious fresh water up into the ready use tanks, the noise of this being drowned out by the infernal din of the charges.

Some of the crew had started to have fits of vomiting, probably brought on by the heat, but of the whole crew, only one or two were getting beyond the 'edgy' stage. The captained summoned me and asked me to go into the torpedo room where Geoff Annear was having a little bother with one of his team. I wasn't very happy about this, but when I got there I found that one very young seaman was rolling about on the deck in a fit of hysterics.

This was a most undesirable situation as, not only was he making a great deal of noise, and the enemy was still tracking us down, but he was having a very bad effect on the morale of those around him. It wasn't that Geoff could not have dealt with the situation, but I had the advantage of being old enough to be this chaps father. As he did not respond to my request for silence, I grabbed hold of him and told him that if he did not pull himself together, he'd have to bear the consequences. This was a threat that I was well prepared to carry out under these grim circumstances, as I wasn't exactly in the most tolerant mood myself. However, this seemed to have the desired effect, and he quietened down, wrapping his head in a large towel so that he could not hear the noise of the charges. I for one was very relieved.

The fact was that by now we were all pretty tired, and not a little anxious. Although in a very tense situation, I think only a few of us really appreciated the extent of the difficulty that we were in. My opinion was that the steering and the hydroplanes would work correctly when needed, but I had little idea of what other snags we would be up against if only we could shake these 'Japs' off. I did not even know if the main engines were workable, nor even if we could surface the boat. Even if we were able to surface it would not do us a lot of good if the 'Japs' were still up there waiting for us, we could expect no mercy from them. We could not risk the boat being captured, but scuttling the boat after surfacing and then swimming for it would have made us very unpopular with the enemy, and I don't think that we would have got very far.

Normally a boat could remain in this state for something over thirty hours, depending on its size, the number and physical condition of the crew, and the condition of the boats atmosphere. In our case, thankfully the main batteries appeared to be undamaged, possibly because none of the depth charges had exploded beneath us, or the fact that individual cells were now mounted on rubber blocks (after *Porpoise's* experiences in the Mediterranean) but to have an undamaged battery was indeed a bonus.

As the afternoon drew on our pursuers seemed to move further away and we lost contact. There was no good reason why they should, as we were stationary on the ocean bed, and they had the use of ASDIC. But as everything was so quiet below they must have thought that they had destroyed us, perhaps deciding to lie off and keep a lookout in case any of our crew made an escape using DSEA equipment.

It was apparent to us that we would have to do something pretty soon. Earlier the captain had decided that with the next pattern of depth charges he would try and move the boat off the bottom and look for deeper water, but we had received no more depth charges for almost three hours.

During the few moments when I was able to rest, I well remember reflecting that after having endured five years of war, and having had so many 'close shaves', it seemed very unfair that things were now going to end in this way. Not long before this had happened, I had been thinking of an early reunion with my family, as, with our recent victories, the end of the war had seemed almost in sight.

I rather ashamedly offered up a little prayer, not that I was ashamed to pray; this I had done almost every day since the war had commenced. I prayed for the strength and the courage to face up to this situation rather than to be delivered from the enemy. I've often reflected on what my feelings really were at that time, I remember that I was quite calm and clear thinking, just a little sorry that this should happen at so late a stage – after all, I had not really expected to have lasted for so long as this. But all these other lads – they were so young.

But I knew that it was no use asking for God's help if we did nothing about the situation ourselves, and I had racked my brains trying to anticipate what problems we might have when we did try to make a move. It wasn't long before I was to find out! At 17:15, all appearing to be quiet topsides, our captain decided to take us off the bottom and to come to periscope depth for a look around.

The first necessity was to pump out the trim tanks with our ballast pump until we regained buoyancy. Our ballast pump was sound insulated and normally very quiet running, but after the deathly hush we had been observing for the past hours it seemed to make a an awful din – but thank heavens, it worked.

We must have pumped out two or three tons of water before we were in trim. Gingerly the captain ordered 'Group down – Slow ahead' on the main motors. I went aft to warn my staff to keep a close watch on all the bearings, thrust blocks and stern glands. Also to listen for any undue noises from our own propellers – not that there was much that we could do about it if there was.

At 17:30 we came to periscope depth only to discover that our high-powered (search) periscope was utterly useless, and the forward (attack) periscope was not much better. Surface objects could barely be discerned, but the captain was just able to make out the line of four vessels about two miles astern of us. As these appeared to be on the same course as we were, we altered course by ninety degrees toward land, this being the best chance of eluding them. Our Sperry Gyro compass being out of action, we were relying solely on our magnetic compass (Faithful Freddie), which luckily, was just about working.

In our condition, and with such limited vision, there could be no question of carrying out any form of attack. The after planes were still a couple of degrees out of phase with the indicator, this was as near as we were able to get them, and the temporary repairs to the steering gear seemed satisfactory.

The enemy had not made contact again, in fact as far as we could see through our one bleary periscope, they had altered course to seaward. At about 18:30 there appeared to be a spate of signalling between them, using lamps. Probably the senior officer congratulating them on the sinking of a British submarine, and giving the order to 'splice the main brace' if the Japanese navy did such a thing..

However, we were not yet out of the woods by a long way, even though we were continually drawing away to landward. The captain, having ascertained that the damage we had sustained was considerable, had a short talk with his officers before deciding that, due to the dreadful conditions now existing within the boat, we would surface at 20:00, quickly ventilate the boat, and make a dash for it in a southerly direction on the main motors, they being more silent than the main engines.

This was going further into the 'lions den' but it would be a move least expected by the enemy. We would then cross to the Sumatran coast into area 'G' if we could get permission from base by signal. This would then give us a chance to properly investigate our damage, and to 'lick our wounds!'

At present our shaft bearings were not getting unduly hot, although the main motors were running at temperatures in excess of two hundred degrees F. despite the opening up of a temporary cooling system. This was a very worrying situation, and except for the one L.T.O. operating the main motors, the motor room was evacuated.

Several of the crew were now 'hors de combat' and the remainder of us were just waiting and hoping for the time when we could draw some fresh air into the boat. This was the highest temperature I had ever experienced in a submarine, it was perhaps comparable with the temperatures found on the top of the boilers of a large ship after a week's steaming, except that it was much more humid.

As 20:00 approached, the captain stopped each motor in turn in order to test the engaging of each engine clutch. As I had feared, both were very stiff to operate, particularly the port engine clutch. These clutches were normally easy to engage manually by one man, now it took all the effort of two lusty lads to do the job. This was more or less what I had anticipated, but I fervently hoped that any misalignment would not result in overheated bearings. We only had to run the white metal in either one of our main motor or engine bearings, and we would be in very serious trouble indeed.

At last came the welcome order 'Surface the submarine'. With a pressure in the boat of over five lbs per sq in above atmospheric pressure, it was wise to run the L.P. Blower on the main ballast tanks before opening the hatch, as well as giving the boat increased buoyancy this would also reduce the pressure within the boat. There had been occasions in the past when surfacing boats had opened their conning tower hatches while there was excessive pressure in the boat, and the sudden release of pressure had taken unfortunate crewmen straight up the tower, in some cases causing very severe injury.

Our temporary repair to the L.P. compressor had obviously worked, and when the pressure within the boat had fallen almost to that of the atmosphere the order was given to open the conning tower hatch. What a relief it was to feel fresh air entering the boat!

The quickest way to ventilate the boat was of course to run the main engines, but the captain deemed it advisable to continue on a southerly course using main motors for a further six miles. All was quiet on the surface, and it was as well for us that it was a very dark night.

At 21:00 we engaged our starboard main engine clutch and started the starboard main engine. Although running satisfactorily, it was making much more noise than usual, small wonder considering the shaking up it had had, as well as the fact that half of its mounting bolts were still slack.

Having been assured that no bearings were getting unduly hot, the captain ordered the port engine to be started. The din was deafening, but probably seemed a lot worse than it actually was because we were so very conscious of the nearness of the enemy. But it was now very necessary to charge up our batteries and to give our poor old main motors a well earned rest.

The Electrical Artificer (E.A.), and Leading Seaman Ridge were busy making repairs to our ASDIC training mechanism. The E.A. had also repaired the delicate mechanism of the Sperry Gyro, but the echo sounder (depth finding machine), was beyond immediate repair.

We now encountered another major snag. As well as charging our main batteries, we were anxious to recharge our H.P. air bottle groups back up to their normal pressure of four thousand p.s.i. But now the C.E.R.A. reported to me that neither of the H.P. air compressors was working. This was a bitter blow indeed. On

213

examination it was found that the shock of the depth charging had bent both shafts. There was nothing that we could do to get them going.

If not before, we would certainly have to dive before it became light, and H.P. air was not only used for surfacing, but for many other purposes. Owing to leaks our reserves were low already, and we would now have to conserve the little we had. Surfacing without using H.P. air to blow the main ballast tanks was a slow business, and it was always important for the captain to get up to the bridge very quickly. Even so, we had to 'gag' the fifteen p.s.i. relief valve on the L.P. blowing system in order to get sufficient pressure without using any of our precious H.P. air.

We were much too concerned with our plight to think about food – we'd had nothing but the odd ships biscuit since early morning – but the chef rustled up something for us to eat by about midnight; that was the time we normally had our main meal.

At 00:20, now the 14ᵗʰ of January, we altered course to 315 degrees toward the Sumatran coast, after the captain had stopped our noisy main engines for a while in order that Leading Seaman Ridge could have a good listen on his H.E. machine. He detected H.E. on our port quarter, and although it was a dark night, vessels were clearly visible on our starboard quarter. This was bad news, as we thought that 'our friends' had returned to harbour. We dived instantly, but without sounding the klaxon, and then proceeded on 'grouped down' main motors.

They were obviously still searching for us, and H.E. as well as ASDIC impulses were detected off our port bow. We turned away, only to find after about ten minutes that our hydrophone-detecting machine was one hundred and twenty degrees out of phase, thereby putting the H.E. bearing on our port quarter. We heard nothing from those on our starboard side.

Gradually the H.E. faded, until at 0130 we surfaced once more, running on the surface for an hour before starting our main engines. This shook our batteries up considerably, and it became very urgent that we charged them before we would have to dive at daybreak. Fortunately we were able to remain on the surface until 0530, getting every amp that we could into our batteries, when, after taking a land fix on the Sumatran coast, we dived.

Whilst dived we removed the face piece of the after periscope to see if anything could be done, but the trouble lay beyond this, probably a leak in the top lens. There was nothing we could do to improve the periscope situation. Three desiccators were carried in the depot ship, but none in the submarine.

There was also a considerable vibration in our port propeller shaft, but fortunately none of the bearings became seriously hot. If we had to go into silent routine again, we would have to use the starboard shaft only. Although the stern glands had now been slackened, they were both very warm and were leaking quite badly.

There were snags on the main motors too; the port side field regulator was very stiff to operate, indicating that the whole of the port motor had moved. We were now gradually discovering that things were not quite as they were before the depth charging. One rather unimportant feature was the control room ladder, secured at the top to a point adjacent to the conning tower lower hatch, and at the bottom to the control room deck. This ladder was normally at an angle, but now it was vertical, indicating that the distance between the hull and the deck of the control room had significantly increased!

We continued on a north by north westerly course without sighting the Japanese anti-submarine patrol that we had had the misfortune of running into on the previous day, but we did sight a plane, that was obviously on the lookout. When the coast was clear we surfaced well up in area 'G' in order to report our position to Captain S/M2 by coded signal. Two hours later we received a reply ordering us to leave the area and return to *Wolfe* for repairs to be carried out.

Our return passage thereafter continued on the surface and fairly close to the Sumatran coast, but we had sufficient air for one more dive if necessary. We did however; have to reduce our speed owing to the excessive vibration in the port shaft.

On the day before our arrival the captain insisted on carrying out a deep dive (350 feet). I could not see the point of this before a thorough examination of our hull and tanks had been carried out. We had already discovered small leaks along the butt strap port side aft. as well as considerable amounts of inter-frame buckling, but apart from the stern glands and the periscope glands leaking badly the dive was reasonably satisfactory.

It was during our return trip whilst I was deciphering signals addressed to submarines in general and to us in particular, that I noticed signals at regular intervals addressed to *Porpoise*. Normally I would have done nothing more than decode the address, as the remainder would not have concerned *Strongbow*. However, as I had spent the first three and a half years of this war in *Porpoise* I made the effort to find out what these signals were about. It became increasingly ominous as these signals repeatedly called for her to report her position. Poor old *Porpoise*! After a few of these signals it became increasingly apparent to me that she was missing. It made me feel so miserable that I could have cried. There wasn't many of her present crew that I knew, but as I have said, one becomes part of a submarine after a while, and I had been with *Porpoise* for a very long time.

This seemed to me to be quite an anti-climax to our fortunate escape. We subsequently discovered that *Porpoise* was lost on her second war patrol in Far Eastern waters, and there were no survivors. There was still a shortage of operational submarines, but *Porpoise* was a little unwieldy for such closed waters.

The captain stated in his patrol report that it was quite a mystery why these four Japanese destroyers had held us for so long, and then appeared to lose contact. I would have described it as a miracle!

We arrived back alongside *Wolfe* on the morning of January the 19th. The depot ship crew lined her guardrails to acclaim our return; news had got around that we

215

had had a very narrow escape, and it wasn't long before the war correspondents came aboard to get their stories. A photographer requested the officers to pose together on the gun platform. A copy of this photograph was given to me twenty-eight years later, together with a contemporary photograph of the same six when we were personal guests of Tony Troup, who at that time was a Vice Admiral and Flag Officer Submarines. (F.O.S.M.). Gosh but it was good to be back alongside again. At one time I really had thought that I'd seen the last of the old *Wolfe*!

Our reserve air had just lasted out. I did try to run the starboard H.P. air compressor on the return journey, but all that I got was much noise and vibration and very little result. It was as well that our 'Heath Robinson' repairs to the L.P. compressor had held.

Now that we were secured safely alongside *Wolfe* once more, I had anticipated a celebration drink, but with the news of *Porpoise* I felt more than a little depressed.

I had to report my findings to the flotilla engineer office, Cdr W.A. 'Gussey' Stewart. OBE. on arrival, but obviously many more examinations and tests would have to be made. For a start, he had arranged for *Strongbow* to be docked in Trincomalee in order that a thorough external examination could be carried out. Before docking several items of machinery had to be removed so that the depot ships staff could commence repairs, for example the L.P. compressor needed three feet of piping welded on to it.

If I had any preconceived ideas about having a nice little rest, these were soon dispelled. As the small dockyard was very short staffed, it was arranged that the depot ship staff should undertake the work on all equipment that my lads could dismantle and get inboard to *Wolfe*. We were to be responsible for the dismantling, and subsequent refitting of all auxiliary machinery, as well as renewing all the main engine holding down bolts (manufactured by the depot ship staff), and the complete re-alignment of the main engines, clutches, main motors, tail clutches and propeller shafts, we were going to be very busy indeed. But at least we were loaned four extra E.R.A.'s from the spare crew.

Without further examination, which would undoubtedly reveal more damage, I could visualize a refit list that would occupy most dockyards for at least three months, and we had very limited facilities. To start with, once we were docked, we would be nearly two miles from our depot ship where, besides transporting large and small pieces of machinery for welding or repair, all except the duty watch were to sleep and eat.

I was given 'Carte Blanche' to get on with, and carry out any work considered necessary, and would be given the assistance of E.R.A.'s, naval shipwrights, or other tradesmen that were required. This was quite a task, and a big responsibility by any standard.

Though not a fitter and turner by trade, I had had a great deal of experience in this sort of work, and almost welcomed the challenge and responsibility invested in me by Captain 'Jacky' Slaughter and Commander 'Gussey' Stewart.

A couple of days before we had limped back alongside, *Shakespeare* had staggered back also in an extremely damaged condition. She had engaged an enemy cargo vessel with her 3" gun, but this vessel had a similar gun, and in the exchange of fire the Japanese vessel either by extremely good shooting or very good luck, scored a direct hit on a portion of *Shakespeare's* hull above the water line.

This is what all submariners dreaded when encountering the enemy in a gun action – just one hit on the pressure hull. The shell, which must have been armour piercing, went right through the ¾" special steel hull and lodged itself in the wireless cabinet, but luckily it did not explode.

It is not for me to recount this incident, indeed I know very little of the detail, but *Shakespeare* found herself in a most unenviable predicament. She was on the surface with a jagged four to five inch hole in her hull, close to enemy occupied territory, (she was in a more northerly area than we were) in broad daylight, and with no wireless. Needless to say the engagement was immediately broken off. Whether or not the enemy were aware of the vital damage they had caused is not clear, but they made no attempt to press home their advantage.

Shakespeare's crew could only ram an old hammock into the hole, and retire at full speed, hoping that there were no aircraft available to the 'Japs' that could be sent out to finish her off. There were several hours of daylight remaining and it wasn't very long before an aircraft appeared. She came in to the attack, but although missing with her bombs she raked *Shakespeare's* casing and bridge with gunfire. *Shakespeare*, fighting back desperately with her Oerlikon and sub-machine guns, lost several men killed or wounded. The Petty Officer, who had volunteered to remain by the hole to see that the hammock was not washed away, was very lucky to escape. This was a crude but effective way of stopping the leak as waves were breaking over the hull. Secured by a line to the casing, this intrepid seaman stayed there for several hours and survived several more attacks by a succession of aircraft, all of which failed to deliver the 'coup de grace'. He was later awarded the Distinguished Conduct Medal.

Throughout the remainder of that day, *Shakespeare* successfully fought off attacks from single aircraft, bringing one of them down into the sea. Her captain was Lt. David 'Shaver' Swanston DSC who naturally wanted all the speed his engineer officer could give him, in order to get as far as possible from enemy based aircraft before nightfall. So it was a calamity when, early on, my young friend and star of our mess piano, 'Shorty' Hodges, in an effort to give maximum speed to his captain, seized the pistons on one of his main engines. Not only did *Shakespeare* then lose speed, she also lost her manoeuvrability.

With her W/T cabinet wrecked she was unable to transmit a signal asking permission to withdraw, or to inform Captain S/M 2 of her plight. But what she did know by means of a previous signal, was the course and approximate position of another of our submarines proceeding on patrol into an adjacent area.

As it was most dangerous to be prowling about on the surface without the knowledge of our own forces, her captain altered course to intercept the outgoing submarine, hoping to establish recognition quickly when sighted.

When the submarine was eventually sighted (a fine piece of navigation by *Shakespeare*) recognition flares were fired. Nevertheless the captain of the outgoing submarine was still not satisfied, he knew that there should not be another British submarine in this position – and suspected a cunning ruse by the enemy, who may well have compromised our recognition signals. Knowing that he would have to act quickly, and while still some way off he flashed in Morse code 'What is your wife's name?' and was greatly relieved to get the correct reply. The captain of the outgoing submarine was then able to send a signal to Captain S/M 2 giving details of this unfortunate incident, and thereby establishing safe conduct for *Shakespeare* back to Trincomalee.

Poor 'Shorty'! He hadn't been in the submarine service for very long, and *Shakespeare* was his first boat. It is very difficult for a junior and inexperienced engineer officer not to increase engine revolutions beyond a safe limit when a very harassed C.O. is calling for more, and yet more speed. We didn't get a great deal of fun in those days, but when we were in harbour such fun as we did get, which was generally around the old piano, generally seemed to emanate from 'Shorty'.

Unlike *Strongbow's* crew, who were ordered to carry out repairs themselves, *Shakespeare*, like *Shalimar*, was ordered to Colombo. Just my luck I thought; it would have suited me admirably to have spent the next few weeks at Colombo, where I could have been accommodated by my charming and hospitable cousins, Lt. Col. Jack and Louise Smith. I was nearing the end of my tether physically, and this would have been a very welcome respite.

If the press boys had thought they had a good story when we arrived back alongside, they had an even more spectacular one from *Shakespeare*, even though our damage was more extensive.

So, from having things going our way since losing *Strategem*, we had now lost *Porpoise* (it was subsequently assumed that she had hit a mine), and we now had two 'S' class boats severely damaged. The enemy was not beaten yet. Our main handicap was having to get so close inshore to seek targets, often skirting known enemy minefields in the very shallow waters.

When *Strongbow* was in the dock, it was no surprise to me to find inter-frame indentations along our port side, abaft the engine room. These 6" H sectioned frames, to which the hull was welded, were positioned at 21" intervals from stem to stern. As many of these dents were over a depth of 1", it was small wonder that our engine holding down bolts had been bent, and the engines misaligned. The rudder and the after hydroplanes, normally about 6" thick and filled with wood, were badly squashed by the tremendous pressures created by the depth charges. Experts agreed that many of the depth charges would have exploded within a distance of twenty feet from us, I would have said that it was half that.

218

Nothing could be done about the hull, except that the shipwrights were employed in welding 4″ steel angle bars to the interior of the hull, in order to strengthen the worst places. The most difficult job was the removal of the bent engine and motor holding down bolts. In places where it was impossible to wield a sledgehammer these bolts had to be drilled out. This was sweated labour under these conditions, and although we did have extra portable ventilation fans pouring air into the confined spaces behind the engines and motors, the atmosphere was not improved by the extensive welding that was being carried out in the boat.

The removal of these securing bolts took us nearly two weeks, and this was followed by a further three or four weeks getting the engines, motors and propeller shafts lined up, and then another three or four weeks fitting the new oversize bolts that had been made by the engineers aboard *Wolfe*. The misalignment caused by the extreme shock was such that it seemed a miracle to us that more of our bearings hadn't overheated, or even melted. The worst of this misalignment was in the horizontal rather than the vertical plane, which told us that the nearest charges had exploded alongside us rather than below us.

We worked from 08:00 to 18:30 each day, with only short intervals for a snack dinner and tea. Then, if *Wolfe's* motor launch arrived on time, we would arrive dirty and tired back on the parent ship by about 1900, ready for our cooked evening meal. Most of the work fell to my own staff, as many of the tradesmen on loan to us were very young and inexperienced. My chaps were 'towers of strength' and worked unflinchingly.

There were domestic as well as engineering problems. During the course of the ten weeks that we were away from *Wolfe*, the motor launch, for one reason or another was often more than a half an hour late, and my staff were left waiting about in filthy conditions, wet through with perspiration, very tired, and very hungry. As no special catering arrangements had been made, by the time they had cleaned themselves, their meal was often cold and inedible. This then meant that I had to dash off to see the depot ship officer of the day to plead their case, and very often having to 'play hell' with him to get my way. Cooks would be called out, galleys reopened, and another meal cooked. By which time I'd probably missed my meal in the wardroom. The whole thing made me furious, because it was all caused by the coxswain of the motorboat simply forgetting to call for us. Having caused a stir – things would then run smoothly for a few days – boats on time, hot water in the bathrooms, nicely cooked piping hot food – then it would happen again, and I would have to go through the whole rigmarole once more.

I had all the sympathy from my own C.O., and from my old friend Captain S/M 2 'Jacky' Slaughter, and each time this situation occurred it was rectified immediately. Tony Troup was quite capable of 'tearing off a strip', but when 'Jacky' Slaughter barked, things happened very quickly. We deserved to be properly cared for; my lads were working like Trojans. However, we did realize that it wasn't all fun for the depot ship crew being stuck for month after month in Trincomalee.

Theirs was a pretty thankless task. No glory for them, just a long and continuous grind.

At long last we finished with the dry dock and the dockyard, returning once more alongside Wolfe where we shipped our repaired machinery and reconditioned periscopes. Another week installing these and we were ready to carry out main engine and diving trials. Just eleven weeks from the time we had started. This was considered by the senior officers in the depot ship to be excellent. (I have mentioned but a few of the jobs done and examinations made.).

The engine and motor trials were a great success, much to my relief, but the deep dive trial gave us all a big scare. All the work we had carried out appeared to be quite satisfactory at a depth of one hundred and fifty feet. Much of this involved me crawling through all the tanks that had been repaired to check for any abnormalities. What an eerie business this was! I would thoroughly recommend it to anyone who wished to feel completely alone and cut off from this world.

Then the captain ordered three hundred feet, our new restricted deep working depth. I was in the control room when we reached this depth, looking around with the outside E.R.A. (Ken Holmes), when there was a sudden alarming noise in the engine room. I immediately dashed through the watertight door of the engine room bulkhead to be met with a terrific column of water, which nearly knocked my glasses off. I should imagine that it was like meeting the jet from a high-pressure fire hose head on, but it was impossible to see where it was coming from.

There was no time to lose. We were already below three hundred feet, where the seawater pressure would be in excess of 135psi. I immediately dashed back to warn the captain so that he could blow main ballast tanks quickly as we were shipping seawater at an alarming rate, he, having already seen the cascade and felt the pressure, had ordered the panel watch-keeper to blow all main ballast. We were almost on the surface before we discovered the cause of the problem. The 4" internal diameter bonded rubber insert in the cooling system had burst, thus allowing a full flood of water at sea pressure into the boat.

It took us a little time to surface, probably in the region of forty-five seconds, in which time we had taken in about twelve tons of seawater. There were two valves which could have been shut to isolate the system and thus stop the flow if (a) we could have determined quickly where the cascade was coming from (it was in the bilge under the deck-plates), and (b) we could get near enough to it, with the water pressure at 135psi.

This mishap was very disconcerting, as we were fitted with six of these large rubber inserts in the cooling system, their purpose was sound insulation, they were very thick and strong, and designed to withstand great pressure. Luckily we had our cooling system shut off during our recent depth charging, or the pressure at that time would almost certainly have burst them all.

There was another concern during this incident. When surfacing we naturally had a big bow up angle, and all this water we had shipped flowed aft to the watertight bulkhead abaft the two main motors. The question was - Had this water been deep enough to destroy the main motor insulation? But thankfully all was well. The electrical staff had worked very hard to make good this insulation after our recent overheating.

It was an awkward, but not a difficult job to replace the burst insert in the cooling system when we arrived back alongside.

I had now reached a stage where I was feeling completely worn out, so as there were still a few days before we were to leave for our next patrol, I agreed with my C.O. that a few of my staff together with myself, should seize the opportunity to take four days leave in order to recuperate. But the very next morning *Strongbow* was ordered to sail on patrol earlier than planned. So much for my rest and recuperation leave.

I certainly wasn't looking forward to this next war patrol, and fervently hoped that we wouldn't be sent down to the nethermost regions of the Malacca Straits again. I was beginning to doubt my sanity in refusing to let someone take my place when I'd had shingles. For the first time in my life I was feeling much older than my age (I had had my 40th birthday while on war patrol). If only I could have spent a couple of weeks with Jack and Louise up in the hills, it would have put new life into me. Surely the war could not last for much longer; the war news from Europe was good and, with the USA forces we seemed to be doing well in the Far East.

I was not prepared for our next mission, although in truth nothing really surprised me now. Before sailing we embarked an RNVR Lt. Cdr. who was a meteorological expert, and it soon became known that *Strongbow* was to be the weather ship to work in conjunction with the Rangoon landings. Now I thought I'd completed the full cycle, having since the beginning of the war, taken part in just about everything that a submarine could be used for

The war had been dragging on for well over five years now, and all those who had been in from the start were beginning to feel war weary. For myself, I'd done more patrols than most who were serving around me now and, heaven forbid, was beginning to grudge the risk of going on another patrol. At this stage, in May 1945, with few enemy targets in this zone, I wondered if it really mattered whether *Strongbow* was on patrol or not. This of course was wrong, and mine was completely the wrong attitude at that time. I realized that I was being tempted to get out, and knew that I must get a grip on myself. It would have been relatively easy to have allowed one of the spare crew E.O.'S to go in my place, but I did not wish to leave *Strongbow* now – I knew that I must carry on to the bitter end, and I prayed to God that I did not come to the end of my tether in the same way as poor young Rob McCurragh had done.

We did not know what to expect on this patrol, it was something quite different. We carried a lot of extra equipment that was to be used for determining weather conditions, and we remained on the surface day and night about fifty miles to seaward of Rangoon the whole time, except for an occasional trim dive. This routine gave us an uncomfortable and very vulnerable feeling. We were a real 'sitting duck' for any enemy submarine that might be prowling around. We could be detected for miles around, especially as we were regularly sending up huge gas filled balloons to determine wind direction in the lower and upper strata. Doubtless the information that we gained was of great value to those gallant soldiers who were now fighting their way inland through jungle and swamp, I wasn't too keen on the job that I was doing, but I certainly wouldn't have swapped it for theirs.

We hadn't been on the billet for many days when we received a signal telling us the war in Europe was ended, and that the German forces had unconditionally surrendered. The 8th of May was set aside to celebrate the victory in Europe. Contrary to the usual practice on war patrol, the C.O. ordered 'splice the main-brace', and invited the officers to have one drink all round, this was indeed joyous news, but not entirely unexpected. My messmates must have considered me a 'miserable old so and so' because I refused to have a drink. I begrudged those at home and on shore their hilarious celebrations; we were still at war out here, and I would celebrate when my war was over.

We did this job for about three weeks, returning to *Wolfe* within the usual twenty-nine days, and jolly thankful I was to get there. Prowling slowly around on the surface in broad daylight, expecting at any moment to receive a torpedo in our belly was not exactly my 'cup of tea'. Submarines had been put to some extraordinary uses since the war had started, but this seemed to me to be the limit.

Actually we hadn't spotted a ship or an aircraft throughout the whole period of the patrol. We had sent hundreds of signals reporting the barometric pressure, and details of various frontal systems. All the while steaming around in circles, sometimes in rough seas, and sometimes in glassy calm.

We hadn't been back alongside for very long before 'Jacky' Slaughter summoned me to his large cabin. He greeted me with, 'Sit down Joe, and have a drink, because I have some bad news for you.' Naturally I was now wondering what in hell's name this was all about. Perhaps he was to announce that I was to be demoted, or that a court martial was pending. He appeared very serious and full of compassion – most 'un-Jacky' in fact.

'Jacky', as he was known to one and all, though not to his face, was quite a character, and could be an unholy terror when the occasion demanded. Nevertheless behind that rugged exterior, and I hope that he will forgive me for saying this, lay if not a heart of gold, at least a kindly streak.

Having poured me a stiff gin (with, owing to the water shortage, very little water) he continued in his inimitable manner 'My heart bleeds for you Joe! After all the work that you and your staff have done to bring *Strongbow* back, now she has been ordered to return to the U.K.'

I was staggered at this news, and wanted to gulp down my gin and shout 'Whoopee!' but I tried hard to hide these feelings, as 'Jacky' seemed quite sincere. He must have realized though, that now that the war was nearly over I would be delighted at the thought of returning home especially as *Strongbow* was going, and that I was simply putting on an act, because I think I blurted out 'Damnit!' However, whatever he thought, it was a great gesture, and I much appreciated what was in effect a 'pat on the back' from the C.O. of the whole flotilla.

Of course I was both delighted and intensely relieved, not that my patriotic fervour was waning, but I really had had a 'belly full' by this time, and did feel utterly worn out. I had spent V.E. day on patrol, and had sulked all day! I certainly had no ambition to be at sea on V.J. day.

Although I had joined *Strongbow* with a chip on my shoulder, (and had never really forgiven the chap who had 'slid out' before she had sailed from the U.K.) I would not now have liked to have returned to the U.K. without her.

We sailed within a week of receiving these glad tidings, during which time we gave two or three 'whoopee' parties for those poor blighters that we were leaving behind.

Even then we nearly departed without 'The Tiger', our C.E.R.A. He had been the very acme of model behaviour since we had had our little talk when he had joined *Strongbow,* but now, as far as he was concerned, his contract had ceased. He had indulged in one of his typical escapades ashore, and was now under arrest, having once more made war upon a naval patrol, in fact on the Provost Marshall himself it seems.

We were sailing the next day, and as Tiger Jones had worked so hard, and had been so loyal to *Strongbow* in pretty grim times, I asked my captain if he would plead with Captain S/M2 to in turn plead with the O.C. Naval Forces in 'Trinco' to allow my C.E.R.A. to sail with us.

What went on in the way of signals I do not know. The affair was not very easy to handle, as the Provost Marshall was, to put it mildly, very cross. However, in the end a certain amount of sympathy prevailed and I was told by the captain that 'Tiger' would after all be sailing with us. He was released on remand, and would be confined to *Strongbow* until she reached the U.K. when, pending his good behaviour en-route, the whole very serious charge of the assault on the Provost Marshall in Trincomalee would be dropped.

Well, here was a 'let off' to be sure, and a marvellous chance for 'Tiger' of getting back to the U.K. with a clean sheet. I had not realized that he had set upon the P.M. himself – no half measures with 'The Tiger'. I interviewed him shortly after he had been brought back aboard under guard, and explained the situation. He in turn was very grateful that I had intervened on his behalf, and explained that it was his nature, and that he couldn't help himself. This I could well believe, since no naval man who could help himself would pick on the Provost Marshall, who was the man in charge of the naval police and all the naval patrols ashore. I warned Tiger' that failure to meet the conditions set would inevitably lead to a court martial – with probably a stay in the 'glasshouse' (naval prison) and a reduction in rank down to 4th class E.R.A. So with this niggling domestic affair on my plate, we finally cast off from *Wolfe*, and virtually bid farewell to warfare, as except for a daily trim dive, we were to proceed on the surface for the whole way. There was very little possibility of encountering any Japanese submarines whilst on a westerly course from Ceylon, they were now having more than they could cope with in the Pacific. Nevertheless, it was a strange feeling.

We breathed more easily as we journeyed westward. Our first port of call was Aden, where we refuelled and took on fresh provisions. The captain allowed half the crew shore leave until 2200. 'Tiger' Jones, who was of course under stoppage of leave, did the duty watch aboard so that the duty E.R.A. could have a 'run ashore' (strictly illegal), although why anyone should crave to go ashore in Aden was hard to imagine; I loathed the place. We didn't expect any trouble with the lads, as they were on their way home, and we didn't get any.

Next stop was Port Said, where the captain allowed the other half of the crew ashore for a few hours. I didn't care much for this place either, but I thought that I might just land for a few hours when we arrived at Malta. Leave expired at midnight, and everyone who was known to be ashore had returned, but our C.E.R.A. was nowhere to be found! Merciful heavens! He had broken out of the ship and had not returned – and with the ship under sailing order too.

We were sailing at 0800 the next morning. If 'The Tiger' didn't reappear by that time there would be a 'rap on the knuckles' for several people, including myself and the captain, for not enforcing the necessary precautions. Also of course we would now be sailing short of one E.R.A. for the rest of the trip home. But then sure enough, just as we were casting off, there was 'Tiger' Jones, strolling along the jetty, tattered, torn and dishevelled (I shudder to think what his assailants would be looking like, because 'Tiger' was as tough as they come). Well, that was that! There was nothing further that I could do for my chief; there were no mitigating circumstances this time. He would just have to 'bear the rub'. He had been under 'open arrest', which meant that he could carry on with his duties, but kept under strict surveillance to make sure that he did not go ashore. In retrospect, I was sorry that I had intervened in the first place, but at the time, it was my duty to have done so. He was one of my department, the senior one, and had carried out his duties satisfactorily, and had been true to his word until 'his war' was over. Now the offence had been aggravated.

It hadn't occurred to me at the time, but if 'Tiger' had been left at 'Trinco' it was possible that our original C.E.R.A. Rob McCurragh might have been able to return with us instead of waiting out there for nearly another year.

We didn't call in at Malta, so I didn't get my run ashore there, bur we did call at Gibraltar where I was able to purchase, not only a few presents for my family, but also a few necessities of life – the rationing of food and clothing was to remain with us in the U.K. for at least another two years.

There was plenty to be had at Gibraltar, and we hoped that the Customs in the U.K. would be lenient with a submarine crew returning from war, but there was no telling.

What a relief it was to be no longer constantly expecting either a torpedo in your belly or an aircraft suddenly appearing out of the clouds, ready to bomb you off the face of the ocean. It was very hard to believe that it really was all over. After leaving Port Said we wore our steaming lights, something that we had not done since August 1939, and when the weather permitted we even opened our fore hatch whilst steaming across the Mediterranean.

I was terribly anxious to get home, but we stayed in 'Gib' for a couple of days. An escort of naval police arrived on board to march C.E.R.A. Jones away to be formally charged. He was returned to us, again under guard about an hour before we sailed. All this was very undignified for a senior Chief Petty Officer, and Jones apologised to me as profusely as he was able, for letting me down. As he had already said, this was his nature, he was a rebel, and could not change his spots. I was thankful that he 'did his stuff' when it was really necessary. 'Tough 'uns' were aplenty in the submarine service, and I had had dealings with many of them, but 'Tiger' Jones was quite unique. He was genuinely sorry for having let me down, but otherwise unrepentant, and willing to accept any punishment the authorities would ultimately inflict upon him.

Our last lap was fairly comfortable; the 'Bay' was on its best behaviour. A little fog up channel was disconcerting; at one time there was doubt about taking the short cut past the Needles and into the Solent, or whether to take the more southerly course around St. Catherine's Point. However, the fog cleared sufficiently for us to take the inshore route, and excitement on board mounted steadily as we neared Portsmouth.

The lower deck was cleared to cheer us alongside Fort Blockhouse – my second experience of this since the war had started, and we were welcomed back with open arms.

One of my first duties was to report to the flotilla engineer officer, who was none other than my friend and classmate in the artificer apprentices, Cdr. (E) A.E. 'Bert' Hollenby. We were both forty years of age, he was promoted to Commander at about the same time as I had been made Temporary Warrant Engineer, and we had quite a long chat. The primary reason for my visit was to inform him of *Strongbow's* condition, and what temporary and permanent repairs were needed, but he was mostly concerned about myself. I explained to him that of the five and a half years we had been at war, I had spent over four in an operational submarine, during which time I had changed from feeling much younger than my years, to very much older. 'Bert' made light of this and consoled me that after a little leave I'd soon feel my old self again – I wasn't so sure.

He then informed me that the Engineer Captain on the Admirals staff wished to interview me. This was the great Sidney Frew, who had risen from an E.R.A. to

225

become Vice Admiral Sir Sydney Frew. So I trotted along to see him, taking with me a couple of our very bent engine securing bolts as exhibits. He was a very shrewd and clever engineer, and was very interested in the effect of heavy depth charging on various types of machinery.

Our rather truculent C.E.R.A. has been whisked away under guard as soon as we had arrived. It was a relief to me that I was not required to give evidence at his trial. I heard nothing of him for several years when quite unexpectedly I met him aboard one of our depot ships. He was no longer a member of the submarine service, and was still a 4th class E.R.A., the result of again being several times in hot water during that period.

Yet serving on a submarine depot ship his knowledge and experience was very valuable. He was still cheerful and quite philosophical about his lot, and realized that it was all very much his own fault.

Our first C.E.R.A., Rob McCurragh DSM and Bar, remained at 'Trinco' for some time after the war had finished, and *Wolfe* had departed, which seemed rather hard luck. He was not married, or it would have been a bitter blow to swallow. He eventually left the Navy after serving for twelve years, and passed examinations to qualify for a teaching post. He later wrote to me, asking for a reference, which I was very pleased to furnish, as I thought him to be admirably suited for this vocation. Strictly speaking I don't think that officers were permitted to give private references, but I gave it just the same.

It was my wish to proceed on leave within a day or so of our arrival, but much to my disgust, we were then given orders to take *Strongbow* up channel to Chatham. Only those who lived in the London or Kent areas were pleased about this.

Normally it was my policy to stand back and let others choose when they wanted their leave, fitting myself in as and when convenient, but this time I asked 'Tony' if I could have first leave. Our C.E.R.A. had not been replaced, so the next senior E.R.A., our 'outside wrecker' young Ken Holmes had to take over the duties of C.E.R.A. and take the opposite leave to me.

It was like walking on air, the war was virtually finished, and I had three weeks leave to come. It was good to get home again and to see the loved ones who, not so very long ago I thought I would never see again. Joan, having endured some of the worst air raids in Plymouth before she was evacuated to Callington, was now also home on vacation.

Having been cheated out of the V.E. celebrations, I was determined to have my own as soon as our small family were re-united. The folk around us must have thought me 'barmy' when, on this beautiful August afternoon we hung out the flags, invited some forty guests to tea, and danced on our tennis lawn. It was certainly quite a party!

Then I took Clare and Joan off to Cornwall for a fortnight to find accommodation in a hotel on the sea front at Falmouth. We were quite comfortable there, but the food was poor. We were of course, still rationed and were served with food, which was out of a tin. Joan was more than pleased to get my share of tinned beans etc.

Early in our stay a telegram arrived informing me that it had been announced in the London Gazette that I had been awarded the Distinguished Service Cross. This was quite unexpected, and made me feel proud but nevertheless humble. The quotation mentioned something about 'bravery and distinguished service'. Our Captain, 'Tony' Troup was awarded his second DSC, and the Coxswain, together with Leading Seaman Ridge and our outside E.R.A. Ken Holmes, were each awarded the DSM.

I was very sorry that Peter Minchiner had been omitted. He was a fine First Lieutenant, and very courageous to have stuck to his task all those hours whilst in a high fever. My next reaction was that I would now be able to take Joan to Buckingham Palace, having felt more than a little guilty for not taking her previously.

We hadn't been in Falmouth for more than a few days when another telegram arrived. This one was not so welcome; it was recalling me to Chatham the very next day, because *Strongbow* was now to return to Fort Blockhouse. I was furious about this, because I did not consider that my presence was necessary for this move; not only was this going to be a surface trip of just some one hundred and sixty miles which our on board E.R.A.'s could have coped with quite happily, but even if an engineer officer was required, there were several at Fort Blockhouse who hadn't been to sea for a considerable time. This was the first leave of over a week that I'd had for five years, except for the 'kitting up' leave I'd had when I was promoted, and we were booked in at this hotel for a fortnight. They did give me an extra three days leave afterwards, but my holiday had been broken up. I voiced my displeasure when I returned to Fort Blockhouse, implying that it would have been an opportunity for one of the 'wallflowers' to have gained a little sea experience – a bit saucy for a very junior engineer officer. On reflection, this really was a poor tempered approach, as I don't suppose they were aware of my predicament, but this after all, was the effect of the war on my powers of tolerance. I sulked all the way back to Falmouth to continue my leave. Toward the end of the war I became very bitter, bearing instant grudges, and incidents like this did not improve my demeanour, although still intensely patriotic, I could not bear the thought of being exploited in any way.

No sooner had I arrived back in Falmouth than we received the news that everyone had been waiting for, the Japanese had surrendered, and the whole population except myself, celebrated V.J. day. I could raise no enthusiasm whatsoever; it all seemed an awful anti-climax. Of course I was glad that it was all finished, but we had lost nearly eighty submarines, and with them so many of my good friends and contemporaries. Very few of the original fifty submarines that we had at the start of the war, now remained.

I received several pathetic enquiries from wives and mothers regarding their loved ones. One wife wrote to me asking if there was any hope for her husband, a friend of mine, who was listed as missing, presumed dead. Well, it wasn't for me to dispel the last vestige of hope, but when a submarine was lost the whole crew usually went with her, unless it happened to be in very shallow water, when any of those fortunate enough to escape became prisoners of war, as in the case of *Starfish*.

The years of captivity seemed to have taken a toll on those ex prisoners of war whom I subsequently met up with, particularly those who had had the misfortune to fall into the hands of the Japanese.

All of our wives had undergone a terrible ordeal, each expecting the next missing submarine to be her husband's. Clare had had more than most to endure, as I had spent such a long time at sea, not to mention the strain of the Plymouth air raids. Thankfully she was unaware of the many times that we came so close to being lost, and of course, I had the drafting office to thank on at least two occasions, for not being aboard a boat that was lost with all hands.

I'd been in *Seahorse* for nearly two years before the war. Alas she had had a very short innings. *Porpoise* had a long, if very precarious innings, and did much valuable work before she was finally lost, again with all hands. My draft to *H31* had been cancelled, and she had been lost with all hands. As each one of these had been lost, a part of me seemed to go with them. I could only consider that I was extremely fortunate to have survived.

Leave over, and feeling somewhat refreshed, I returned to *Dolphin* to find myself temporarily out of a job. The experts had examined poor old *Strongbow*, and with the war now over, decided that she should be scrapped. It was obvious that many of our submarines would now have to be sent to the breakers yards, and the first to go would be the oldest and the ones who had suffered most damage. What was in store for me now? I did hope that I too would not be put on the scrap heap, at least not for a while yet. It was a very unsettling time for me in that respect. I hadn't even considered what I would do if I left the navy. Under normal circumstances I would have left the Navy at forty, and would have been prepared for it. Those who had enlisted only for the duration of the war now had jobs to return to. I suggested to Clare that it would be better for her to remain in Plymouth until I found out what was going to happen to me.

Part Three - The Post-War Years

So what I wondered, did their Lordships have in store for me now that the war was over? Little did I realize at that time that I would still be going to sea in a submarine at the ripe old age of forty-nine!

Chapter Eleven

I did not have very long to wait before finding out what was going to happen to me next. Within a matter of weeks I was appointed as engineer officer to the newly formed Reserve Submarine Group. (R.G.F.) The 'F' stood for Falmouth. Gosh, but this sounded good!

A job at Devonport would have been ideal, but this was more than I could have hoped for. I was thankful now to have been born in the little village of Budock Water, near Falmouth, many relatives and friends lived in that district, and my uncle, Superintendent E. Norish was Superintendent of Police in Falmouth. It was my wish now to get Clare down there as soon as I was settled.

This group was to comprise submarines of all classes that were now destined for the breakers yard. This must include *Strongbow*. The C.O. of the group was Lt. Cdr H.D. Bowker RNR., who had been a prisoner of war in German hands for almost four years. The only other officer was a young RNVR lieutenant who was to be our First Lieutenant; otherwise we had a full *'T'* class submarine crew.

Captain G.C. Phillips' old command, *Ursula,* one of the old *'U'* class boats, was commissioned, and was to be our base ship. We made a surface run to Falmouth, where we berthed alongside one of the jetties at Siley Cox Ship Repair Docks.

All the other submarines, which were awaiting purchase by the ship-breakers, were to be de-stored, de-fuelled, and were to have their main batteries removed before being towed to Falmouth. Our job was to have them towed to the beautiful Restronquet Creek, and berth them high and dry on the mud bank at high water, to await disposal.

All the Reserve Group crew had to find private accommodation ashore, and were paid a subsistence allowance. I was lucky because my Aunt Alice was pleased to have me board with them, and I travelled by train to Plymouth at every weekend so that the allowance paid to me was sufficient to pay for my keep in Falmouth during the week, and to cover my weekend train fare to Plymouth.

It was a peach of a job, no major worries and just enough work to keep us fairly busy. It was apparent to me that I had been given this 'cushy number' in my own interest, in order to find my feet, and to recuperate a little before enforced retirement; the war was over and there was bound to be a large reduction in the numbers of naval personnel.

My aim was to get Clare down to Falmouth, but there were problems. Joan was now studying for the Chartered Institute of Secretaries examination at Plymouth Technical College. Moreover, it was not long before Clare became poorly, and in the November had to undergo a not very serious abdominal operation from which she appeared to recover very quickly.

As soon as we had arrived at Falmouth, the submarines began to arrive. *Strongbow* and *Shakespeare* were among the first, followed by many other famous names of submarines whose C.O.'s had accomplished great deeds during this war. Amongst them was *Torbay*, whose C.O. was 'Tony' Miers (Later Rear Admiral Sir 'Tony' Miers), who was awarded the V.C. as well as two DSO's. *Thrasher*, whose C.O. 'Rufus McKenzie (Later Vice Admiral Sir Hugh 'Rufus' McKenzie) also the holder of two DSO's. Lt. P. S.W. Roberts and Petty Officer (later Lt.) T.W. Gould, both awarded V.C's for the thrilling exploit in removal of a live bomb from under *Thrasher's* casing. *Rorqual*, the only surviving *Porpoise* class - whose C.O., Cdr R.H. Dewhurst (my C.O. of *Seahorse* days) was awarded three DSO's; *Tribune, Terrapin* (whose port side, like that of *Strongbow's*, was stove in by depth charges), and many others, fourteen in all.

We were given a small landing craft to transport us to and from Restroquet Creek, and it was our captain's duty to arrange for the local tugs to tow these war weary submarines to the creek for mud berthing at high water. There was little of value left in them when they arrived, nevertheless we secured all except one hatch from the inside and that one was padlocked shut from the outside after we had opened the main vents by hand to allow the boats to settle on the mud.

Needless to say, the mud berthing of these submarines in Restroquet Creek was not very popular amongst the local inhabitants, and I had to agree that they didn't exactly enhance the view. It was a beautiful creek when the tide was in, and was a popular spot for sailing in the summer. One of our problems was that we were unable to berth them in an orderly fashion; they were mostly facing in the same direction, but the distance from the shore depended on the height of the tide and the handling by the tug captains. The submarines were totally devoid of power, and the draught of each one varied considerably. We did our best, but it still wasn't a very pretty picture.

The winter of 1945/46 was one of the coldest on record, and we had to cope with snow and ice for several weeks. Those trips up to Restronquent were perishing cold. We had difficulty in starting the diesel engines of the landing craft; dramatic measures, not entirely conforming to Admiralty rules and regulations, often had to be employed.

'Dolphin', under whose jurisdiction we came, regarded us as a very useful spare gear store and we were constantly receiving orders to dismantle portions of machinery for transport back to Fort Blockhouse. This I was very pleased to do, except that it meant a very cold trip up to the relevant submarine, a distance of about five miles.

Luckily there was a very nice 'old world' inn situated on the southern bank of the creek where we often stopped for a 'warm up'. The Pandora Inn could be approached easily in our small skiff, but only when the tide was fairly well in.

Having mud berthed our entire flotilla except *Ursula*; we then received orders to re-float the boats that had now been sold, in order that they could be towed to the ship-breakers. Where it was relatively easy to mud-berth a submarine, it was rather a different 'kettle of fish' to re-float one after it had been settled on the mud for several weeks or months. To start with, a large quantity of mud would have found its way into the free-flood holes in the bottoms of the main ballast tanks, making her three or four tons heavier than before she was berthed. Although we were fitted with an air compressor on the landing craft, it had not nearly the capacity of the submarines own compressors, which of course we could not use.

Our only hope was to hire two large harbour tugs, and commence the removal operation on the high spring tides. As these lasted for only three to four days we had to work very fast, aiming at floating off one boat each day. Sometimes we did not succeed, and had to have a second attempt. The submarine would then be towed down to Falmouth docks where we would prepare her for her final journey to the breakers yard, towed by a couple of ocean going tugs.

There was still a naval officer in charge at Falmouth, it had been a Rear Admiral during the war, but now the post had been downgraded to a Commander. His must have been a very quiet number, as we were the only naval vessels in the port. He probably furnished us with high water times, and arranged for the charter of the tugs for our operations. However, he was a very pleasant officer, and we were pleased to entertain him to pre – lunch drinks on several occasions. This pleased him immensely; it was the environment more than the pink gin that appealed to him, though as a 'big ship' man it was certainly not the size of wardroom that he was accustomed to. A 'U' class submarines wardroom was almost overcrowded with five of us, as my uncle the police superintendent usually attended these functions as well.

Although these mud-berthed submarines were securely locked up each time we left them, we did have a little trouble with looters who, in the dead of night, picked the locks and entered the submarines to see what they could take away. There was very little of any value that could be taken away easily, all furniture and stores had been removed. Our main concern was that these 'pirates' might tamper with things that could affect the watertight integrity of the boat.

Someone had gained access to *Tribune*, for on one of our daily visits I discovered that her after two compartments, the engine room and after ends were flooded to the level of the last high tide. This was an alarming discovery. The matter was reported to *Dolphin*, and I set about getting the water out.

I decided that rather than borrow a submersible pump, having several lengths of 4″ diameter fuel hose; we would attempt to siphon the seawater out at the next low tide. It was a beastly and dangerous job, working in those flooded compartments. The hoses were very heavy, and we had quite a problem to get the siphoning action started. But once started it did not take long to empty both compartments to within a few inches in the bilges- a very successful operation.

But how did the water get in, and why did it not flow out again when the tide dropped? A thorough examination did not reveal the answer, and all valves were checked shut. I was very concerned that this may have been an act of sabotage. However, those at *Dolphin* did not seem too concerned about the matter, especially when it was reported that we had cleared the water. The whole affair remained a rather disconcerting mystery, and mysteries are not very popular in the submarine service.

Luckily we had no further trouble. It was as well that the boats were to be scrapped, and were unable to proceed under their own power, or the damage would have had a very serious effect. There would inevitably been a court of enquiry, and possibly a court martial.

We had only re-floated eight of these submarines when, in April 1946, I was appointed to *HMS Dolphin* for duty with submarines. Naturally I was very sorry to leave this 'plumb' job, and at the same time concerned lest my service career was now to be terminated. We had been a friendly little group in *Ursula* and I had a splendid staff, who having endured the rigours and torments of war were very appreciative of this relatively quiet number in Falmouth. Throughout the eight months that I was there we had practically no defaulters, and no trouble with the local inhabitants. *Ursula* was kept in seagoing condition, in consequence enjoyed the normal privileges of ships in commission (duty free liquor and tobacco), in fact on one occasion we steamed her back to Fort Blockhouse with some heavy machinery from one of the berthed submarines.

But now I was to leave this, and return to …what? What had their lordships in store for me this time? I couldn't see myself being in Blockhouse for very long, but I did not want to leave the Navy at this juncture as every extra year meant an increased pension

Within weeks of my return to *Dolphin* I was appointed to *HMS Maidstone*, which had returned from Australia and was now parent ship for the submarine flotilla at Portland. I was to be the spare crew engineer officer. This was certainly better than a commission abroad. Being duty engineer officer only once in every five days enabled me to take three weekends out of five to travel home to Plymouth. Other duties varied from being the Divisional Officer for the whole engineering staff of the spare crew, numbering about thirty, to arranging for the instruction and examination of all submarine engineering ratings in order that they could be advanced. Also preparing the E.R.A.'s for their advancement examinations. I also had to acquaint myself with the boiler and engine rooms on *Maidstone*, as a watch-keeping engineer when she made one of her rare trips to sea, as well as deputizing for any submarine E.O. who fell sick In fact I was a 'general dogs body'.

If Clare could have been with me this would have been an ideal job, as *Maidstone* very rarely went to sea, and it wasn't that often that I had to go to sea in a submarine. Our captain was none other than the rugged 'Jacky' Slaughter who seemed to crop up so frequently in my life. The senior engineer was Lt. Cdr. (E) 'Ken' Dunlop, excellent at his job, and a splendid messmate.

Strangely *Maidstone* had a gunroom, - a separate mess for midshipmen and young Sub. Lieutenants – previously reserved only for large battleships and cruisers. But now there were very few large battleships and cruisers, and as a result, *Maidstone* now accommodated about twenty of these fine lads – the budding officers of the Royal Navy.

Though only permitted a very restricted wine bill which allowed them nothing more than a couple of glasses of ale each day, they were noted for their exuberant spirits and high jinks. On one evening they entertained the whole of the W.O's mess to dinner, and very good hosts they were. After dinner it was time for 'high jinks', they challenged us old timers to all sorts of boisterous games. I was not adverse to a 'rough and tumble' but nipped smartly away after dinner to change out of my best mess undress, as new uniforms were very costly.

I think they anticipated an easy victory, but we had been brought up the hard way, and were a tough, even agile bunch, soon putting these youngsters into their proper place. One of the things I had to do was to hoist myself up on a pipe and get myself between it and the deck above (a gap of not more than ten inches) which was accomplished with a great deal more ease than I had imagined. We really enjoyed our frolic, even though we were a little stiff and bruised on the following day.

I hadn't been on *Maidstone* for more than four months when I received yet another appointment. This was to join *HMS Montclare* at Devonport, again as the spare crew engineer. This came as a big surprise as I had expected to be on *Maidstone* for the usual two years. Clare was still not fit to move house, and I could have applied for a job a little nearer home for compassionate reasons, but I didn't relish asking favours, especially as I'd just spent eight months at Falmouth. I did not broadcast my predicament, but someone had obviously pulled a string or two to get me to Devonport, most likely it was 'Jacky' Slaughter himself.

Montclare was the sister ship to *Montcalm* (later *Wolfe*). In pre-war Canadian Pacific days she had been converted for service as a fleet repair ship in the Far East during the war. H.M. Dockyard Portsmouth had commenced the job of converting her to a submarine repair ship, but for some reason, with only about one third of the work completed she was transferred to Devonport where she was to complete her refit for the next five to six months, carrying only a skeleton crew.

Toward *Montclare's* completion, Captain 'Jacky' Slaughter was appointed Captain S/M 3. My immediate bosses were the flotilla E.O. Cdr. (E) B.H. Pike, and the Senior Engineer, Lt.. Cdr. (E) Peter F. Parker. Both of these were submariners. The senior watch-keeping engineer was Lt. (E) H. Wilkinson (Wilkie), with whom I became very friendly; he had been promoted from Warrant Officer rank, and was in charge of *Montclare's* engine and boiler rooms.

I was given the job of engineer in charge of workshops, the new and very modern laundry, and the installation and subsequent maintenance of two large diesel dynamos, as well as being divisional officer for all the engine room spare crew ratings. This was no mean assignment as, when in full commission with a flotilla of at least eight submarines, the workshop job alone would be a full time one. We had a repair staff of about twenty-five Chiefs and E.R.A.'s. These comprised fitters, turners, coppersmiths, boilermaker welders, moulders and pattern makers, as well as a full complement of stoker petty officers, leading stokers and stokers

Montclare had modern machinery and equipment that would enable her to tackle almost any repair work that might be required for any class of submarine, the depot ship, or accompanying tenders. To me it seemed that I had more than my fair share of responsibilities, however for the present, and before our submarines joined us, I could cope comfortably, and at least while still in dockyard hands, there were no duty watches to be kept on board.

To say that I was wildly apprehensive about my duties would have been mild understatement. The diesel engines presented no problems, but my experience and knowledge of workshop practice was practically nil, and I knew nothing of the function of laundry machinery. There was no doubt that I would have to lean heavily upon my C.E.R.A. and his staff. Fortunately for me, and for the whole flotilla, when they eventually arrived on board, they were of the highest calibre, some being outstanding craftsmen. The senior C.E.R.A. and my right hand man to be, was 'Bill' Burden, a talented fitter and turner, who was also the very popular president of the C.E.R.A.'s mess.

Although as time went on I became increasingly busy, I thoroughly enjoyed our stay at Devonport, although there were of course problems. The war was over; the country was heavily in debt. To get essential work done in order to make us an efficient parent ship would have been a lot more difficult had it not been for my neighbour and very good friend, Mr. 'Les' Merret M.B.E. who was foreman in charge of *Montclare* during her refit. He really was a tower of strength to me.

It was during this refit period that I was able to do a good turn for one of my oldest friends, C.E.R.A. 'Phil' King. 'Phil' at that time was a member of the spare crew at Portland, and was very concerned that his wife, who at that time was living at Devonport, was unwell. I suggested he should be loaned to *Montclare* for a period to supervise the installation of the diesels, and this was agreed. It was a privilege for me to be able to help 'Phil' in this way, as he had relieved me of a great deal of my burden when I was so hard pressed at Beirut. Of course this helped me as well, as there was little that 'Phil' King didn't know about diesel engines, and I already had enough on my plate anyway. We were at Devonport for nearly six months in all, and 'Phil' left us just before we sailed.

Our captain, 'Jacky' Slaughter, joined us just before we sailed. It was a pleasure to serve under him once again. It was never mentioned by either of us but I was pretty sure that it was he who had seen to it that I'd had this refit in Plymouth, and I was mighty grateful. But then, all good things must come to an end, and at last we raised steam to sail for Rothesay.

Chapter Twelve

All E.O.'s had to be in the engine room for leaving harbour, and I was genuinely amused and intrigued by the rather antiquated set up in *Montclare's* engine room. There was literally hardly any room to move, and considering myself as a mere onlooker, I stood unobtrusively in the background hoping to pick up a few tips lest at some future date I should be required to keep a watch in this very engine room.

There was a multitude of E.O.'s, Chiefs and E.R.A.'s, stoker P.O.'s, and stokers milling about, most of whom had something to do, or were at least, doing something. I had certain knowledge of main and auxiliary machinery, having kept watch in *Maidstone,* but she was much more up to date. This to me was a bit like a comic opera, and very confusing. Having had little opportunity of looking over the boiler and engine rooms, I decided that in my own interest I should remain a little longer after this motley throng had disappeared on falling out from Harbour Stations. We had been at Harbour Stations for full three quarters of an hour before this order was finally given, and must by that time have been well clear of the Hamoase, if not the Sound. There was no particular hurry for me to leave, and I was watching the E.R.A.'s on the main throttles when Lt. Wilkinson (Wilkie), the senior watch-keeper, came across to me. There was still much steam about, and the noise although not comparable to a submarine engine room, made it necessary to almost shout to be heard. I thought he was going to ask me why I was still loitering in the engine room. Instead he informed me that they had drawn lots for the first watch in the engine room after leaving harbour, and that I had 'won'. This meant that I was now fully responsible for the running of this 'contraption' for the remaining one and a half hours of the last dogwatch. How naive I'd been! I was speechless. Here was I, having spent over twenty years in submarines, and being borne for duty with submarines, being 'browned off' to take over this antiquated contraption at a moment's notice – truly shabby treatment. Pride forbade me making any statement, but frankly I was scared stiff. I tried to put on an authoritative and confident air and prayed that I was left with a competent and knowledgeable staff. In this I was fortunate in having 'Bill' Burdon as C.E.R.A. of the watch; he was one of the old commission, and very experienced.

Apart from one or two minor snags, which the E.R.A.'s dealt with efficiently, revolutions ordered from the bridge were maintained, and having learned a little more of what was going on by then, I was thankfully able to turn over to my relief, who was a little late for the first watch (2000 till midnight) that all was well,

I was a little cross with 'Wilkie' for my initial discomfiture, but did not feel too bitter about it. He had informed me earlier that I would probably be required as a watch-keeper; nevertheless it wasn't a pleasant experience to be in charge, knowing less than those junior to you. The joke was on me, but it was some time before I could appreciate the funny side of it. I didn't always have 'Bill' Burdon to carry me because the E.R.A.'s were in three watches while we the officers, enjoyed a rather luxurious one in five. but I was learning very quickly. Of course, one E.O. is supposed to be as good as another, but we who had spent many years in submarines were expected to know as much about turbines, boilers, condensers, Weir's pumps (with their weird shuttle valves) etc. as the chaps who had spent the majority of their naval lives with this equipment. Admittedly they were expected to cope with any diesel engine problems, but I had already been 'palmed off' with the responsibility for the diesel dynamos on *Montclare*.

The remainder of the trip north to Rothesay Bay, where we were to rendezvous with our brood of about eight 'A' and 'T' class submarines, was uneventful and we arrived a couple of days later. After mooring about three cables offshore, our submarines were soon secured alongside, and *Montclare* was in business. Who looked after these boats before our arrival I do not know, but most of them had several repair jobs upon which we had to start immediately.

We were prepared for almost anything, and had developed a very efficient system of dealing with any piece of machinery needing repair or renewal. Needless to say I leaned heavily on my workshop staff as to methods of dealing with jobs, metals used in manufacture or repair, and largely the times that were estimated for the completion and test of each job. I also had to seek the advice of the senior engineer as to the priority of the work.

Every submarine engineer officer who submitted a piece of machinery for repair thought his to be the most important job, and wanted it to be given highest priority. Being well acquainted with the requirements of submarines and having some access to the submarine exercise programmes, I also had a good idea of how long it would take the submarine staff to refit the equipment once it had been repaired. On the other hand it was not good policy to promise a repair completion time when there was likely to be delays through unforeseen circumstances. Not only had we to care for our submarines, but also their crews. My up-to-date laundry was soon in great demand. I had taken the precaution of visiting a large laundry at Plymouth to see how things worked. This was just as well; I had taken on board three tons of washing powder that was completely unsuitable for our requirements. Luckily I was able to procure the correct commodity before leaving Plymouth, but had to sell the other very cheaply to the dockyard laundry – a financial loss to start with. It surprised me that the laundry was not to be an Admiralty commitment. They financed the installation, but thereafter it had to be run on a sound financial basis; a queer set up! Three or four sailors were detailed to operate the machines, and the parent ship and submarine crews were charged for all articles washed, and the engineering and electrical departments undertook to keep the numerous machines in good working order.

After installation of the laundry machinery, my sole responsibility where the laundry was concerned was the repair and maintenance of the machinery. Though many sailors still preferred to do their own dhobying as they had always done, the laundry was still kept very busy. Not only were we responsible for *Montclare* and her eight submarines, but there was always a tender destroyer, at present *HMS Douglas*, one or two smaller vessels for torpedo recovery, and a floating dock, a 'family of over sixteen hundred men in all.

This large brood kept our workshops very busy too. Submarine work had priority, but most of the other vessels were old, particularly the floating dock, and *Montclare* herself. The former was moored in Ballantyne Bay about a mile distant, and all work resulting from a submarines periodical docking had to be transported across to *Montclare*, and back again when completed.

The dock-master (a commissioned warrant shipwright officer), had his own staff of shipwrights, welders and painters, but any mechanical repairs such as re-tipping damaged propeller blades or repairs to underwater fittings, had to be carried out in *Montclare's* workshops.

There was much overtime work to be done, sometimes working right through the night in order to get a submarine to sea on time, or even just to get her un-docked. Although prepared to work the staff in watches (shift work), I soon found out that the majority of our E.R.A.'s much preferred to complete a job once they had started it. It was fortunate that we had an excellent staff, or we could not have kept pace with this work.

I have already mentioned the senior C.E.R.A. 'Bill' Burdon, not only was he a good fitter and turner; he was also a fine organizer. E.R.A. Peter Gill, our boilermaker welder (an ex submariner who had lost a forefinger feeling bottom end bearings of a diesel while doing 400 rpm), was the finest welder I'd ever come across. I'd had some experience in welding, and could well appreciate his uncanny skill. He could weld almost anything – a great asset, as much of our work involved welding at one stage or another, even if it were building up a damaged or worn bearing before grinding it down to size.

Perhaps the most outstanding craftsman of them all was E.R.A. Albert Hinks. Albert, a product of the artificer apprentices, was a fitter and turner; he was also an ex-submariner where, owing to his incompatibility with his E.O. (or indeed a succession of E.O.'s) was transferred back to general service. In many ways Albert was similar to my old friend 'Tiger' Jones, having scant respect for authority of any sort, except that unlike 'Tiger' he rarely got into trouble.

Although I had much experience in dealing with 'awkward coves', there was a little difficulty with Albert in the early stages, and I lost no time in telling him that if he didn't wish for more senior officers chasing him around, then he would have to put up with me keeping them acquainted with the progress of the work. Both the Senior Engineer and the Flotilla Engineer Officer were very much concerned with work progress, and I thought that if I could reassure these officers that production would be maintained and completion times met, there would be no need for them to visit the workshops except on special occasions.

Quite soon Albert Hinks and I began to get on very well together, and I asked the senior C.E.R.A. to keep clear of him as much as possible, as this E.R.A. could produce more work of a very high standard than any two others. It was nothing to see this man operating a 12″ lathe, a large boring machine, and a milling or shaping machine at the same time. This suited me well as I could only spare two or three E.R.A.'s for the heavy machine shop, whereas twelve or fourteen were required for the light machine and fitting workshop.

One had to be discreet with these highly skilled men, and I gradually got much wiser, cunning even. I wouldn't tell them how long a job should take; I'd let them tell me. If a job was required urgently and would necessitate working overtime, the technique would be to tell the chaps concerned that I'd already informed the senior engineer, or the E.O. of the submarine that it was impossible to complete the job in the time that they had asked for. This then would set the lads a challenge, which they would always accept, often working all night to get the job done. In the meanwhile I would have told the senior engineer or the E.O. of the boat concerned that the job would be finished and tested in a time better than he had hoped for, and the submarine would sail on time.

This workshop job was extremely interesting and worthwhile, but there were the inevitable problems. We had the facilities, much of our machinery was brand new and modern, we also had the skilled men, but it was a question of keeping them satisfied. Very few of the lads had their families living in Rothesay because many of them were expecting to leave the service within a year or two. Rothesay was quite a pleasant place to live, but there were very few attractions for naval men ashore.

Many of my workshop staff loathed attending Sunday morning Divisions, where we all had to tog up in our No.1. suits and fall in for inspection, followed by a church service. It was difficult for me to appreciate this attitude; I personally, welcomed the chance to get away from the humdrum of work. But it seemed that most of the lads would rather do four hours hard work than attend a mere one and a half hours of divisions and church. However, in order to compensate them for the overtime work that they readily endured often at very short notice, I made a practice of saving several fairly urgent jobs until the end of the week in order to create the need for at least eight or ten of them to work on a Sunday morning; jobs that previously had no priority, suddenly became most urgent.

I am sure that my departmental bosses, and even 'Jacky' Slaughter himself must have known that I was working a 'bit of a racket', but they were all very understanding. Nevertheless there were occasions, about once in every two months when Captain S/M would insist that there were to be no absentees from divisions. Even then, exceptions were made for really urgent work.

Rarely did I go ashore myself, and when I did it was to play golf on Canada Hill, or the occasional game of tennis. Lt. Wilkinson (Wilkie) was my golfing partner, and a round of golf cost us a mere two shillings.

The weather during our first year at Rothesay was marvellous even during the winter, and the west coast of Scotland in these conditions compares favourably with any of the world's beauty spots. It was a great pity that Clare could not be with me at this time, but Joan's education was very important. I decided however, that Clare could join me after twelve months.

During this year King George V1 inspected the whole of the Home Fleet, which had assembled in the Clyde opposite Greenock. This gave us a temporary relief from the monotony of being moored in Rothesay Bay. His Majesty, together with Queen Elizabeth and the two young Princesses, boarded *Montclare* and inspected her crew, as well as the crews of her submarines.

Another outstanding event during this period was the closing down of the warrant officers mess as such. Their lordships at the Admiralty had decided to upgrade this bastion; instead of being termed Commissioned Warrant Officer, or merely Warrant Officer, depending on whether a thick stripe or a thin stripe, we were now to be known as Branch Officers, and were to be transferred to the wardroom. This meant that we would lose our age-old privilege of being addressed as Mister, and would no longer be able to manage our own mess. We regarded this as a very dubious up grading, more like an Irishman's rise' as it were, with not even a rise in pay to compensate.

A few of my messmates carried out a fairly thorough research into the history and origin of this ancient rank with all its peculiarities. No doubt the Admiralty were under the impression that we were being favoured, but our mess president (Mr. R. Farmer, a commissioned gunner) had discussed this with 'Jacky' Slaughter who offered us a happy compromise. Of our proposed nomenclature he could of course do nothing, but he suggested that if we wished, we could retain our old mess, having our own president and vice president, but to rename it wardroom 2.

This was a very acceptable arrangement as far as we were concerned. It also suited 'Jacky' very well because there was nothing he liked better than being invited to join us in our mess, and this we did quite frequently, where we'd either stand around our small bar telling tales over a 'pink' gin, or get down to a serious game of poker, of which 'Jacky' was an exponent.

Captain S/M2, who had his own suite, but many of the other wardroom officers were in turn invited down to our mess; they not only enjoyed it but also deemed it quite a privilege. Our mess, and indeed warrant officers messes throughout the navy was quite an institution, and contained all the working heads of all departments – gunners, boatswains, marine, electrical and ordnance engineers, shipwrights, writers, stores and catering officers and others. Much of the ship's work and planning literally took place in our mess.

We could not let this occasion, 30th of June 1948, pass without some form of recognition, and so we duly arranged a formal 'dinner. Our guests included 'Jacky' and as many of the wardroom officers as could be accommodated.

Before dinner, and after a stiff gin to fight back our tears, we formally, and with a dignity befitting the solemnity of the occasion, covered the old mess title with a small Union Jack and committed it to the ancient realms of King Neptune, through one of the port holes. This was followed by a splendid dinner with speeches and festivities that continued into the early hours.

A small commemoration plaque was given to each member of the mess, on which was stated:

"We, the members of the ancient order of Commissioned and Warrant Officers, are hereby gathered together on this very solemn occasion to commit to the deep the title of our worthy mess, which, throughout the centuries has been the rendezvous of all and sundry illustrious seafarers. It is extremely gratifying to us, the members of this ancient order, that King Neptune, himself an honorary member of this fraternity, has commended us for our social activities, and we, the present members, trust we have fulfilled this noble duty which was laid upon our shoulders, and that we have maintained the high standards set by our forbears.

We, the present members of this order, have the honour to commit this glorious and noble title to the realms and safekeeping of his Titanic Majesty King Neptune and his minions."

Thereafter we continued as before under our new title. Probably we were the only ship in the navy to do this, since hitherto as in submarines, all small ship wardrooms absorbed the one or two warrant officers they carried.

It was a monumental stag party, and there were many severe headaches the following morning. But it was an unwritten law amongst our kind that no matter the extent of the festivities on the evening before, there was no excuse for turning up late at the workplace on the next morning, or for that matter, for even looking 'under the weather'.

Montclare and her flotilla then embarked on a very pleasant summer cruise, which took us through the Skagerrak and Kattegat into the Baltic Sea on a goodwill visit to Copenhagen. We then had permission to proceed via the Kiel Canal to Rotterdam followed by a visit to Cherbourg. It was still not long since the end of the war, and the enthusiasm accorded to us on passing through the Kiel Canal was rather subdued, quite different from the enthusiastic reception given to us by the Dutch at Rotterdam. The Dutch naval submariners laid on a big party in our honour; they appeared to drink Bols gin as we would drink ale. Although having an intense dislike for the stuff, diplomacy was the order of the day, and I must have consumed at least a half a bottle.

Having now been in the submarine service for twenty-two years, it was only to be expected that I would be on familiar terms with many of the senior officers, and submarine captains. Amongst my friends was the C.O. of *Alderney*, my shipmate of *Porpoise* days, and now Lt, Cdr. Ian McIntosh, who frequently invited me down to his boat, one of the post war 'A' class, as a guest. .

On Christmas morning 1948, as early as 10:30, a messenger came to my mess stating that my presence was required in *Alderney*. This I thought was a little early to have a drink, even on Christmas day, and, as the whole of our mess had been invited to the wardroom at 1145, I respectfully declined. Less than ten minutes later *Alderney's* First Lieutenant was knocking on our mess door asking to speak to me. Unsuspectingly I went to the door, only to be grabbed by Lt. 'Mike' Badham and his navigator, and literally carried off into the bowels of *Alderney*. I couldn't be angry with these grand fellows and lingered over a couple of stiff pink gins before making my way to *Montclare's* wardroom at noon, where we continued our Christmas festivities. At 12:45, when I was about to depart for my Christmas dinner, a steward informed me that C.E.R.A. Burdon wished to speak to me. Bill Burdon being the chief of the workshops, I immediately started to wonder what had gone wrong. But when I met him at the wardroom door he informed me that there were no problems, it was just that the E.R.A.'s mess were very disappointed that I had been absent when Captain S/M had made his traditional Christmas day rounds of the mess-decks that morning. Feeling more than a little ashamed of myself I explained that I had been called down to *Alderney*, and immediately accompanied Bill down to the E.R.A.'s mess to wish them a belated Merry Christmas. As soon as I had walked into their mess, a glass containing at least two full tots of rum was thrust into my hand in order to drink their health. Explaining that I had already consumed a considerable quantity of gin, and that I'd better just have a sip, the cry went up 'Bottoms up'! Whereupon I sank the lot. Knowing full well that this was a little more than was good for me, I dashed off to my cabin, changed into 'mufti' grabbed my golf clubs and within five minutes was on the 13:15 boat ashore.

Feeling pretty good when I reached the golf course, I solemnly played my way around eighteen holes. The weather however, was not good, and apart from getting pretty cold and wet, I took far too many strokes to get around. But having finally achieved my objective of getting all that alcohol out of my system, I caught the 17:00 boat back to the ship feeling thoroughly tired and hungry, not having eaten since breakfast that morning. After having a refreshing hot bath I remembered having promising the padre that I would attend evensong at 18:30. What a Christmas day! My dinner of turkey and Christmas pudding had been ditched with the gash and all that I had at about 20:00 was a little cold meat and salad.

Normally I tried to avoid consuming anything that was not good for me, but what would the lads think of a boss who could not down a couple of tots? These were the type of situations that had to be resolved in the normal course of duty.

My good friend Ian McIntosh had unwittingly landed me in this situation, as otherwise I would have gone on the rounds with the captain, and have had perhaps a half a tot to wish the lads a merry Christmas. But I couldn't be cross about it; Ian McIntosh (later Vice Admiral Sir Ian) was one of the most splendid officers I'd met in the service.

Many years later, when I had retired, and he was then Captain S/M 2 Ian kindly invited Clare and I to dinner in his suite aboard *HMS Adamant* at Devonport. Travelling down from our home in Newton Abbot, we fully expected to be guests at a small dinner party, but instead found that we were the principle guests of a party of about fifteen people including another old friend, Sir Tom Barlow Bart, who was at that time the Commodore of *HMS Drake*.

After I had been at Rothesay for twelve months, Joan had taken her final examinations, and Clare was at last able to join me. Accommodation was not easy to find, and all I could procure was a small and rather dismal furnished apartment at Ardbeg in the Port Bannatyne area overlooking the floating dock, which spoiled an otherwise beautiful view across the Kyles of Bute.

Winter was approaching and all we had for warmth was a small gas fire. Later in my further search for accommodation I eventually secured a flat at the other end of Rothesay. This was on the waterfront overlooking Loch Striven and would have been ideal had it not been for the fact that it was enveloped almost completely in a thick scotch mist for most of the winter. For practically the whole of the next year that Clare was with me the weather was in complete contrast to the marvellous weather that we had enjoyed previously. I remember that we scarcely had more than two consecutive days without rain for the whole of the remaining time that we were there. Clare and I escaped this miserable weather when I took a whole fortnight's leave to visit Commander 'Reg' Lockley and Clare's sister at Arbroath on the eastern seaboard, where 'Reg' was at that time Commander of the Fleet Air Arm base.

The time finally then came for 'Jacky' Slaughter to be relieved. As he had been a very popular and understanding captain with both the officers and the men, I suggested to my hard worked team that we made some suitable farewell gift for him. Having done this I left it to these superb craftsmen to get on with it. The finished article, which was made entirely in their own time, was a truly magnificent piece of work; a fire screen and curb, the woodwork of which was mostly fashioned by the pattern maker, C.E.R.A. Colley, and bore the *Montclare's* crest moulded by C.E.R.A. Glazebrook. The curb carried a fine detailed model of an 'A' class submarine on each side, (either one of which would have made a very fine gift on its own). The ever-popular 'Jacky' was quite overwhelmed when we presented him with this parting gift from the engine room department.

I was very sorry to see 'Jacky' go: we'd been together 'off and on' since our old *Valiant* days (1925-26). He had been kind to me on two or three occasions when I had needed it most, and Clare and I had been his guests at 'Kames Castle' his official residence as Captain S/M2.

'Jacky's' successor was that old warhorse, Captain H.F. 'Boggy' Bone. DSO and Bar. who had been Commander S/M on *Wolfe* at Trincomalee. He was a fine captain but a stark contrast from his predecessor, being very dour and uncommunicative (at least to ratings and junior officers). Yet I had often played bridge with him aboard *Wolfe*. He did not seem to hold it against me that I had snapped at him when he had made that somewhat derogatory remark about *Strongbow's* stokers.

All went well in the workshops for about fifteen months, when Peter Parker our senior engineer, despite my appeal, lingered a little too long while watching 'our Albert' at work in the machine shop. The latter was rude, even insubordinate, and probably could have been court-martialled, but the effect was that Albert Hinks was quickly drafted back to his depot at Chatham barracks, and workshop production then fell considerably.

I was a bit cross with Peter Parker for ignoring my previous appeal to tread warily around Albert Hinks; Peter was well aware of the situation regarding this very eccentric man. I of course, pleaded leniency for Hinks in consideration for all the fine work that he had completed while in *Montclare,* and it was both surprising and gratifying to me that Captain Bone was able to take a lenient view of this incident as he had not been with us for long enough to appreciate the remarkable skills of E.R.A. Albert Hinks. Of course I did not condone Hinks' surly behaviour and realized that discipline must be maintained whatever the situation, but this man had worked many hours overtime, and much of this voluntarily, in order to keep our flock of submarines seaworthy, and he had in fact on two occasions received a monetary award from the Herbert Lott Trust Fund for useful inventions. However, Hinks now had only a few months to serve before leaving the navy, and he would certainly be a priceless asset to any big engineering firm, as of course would several others on my staff.

Soon Peter Parker was to be relieved by Lt. Cdr. (E) H.A. 'Tony' Kidd. DSO. Tony had served in *Torbay* when 'Gamp' Miers had earned his VC.

Meanwhile my old friend Ian McIntosh had been promoted to Commander and given one of the most exacting jobs in the submarine service, that of Commander in charge of the C.O's Qualifying Course, more commonly known as the 'Perishers Course'. Consequently we saw quite a lot of him, as the course spent a lot of its time with our flotilla.

Another great friend with whom I had served many times, now appeared upon the scene once more, this was Temporary Commissioned Engineer H.J.C. 'Bert' Pinch. Bertie was appointed to *Montclare* for duty with submarines.

Shortly after Bert's arrival, and having by now served aboard *Montclare* for just over two years, I was again appointed to *HMS Dolphin* for duty with submarines. It had been a very pleasant couple of years for me in Scotland, despite the ghastly weather during the latter half of my time there. Clare had enjoyed the second year with me, with Sunday evenings being a highlight of her week, as whether I was duty engineer or not, she would always come aboard *Montclare* on Sunday evenings for a film show and dinner.

They dined me before leaving. Another rather hectic evening, with 'Dutchy' Holland up to his tricks again. His 'piece de resistance' on that particular evening was to remove the armature from one of the large fan motors almost above where the mess president and myself as guest of honour would sit. and replace it with flour and pepper. When the fan switch was made, luckily after the meal had finished, the whole lot poured down upon us, and chaos rained. The speeches that evening were completed to an accompaniment of loud coughs and sneezes. 'Duchy' was a grand fellow, but he could be an unholy terror on these occasions.

Clare and I travelled south together, and found accommodation in Lee-on-Solent until I was appointed to *Sanguine*, which was shortly due to refit at Devonport. *Sanguine's* E.O. had previously fallen sick, and so one of my first jobs on joining her was to hastily prepare a comprehensive defect list from the information that I had at hand. *Sanguine's* refit would probably last for about five months, which suited me admirably, at last Clare and I would be able to live in our own home once more.

With my past experience of refitting submarines, and my knowledge of so many of the dockyard personnel at Devonport, I judged that this job after the initial sweat, would be both easy for me and beneficial to the boat. *Sanguine's* C.O. was Lt. Cdr. (Roger) Stone, and her 1st. Lt. Lieutenant 'Hubby' Hubbard, both of whom would remain with her for the duration of the refit.

It was good to be back living in our own home once more, and Clare and I determined to make the most of it. It was a very pleasant period, the weather was good, and having a very nice tennis court, we entertained a lot. There were two 'T' class submarines refitting in Devonport at this time, whose officers enjoyed our parties. 'Hubby' Hubbard in particular was a very regular visitor; a powerfully built man, he was not a good tennis player, but what he lacked in skill he made up for with his boundless energy and enthusiasm.

One incident marred this otherwise idyllic period. Our C.E.R.A. owned a powerful motorcycle, and on one weekend he took our 'outside wrecker' E.R.A. Keysell with him to Portsmouth as a pillion passenger. They were involved in a road accident, and sadly Keysell was killed. This was a great loss to *Sanguine* as it was late in her refit. I travelled to Portsmouth to attend requiem mass for our dead shipmate, who was a Roman Catholic and lived in that area.

As we neared the end of refit, a signal arrived stating that I had been promoted to Temporary Commissioned Senior Engineer. I was genuinely surprised, and of course very pleased. Surprised because having just missed the wartime measures of automatic promotion after four years, the normal time to wait in the rank was eight years, and then only with good recommendation. I had received my thin stripe only six and a half years previously. Pleased, because although this promotion carried no extra responsibility, it gave me a much needed increase in pay, and ultimately of course, an increase to my pension.

It was at this time that I badly strained my back, probably whilst tending to our very large garden. I was foolish enough to ignore the pain and to play a round of golf with Reg Lockley who was spending his leave with us. The result was a severe attack of sciatica. I was in such great pain that I was not able to get into the Dockyard on the following morning. Clare telephoned the C.O. and within an hour an ambulance had arrived to whisk me away to the R.N. hospital at Stonehouse. This was the first and only time during my naval career that I had been a patient in hospital – and I am sorry to say, a rather impatient one at that.

The following two weeks were spent lying prostrate on a board, the first week in great pain, sleeping only with the aid of pills. My companion in the ward was a young marine commando captain. I never quite understood why he was there, as he seemed to me to be in the peak of physical condition. I had little interest in him, or indeed in anything else during that first week, but as my pain eased we began to play cribbage or, if he could make up a four from the other wards, we would play bridge. This young officer was always up to some sort of mischief, and he inevitably managed to involve me in this, we were certainly not too popular with the rather sombre and severe ward sister.

It was the month of July and stifling hot in the ward. I was mighty thankful to be discharged after two weeks, which had seemed to me longer than the average war patrol. The Surgeon Admiral interviewed me before I left, strongly advising me not to indulge in any sport for at least three months. This advice I am ashamed to say, was not strictly adhered to.

As Clare and I had been the guests of Claude and Dorothy Bedard at bridge evenings many times during our refit, I invited them aboard *Sanguine* for a drink on the evening following our commissioning party. Not ever having been in a submarine before, they eagerly accepted my invitation. Claude, a fellow of the Royal Society was splendid company, having a succession of suitable stories for the occasion. The 1st Lt. also had two or three guests, so it was a small and friendly party for *Sanguine's* wardroom that evening.

At about 20:30, just when we were preparing to leave, a messenger arrived and asked to speak to me. He informed me that the Chief Engineer of *Amethyst* wished to entertain Clare and myself to a party on board, in order to celebrate *Amethyst's* return to the U.K. The whole country knew that *Amethyst* had just returned that day, fresh from her epic run down the Yangtze river to escape from a Chinese ambush: it was splashed all over the daily papers. Only superb handling by her C.O. Lt. Cdr. J.S. Kerens DSO had saved *Amethyst* from disaster at the hands of the Chinese manned batteries along the banks of the Yangtze. She was absolutely riddled with shell holes and had suffered many casualties. What I did not know was that my old golfing chum of *Montclare* days, now Lt. Cdr C. 'Wilkie' Wilkinson, was her engineer officer. Even more surprising to me was how could he have possibly known that I was aboard *Sanguine* at that time?

I had naturally to decline 'Wilkies' very kind offer, as I had guests of my own and we were about to return home for food. But only a very few minutes had elapsed when the messenger returned and breathlessly extended the invitation to my two guests, stating that there was plenty of food aboard *Amethyst*. Claude and Dorothy were thrilled at the prospect and so away we went to meet 'Wilkie', his captain and fellow officers, the Lord Mayor of Plymouth, the C in C Plymouth, and many others.

The party was most enjoyable and went on for longer than we had anticipated, all guests were supposed to be clear by 23:00, but the C.O. had arranged for special dispensation until midnight. Claude and Dorothy were delighted with their evening and slept the night at our house before leaving for their home at Postbridge on Dartmoor the following morning.

There had been a frustrating delay with the main engines on Sanguine: an incorrect assembly of a portion of the fuel pump camshaft presented a difficult diagnosis both for the dockyard-engineering experts and myself. It caused quite a headache, but at least the fact that it was myself who discovered the reason for the fault was of some consolation to me.

Sanguine was now ready for her sea trials – full power and diving. The former went off without a hitch, and we disembarked the engine trials team before diving.

Now all was set for our trial dive, but poor 'Hubby' was having trouble with the trim; the boat seemed terribly light. Eventually we got down to periscope depth with twelve tons more water in our compensating tanks than our very experienced 1st Lt. thought that we should have. Asked by the captain for my opinion, I replied that unless we had accidentally lost our drop keel (and that weighed only seven tons) I could not account for the situation. The drop keel mechanism is exercised from time to time, but always under the supervision of the engineer officer.

On our return to the dockyard a diver went down to check the keel, and this, much to the relief of the 'outside wrecker', and myself was found to be intact. Eventually it was discovered that our new battery weighed twelve tons lighter than the old one. This was a dreadful oversight on the part of the dockyard. We sailed again the next morning with pig iron castings totalling twelve tons secure in our tanks and bilges to compensate for this differential in weight, and this time the dive being successful, we returned again to Fort Blockhouse.

Understanding that I would be *Sanguine's* E.O. for the next eighteen months or so, and that she would be operating from Fort Blockhouse, I suggested to Clare that she come up to Gosport once more. Reg Lockley, who was then Commander (E) of the Fleet Air Arm base at Lee-on –Solent, was at that time renting a beautiful house named 'Homeport', offered us accommodation with him, and we were pleased to accept.

But within a very few weeks *Sanguine* was ordered to join the flotilla at Malta. This was entirely unexpected but, as Clare would almost certainly be able to join me at Malta, I was not unduly perturbed. Alas, within a couple of days before sailing, a young engineer officer replaced me, and once more I was appointed back to *Dolphin* for duty with submarines. Here in the workshops I was employed as deputy to Lt. 'Jacky' Northwood.

'Jacky' was a great character, and we got on well together, having much in common. About two years older than me he was an exceptional games player; rugby, tennis, golf, billiards – he was very good at them all. We played golf many times; although it was seldom that I beat him. Like myself, 'Jacky' Northwood was very lucky to have survived the war, having had the courage to volunteer to be E.O. of *Thunderbolt,* which was the ill fated, reclaimed and renamed *Thetis.* He was given another appointment after a gruelling year with *Thunderbolt* in the Mediterranean Sea just before she was lost with all hands. 'Jacky' Northwood was one of the truly 'old school' submariners.

This quiet number understudying 'Jacky' did not last for long. Early in the January of 1950 I was once more appointed to *HMS Maidstone* for duty with submarines at Portland. Given the same job as I had previously – spare crew 'dogsbody', the majority of my time was taken up with educating submariners in steam, ready for their promotion exams. *SWEDISH MV*

Soon after my arrival at Portland there occurred a tragic submarine disaster. *DIVINA* *Truculent* was carrying out trials in the Thames Estuary when she was run down by a merchantman and lost with very few survivors. Among the few survivors was the son of Vice Admiral Sir Sydney Frew. It was always depressing to lose a submarine in peacetime, however, before 1932 our loss rate had been almost one boat per year, so at least this was a comforting improvement in statistics. Apparently many had actually escaped from *Truculent* using D.S.E.A. suits, but on reaching the surface in the blackness of the night, were swept seawards in the strong and bitterly cold currents.

When I first arrived at Maidstone her captain was C.J. 'Joe' Blake, a very congenial and fatherly figure. My flotilla Engineer Officer was the exuberant and friendly Cdr. W.A. 'Gussy' Stewart, and the senior engineer was Lt. Cdr. 'Jerry' Mellors.

Here I had nothing to do with the workshops, although I recollect that I was responsible for the work carried out in the periscope workshop. There was always one C.E.R.A. or E.R.A. on each parent ship that specialized in the maintenance of submarine periscopes. These people usually held this job for several years, having completed very detailed courses of instruction from the periscope makers Barr and Stroud, as well as regular refresher courses. They were the experts in their field, and this was a much sought after job. Theirs was an extremely important job, not only because they were responsible for the repair and servicing of all the periscopes in the flotilla, but for the personal supervision of the removal and replacement of all these periscopes. This could be an extremely delicate and tricky job, especially if there was a swell and the boat was likely to move. There was only a few thousandths of an inch clearance in the periscope bearings and glands.

Captain 'Joe' Blake was very soon to be relieved by Captain R.L.S. Gainsford OBE, and my daughter Joan, who had by now completed her studies, was living with us again. She had found a secretarial post with a firm of accountants in nearby Dorchester.

It was now that my 'quiet number' came to an abrupt end. In the late summer *Maidstone* left Portland to refit at Chatham dockyard, where she was to remain for almost six months. Our flotilla of four 'T' class and four 'S' class submarines were to remain operational at Portland. Just before *Maidstone* sailed I was summoned to the presence of 'Gussy' Stewart who explained that I was to be left behind together with Cdr. T.C. Barlow, Lt. Cdr. P.E. (Bill) Newstead (Staff Operations Officer), and a young RNVR officer Lt. 'Tubby' Hannan, to look after the flotilla. We would have a temporary workshop allocated to us, and an office from which Cdr. S/M and S.O.O. could organize the submarine operations. As the only technical officer I was given a repair staff of one C.E.R.A., three E.R.A's, one electrical artificer, two shipwrights, and one each P.O. Radar, ASDIC, LTO, a TGM and a Stoker P.O. as well as six junior ratings.

This all seemed quite a monumental task to me, not only was I to be in sole charge of all the mechanical repairs to eight submarines, but I would also be responsible for area's of repair work of which I had little or no previous knowledge. But at least I had an expert in all fields, and of course would not presume to advise them on their own work, or how long a job should take. It was hoped that they were decent guys who would be willing to work hard when the need arose, get on well together, and not try to hoodwink me. Heaven knows what the modern day Trades Union would have made of this peculiar and unusual set-up! But it suited me nicely to remain behind, although I could not understand why I was elected for the job, as there were several E.O.'s senior to me in *Maidstone*.

I foresaw domestic and technical problems galore, but was assured that all would be well. There was always the small R.N. Dockyard at Portland that I could call upon in an emergency. They had experts in all fields, and if necessary the technical officer from *Maidstone* could always be flown down.

The submarine crews were to live aboard their boats, and would thus get 'hard layer' money over the whole period. My staff would be required to find their own accommodation ashore, for which they would be paid the princely sum of just under 5/- per day.

The workshop allocated to us was situated in the small torpedo establishment just outside the dockyard gates. It contained a very limited amount of machinery, which seemed very inadequate to me, since the amount of work that I was expecting would be as much as that which I had handled previously while aboard *Montclare*.

'Bill' Newstead formulated some rules to be adhered to, fervently hoping that things would run smoothly and that the staff would not be too overworked. In the event we coped with all the repair work given to us, and no boat was ever held up for want of repairs during the whole of that period. There were five or six submarines at sea on exercises each day. The staff were magnificent – no grumbling, and no domestic troubles; they were all submariners, and took a pride in keeping the flotilla going throughout that period.

Of course we had our anxious moments. There were a few breakdown jobs that were beyond our scope, or rather beyond the scope of our workshop. These I was authorized to take to the R.N. Dockyard with the appropriate paperwork requesting urgent attention. Once these jobs were given to the dockyard I had no further control over them, except to politely impress the need for urgency of completion.

Unfortunately the manager of the engineering department of the dockyard was a rather elderly naval captain who did not share our enthusiasm. He invariably questioned my application for jobs to be treated as 'urgent', and continuously sought to downgrade my priorities. I would have to state my reasons for each priority, giving the sailing times for the various submarines concerned, and the estimated time that it would take the submarine crews to reassemble a piece of machinery back on board when the repair was complete.

Nevertheless this old 'so and so' would still argue that all the work that he received was urgent – 'Submarines were not the only pebbles on the beach'. He was not an ex-submariner, and knew little of the work that these boats were called upon to do, or indeed the conditions under which their crews worked.

In spite of all this 'hoo-hah' work was usually completed within the time requested, but eventually I did grow tired of these continual arguments over priorities. I felt that I was wasting my time, and so one day I stated to the captain as politely as I could that no further jobs would be given to the dockyard unless they were vitally urgent, and my staff could not cope with them. I told him that we were endeavouring to keep a whole submarine flotilla seaworthy and that if jobs could not be done in the time requested, then I would have to make a written report to my superior officer etc – very saucy behaviour to a senior officer, and I feared for my thick stripe – pity really, I'd only had it for six months.

The old boy weathered this storm without interrupting me. He made no pretence at apology, but thereafter he never once questioned my priorities. In fact we then began to get along very well, he even invited me to his house in the dockyard for a drink on one occasion. I later told my C.O. 'Tommy' Barlow (later Sir Thomas Barlow Bart) about my confrontation. He grinned, and assured me that he would have backed me up if necessary.

We were all mighty pleased when *Maidstone* eventually rejoined us. Although we had enjoyed the challenge, it was a long time for a flotilla to be without a proper parent ship. I was deeply indebted to the electrical, radar, and torpedo experts for their co-operation, and made many friends among the submariners during that period. Apart from summoning the services of the periscope E.R.A., and on one occasion the flotilla radar officer, I cannot recall bothering *Maidstone* for anything except a few pieces of spare gear, which were sent by rail. Captain S/M warmly praised our efforts, and it was very restful to get my old job back once again, and to be able to catch the first liberty boat ashore each evening.

Tragedy struck again within a few weeks. My young friend, Lt. 'Dusty' Miller, E.O. of *Totem*, invited me down to his boat where they were entertaining a few friends. I had become acquainted with this brilliant and congenial young engineer officer while *Maidstone* was away, and I held him in great esteem. I t was good to be invited down to the boats by these young officers, although I do not know what the occasion was – one needed but a flimsy excuse to invite a few officers down to one's boat for a drink. It was a stag party, and a very well conducted one- no raucous behaviour – it lasted from 18: 00 to 19:30, but for some unknown reason 'Dusty', who had recently married an Admiral's daughter, had asked his captain's permission to leave at 19:10. This caused me no embarrassment, as I was friendly with the captain, and with the 1st Lt.

I was leaving the boat for home at about 19:30 when a messenger rushed up the gangway with the stunning news that 'Dusty' had been killed in a road accident. It was natural to assume that he was suspected of drinking, but I was with him before his departure and I knew that he had only had two half pints of ale. His death was a big loss to the submarine service, for I think that he was destined for high rank, but what a tragic loss to his poor young wife!

It was not often that I was called upon to deputize for a sick engineer, but early in the April of 1951, the E.O. of *Sea Devil*, George 'Baldy' Shimmings BEM fell sick, and I temporarily took over his duties.

One day we took *Sea Devil* to sea for just a one day exercise with the local anti-submarine flotilla, and would normally have tied up alongside *Maidstone* again by about 18:00 that evening. Surfacing at about noon after a two-hour hunt by a frigate, for the benefit of young A/S operators, we were instructed to cease exercising and to proceed south to a position where the submarine *Affray*, operating from Dolphin, was apparently overdue. She had signalled her position on diving, and should have sent a surfacing signal several hours previously. Several ships including us were deployed in an endeavour to make contact with her, or to search for survivors. This we did for the next five days without returning to harbour, looking, listening for H.E., and trying to locate her with our ASDICS and our echo-sounding machine.

This was a dismal and depressing task, the weather was poor, and once darkness set in there was little hope of sighting anything. Dangerous for us as well, as there were so many ships milling around close by. We had only taken enough food for one lunch aboard, and most of us had no bedding or toilet gear. True, *Sea Devil* carried emergency rations in the form of tinned food and biscuits, but no bread.

After five days we were recalled, not that we wouldn't have been pleased to continue this search and to endure the discomfort for weeks if there had been any chance of achieving something tangible, but any hope of contacting or rescuing survivors had long since become remote. *Affray's* crew could never have escaped from the depth of water in the position we were searching anyway.

Fortunately *Maidstone* had taken the precaution of informing our folks in Portland and Weymouth that we had been detained at sea, so there was no unnecessary anxiety.

HMS *Reclaim*, using new underwater photography techniques, eventually located *Affray*; she was lying in forty-three fathoms of water. This was yet another tragic loss to the submarine service, as *Affray*, was on a training cruise, and was carrying on board the whole of a Sub Lieutenant's training course and their training officers as well as her normal crew. *Affray's* C.O. was Lt. Cdr. John Blackburn. Among those lost was young Sub Lt. Frew, a survivor from the *Truculent* disaster, not fourteen moths previous.

The subsequent court of enquiry concluded that *Affray's* loss was due to a fractured snorkel (snort mast). The snort mast, used extensively by the Germans during the war, was now being fitted to our boats. It was of course a great asset, as it negated the need to surface in order to charge the batteries, thus avoiding the submarines greatest vulnerability. The large quantities of air required by the main engines could now be drawn down this snort induction mast when it was raised to the vertical position and the boat was at periscope depth. (About forty feet in the 'A' class and thirty-two feet in the 'S' class). This then allowed the submarine to remain dived for weeks, as navigational fixes and star sights could be taken from the periscopes.

All was well until the trim was lost, or the weather was very rough, causing the boat to go deeper than periscope depth with the engines still running. A float-operated valve at the snort masthead would then shut off the air supply and thus prevent volumes of water from pouring down into the engine room. But unless the engines were very quickly stopped, they would draw a huge vacuum in the boat, which was most uncomfortable to the eardrums. At seven inches of vacuum the E,R.A. of the watch would stop the engines immediately.

Shortly after this I received another unexpected appointment. Having been with *Maidstone* for a little less than eighteen months, I expected to be with her for at least six more months. But this new appointment was as E.O. of S/M *Sidon*, which surprised me somewhat, since, now at the ripe old age of forty-seven I was no longer seeking, or expecting to be a permanent member of a submarine crew.

Chapter Thirteen

Sidon was based at Portland, and apparently due for a refit at Devonport within five months. I was paid as a spare crewmember, and therefore couldn't really grumble, but there must have been many young E.O.'s hankering after such a job.

The C.O. of *Sidon* was Lt. P.A. (Peter) Fickling, her 1st. Lt. was Lt. G. Baker, her 3rd officer was Lt. A.E. (Tony) Newell-Johnson, and the navigator was Lt. Tom Nosworthy: all very young but nevertheless very pleasant officers to serve with, even though there was a great disparity in our ages. None except the C.O. was even born when I started my service in submarines. This age gap was even greater than when I was in *Strongbow*, where Tony Troup was twenty-three, and I was forty.

Exercising from Portland for four, sometimes five days each week made a big difference to the time I could spend at home, having to breakfast before 0800 and often having to remain behind at the end of the day to supervise work which had to be completed before sailing on the following morning

This was my first practical experience of the 'snorkel', and although I was quite familiar with its layout and operation, I must admit that at first this contraption seemed to me to be a very mixed blessing, it's obvious operational advantages being somewhat detracted from by the very acute discomfort it could cause if the boat was not in good trim. My poor eardrums, already accustomed to excess pressure, would now have to cope with partial vacuums

Life wasn't too bad while operating from Portland, but there were of course times when we had to embark upon cruises, mini war patrols, and exercises further a field. It was as well that Joan was at home to be company for Clare.

On one occasion we spent three weeks off the west coast of Scotland with other submarines, on submarine versus submarine exercises. Working in pairs, the 'hunter' at periscope depth, and the 'hunted' at one hundred and fifty feet and at watch diving stations, keeping a strict silence throughout the boat. Those off watch were turned in either catching up on their sleep, or simply reading. It was blissfully peaceful and quiet. Suddenly with a loud crash, the boat jarred to a stop. Horror of horrors! Our first reaction was that we had collided with another boat. Luckily we had been running at a very slow speed, and there was no immediate sign of serious damage, no sudden inrush of water, and no sudden increase in pressure, in fact the trim appeared to remain unaffected.

We blew main ballast up to one hundred feet, and the captain, who had reached the control room in a flash, prevented her from coming up further and soon had her back down to one hundred and fifty feet. What had we hit? Perhaps more importantly to us at the time was. "What damage had we sustained?" Tom

Nosworthy our navigator carefully rechecked his chart, and confirmed that there was plenty of depth where we were operating.

Certainly we would have to surface without delay, in order to ascertain the damage, and we promptly signalled our partner of our need to surface. We then had to wait for her to surface before she would give us permission. On reaching the surface we found that there was considerable damage to our bows, but the exact extent of this damage could not be proved until we could get into a dry-dock. At the subsequent court of enquiry it emerged that we had hit what was an uncharted submerged pinnacle. Well at least it was charted now! But to me, a mere layman in this subject, it seemed quite incredible that we, one of the leading maritime nations in the world, should still have an uncharted pinnacle so close to our shores. Rather unsettling news for submariners operating in these waters.

The floating dock, which I knew so well, was made available to us on our return to Rothesay and as soon as we were docked down and the staging rigged I made a thorough inspection. The damage was largely superficial, and our forward torpedo tubes had not been thrown out of line, as could so easily have happened. Had this been so, then we would have needed major surgery at one of our main dockyards. As it was, the cutting away and the renewal of several damaged plates by the shipwrights, assisted by my E.R.A.'s took only ten days, and we were again ready for sea. Some of the repair work was of a temporary nature but would be quite satisfactory until our next refit, which was due very soon.

Another couple of months, and we were on our way to Devonport for this refit, with me keeping my fingers crossed that I would remain with *Sidon* for the whole of the period that she was in the dockyard. I had already given notice to vacate our service hiring in anticipation of this, and Clare and I were looking forward to moving back into our own home once more. Joan however, did not wish to leave her job in Dorchester, so she found alternative accommodation locally.

Peter Fickling left us to take up another command shortly after we arrived at Devonport, and the only other officer to remain for the refit was Lt. C. (Chas) Hunt, who was now our 1st Lt.. He and I shared a small office that had been allocated to *Sidon*, down at Moon Cove, together with the 1st Lieutenants and Engineer officers of two 'T' class submarines already in refit.

The situation was to me, a familiar one. Many of the dockyard officers were old friends of mine, which meant that we could dispense with much of the usual 'red tape'. Chas Hunt and I got along very well, and I was able to assist him in familiarizing himself both with the dockyard routine, and many of the dockyard personnel.

There was however, one thing that had changed since I refitted *Sanguine* in this yard. The Customs and Excise had now prohibited the use of duty free tobacco and liquor to refitting submarines. This was a bitter blow. Ironically, just some twenty yards away on the other side of the cove was a huge brewery. However, I knew several aboard nearby ships in commission, and was frequently invited aboard for drinks. One of these was my old friend of wartime days 'Shorty' Hodge, who had such fun and games with *Shakespeare* in the Far East. His C.O. liked to throw a stag party almost every Saturday lunchtime.

Another innovation of this refit was the officer for the submarines refitting had to be accommodated in barracks. He then had a very long walk down to the boats to do his rounds at 21:00 and 02:00, or on any other occasion when his presence was required. This was a real nuisance, and anything but pleasant when there was a howling wind blowing, or driving rain. But at least with three boats in refit, it meant that we were only required for duty one day in six.

My Sunday morning routine was to attend service at the barracks church, and then on to the wardroom for coffee. Clare would come along with me, and it was here that we met up with an old shipmate of mine, none other than the Commodore of the barracks, 'Ben' Bryant. 'Ben' was that gangling young Sub Lt. of *L52* days, who had since made himself famous during the war by being awarded three DSO'S and a DSC. For his great onslaught on enemy shipping, mostly by gun action, of which he was a staunch advocate.

At about this time a workman's strike resulted in a complete loss of electricity in the dockyard. HMS Adamant, with her flotilla of submarines was sent to Devonport to provide the electricity for the essential work in the yard. This was very appropriately named 'Operation Blackcurrant'.

Nearing the completion of our refit, Lt. J.H. (Ginger) Blacklock was appointed, as our C.O. Ginger was a huge north-countryman, and another old friend of mine. I had known him previously both as a 3rd officer and as a 1st Lt. and we enjoyed several games of golf together before *Sidon* finally left Devonport. Ginger was a little older than most lieutenants on their first command, because he was promoted from the lower deck. He and his charming wife Pat became our great friends, but this of course in no way interfered with our C.O E.O. relationship while aboard the boat. There is one thing that I have to be especially grateful to 'Ginger' for – he was a staunch Roman Catholic, and on this particular Ash Wednesday he bluntly asked me if I was making any Lenten sacrifice. I hadn't even given the subject a thought, but glibly answered 'Yes – cigarette smoking! As if I'd been giving the matter careful consideration. But having made this bold statement, I would now have to stick to it. It was no very great hardship for me as I rarely smoked more than ten a day, and had frequently given it up for short periods in the past; for instance, I never smoked while at sea on patrol. All of *Sidon's* officers committed to giving up something for lent that year, which must have been Lent of 1952.

I have not smoked a cigarette or a cigar since, although I did continue to smoke my pipe for many years.

At last we were ready for sea trials, and no matter how long the refit, inevitably the last few weeks were abject chaos. There was always the rush to complete those last jobs on time in order to meet the date for sea trials. I have never known it otherwise. This is partly because some work cannot be completed, or some piece of machinery installed until either a certain tank has been tested, or another piece of equipment has been installed and tested, or indeed, for a variety of other reasons. Due to the very nature of the job a last minute panic is largely unavoidable, and is accepted as such. Furthermore, all the spare gear removed for checking and cleaning at the start of the refit, now has to be replaced, together with all the other stores. Also fuel and freshwater now has to be embarked, and often this cannot be done until literally the very last minute.

Just a few days before our completion date a signal arrived authorizing significant modifications to our telemotor system. This is the pressurized oil system that operated our hydroplanes and steering, main vents, and many other vital units. This of course was highly inconvenient and very bad timing as far as I was concerned. My full attention, and that of the dockyard was at this stage required for a whole host of other details if we were to meet the date for the sea trials. However, the dockyard staff carried out this modification and completed it by the due date. I had just time to study the drawings which were returned to me the day before our sea trials.

Our main engine full power trials were carried out successfully, after which more than half of the dockyard trials party were disembarked to a waiting Tender, while we prepared for our diving trials.

Our 1st Lt. 'Chas' Hunt had now been relieved by Lt. Ben Golding, who had carefully made adjustments to our trim, discreetly erring a little on the light side. The captain ordered 'periscope depth', and on arriving at that depth we suddenly assumed a large bow down angle, and careered toward the seabed. - Which, fortunately for us was only one hundred and fifty feet below us.

The captain immediately ordered all main vents shut, and to blow on number one main ballast tank. But for some reason we had lost telemotor pressure, and so the vents would not shut, and therefore main ballast could not be blown until the main vents had been shut in hand control, using a ratchet lever. This was a long and laborious task, especially with the boat being bow down by thirty degrees, and with a new crew, many of who had not been in a submarine before, except for training.

Neither of the planes could be put to rise as there was no telemotor pressure, and these too would have to be operated in hand. But before that, we hit the seabed with a resounding thump. At this angle, unless you are hanging on to something solid you would slide forward and end up at the forward end of the compartment together with many other moving objects, in an undignified heap of humanity and equipment. Movable objects are reduced to an absolute minimum in submarines, as indeed they are in any sea-going vessel, but practically all of the crockery that the 1st Lt. had just drawn brand new from the stores, was now in fragments.

This whole affair was more than a little unnerving, as at first I had visions of a similar accident to that which had happened to *Thetis*, the flooding of a forward compartment through an open torpedo tube. I was very relieved to discover the real cause, although in retrospect this could have been very serious indeed for us had we been in deeper water at the time.

As soon as our main vents were reported shut our captain, who had remained completely calm throughout this incident, ordered the forward main ballast tanks to be blown. The 'outside wrecker', in this instance having little regard for the conservation of his precious high pressure air, blew with gusto, with the result that poor old *Sidon* came up with as much bow up angle as she previously had bow down. Again all moving objects and those who were not holding on, slid unceremoniously from the forward ends of each compartment to the after ends. Fortunately there were no serious injuries, although several of the lads were quite badly bruised. Had the seabed been mud instead of shingle we would of course have had much more difficulty in extracting ourselves and getting back to the surface.

I was extremely concerned with this telemotor pressure failure, and on return to harbour immediately got into a huddle with the inspector of ship fitters responsible for the installation of our modified system. As we were the first boat to be fitted with this modification, no one seemed to be very familiar with it.

Eventually we discovered that any slight over charging of the air pressure in the telemotor accumulator would render the new fitting inoperative – a very serious impediment. Several quick experiments were then carried out, which proved our case quite conclusively, and I forwarded a full report to *HMS Dolphin* so that this modification could be 're-modified' before being installed in other submarines. I was still very cross that this modification had been sprung on us in the way that it had been, when neither the dockyard staff or myself had had the opportunity to properly study the design or the operation. We were delayed sailing while this modification was removed and the system returned to normal.

The next day we sailed for Portland to secure alongside *Maidstone* once more. And no sooner had we arrived than we were bustled off to join *Adamant* who had now taken the place of *Montclare* at Rothesay, for a three-week work up period.

An amusing incident occurred when we arrived alongside *Adamant*. On our arrival most of the crew disappeared into the depot ship, except those who were to start the battery charge, and myself who had stopped behind in order to bring my logs up to date. Our captain, as was customary, was the first to leave the boat. It was his duty to report immediately to Captain S/M. I was about to depart for the depot ship to find my cabin and take a much needed bath, when a petty officer came to the wardroom to tell me that Captain S/M wished me to report to him straight away.

Following the P.O. to the upper deck aboard *Adamant,* and into the Captains suite – a huge well furnished cabin cum office, I felt a certain amount of apprehension since I had no idea why I had been sent for in this manner, or indeed who the current Captain S/M was - but this apprehension was soon dispelled. As I walked into Captain S/M's suite, there was my captain standing to attention in the presence of Captain S/M, who was none other than my old C.O. and friend, Captain 'Benny' Bennington.

Upon seeing me 'Benny' dashed across to shake my hand and greet me with 'Wotcher Joe, How nice to see you again!' I was equally as pleased to see him, even though it was a little embarrassing for my own C.O. who was still stood rigidly to attention, and must have been feeling rather left out. Actually 'Ginger' was quite 'tickled' by the fuss that 'Benny' had made of me, greeting me like a long lost brother. 'Benny' was not an effusive type, friendly, but not usually demonstrably so. However, it was not long before we three B's, Bennington, Blacklock and Blamey, were seated over a glass of gin and talking of old times. 'Benny' was obviously surprised that at my age of forty-eight I was still an active member of a submarines crew. We had not seen each other since the Trincomalee days, some eight years previously.

We then had a strenuous working up period, with Captain S/M's inspection at the end of it. Many of those who had joined us at Devonport were new to submarines, and this was our captain's first command, but by the end of this work up we were ready and fit for anything, having now overcome all our dockyard teething problems.

'Benny' came to sea with us for a few days to put us through our paces, and he did not 'spare the rod'. But he was pleased with our performance, and gave us a good 'write up' to take back to our own flotilla.

On our return to Portland I found some very good, if rather expensive accommodation at Greenbank on the eastern side of Weymouth. Again we let our house in Plymouth, to offset the rent that we had to pay for this very pleasant flat overlooking the sea.

Life went along pretty much as it had previously, *Sidon* was a good boat with a very good captain and crew, and we continued to carry out our daily exercises at sea, with the occasional cruise thrown in. I had been in *Sidon* for some considerable time now, and having a good staff, the job was relatively easy for me; nevertheless it really was a younger man's job.

Press-ganged into *Sidon's* football team I sustained a rather severe knee injury, and being conscious of the fact that it was rather irresponsible of me to be playing football at my age, I did not report sick. The tendons of the knee had been badly stretched, subsequently causing the knee to collapse when least expected. This injury proved to be a great handicap when climbing the vertical ladder to the bridge, or when crawling into an awkward corner to examine a piece of machinery.

Eventually the time came when, having been in Sidon for nearly two years, I was appointed back to HMS *Dolphin* as Assistant Engineer Officer (Training). The E.O. (T) was an old friend, and a contemporary of my brother's. Commander (E) A.A. 'Ginger' Summerhayes DSC had apparently applied for me as a replacement for Senior Commissioned Engineer 'Bert' Lacey who was due for relief.

This was a very vital job, and although I felt privileged and proud to have been selected for it, I could not quite understand why, as there were many Senior Commissioned E.O.'s who I felt would have been much more suitable for this post. Although having a wealth of practical engineering experience both in peacetime and war, I had no experience as such in teaching, except in a very modest way with my junior ratings on *Maidstone,* and I certainly had more than a few misgivings on my potential capabilities as a lecturer.

Having had very little opportunity for study since joining the submarine service, mine was essentially a practical background, and my pupils would be young Lieutenants (E), most of whom would be coming straight from college and would hold degrees in engineering. Small wonder that I approached my first lecture with more than a little trepidation.

There were three separate courses held each year, each course spanning about fourteen weeks. The numbers in each class would vary between six and twelve, at least one of who would be an Electrical or an Ordnance Lieutenant. I had very little time to prepare my lectures before being introduced to my first class, in which there were five Lieutenants (E) and one Lieutenant (E.L.), as well as three Warrant Officers. The former were of course, all senior in rank to me, and not only had I to teach them all aspects of submarine construction and auxiliary machinery, but I had to be their general organizer and 'mother superior'.

Practical experience for them was one whole day at sea each week, which I had to arrange in advance with the Staff Officer (Operations) and the C.O. of the submarine detailed for the job. At the end of their fourteen weeks I would then arrange to take them to sea on an eight day simulated war patrol.

With sea training classes being in addition to, and not replacing some of the boat's crew, (a policy introduced since the tragic and catastrophic loss of *Affray*), there was practically no accommodation for the trainees, their sleeping facilities were just a camp bed and two blankets, not that they were given much time to sleep.

I was afforded the privilege of a bunk in the wardroom when I wasn't fully occupied in overseeing and carrying out all the many drills and evolutions normally practised by a boat's crew on exercises. I had previously made out a watch bill so that each trainee could gain 'hands on' experience in all aspects of these breakdown drills, torpedo and gun actions etc. The trainees really had to rough it, especially during foul weather, not being used to submarine smells and motions, many were inclined to seasickness. They had to eat and sleep in the after ends, where the motion of the boat would be felt at its worst. I usually got a table fixed up for them, but it was almost impossible to secure the camp beds which, with the inevitable surfeit of oil and water running across the decks in these conditions, would slide about everywhere. I must admit to feeling sympathetic toward them at times, especially having the comfort of a wardroom bunk myself, but at the same time they were here to learn and to tolerate the discomforts of submarine life, as well as learning the many jobs and tasks allocated to them.

The submarine C.O.'s were always very co-operative and happy to carry out any special exercises considered beneficial to the trainees. The training programme was arranged before going to sea, and a copy given to the captain, although in the event, these programmes could not always be strictly adhered to, possibly because of actual breakdowns, adverse weather conditions.

Immediately following this hectic and busy period at sea were the examinations, in which the trainees were examined on everything they had been taught during the course. Very often, while my own trainees were sitting their exams, I would be setting or marking papers for the E.R.A.'s and the stoker mechanics, who would have been trained by someone else – these were very busy times for me.

On two occasions I had full classes of twelve officers, this made for very heavy going both for them and myself, particularly during the sea training stages. Other classes undergoing training at the same time as mine comprised young executive officers (mostly sub-lieutenants) whose tutor and 'mother superior' was my friend Lt. R.R. (Tubby) Squires (later Vice Admiral) while C.E.R.A. 'Sid' Denham instructed the E.R.A.'s,

Ceasing work for an hour and a quarter at noon each day, it appeared that another one of my many duties was to entertain these young officers during their lunch break. We would repair to the bar for a beer, and invariably one or two of them would challenge me to a game of billiards, or 'shove halfpenny', or perhaps a frame of snooker. They seemed to enjoy having a tilt at me, no doubt hoping to beat me for the hardships I caused them while they were at sea, but I rarely lost. In the eighteen months or so that I was in that job I don't think I lost more than six games of 'shove halfpenny'.

For the first six months while I was at the submarine school, Clare had remained at Weymouth with Joan, and I dashed off down there at every weekend that I was free of duties. Even so, it was usually noon on the Saturday before I could get away, as I often had lectures to do in the forenoon

The training syllabus included instruction at various other establishments where the work or research had some bearing on the work or environment the students were about to embark upon. Each class had a three-day visit to Barrow-in-Furness in order to examine a modern submarine under construction. I also had to take them to the Admiralty Physiological Laboratories, the Admiralty Experimental and Research Station in Surrey, and numerous other places. With the exception of Barrow–in–Furness, a place, which I think I had had my fill of as a member of the trials party in my younger days, most of these visits were very interesting for me, never previously having had access to them. One such experience that I remember was when we had to enter a large steel cylinder, about six of us at a time, and be subjected to an air pressure of about sixty psi. (This would be the sea pressure at one hundred and forty feet below the surface). There was not a great deal in this except that some had difficulty in clearing their ears. This could be terribly painful, indeed even dangerous, as it indicated that owing to a blockage between the nose and the eardrum, there was pressure on one side of the eardrum and not the other. Not being able to clear one's ears properly is sufficient cause to medically disqualify that unfortunate person from service in submarines. If it were necessary to escape from a submarine, then the ears would be subjected to a pressure of approximately half the depth in feet; at two hundred feet the pressure would be ninety psi.

A lighter side of this experiment was that a pressure in excess of forty-five psi would restrict the operation of a man's larynx, causing him to speak in a high falsetto voice. On one occasion an old friend of mine, Lt. Ken Vause (later captain, but at that time the First Lieutenant of an 'A' class submarine) asked if he could accompany us into this cylinder. Ken had a particularly deep voice and normally spoke in deep stentorian tones, it was so funny to hear him uttering in these clipped choirboy's tones.

This experimental pressure cylinder was extremely beneficial, as shortly the twenty-five feet deep D.S.E.A. escape tank at *HMS Dolphin* was to be replaced by a new one hundred feet deep tank, where mostly the Davis Submerged Escape Apparatus was dispensed with and free ascent encouraged. As this new form of escape came into operation before the end of my term in office at the training school, I felt it my duty to be one of the first to qualify from this depth, but I must admit that now nearing the age of fifty, I was rather relieved when my application was turned down. There had been much delay in the completion of this new tank, resulting in a large waiting list of active submariners to undergo this training.

Although perfectly at ease in the water myself, and regarding escape from the twenty-five foot tank as little more than healthy exercise, it was not always so easy. For many years submarine crews had to re-qualify in escape at least annually. This was often fitted in while their boat was in refit. It was whilst re-qualifying during *Sidon's* refit that I entered the quick escape chamber with my friend C.E.R.A. 'Sid' Denham. There was barely room for the two of us in this small tank, and the chief was above me on the ladder. After adjusting our breathing apparatus, and signalling that we were ready, the small tower was flooded from the outside, and I signalled to the chief to open the hatch and be the first away. It was as well that he was quick, because on his way out he accidentally kicked my mouthpiece away and it was necessary for me to just hold my breath until he was clear of the hatch. I was quite pleased to reach the surface on that occasion.

During the summer of 1953 the newly crowned Queen Elizabeth II ordered a Naval Review at Spithead. This was a very big naval occasion, not only was it attended by nearly all the ships of our then, very large navy, but by many ships of foreign navies. Even the Russians produced three or four large ships. Three long lines of ships, both large and small, stretched through the Solent as far as the eye could see - a very impressive and satisfying sight. It so happened that there was no better viewpoint of this rare spectacle than from the window of my cabin, which was on the first floor of Maidstone block, facing out to the Solent. Clare had come up from Weymouth for the occasion, and we were hosts to a further eight friends and relatives, tightly packed into the small cabin. From the large window, and with the aid of binoculars we had a first class view of all that was going on, especially of the Queen and her family proceeding out of Portsmouth harbour in the royal yacht, followed by the Trinity House pilot boat carrying the famous Sir Winston Churchill, the then Admiral of the Cinque Ports, and other escorting vessels.

I was pleased when Clare was able to join me toward the end of 1953. We found a pleasant furnished bungalow in Lee-on Solent, which at least allowed me to spend a little more time away from the job. My daughter Joan, who was now twenty-three, had become engaged to a smart young naval officer of the Supplies and Secretariat branch, Sub. Lt. Peter Lockley, who was the nephew of my old friend and brother-in-law Commander Reg Lockley. As soon as he was promoted to Lieutenant they decided that they would get married. I suggested that perhaps they could get married in the small Church of St Ambrose in Fort Blockhouse. This they considered a splendid idea, and I had very little difficulty in not only making this arrangement, but also for the reception to be held in the long billiard hall immediately below my cabin where I had spent so much of my free time in the past – an ideal setting, and one that would cause a minimum of inconvenience to the wardroom officers.

The Padre of *HMS Dolphin* was the very senior naval chaplain, the Rev. R.L. Scarffe, who assured me that that this would be the first wedding to be held in *Dolphin* for very many years, the last one being the marriage of the Admiral's daughter.

The 19th of December was in the middle of the first Christmas leave period, the whole establishment was decorated with fairy lights and there was a huge Christmas tree on the lawn outside the wardroom. The officers on duty on that memorable Saturday were cordially invited to the reception. The captain's wife, Mrs. Gainsford, a most charming lady, insisted not only in purchasing, but also in arranging all the flowers for the tiny little church of St Ambrose, which just held my one hundred guests. She did this both generously and very beautifully, pointing out that she undertook this task as a matter of course for most Sunday services.

Joan was fairly well known in submarine circles, having helped her mother to entertain, and also having attended submarine functions on many previous occasions. Peter, still a very junior officer at this time, was accorded a very senior guard of honour, not only of Lt. Commander's and Commanders, including his uncle Reg Lockley, but also Captain Gainsford himself.

It was a unique occasion, which thankfully went smoothly and without a hitch, thanks largely to my messmates and the stewards. Well - perhaps just one small hitch! It appeared that the Rev. Scarffe, who had been humorously advising the bride and groom, and indeed myself, 'not to panic', had himself made a slip. When the happy couple returned from their honeymoon, this worthy padre informed them that although they were truly married 'in the eyes of God' there was however, some doubt about the 'eyes of the law'. Apparently he'd got a little mixed up with his documents, and they had to be re-signed. We all had a good laugh at the reverend gentleman's expense.

Dolphin certainly served me well on that day and I felt amply rewarded for all the service that I had bestowed upon her in the past. The little church, named after a previous depot ship, and barely holding one hundred people, appeared completely unobtrusive, almost grotesque from without, but looked beautiful from within, not only with an abundance of flowers, but also with the hundreds of brightly coloured submarine crests that adorned the walls and pillars. The civilian organist and the choir had gladly given their services. Clare had often deputized as organist in the past, and I had often pumped the organ before the electrical blower was installed.

After this minor upheaval, life returned to normal once again, that is – until I received my mess bill at the end of the month. Clare and I had planned to have a celebration for our silver wedding anniversary in November, but this was completely overshadowed by Joan's wedding.

Captain Gainsford was now relieved by none other than my old C.O. of *Porpoise* days, Captain E.F. (Bertie) Pizey D.S.O. It seemed that this was a period in Fort Blockhouse that officers were either those with which I had previously served, or were friends that I had known for many years.

Of all the establishments we visited during the course of my time at the submarine school, I found the Physiological Laboratories in Alverstoke by far the most interesting. Although not specifically concerned with submarine personnel, much of the research carried out there was particularly significant to their welfare.

Situated very near Fort Blockhouse this establishment was run by an entirely civilian staff, many of whom could be termed as 'boffins'. A very remarkable scientist called Dr. Taylor headed it up. Remarkable because he courageously offered himself as 'guinea pig' for many of his own experiments pertaining to human endurance. On more than one occasion he had rendered himself unconscious by subjecting himself to shock pressure caused by depth charging whilst in the water. He and his staff also subjected themselves to experiments regarding survival in atmospheres containing too much carbon dioxide and too little oxygen; this of course was of particular interest to submariners, as at that time we had not developed an adequate or efficient method of reducing one or increasing the other. I had been subjected to both of these conditions many times in the past, and found it very depressing to be almost gasping for breath at the slightest physical or mental effort.

It was almost like visiting a zoo at this establishment, as most of the original experiments were carried our on rodents and other animals. Needless to say there were the periodical demonstrations by the Society for the Prevention of Cruelty to Animals. But being familiar with many of the staff, particularly Dr. Taylor, I am certain that any experiments carried out on livestock were minimal and then absolutely necessary for the completion of his very valuable work. One had to take into account that his research was in order to aid human beings who were in grave danger. The staff certainly did not spare themselves. Once, as a demonstration on the effects of depth charging, we all put our arms in a tank of water where a charge of just a few ounces was detonated, and that was enough for me! A depth charge would normally consist of between two and four hundred pounds of explosive.

My time in the submarine service, and indeed my career in the navy, was now fast coming toward its end. The retiring age for those of my rank was fifty, and I was now but a few months away from that age; one more training class would take me beyond it.

Dolphin had grown enormously since I had joined twenty-eight years previously. Submarines had become such an important and vital part of our defence, that to make the depot really up to date and efficient, the whole establishment needed to be completely demolished and rebuilt Primarily there had never been sufficient money in the naval estimates to do this, and secondly, this old fort had become so much a part of submarine life that no one had the heart to do it anyway. The place was steeped in tradition and, although the whole service grumbled about its general inadequacies, at heart they loved it.

By this time so many new accommodation blocks, training buildings and workshops had been added over the years, that the main gate had been pushed out three times until it had now reached the limit of the playing fields, just across the road from the Royal Naval Hospital at Haslar, with the old original Fort Blockhouse standing intact at the western entrance of Portsmouth harbour. Apart from St. Ambrose church with all its submarine crests, a small part of Onyx Block was designated for a future library and museum; this has grown considerably over the years and now has its own curator. My dear old friend 'Jan' Honeywill, who made a life study of submarines and submariners, did much to help this museum and library, and ensured that the whole of his vast collection of books and writings passed to the library on his death. It was my privilege to help in this matter.

With the many extensions that had been made over the years when money and space became available, *Dolphin* must be the 'patchiest' of all service shore establishments. In many cases where a building could not be extended outward, then a further storey was added. Furthermore, workshops and buildings would soon have to be modified to meet nuclear requirements. In my young days, E.R.A.'s used to live on the ground floor of Bonaventure Block, they continued to live there whilst a third storey was added to this block without even removing the roof, a fact that has never ceased to amaze me. A new accommodation block was subsequently built for the E.R.A.'s just outside the original main gate, the ground and first floors to accommodate the Chiefs and E.R.A.'s with the second floor to be used as a church, but before the church was consecrated, the whole building was given over to E.R.A.'s accommodation.

My old friend and contemporary 'Bert' Pinch, who had served in submarines for almost as long as myself, had already retired. We had served many times together. It wasn't long before his retirement that he fell sick with pneumonia and was taken to the nearby Haslar hospital. Despite the fact that he was really ill I could not resist the temptation to visit him with a beautiful bunch of flowers. He gave a wan smile, had he been stronger I am sure he would have belaboured me with them. This little incident did not seem so hilariously funny in retrospect, but 'Bert' wasn't the 'flowery' type; he made very little of his ailments and must have been very sick to allow them to cart him off to hospital in the first place. He too had had plenty of 'narrow squeaks' during the war, and had been awarded the D.S.M. while serving with 'Gamp' Miers in *Torbay*.

I still had to take my last class to sea for their final week's training when senior commissioned Engineer 'Buster' Crabb was appointed as my successor. I was appointed to HMS *Raleigh*, a stoker's training establishment near Torpoint to serve my final two or three months. This of course, suited me admirably; being very near my home I would now be able to start looking around for future employment.

My final week at sea was to be in the submarine *Ambush*, who's C.O. was yet another an old friend of mine, Lt. Cdr. Geoff Bourne, who lived near me in Alverstoke. This was a full class of twelve trainees, which meant that the boat would again be very crowded. Geoff did all that he could to help me, and certainly made me as comfortable as possible, he even dropped anchor off Brixham one evening in order to give his crew and us a short break ashore.

On the eighth day we headed up channel toward Fort Blockhouse. We had all worked very hard and I thought that I'd now had my last dive in a submarine. The weather throughout the past week hadn't been very kind to us and we were all fairly exhausted.

Rounding St. Catherine's Point, the order 'Diving Stations' was suddenly given. I was soon to discover that this extra dive was in my honour, and not ostensibly for additional class training. The C.O. stated over the main broadcast that I was deputizing for the outside E.R.A in diving the boat, namely opening all main vents etc., then for the First Lieutenant in adjusting the trim, and on surfacing a few minutes later I was to blow main ballast before finally repairing to the engine room to start both main engines

All this was of course, rather unconventional and perhaps a little frivolous, perhaps it may even have cost the tax payer a few extra pounds, but at least it made for a little light hearted humour among the hard working crew, and after all, it gave my trainees the benefit of one extra dive. The whole thing was done with a great air of solemnity, and of course, all the usual care, but it gave a great deal of amusement to the crew, especially the younger members. This was my last dive in one of Her Majesty's submarines, and the last time that I was ever to start a submarine diesel engine, rather a fitting climax for one who had spent over twenty-eight years in the submarine service, and it certainly was a jolly nice gesture on the part of Geoff Bourne.

I shudder to think of how many dives I have done during my time, but it must be a record that will stand for all time. My period of service, a record in itself at that time, may have now been exceeded, but as the modern submarine is either fitted with a schnorkel, or had nuclear propulsion, it is very unlikely that anyone will dive and surface as many times as I did.

Having dealt with the end of term duties, marking exam papers etc. I proceeded on a fortnight's leave before taking up my next appointment at *Raleigh*, and on return from this leave I was informed by the commander that I was to be 'wined and dined' before leaving *Dolphin*. This was not an unusual practice for an officer leaving a ship. Clare was duly informed that I would be sleeping aboard that night; at least I hoped to get a little sleep!

It was quite an evening; not only was I the guest of honour, and seated beside the president at dinner, but *Dolphin* was also entertaining the Lt. Colonel and eight officers of the Hampshire Regiment. Many of my contemporaries had forfeited their evening ashore to be present, including my friend of *Porpoise* days, Cdr. (later Vice Admiral Sir Ian) McIntosh (who I hope will be kind enough to write a forward to this account when finished), and Cdr. (E) (later Rear Admiral) Tommy Maxwell D.S.C. whom I had known for many years.

To Tommy was delegated the job of proposing my toast. He showed not the slightest embarrassment in according praise for the service that I had given to submarines – and in the presence of all these army chaps. It was kind of him to shower me with all those tributes but it made my reply very difficult. I felt like nudging him and muttering 'For hell's sake sit down Tommy'. Needless to say my reply was very brief, but I remember that my feelings were a strange mixture of pride and humility.

We eventually retired to the 'Blue Room' for further drinks, the younger officers gathering around bent on replenishing my glass at every opportunity. It was my pleasure to drink with them for as long as they wished, but I requested that I might be allowed to empty my glass before it was again 'topped up'. Whiskey was never my favourite tipple, but experience had taught me that I could take a considerable quantity without becoming a bore.

At 23:59 when the party finally broke up, I was as 'sober as a judge'; in fact the occasion was such that it seemed unlikely that I could get inebriated. Although it was rather a sad, and certainly very nostalgic occasion for me, I made every effort to join in the fun and games.

And so after twenty-eight long years, almost three fifths of my life at that time, I left the submarine service. There had been many changes during that period. I had met many extraordinary characters, had thrills aplenty, and regarded myself to have been most fortunate to have survived the Second World War. Despite all the prolonged periods of physical hardship, and the physical and mental stress that I had suffered, now at the age of fifty, I was still a very fit man.

Nuclear submarines would soon be appearing, and I did not envy my successors who would have to remain at sea beneath the waves for two or three months at a stretch, although of course their living conditions would be much improved. These submarines would be capable of remaining at sea for very long periods, but in the final analysis this would be limited by the endurance of their crews.

I had no idea of what my duties would be for my remaining two or three months at *HMS Raleigh*, and I arrived there rather like a 'fish out of water' to find that I was to be boatswain of the establishment. I would be directly responsible to the First Lieutenant, who happened to be my friend of *Shalimar* days, Lt. Cdr. Mike Chambers D.S.C., for the maintenance of the gardens, the large flotilla of rowing and sailing boats (over twenty of them), all bunting, ropes and halyards, and all work carried out by the sail maker. All this rather amused more than frightened me, although I know that my father, one of the finest professional boatswain's in the navy by all accounts, would have been very amused.

Most of the officers at *Raleigh* were engineers, and engaged on the training side. Several were ex-submariners. The C.O. was Captain (E) I.O. Backhouse, who insisted on playing golf with me at least once a week, and some great games we had. 'Mr Blamey' he would say' 'Do you think that you could make yourself available for a round of golf this afternoon?' As it was not prudent for a junior officer to refuse his C.O, I would have to hastily make arrangements with Mike Chambers, and then ring Clare to tell her that I would probably be late.

It was then quite unexpectedly that I was given the chance to serve for a further two years, and with my pension in mind I accepted this opportunity gladly, continuing with my appointment at *Raleigh*.

Thus in this very relaxed fashion, I ended my period of nearly thirty-seven years in the Royal Navy, which included my pre-submarine years and my halcyon years at *HMS Raleigh*, leaving a little over twenty-eight years of service in submarines – most of which was spent in a boat.

This was the luck of the draw, and not my original choice. True I subsequently volunteered for further service in submarines, but after all, this was under a certain amount of pressure from the engineer commander at *HMS Dolphin* all those years ago. But in retrospect it is doubtful that I would ever have done otherwise. There certainly was rarely a dull moment during my service in submarines, or indeed throughout my whole service career. There were moments that, at the time I would gladly have foregone, I was extremely fortunate to have survived those war years, more fortunate perhaps than I ever knew. It is my choice to think that this may well have been influenced by the little prayers that I offered up to God during practically every last dogwatch throughout this period, not only for my own survival (though I had much to live for), but also for mankind in general, that they should live at peace and not at war, where all were losers.

I had been in many extraordinary situations, and had met men of all ranks for whom I had the greatest admiration. More than half of my service in submarines had been served as an Engine Room Artificer, or as a C.E.R.A., and I feel very proud to have served in that branch

On my final retirement from the Royal Navy, I was wined and dined once more at *Raleigh*, but for me this was not the same emotional experience as when I had left *Dolphin* for the last time. In fact, although not my strong point, I almost enjoyed responding to my toast.

I have enjoyed very much attending the submarine reunions each year, where old acquaintances meet to talk, not only of the old times, but with the new generation of submariners. We thought that a boat of fifteen hundred tons surface displacement was relatively large, and an underwater speed of ten knots was fast, now we have our huge nuclear propelled boats with underwater speeds of circa thirty knots, and which are able to remain dived for months at a time. These men have as many problems as we had, although their problems may be of a slightly different nature to the ones we had. The men however, are of the same sturdy breed, and will doubtless cope with their difficulties just as we did.

Epilogue

It is now over thirty-one years since I completed these memoirs, which were originally written solely for my family archives. Now well into my ninety-eighth year, I am trusting in the grace of God and the expertise of my good friend and G.P. Dr. Richard Ward to assist me in my slow recovery from the activities of the Submarine Service Centenary year which although being both thrilling and exciting, was rather hectic for someone of my advanced years.

Some eighteen months ago I loaned my original manuscript to my good friend and fellow ex-submariner John Kiff, and after reading these memoirs, John has convinced me that they should have been published long ago. Since that time we have together spent many hours preparing my manuscript for publication, he having undertaken to do the major part of the work, for which I am most grateful. I believe that many of my experiences are unique, and will never be repeated.

Present day submarines being nuclear powered, can remain dived for almost indefinite periods. Creating their own atmosphere and fresh water, their only limits being the amount of stores they can carry, and the ability of their crews to cope with these extended dived periods away from what is now known as normal civilization. Although the modern day submarine provides more comfortable living accommodation for its crew, the submarine is, as in my day, filled from stem to stern with a diverse variety of machinery and life aboard a submarine can never be described as comfortable. Furthermore, as my book has shown, the inherent dangers in a submariners life although perhaps reduced to a degree by technical advances, will always be present in both peacetime, and while at war.

I regard it as my good fortune that I survived over twenty-eight years in the submarine service; during the war whilst serving in *Porpoise* and *Strongbow* I encountered more than my fair share of depth charging attacks, I would estimate at least two hundred charges between them, and I have tried to make the most of my good fortune in the years since leaving the service.

Sadly, my boyhood sweetheart Clare, who I married whilst in my first submarine *L52,* passed away in 1991. We enjoyed being wed for sixty-three years, and I always felt that Clare suffered as much worry and discomfort as I did during those six long years of war. Moving to Newton Abbot on our retirement, I think we both made ourselves useful members of the local community, Clare with her musical talent, and myself becoming a member of many societies, associations and committees. Many of my wartime colleagues have now crossed the bar, but I continue to enjoy the friendship of my last wartime C.O. Vice Admiral Sir Tony Troup KCB. DSC**, and that young Sub. Lt. who joined dear old *Porpoise* in 1941, now Vice Admiral Sir Ian McIntosh. KBE. CB. DSO. MBE. DSC. who has been kind enough to write the foreword to these memoirs.

Joel. C.E. Blamey

INDEX